The

VIENNA URTEXT
Guide to Piano Literature

Written by the Editors of The Vienna Urtext Edition
Compiled and Introduced by Maurice Hinson

EA 763

EUROPEAN AMERICAN MUSIC CORPORATION
Valley Forge, Pennsylvania
B. Schott's Söhne, Mainz • Universal Edition Vienna
Alfred A. Kalmus (Universal Edition) London Ltd • Schott Japan Company Ltd, Tokyo

Contents

*The thematic indexes, prefaces, and notes on interpretation are reprinted with the kind permission of
the copyright owner Wiener Urtext Edition Musikverlag G. m. b. H. & Co., K.G., Vienna, a co-
production of the publishers B. Schott's Söhne, Mainz, and Universal Edition, Vienna.*

For European American Music Corporation / Series Editor: Corey Field
© Copyright 1995 by European American Music Corporation
All Rights Reserved   International Copyright Secured   Printed in U.S.A.

Introduction

The Vienna Urtext Guide to Piano Literature is finally here! This book has long been needed by the profession, ever since Vienna Urtext Edition (in German: "Wiener Urtext Edition") began publishing keyboard music with outstanding front matter. This great edition has the advantage of being one of the most modern Urtext series. It is published by the Universal Edition of Vienna, Austria and B. Schott's Söhne of Mainz, Germany, two of the oldest and largest music publishers in the world, and distributed in the United States by European American Music Distributors Corporation of Valley Forge, PA. This edition began in 1972 and has issued many of the great masterworks.

It is the important and crucial front notes of these great masterworks, the in-depth discussion of sources, critical notes, historical background and suggestions for interpretation that have been compiled to form this superb literature guide. Most of the writers of these front notes are outstanding performers and scholars in their fields including Vladimir Ashkenazy, Paul Badura-Skoda, Michel Béroff, Alfred Brendel, Jorg Demus, Christa Landon, Menahem Pressler, etc.

Some background on the word urtext is necessary to understand the basic philosophy of the Vienna Urtext Edition. The German word *urtext* indicates a text in its original state without additions by an editor. There are two main processes by which an urtext can be prepared. The first is for the editor to solve all the problems and thus take the full responsibility. This method is acceptable only when the source situation is relatively uncomplicated (e.g., a single clear and authentic source) or when the musical object itself can be described as unusually difficult (as in an edition of works by Arnold Schönberg). If, however, the source situation is more or less confused—as in Bach, Haydn and Mozart—and is additionally complicated by the absence of autographs and carefully-made contemporary editions, a different method will almost certainly prove to be the better: namely, to inform the reader about two (or more) traditional readings and to compare them, especially when it can be assumed that a later reading is definitive—conclusions made on the basis of analogy and musical quality having to substitute for documentary evidence. Fortunately the Vienna Urtext Editions are basically approached this way. For this reason they stand on a plateau above many other editions. The student and teacher using this edition will have to make decisions for themselves occasionally, but careful study of the text and notes will help them to arrive at a stylistically and historically informed decision.

A large number of masterworks are included in the Vienna Urtext Edition and this writer has felt it vitally important to make available in a separate publication for broader use the commentaries included with the musical editions. This need has now been realized in *The Vienna Urtext Guide to Piano Literature*. A quick glance at the Contents will let the reader see the broad scope of this book: standard keyboard works from J. S. Bach to Paul Hindemith. The compilation of these commentaries make this one of the most valuable books available in English for any person interested in the great literature for the piano. Each volume contains even more detailed information, including some critical notes, that are not included here.

It is my hope that the piano profession will find as much help and enjoyment from *The Vienna Urtext Guide to Piano Literature* as has this writer.

Maurice Hinson

PREFACE

Johann Sebastian Bach's *Clavier-Büchlein vor Anna Magdalena Bachin ANNO 1722* begins with five suites. Three years later Anna Magdalena, Bach's second wife, incorporated the first two suites in the second Klavierbüchlein, although here – for reasons which are not known – the second suite has been left incomplete, breaking off in the Sarabande. The five suites in the first Klavierbüchlein are also not extant in complete form, because some of the individual sheets have been lost. Together with the sixth suite in E, which was in all probability added only a short time later but has not been preserved in autograph form, they constitute what subsequently came to be known as the *French Suites* BWV 812–817. Several copies dating from the mid-18th century present the suites as a cycle in the sequence given in the Klavierbüchlein of 1722 with the suite in E appended. Earlier copies arrange them in a different order, some of them together with the separate suites BWV 818 and 819.

In the case of some of the suites Bach made several revisions and added new movements. In two cases even in the Klavierbüchlein of 1722 he wrote in the Minuets as a later addition at the end of the book. This means that the sequence of the individual movements is not always beyond doubt. The present edition attempts to give a definitive version of the suites. In borderline cases variant readings are given as footnotes; the editor considers that these can be regarded as alternative readings. All other editorial questions are dealt with in the Critical Notes at the end of this volume.

Bach entitled these works simply *Suites pour le Clavessin*. Altnikol describes them as "Six Suites consisting of Allemandes, Courantes, Sarabandes, Gigues, Minuets, Bourrées and other galant pieces. Composed for the edification of music-lovers . . ." The necrologue of 1754 lists under No. 12 of the unpublished works: "Another six similar [Suites] somewhat shorter". The designation *French Suites* occurs for the first time in a collection of keyboard compositions edited by Friedrich Wilhelm Marpurg, Berlin 1762, which contains the sentence: "Authentic examples of the composition of Allemandes are to be found primarily in the VI French Suites by the late Capellmeister Bach". The copies in the possession of Princess Anna Amalia of Prussia also describe the works as *French Suites,* and J. N. Forkel writes in his book *Über Johann Sebastian Bachs Leben, Kunst und Kunstwerke . . .,* Leipzig 1802, p. 56f.: "8) Six short Suites, consisting of Allemandes, Courantes etc. They are known generally as French Suites because they are composed in the French manner. In these works the composer has set out to be less academic than in his other suites, and the melodies which he employs tend to be more prominent and ingratiating. In this connection the fifth suite is particularly worthy of mention: each of its individual movements has the gentlest of melodies, and in the final Gigue only consonant intervals – above all sixths and thirds – are used".

Bach composed the *French Suites* for his second wife Anna Magdalena shortly after they had married. They are shorter than the *English Suites* (whose composition must immediately have preceded that of the present works), dispensing as they do with a large-scale Prelude; and they are also technically less demanding. The *French Suites* and the two separate suites BWV 818 and 819 were followed by the set of six *Partitas* – two of them contained in the Klavierbüchlein of 1725 – which Bach published as *Klavierübung I.* He used all of these works as teaching material for his pupils, as the latters' extant copies prove. It is known that around the year 1725 Heinrich Nicolaus Gerber was

required to study the works in the following order: *Inventions,* French and *English Suites, Welltempered Clavier*[1]. In Bach's day the keyboard suite was composed for performance purposes only: the individual movements were not intended as dance music, although many of the dances contained in the suites were new and fashionable. The sequence of dances in the keyboard suite had been established since the 17th century: Allemande, Courante, Sarabande and Gigue. Thus, Mattheson writes in his *Der Vollkommene Capellmeister*[2]: "The Allemanda, an authentic German invention, before the Courante, and this before the Sarabande and Gigue, this sequence of melodies being known as a suite". In this established order of movements Bach inserts between the Sarabande and the Gigue two to four French dances in each suite: the then modern dances Minuet, Gavotte, Anglaise, Bourrée and also Air, Loure and Polonaise.

A number of Bach's contemporaries were amongst those writers who expressed their views on the character of the individual suite movements. Johann Mattheson's *Der Vollkommene Capellmeister*[3] and Johann Gottfried Walther's *Dictionary*[4] are two cases in point; and there are also relevant entries in the *Musical Dictionary* by Heinrich Christoph Koch (1802)[5].

Walther describes the Allemande thus: ". . . as it were the proposition in a musical work, from which the remaining movements – Courante, Sarabande and Gigue – derive as components . . . it is serious and ponderous in mood and must also be performed as such". And Mattheson, who is also quoted by Koch, adds: ". . . a many-layered, severe and wellexecuted harmony suggesting the picture of a contented or felicitous mind contemplating orderliness and tranquility with satisfaction".

A feature of the Courante is "a continuous flowing" (Mattheson). The Courante (to give it its French designation) or Corrente (Italian) "is a melody for instruments in two repeated sections, consisting more of short and flowing notes than of long notes, in $^3/_4$ or $^3/_2$ time, in such a manner that it could actually be danced to. It begins with one very short note as an upbeat. The time signature of the Courante, or more precisely the rhythm which it requires as a dance, is the most earnest to be found". Koch adds: "It requires an earnest, urgent rather than dragging performance . . ." And Marpurg writes in his Critical Letters on The Art of Composition[6]: "The actual time signature of the Courante in the French manner, while belonging to the heavy $^3/_2$ category, in the external form of its rhythm in a number of passages comes closer to $^6/_4$ time. The only difference is that these $^6/_4$ passages have to be played in true $^3/_2$ time. The late Capellmeister Bach left us numerous authentic examples of this proper Courante rhythm".

"The Sarabande is a serious, rather brief melody particularly common and popular in Spain, which is always in $^3/_4$

---

[1] Hermann Keller. *Die Klavierwerke Bachs. Ein Beitrag zu ihrer Geschichte, Form, Deutung und Wiedergabe,* Leipzig 1950, p. 165.

[2] Johann Mattheson, *Der vollkommene Capellmeister* (reprint of the edition Hamburg 1739), Kassel, Basle 1954, p. 232.

[3] J. Mattheson, ibid., p. 224 ff.

[4] Johann Gottfried Walther, *Musicalisches Lexicon* or *Musicalische Bibliothec* (reprint of the edition Leipzig 1732), Kassel, Basle 1953.

[5] Heinrich Christoph Koch, *Musikalisches Lexikon* (reprint of the edition Frankfurt 1802), Hildesheim 1964.

[6] Friedrich Wilhelm Marpurg: *Kritische Briefe über die Tonkunst,* vol. 2 (reprint of the edition Berlin 1763), Hildesheim, New York 1974, p. 26.

time when danced to but can be in a slow ³/₂ time when written for performance purposes", writes Walther. Koch adds: "It can incorporate figurations of all kinds and, like an Adagio, requires embellishments".

On the subject of the Gigue, which "is of a happy and jolly nature", Koch quotes Mattheson who describes two further genres apart from the Gigue itself: the "Loure, which has a slow rhythm and whose first quaver is dotted to give ♩♪♪, and the Canarie". Walther describes the Gigue as "an instrumental piece which, as a fast English dance, is made up of two repeated sections in ³/₈, ⁶/₈ or ¹²/₈ time . . ."

The Minuet, which according to Mattheson "sets out to convey only a moderate jollity", is, writes Walther, "a French dance and dance song, in fact from the province of Poituo, its name deriving from the short, rapid steps; for menue, menüe means small". And Koch writes that it is in "a very moderately fast ³/₄ time". According to Keller[7] embellishments are not permissible in the Minuet – a remark which is borne out by the scarcity of embellishments in Bach's Minuets.

Mattheson writes of the Air or Aria as an instrumental piece that it is "generally a short, singable, simple melody divided into two parts, which is frequently kept so simple in order that it can in any number of ways be decorated, embellished and varied so that the performer, while retaining the music's basic structure, can show off the dexterity of his fingers".

"Gavotte (Gallic) is a dance and a dance song made up of two repeated sections, the first of which comprises four bars, the second usually eight, in simple mensuration. It is often played fast but sometimes slowly. Each section has an upbeat of either a minim (which occurs seldom) or – more commonly – two crotchets, and both the two sections and the piece as a whole end with a half bar . . .", writes Walther. Koch lists five characteristics of the Gavotte: the two-minim bar in not too hurried tempo; the even-numbered rhythmic units with a noticeable caesura in the second bar; the upbeat with two crotchets; the two sections of the Gavotte with eight bars each; and the quavers as the fastest notes. Mattheson describes its emotional tenor as "a jubilant joyousness" and calls "its skipping nature a true feature of these Gavottes".

The Anglaise or Angloise is similar to a Gavotte but begins with a full bar. The salient characteristic of this English dance, writes Mattheson, is "in a word its idiosyncracy".

The writers fail to agree on the origins of the Bourrée. Richelet states that the Bourrée has its roots in the Auver-

gne, while Taubert considers it to have originated in Biscay[8]. Koch calls it "a French dance melody of a cheerful and happy character . . . dressed in ²/₂ time . . ." And Mattheson in his *Neueröffnetes Orchester* writes: "It has a dactyllic metre, so that a crotchet is normally followed by two quavers . . ."[9]. In his *Vollkommener Capellmeister* Mattheson remarks: "The word Bourrée in actual fact denotes something filled, stuffed, robust, strong, important and yet soft and gentle . . ."

The Polonaise or Polonoise is described by Koch in the following terms: "A short piece based on the Polish national dance, of a festive, serious character, which is quite distinct from all other compositions in its melodic structure . . . its tempo approximately half way between Allegro and Andante . . . Its most conspicuous feature, however, and that which makes it utterly unmistakable, is that all of its caesuras between sections or phrases or cadences must without exception occur in the wrong beat of the bar . . . The Poles always lead up to their cadences with four semi-quavers, the last of which takes the music into the semitonium modi which is held on the final note . . . Moreover, a genuine Polonaise never contains a combination of notes involving a quaver followed by two semiquavers, this being a common constellation in the German Polonaise . . ."

Bach provides few articulation markings. Occasionally he gives slurs in slow movements and Minuets, but he hardly ever writes staccato dots. The copies made by Bach's pupils give little articulation that is not stipulated in the composer's own manuscripts. The embellishments are a different matter, however. As early as the Klavierbüchlein of 1722 Bach himself wrote in a number of embellishments, but many of the pupils' copies are complete with embellishment markings, and these have on the whole been adopted in the new edition. Detailed information on these is to be found in the Critical Notes. As a rule the embellishments have been selected in their older form, as they appear, for instance, in the copies made by Gerber. The later copies give a modernized form of embellishments. In the Klavierbüchlein for Wilhelm Friedemann, Bach wrote out a table of embellishments (see below) with their corresponding equivalents.

The editor wishes to thank all those libraries mentioned in the Critical Notes for permission to scrutinize the source material during preparatory work for this edition. Especial thanks are due to Karl-Heinz Köhler, former Director of the Music Department in the Deutsche Staatsbibliothek Berlin, for providing valuable information.

Hans-Christian Müller

---

[7] H. Keller, ibid., p. 168.

[8] Quoted from Walther, *Lexicon,* article on Bourrée.
[9] Quoted from Walther, *Lexicon,* article on Bourrée.

Explanation of various signs, showing how to play certain ornaments properly

INDEX

Inventio

1   C-Dur / C major BWV 772

2   c-Moll / C minor BWV 773

3   D-Dur / D major BWV 774

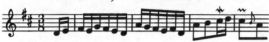

4   d-Moll / D minor BWV 775

5   Es-Dur / E flat major BWV 776

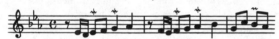

6   E-Dur / E major BWV 777

7   e-Moll / E minor BWV 778

8   F-Dur / F major BWV 779

9   f-Moll / F minor BWV 780

10   G-Dur / G major BWV 781

11   g-Moll / G minor BWV 782

12   A-Dur / A major BWV 783

13   a-Moll / A minor BWV 784

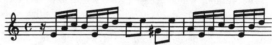

14   B-Dur / B flat major BWV 785

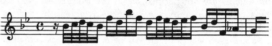

15   h-Moll / B minor BWV 786

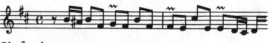

Sinfonia

1   C-Dur / C major BWV 787

2   c-Moll / C minor BWV 788

3   D-Dur / D major BWV 789

4   d-Moll / D minor BWV 790

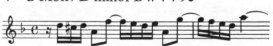

5   Es-Dur / E flat major BWV 791

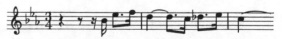

6   E-Dur / E major BWV 792

7   e-Moll / E minor BWV 793

8   F-Dur / F major BWV 794

12   A-Dur / A major BWV 798

9   f-Moll / F minor BWV 795

13   a-Moll / A minor BWV 799

10   G-Dur / G major BWV 796

14   B-Dur / B flat major BWV 800

11   g-Moll / G minor BWV 797

15   h-Moll / B minor BWV 801

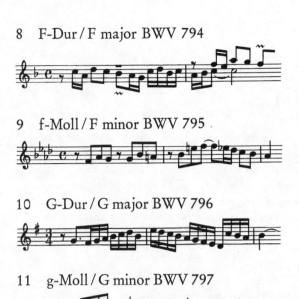
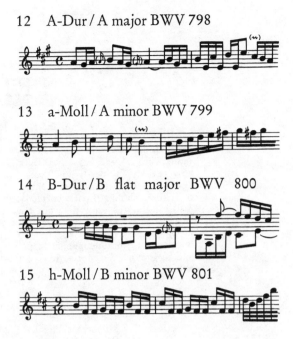

Anhang / Appendix

Verzierte Fassungen / Embellished Versions

Sinfonia

3   D-Dur / D major BWV 789

9   f-Moll / F minor BWV 795

4   d-Moll / D minor BWV 790

11   g-Moll / G minor BWV 797

7   e-Moll / E minor BWV 793

13   a-Moll / A minor BWV 799

Rhythmische Variante / Rhythmical Variant

Inventio

1   C-Dur / C major BWV 772 a

BWV = Bach-Werke-Verzeichnis. Wolfgang Schmieder: *Thematisch-systema-tisches Verzeichnis der musikalischen Werke von Johann Sebastian Bach*. Breitkopf & Härtel, Leipzig, 1950

PREFACE

A sincere guide, in which lovers of keyboard music, and particularly those desiring to learn, are shown in a clear way not only (1) how to play faultlessly in 2 parts, but also, upon further progress, (2) how to treat three obbligato parts correctly and well; and at the same time not only to be inspired with good inventions but to develop them properly; and most of all to achieve a cantabile manner of playing and to gain a strong foretaste of composition.

Prepared
by
Joh: Seb: Bach.
Master of the Chapel to
His Serene Highness, the
Prince of Anhalt-Cöthen

A. D. 1723

This preamble tells us what Bach considered essential in the training of young musicians. Bach's first pupils were his own sons. For the eldest, ten-year-old Wilhelm Friedemann, he put together in 1720 a "Klavierbüchlein" containing little pieces by himself and other composers, as well as an introduction to musical fundamentals such as *claves signatae*, ornaments and "applicatio" (fingering). Part of the book, however, is in Wilhelm Friedemann's hand: copies of some of his father's pieces (among them several of the Inventions), and his own initial ventures in composition. Again and again the elder Bach made corrections in the Inventions and Sinfonias, and the avowedly didactic purpose of the "Klavierbüchlein" may have made necessary the fair copy which was written three years later.

A new edition of a work so universally known requires some justification, and this cannot be drawn exclusively from the musical text. The sources basic to the preparation of an authentic text, and the assessment of those sources, have long been the subject of the most intensive kind of musicological research, the results of which are available not only to scholars but to the interested musical layman as well. From the wealth of publications, the editors of the present edition would single out the study by Ludwig Landshoff (1933) and two products of more recent investigation: the 1962 edition by Wolfgang Plath of the "Klavierbüchlein für Wilhelm Friedemann Bach" (Neue Bach-Ausgabe, Series V, Vol. 5), a rare and eminently successful union of musicological accuracy and musical knowledge; and the edition of the "Inventionen und Sinfonien" (Neue Bach-Ausgabe, Series V, Vol. 3) by Georg von Dadelsen (1970), whose editor's report had not yet been published

when our edition was prepared. In these two source-editions, both the Bach holograph sources of the work are thoroughly examined and illuminated. Our edition can therefore dispense with citing and assessing all the sources yet again. Instead, we prefer to concentrate on an aspect which has so far been neglected. In his preamble, Bach mentions it last but by no means least: "to gain a strong foretaste of composition."

In "Eigenart und Bestimmung des Klavierbüchleins"[1] (Nature and Purpose of the Klavierbüchlein), Wolfgang Plath writes that the traditional view of the Klavierbüchlein as "something on the order of a keyboard course by J. S. Bach" does not hold good. "In this regard, it may be enough to observe that keyboard instruction devoid of further ramifications and aiming at imparting merely technical dexterity is utterly foreign to Bach's method ... Bach may have made the first, purely didactic, entries as it were 'pro memoria', and to illustrate a dry table of ornaments. But the real purpose of the book becomes clear, at the latest, at the point where Wilhelm Friedemann's uncertain hand sets in imitation of his father: the Allemande No. 6 is ... a composition exercise. And the further exercises are doubtless to be understood as the continuation of an initiation into compositional principles. The pieces written down by J. S. Bach are primarily composition models, although they may certainly have served as performance pieces besides. When Wilhelm Friedemann copies, it is not only to train his hand at writing notes, but also to grasp the compositional principles in his father's model pieces, by the simple expedient of writing them down."

The "Invention" is not a musical form; as the name states, its point is the invention and treatment of a musical idea. What we have here is the only composition manual ever written by a great master. Erwin Ratz, co-editor of the present edition, writes in this connection: "There are of course manuals written by masters on thoroughbass, counterpoint and fugue (C. P. E. Bach, J. J. Fux, Marpurg, etc.); but when it came to teaching what we understand as the technique of composition in the higher sense — the technique leading from craft to art — the masters took musical works themselves as demonstration objects for their pupils. Almost without exception, the textbooks written in the 19th century were quite defective attempts to show,

[1] NBA, V/5, Kritischer Bericht, Bärenreiter, Kassel etc., 1963, p. 70 f.

as a system, the axioms on which works of art were based. These textbooks were defective in two ways: when the authors quoted examples from masterpieces, they often failed to grasp the essential point; and when they gave original examples, they showed more than ever how little they had comprehended of what actually makes a master great. Thus we may count it a fortunate circumstance that Bach has given us, in the Inventions, a work that — if we seek to understand it correctly — points far into the future, a work that can help us to understand compositions by later masters as well."[2]

In some instances we have considered it indispensable to contrast (either in the Critical Notes or in the section entitled "The Formal Principles") the familiar definitive version of a piece from Bach's fair copy of 1723 with the earlier version in the "Klavierbüchlein". The compositional variants — divergencies, improvements, subsequent expansions — as well as occasional "ante correcturam" readings, provide an ideal basis for explanations of a compositional nature. Apart from the material presented by the works in their definitive form, knowledge of the earlier readings in many of these pieces offers further material which enables us to discover the reasoning behind a given alteration, and even the sequence of compositional processes.

Our edition is based on four sources. Two of them were written by J. S. Bach, the other two originate from his immediate circle of pupils.

The principal source (A) is the autograph of 1723, a fair copy showing only a few corrections and slips of the pen, but numerous ornaments added later.

The "Klavierbüchlein" of 1720 (B) contains inter alia the first version of all the works in our edition; a few pieces were copied by Wilhelm Friedemann.

The other two manuscripts are significant for their ornamentation. One is by an unknown Bach pupil (C) and dates from c. 1723 (?); it was earlier thought to be a J. S. Bach autograph, and was owned by Wilhelm Friedemann. The other (D) is a copy of A (completed in 1725) in the handwriting of Heinrich Nicolaus Gerber.

A later copy of the "Klavierbüchlein" was occasionally consulted; see the Critical Notes for particulars.

A relatively large amount of space is devoted in this edition to comments on ornaments. We know from experience that here a large gap — particularly apparent in the field of music instruction — remains

to be closed. Musicians tend either to believe uncritically whatever they may have heard about ornamentation at one time or another, or to become confused, intimidated and discouraged by the heated scholarly debates on the subject, and thus resolve to avoid, if possible, something about which there can be no unanimous opinion. It is our aim to awaken the practical musician's interest in the matter and to encourage him to experiment in this direction.

In both of his manuscripts Bach began by being extremely sparing in his use of ornaments — probably for pedagogical reasons. It is interesting to observe that precisely those pieces whose initial version shows little ornamentation (e. g. Sinfonias 5, 11 and 13) or none at all (Sinfonias 7, 9) became in time the ones which were the most lavishly embellished, either in the autograph or in the copies made by Bach's pupils. It is apparent that Bach's method of instruction included giving his pupils not a mechanical manual dexterity aimed at merely playing off a musical text, but rather "a musically-active sensing and shaping of the vigorous emotion inherent in certain melodic notes, which could not be properly expressed in notes in strict rhythm."[3] This is a point which is unfortunately neglected in present-day music instruction. Bach's reason for leaving out the ornaments at first, and adding them later, was surely to show his pupils when and where one or another ornament was "indispensable" in helping to "explain the musical content" (as C. P. E. Bach put it thirty years later), in allowing the sounds to "sing and speak", in short, "to achieve a cantabile manner of playing".

Study of the sources and study at the keyboard have served to strengthen our conviction that, with regard to the compilation of more or less authentic ornaments in this edition, an "intermingling" is admissible. Our reason for committing what is usually a capital crime in an "Urtext" edition is that the ornaments, despite their origin in several different sources, do not, taken together, exclude one another; instead, they combine to form a quite lively and impressive picture of the musical practice of the time. We are convinced that all the ornaments appearing in the main text and in the "embellished versions" printed in the Appendix have, in addition to their instructional value, an artistic significance for each and every piece. This latter point is discussed in detail in the section entitled "Ornamentation".

The origin of ornaments is shown in the musical text as follows:

Ornaments from A: normal print;

[2] Erwin Ratz, „Einführung in die musikalische Formenlehre. Über Formprinzipien zu den Inventionen und Fugen J. S. Bachs und ihre Bedeutung für die Kompositionstechnik Beethovens" (Introduction to Musical Form. The Formal Principles in J. S. Bach's Inventions and Fugues and Their Meaning for Beethoven's Composition Technique). 1st impression: Vienna, 1951; 2nd impression: Universal Edition, Vienna, 1968, p. 17 f.

[3] Rudolf Steglich: Inventionen und Sinfonien, Preface. G. Henle, Duisburg, 1955.

ornaments later added to A: small print;
ornaments from B: normal print in round brackets;
ornaments from C and D: small print in round brackets.

In the "Ornamentation" section, mention is made only of the source in which given ornaments are lacking or are notated differently than in A.

Some of the Sinfonias are richly embellished in C and D; the ornaments in Sinfonia 5 in Source D are in fact in J. S. Bach's own hand. For the sake of an uncluttered page we have dispensed with incorporating into the main text the ornaments subsequently added to the MS. copies, since this would have meant strewing a large number of bracketed additions about. The musical text of Sinfonias 3, 4, 7, 9, 11 and 13 therefore contains a note referring to the "embellished version" printed in the Appendix. The embellished version of Sinfonia 5 is left in the main text; this is a special case, in that Bach himself added the ornamentation in his autograph of 1723 and also — with slight divergencies — in Gerber's MS. copy. The origin of the ornaments is designated in a different way in this one instance (see the footnote on p. 52).

There is, in the "Klavierbüchlein", an "Explication" of the common ornaments in Bach's hand, which we have reproduced following the Preface. Apart from an introduction, the section on ornamentation includes a short and general discussion of the individual signs, together with our suggested execution in the various pieces. Scattered footnotes on important details also appear now and then in the musical text; they concern *inter alia* the execution of ornaments missing in Bach's table, or certain signs (*e. g.* ⌇ for a long trill) which the player must be aware are ambiguous, or which permit various manners of execution. Appoggiaturas are notated in two ways in the sources (as a little note and as an "accent" sign — ⊂ or ⊃); for the sake of simplicity we print them in the musical text in the customary modern notation as a — variable — little note, except for the "embellished versions" in the Appendix.

In the musical text of the sources, no accidentals are added for the ornaments; therefore we have not seen fit to add them here. The neighbouring tones of ornaments either belong to the scale or are determined by accidentals in force — the lower neighbouring tone of a mordent or turn on the tonic of a minor scale, for example, will obviously be a minor second. Doubtful cases are dealt with in the "Ornamentation" section.

The placing of fingerings — above the notes for the right hand, below the notes for the left hand — makes clear the distribution of parts between the two hands. Execution of ornaments is not indicated by fingerings, so as not to imply that only a single execution is possible. Fingerings appearing in a piece, then, apply both to the embellished and the unembellished text, and are so worked out that they need not be altered when the ornamentation is added at an advanced stage of study. If, for reasons of playing technique, a fingering appears above or below an embellished note, it applies without exception to the principal note of the ornament.

The original clefs (soprano, alto and bass) have been changed to treble and bass; this meant that the distribution of parts on the two staves had to be altered from the original notation, although the original has been retained whenever possible. The placement of beams follows, almost without exception, the autograph of 1723. Accidentals have been placed in accordance with the conventions in force today; any problems arising as a consequence are mentioned, in doubtful cases, in the Detailed Notes. Missing whole rests have been tacitly added; slips of the pen in C and D are not mentioned.

The editors wish to thank Christa Landon, Vienna, and Dr. Hans-Christian Müller, Mainz, for their ready aid in discussions of textual problems; Dr. Clemens v. Gleich, Haags Gemeentemuseum, The Netherlands, for premission to examine the Gerber MS. and to reproduce parts of it; Dr. Wolfgang Plath, Augsburg, and Bärenreiter, Kassel, for kindly allowing us to utilize in the present edition some of the results published in the Kritischer Bericht of NBA, V/5.

Karl Heinz Füssl

ORNAMENTATION

For a long time musical theorists, and practical musicians too, believed that ornamentation in old music could and should be dispensed with, especially in the case of the great, "austere" Bach. Their arguments were many and varied. In the object of their aversion the opponents of embellishments saw only the notated "trimmings"; they overlooked the fact that embellishments did not suddenly cease to exist at a certain date, but rather lived on in the masterpieces of the Classic and Romantic periods in an altered guise, written out in fixed note values and thus robbed of their improvisatory nature. Thus it does not come as a surprise that with increasing research and an increasingly objective interpretation of past artistic epochs, the arguments of "ornamentophobes" have been answered by counter-arguments.

Here is the viewpoint of Ludwig Landshoff:

"In Baroque music, ornaments are not an inane play of patterns and they are not added trimmings; their formation obeys strong inner impulses. They have an important mission to fulfil, and belong, as a means of heightening expression, to the primary components of the work of art[1])."

Compare that with the standpoint of Hermann Keller:

"Listeners educated in the musical thought of the 19th century are accustomed to regard embellishments in Romantic music as an intensification of feeling . . .; but the Baroque musician, who set out to embellish a simple melody, raised ornaments to a sphere removed from all feeling, where he presented them like costly bits of jewelry. The indispensable pre-requisite to a proper use of ornaments, therefore, was an aristocratic attitude . . .[2])"

Recently, the Bach scholar George von Dadelsen has put forward the following views which take a stand midway between the above interpretations of the meaning and purpose of ornamentation:

"Like everything that has to do in music with transition, emphasis and animation, embellishments are a matter of an immediate playing impulse; therefore, their precise rhythmic and dynamic values often cannot be determined exactly, either in the player's mind or in notation. This feature, namely that a suitable rhythmic solution is left to the player's taste and skill, is the source of the particular charm inherent in ornamentation[3])."

Is embellishment, then, a means of heightening expression? Or does it involve withdrawal to a sphere removed from feeling? Or is it a matter of immediate playing impulse? We believe that all three viewpoints hold water and need not exclude one another. Ornamentation is not superfluous adornment; not is it a catalogue of instrumental effects occasioned and excused — to advance a strictly "practical" argument — by the lesser volume of sound produced by the instruments of the time. "Placing the whole system of ornaments in a causal relationship with the poor tone of the instrument has in fact always been the most popular and widespread argument, which has received substantial support from a seemingly authentic quarter, namely our forebears, who thought so themselves and handed down their opinions to that effect in writing . . . [C. P. E] Bach's view of the matter, however, is as follows: ornaments belong to the *clavier*, not because its tone is too short or too thin, but simply because the clavier is a clavier, and not a voice or organ. The instrument and its mobility demand a certain brilliance by nature; this is expressed by all sorts of patterns, passages and ornaments, in short, by all those things which can be called ornamentation in the broader sense[4])."

In our edition we have attempted not only present the relevant authentic material, but also to prepare it for practical use. This is done in the form of suggestions and recommendations. These must never be taken as the authoritarian final word on the subject; this will be obvious as soon as one realizes that embellishments — as a matter of improvisation — need not only knowledge, but taste as well. A philological determination and definition of markings can provide only a basis. Beyond that it is no help; on the contrary, it seems initially to cloud the picture still more — even in the case of comparing the divergencies between only the authentic sources.

As it happens, it is entirely possible that divergencies and inconsistencies in the ornamentation crept into even the earliest MS. copies for the reason that many of the markings were hastily written in by ear, that is, on the basis of an aural impression during a class lesson "when Bach, with the excuse that he did not feel like teaching, sat down at one of his excellent instruments and transformed the hours into minutes," as the son of Bach's pupil Gerber tells us[5]). This may be the most natural explanation as to why it is that the freer executions of trills (Inventions 1 and 7) and even a tirata (Invention 15) occur only in the painstakingly written MS. copy by Bach's pet pupil Gerber. For "Johann Sebastian, when he got carried away while playing for his pupils and friends, will not have followed the musical text slavishly, but will have given free rein to his imagination, sometimes embellishing one piece more richly, sometimes another, now highlighting one phrase with an ornament, now heightening the expression of another by free melismatic flourishes[6])."

Concerning the pieces in this edition we may proceed from the fact that even the sometimes lavish ornamentation in the sources gives us only a faint impression of Bach's art of improvisation, and that it would therefore be wrong to accept a fragmentary tradition as a complete and perfect whole, to which nothing more need be added. When playing the Inventions and Sinfonias, the performer should be inspired — not only for the sake of practice — to go beyond the very few recommendations given in footnotes to the musical text; he can, for example, work by "intimation" (*i. e.* on the basis of parallels) and embellish the passages similar to the one

[1]) Ludwig Landshoff, "J. S. Bach. Inventionen und Sinfonien", Editor's Report, C. F. Peters, Leipzig, 1933, p. 26.

[2]) Hermann Keller, "Die Klavierwerke Bachs", C. F. Peters, Leipzig, 1950, p. 32.

[3]) Georg von Dadelsen, "Verzierungen", MGG, Bärenreiter, Kassel, 1966.

[4]) Heinrich Schenker, "Ein Beitrag zur Ornamentik", Universal Edition, Vienna, 1908, p. 6.

[5]) Ernst Ludwig Gerber, "Historisch-Biographisches Lexicon der Tonkünstler", J. G. Breitkopf, Leipzig, 1790, I, p. 492.

[6]) Ludwig Landshoff, *loc. cit.*, p. 37.

Bach himself has ornamented, usually at the beginning of a piece, but sometimes at a later point. And when the player has achieved a degree of freedom which permits him to vary the ornamentation at later entrances of the passage (a wonderful example of this is the embellished version of Sinfonia No. 5), he will realize how ornamentation — its significance misunderstood or ignored for so long — helps him to determine tempo and agogics, to heighten the expressiveness of his playing and thus to approach the correct interpretation. This degree of freedom, which nowadays seems almost like capriciousness, is granted the interpreter by C. P. E. Bach: "... anyone with the requisite dexterity is free to combine more elaborate embellishments with ours. Care must be taken, however, that this be done sparingly, at the right places, and without disturbing the affect of the piece[7])."

The problems presented by the execution of ornaments — eyed uneasily by performers, editors and theorists alike — are in fact more theoretical than practical; they are overestimated, due to our peculiar tendency to trust more and more only in what we see in writing or print, in the (not always warranted) hope that we will not go astray that way. Our first recommendation, therefore, is to theorize less and play more, to try things out, to experiment so as "to train one's ear". Even C. P. E. Bach's textbook, "Essay on the True Art of Playing Keyboard Instruments," is not free from contradictions regarding ornamentation; it could not possibly be, because the interpretation of the signs resists all attempts at generalization. "It is in the nature of things that at the moment when rules of ornamentation give exact rhythmic solutions they are injurious to art. In this respect, a table of ornaments with rhythmically unambiguous transcriptions of little notes and signs which were meant only as hints, is self-contradictory; it can be excused only by the special pedagogical purpose it fulfils — providing, for those unacquainted with them, an initial indication of the various meanings of the signs ... The endless controversies about the one correct rhythmic solution are comparable to attempts at squaring the circle[8])." As part of a work of art, embellishments are, strictly speaking, always as much of a special case as is the work of art itself.

"It is difficult to prescribe the correct context for every ornament, for all composers are free to introduce at most places any ornament they wish, so long as good taste does not suffer. It is enough if we instruct our readers by means of a few established precepts and examples — at least by illustrating the impossibility of placing a certain ornament at a certain point[9])," i. e. an ornament which goes against the musical sense.

Here we should point out that much of what C. P. E. Bach says about ornamentation can certainly be considered as deriving from his father. But the validity of certain detailed statements is questionable; after all, Bach's son was a theorist of his own time, and his "Essay" was written thirty years after the Inventions and Sinfonias were composed. Furthermore, C. P. E. Bach's statements were intended for a different kind of music which, unable to surpass the peak attained by Johann Sebastian, had had to make a new beginning under new conditions. To be sure, the new music retained the old thoroughbass and ornamentation to start with.

But increasingly crowded rows of thoroughbass figures (notably in C. P. E. Bach himself) became more and more an impediment to the new musical ideas, and were soon given up in favour of a written-out realization. Not long after, ornaments suffered the same fate: just a decade later they became, in Bach's music, a fixed ingredient of the composition.

Nevertheless, precepts like the following are still valid: "Since the mastery of this material and its intelligent use involve a great many details, it is necessary to train one's ear as much as possible by listening to good music; but above all, the player must have a knowledge of thoroughbass if he wishes to understand many things more clearly. We know from experience that those without a thorough grounding in harmony fumble in the dark when it comes to ornaments, and must thank their good fortune, rather than their insight, if all goes well. For this reason, I will add a bass to the examples whenever it is necessary[10])."

The execution of ornaments, then, depends not only on the affect, the tempo, and the immediate context (i. e., the direction in which the part in question is moving), but also very much on the bass, that is, the harmonic situation. Even so, we have refrained from putting the slightest editorial marking into the musical text of the present edition. "When reading, the eye of the player reacts immediately to all the markings it meets in connection with the notes. A superfluous editorial marking, therefore, is dangerous in that, via the eye, the hand will be led to play something more than it probably would have if there had been no editorial marking. There is a vast difference between deciding — off one's own bat and in the heat of performance — to put in an indefinable dynamic or rhythmic nuance, and following, as the result of a purely optical stimulus, a specific editorial marking whose principal error lies in its very clarity (its too real existence, as it were) — quite apart from the fact that the marking may be erroneous in other respects[11])."

In the detailed comments which follow, we do not discuss every embellished passage; instead, we treat the ornaments only once with reference to single instances in which the most logical possible solution is desirable. Obviously, this will happen more often in the first pieces than in the later ones, in which the results of earlier discussions can be applied or varied as required (so that only special cases need to be mentioned); this is in accordance with our view that rules are general terms of reference, but not uniformly applicable regulations.

Invention 1

Bar 1 (and analogously in bar 2):

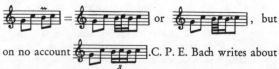

on no account .C. P. E. Bach writes about the pralltriller in general[12]): "This trill is the least dispensable and the most attractive, but at the same time the most difficult ornament. [Badly executed,] it is either not heard at all, or sounds clumsy and ugly, which is just the opposite of its true nature. Unlike other ornaments, it cannot be demonstrated slowly to pupils. It must really crackle. The last upper tone of

[7]) C. P. E. Bach, "Versuch über die wahre Art, das Clavier zu spielen", Berlin, 1753, II, 1, "Von den Manieren überhaupt", § 8.
[8]) Georg von Dadelsen, *loc. cit.*
[9]) C. P. E. Bach, *loc. cit.*, § 11.
[10]) C. P. E. Bach, *loc. cit.*, § 13.
[11]) Heinrich Schenker, *op. cit.*, p. 13, note.
[12]) C. P. E. Bach, *op. cit.*, II, 3. "Von den Trillern", § 32.

this trill is snapped. This snap alone makes it effective ... and occurs with such exceeding speed that the individual tones of the trill will be heard only with difficulty. This gives it a quite special incisiveness which is beyond comparison with even the sharpest other trills ... so that the listener will not feel that the note to which it is applied has lost any of its value, but rather that it has entered precisely at the correct moment ... It makes the performance especially lively and brilliant ..."

C. P. E. Bach insists that the pralltriller is to be used only on a falling second, "namely as the sole interval which permits a suspension from above[13]." According to an example given by C. P. E. Bach (Tab. IV, Fig. XLV), an execution which brings out the suspension clearly would be conceivable; in terms of our example, something like [musical example], although this would involve a somewhat more leisurely tempo.

Schenker doubts, however, that C. P. E. Bach's remarks are also applicable to the trill in J. S. Bach.

Bar 6 (and analogously in bar 20): [musical example] = [musical example] (this is Landshoff's solution too) D has a freer execution in

bar 6/7: [sic!] [musical example].

The harmonic function of both bars is cadential; therefore, the shortest form of pralltriller would not be suitable. In bar 6 the principal note is a sixth removed from the note preceding it, and in bar 20 a third; therefore, it is advisable to begin the trill in both instances with the upper neighbouring tone, in contrast to

Bar 14: [musical example] = [musical example]. Here Landshoff recommends beginning the trill with the principal note because of the interval of a second, unless one prefers the execution [musical example] which matches the C. P. E. Bach example given above. "An ancient law governing trills, quoted by C. P. E. Bach in his book[14], tells us that 'a trill always begins with the tone above the principal note.' It seems to me that this law does not really require what it says, namely that the trill really does always begin with the upper neighbouring tone; instead, it seems merely to refer to the scarcely noticeable — and rarely observed — suspension from above in the trill[15]." (See in this connection Invention 2, bar 3.)

Bar 8: the note embellished here with a pralltriller also needs to be embellished in the next two bars. In bar 9, where the note is approached from below rather than above, a mordent would be preferable: bar 9 [musical example], bar 10 [musical example]

Sources: In D all ∿ are notated *tr*. Bar 5, 13: D gives *tr* instead of ∿, in bar 5 later corrected to ∿ ∾ (for the execution *cf.* Invention 7, bar 1 etc.). Bar 6: no ornament in B. Bar 20: ∿ also in C and D.

[13]) Heinrich Schenker, *op. cit.*, p. 41.
[14]) C. P. E. Bach, *loc. cit.*, § 5.
[15]) Heinrich Schenker, *op. cit.*, p. 34.

Invention 2

Bar 2 (and analogously in bars 4, 12, 14 and 24, since *tr* and ∿ and ∿ mean the same thing here):

[musical example] = [musical example].

Bar 3 (and analogously in all parallel bars):

[musical example] = [musical example].

"The short, accented, suspension-like appoggiatura and trills beginning with the upper neighbouring note came to be so common in the 18th century that these manners of execution were obviously used even when they made no sense in terms of the musical context. This applies to suspension-like appoggiaturas preceding notes which are appoggiaturas themselves, and to trills in which beginning with the upper neighbouring tone leads to parallel fifths or octaves. Making fixed formulas of ornamentation was a fashion which not only the lesser lights of the epoch were addicted to, but also some of the leading musicians of their time, for example C. P. E. Bach and G. Tartini, in their theoretical works at any rate[16]." Here the principal note is a suspension itself; for that reason this pralltriller may on no account begin with the upper neighbouring tone. In bars 3, 23 and 25 the execution from above would result, moreover, in parallel octaves, and in parallel unisons in bar 13. (It is only possible to play the pralltriller in bar 13 on a two-manual instrument.)

Bar 8 (and analogously in bar 16 and 26):

[musical example] = [musical example].

In bar 26 the trill can possibly be played with one or two more repercussions, *e. g.* [musical example] or [musical example]; we recommend that the dotted quaver-semiquaver in bars 6 and 18 be embellished the same way (but without additional repercussions and with the last note as a semiquaver in agreement with the bass); bar 12, however, should not be embellished, because of the trill in the bass.

Sources: In D all ∿ are written as *tr*. Bar 2: B reads ∿ instead of *tr*. Bar 4, 6, 8, 12, 13, 16, 24: B, no ornament in bass. Bar 14, 24, 25: B, no ornament in soprano. Bar 26: B, no ornament on 4th beat.

Invention 3

Bar 4 (46):

See the footnote in the musical text. "Anticipatory" or passing appoggiaturas like this (*i. e.* appoggiaturas which, contrary to the rule, are not counted as part of the value of the principal note) seem to occur most often in the interval of a third, which they fill. They do not represent a suspension, and are therefore to be played unstressed on an unstressed part of the beat. The same ornament should be played in bar 34.

Bar 10/11 (and analogously in bar 22/23 — where the turn should be inserted — and 52/53):

[musical example] = [musical example] or (better):

[musical example]. The execution recommended by

[16]) Georg von Dadelsen, *loc. cit.*

14

Hans Bischoff[17]) is also acceptable:  although this version was perhaps not valid until the time of C. P. E. Bach, who wrote that "the tied note is the last tone of the turn[18])." None of these suggested executions involves an infraction of the rules of part writing when placed against the bass. If, however, one were to use here the turn written out by Bach in Invention 9, bar 16, Source B (theoretically admissible, since ⌐⌐ in Invention 3 and ♩ ♩. ♪ in Invention 9 — as the 1st third of a hemiola — are similar situations, both with cadential function) would have to be rejected due to the resultant parallel fifths.

Bar 11 (and analogously in bars 23, 37, 53, 58):
The trill (*tr* or ~) begins with the upper neighbouring note, e. g. . Normally, the rule applying to would require double-dotting, i. e. shortening the last note (); C. P. E. Bach states that "short notes which follow dotted ones are always played shorter than their notated length[19])." Here, however, that rule can be ignored in view of the continuously flowing semiquaver motion. The trill in bar 22 also begins with the upper tone.

Bar 39/40:

Bar 26/28 (and analogously in bar 28/30, 30/32):
"Our modern piano, especially the concert grand with its full tone, does not lend itself to the playing of embellishments in old music in the same way as the old instruments did; it lacks both the clarity and incisiveness of the harpsichord and the delicacy of the clavichord. In particular, pedal-point trills in the bass, with other parts in lively motion above it, rarely sound good on modern pianos. In such instances I think it permissible to play a short trill instead of a long one, or even perhaps to omit one completely[20])." If the performer decides, however, to play a long trill as recommended in the footnotes to Inventions 4, 7 or 10, the trill should begin with the principal note, as is customary with unprepared trills, so that the goal tone — reached by a leap — is made clearly audible, i. e.

or .

The second manner of execution ends the trill in the most natural way ; but if the first manner of execution is used, it is best to end it .

Sources: Bar 3: D gives *tr* instead of ~. Bar 11, 37, 53, 58: *tr* from D. Bar 11, 39, 40, 53: no ~ in B, C, D. Bar 23: D gives *tr* instead of ~. Bar 34: no ornament

---

in B. Bar 46: in A the appoggiatura is written as an "accent," likewise in B, bar 4 (but ~ over a[1] there); in B the solution of the ornament is written out in bar 46; ~ is lacking in C and D.

Invention 4
Bar 15:
we suggest  .
Bar 17, 37, 48:
suggested execution as in Invention 3, bar 11.
Bar 19ff., 29ff.:
for the various manners of executing a long trill, see Invention 3, bar 26/28. In contrast to that passage, both trills in Invention 4 may begin either with the principal note or the upper neighbouring tone. But to emphasize the dominant function of the trilled bass tone in bar 29ff., the note e should fall on a stressed part of the beat when the trill is continued
(*etc.* or *etc.*). In bar 51 a pralltriller should be added to the f[1]. For the execution see Invention 1, bars 6 and 20.
Sources: Bar 15: B's ~ is probably in Wilhelm Friedemann's hand. Bar 17, 48: *tr* from D. Bar 29: B, C, D read ~ instead of ~.

Invention 5
The pralltrillers in bar 3 and all comparable bars begin with the principal note, since it is approached from above.
Bar 32:
means . Possible execution
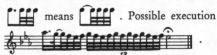
In bars 16, 23 and 27 a mordent should be added on the third quaver of the bar.
in bar 11 means .
Sources: the added ornaments were (according to Landshoff) presumably written in in the 1740s. No ornaments in B, C, D (including the appoggiatura in the final bar), except for the 2nd beat of bar 32: ~ instead of ~. In A the appoggiatura was also added later, as was the vertical line through the trill marking. In B the 1st soprano tone is a crotchet (g[2]).

Invention 7
Bar 1 (and analogously in bars 6, 10, 13, 20, 22):
= . See also the execution of this ornament in Sinfonia 5, bar 1 etc. In conformity with the flowing semiquaver motion in this piece the last note of the ornament should not be shortened and the penultimate note should not be dotted.
Bar 2:

Bar 2, 10:
the pralltriller over the quaver begins with the upper note.

[17]) Hans Bischoff: Inventionen und Sinfonien, Steingräber, Leipzig, 1880.
[18]) C. P. E. Bach, *op. cit.*, II, 4, "Von dem Doppelschlage", § 23.
[19]) C. P. E. Bach, *op. cit.*, III, "Vom Vortrage", § 23.
[20]) Hermann Keller, *op. cit.*, p. 33.

Bar 6:

(long trill agreeing with cadential function) or [music] following D ($\curvearrowright$ instead of $\mathtt{\sim}$).

Bar 7ff., 15ff.:
the unprepared long trill should begin with the principal note [music] *etc.* ; but a trill beginning with the upper note [music] *etc.* also has a certain charm here. The principal note of the bass trill, on the other hand, should be stressed so that the dominant function of the trilled note is brought out, *i. e.* [music] *etc.* . The soprano trill ends at the start of bar 9 (with a ligature across the bar line as in Invention 3, bar 26/28); the bass trill does not end until the 13th semiquaver of bar 17.

Bar 9:

[music] (as in bar 6) or

[music] following D ($\curvearrowright$ instead of $\mathtt{\sim}$) or, according to a later addition in D

[music] for the 1st half of

the bar, an embellishment which (like the subsequently added ornamentation in bar 21) points to a somewhat slower tempo.

Bar 11 (and analogously in bar 15):

Bar 13:
2nd beat, suggested execution [music] , or

[music] following D ($\curvearrowright$ instead of $\mathtt{\sim}$).

Bar 21:
the pralltriller on the suspension c^2 begins with the principal note, or (better) [music] as in D ($\curvearrowright$ instead of $\mathtt{\sim}$), or, according to a later addition in D, [music] . The pralltriller on the last beat is executed as in bar 13 (2nd beat).

Bar 23:

 ; or else as in B ($\curvearrowright$ instead of $\mathtt{\sim}$ on 2nd beat — perhaps this is the ornament intended in C too) [music]

Due to the sequence in bars 3 and 4, the highest tone in bar 4 (b^2) should also be embellished with a mordent.
Sources: the bracketed ornaments in small print are from D, except for those in bar 3 and 11, which are found only in C. Bar 1, 2, 20: B, no $\mathtt{\sim}$ and $\curvearrowright$ resp. on 4th beat. Bar 9: B, no ornament. Bar 21: B, $\curvearrowright$ instead of $\mathtt{\sim}$ on 1st beat. Bar 23: the appoggiatura, notated as an "accent," is in B, C, D.

Invention 9
Bar 15/16:

(1st beat, bar 16 as in B). If $\curvearrowright$ should be read as $\mathtt{\sim}$, however (the marking in A cannot be absolutely identified), the mordent should be given one repercussion more: [music] .

Bar 33:
Taking into account the written-out turn in bar 16 of B, the rhythm is the same as that given immediately above.
Sources: bar 15, 33: B, C, D have no ornaments except D's *tr* instead of $\mathtt{\sim}$ in bar 33.

Invention 10
All pralltrillers can begin with the principal note.
Bar 20/21 (and analogously in bar 22/23 and 24/25):

[music] *etc.* [music] or

[music] *etc.* [music] (but with ligature across

the bar line in bar 23 and bar 25, bass). In D, bar 20 and 24, $\mathtt{\sim}$ could also be read as $\curvearrowright$

(= [music] *etc.*). In B the repeated trill markings on c^2 and b^1 seem only to indicate that the trill is to be continued.

In bar 14 a longer mordent ($\mathtt{\sim}$) can be played: [music] . If the mordent in bar 15 is played (with the neighbouring tone g sharp for the sake of greater "sharpness[21]"), it should also be played at the corresponding point in bar 17, and perhaps also in the soprano, bar 16 (with c sharp[2]).

Sources: bar 3: B, no ornament. Bar 7, 12: bass $\curvearrowright$ also in C, D. Bar 14: $\curvearrowright$ also in C, D. Bar 15: $\curvearrowright$ also in C (but not in D). Bar 15, 17: $\mathtt{\sim}$ also in B, C, D. Bar 24: B, C, give *tr* instead of $\mathtt{\sim}$ (here too — as in bar 15 — C shows its derivation from B).

Invention 11
Bar 10:

[music] = [music] .

This execution of the turn, given by Bach in bar 16 of Invention 9, prevents the two embellished dotted quaver figures from being too much alike.

Bar 16:

[music] .

Bar 23:
the mordent on the final note can be increased by one repercussion: [music] .

Sources: except for $\mathtt{\sim}$ in bar 17, B, C, D have no ornaments.

Invention 12
Bar 1 (and analogously in bars 3, 9, 11, 18, 20):
the ornament itself and the pitches of the semiquavers immediately following it make it appear possible that what is intended here is not a long trill at all, but only an accentuation on the note which, moreover, lasts

---

[21] C. P. E. Bach, *op. cit.*, II, 5, "Von den Mordenten", § 11.

only half a bar:  . The arguments against a long trill are: 1) the relatively short duration of the trilled note; 2) the fact that the note immediately following the long note is always the lower second, a note also contained in the marking ᴧᴧᴧ — two appearances of that lower second just after one another is annoying and meaningless.

Bar 21:

in both sources, ᴧᴧᴧ is over f sharp²; we print it over e² to prevent 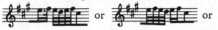 from being played.

There are three possible manners of execution:

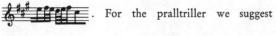

 . For the pralltriller we suggest

Sources: the ornaments later added in A were also subsequently added in C and D; in D, bar 21, both ornaments may have been written in by J. S. Bach. Bar 1: B initially ᴧᴧᴧ, perhaps ᴧᴧ still earlier, then corrected to ᴧᴧᴧ. Bar 3, 9: no ᴧᴧᴧ in B. Bar 14: B, 2nd ᴧᴧ lacking. Bar 18: no ornaments in B. Bar 20: B, both ornaments ᴧᴧᴧ .

Invention 15

All pralltrillers in this piece should begin with the upper note.

Bar 3:

 .

Bar 5:

 , or else 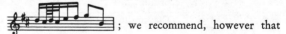 as indicated by D (ᴧᴧᴧ instead of ᴧᴧᴧ). In bar 21, 3rd beat, D writes a tirata ().

Sources: bar 3: no ornaments in B; in C and D the appoggiatura (notated as an "accent") was possibly added later. Bar 4: B, 1st ᴧᴧᴧ lacking. Bar 5, 11, 18: no ornament in B. Bar 15, 21: B, 2nd ᴧᴧᴧ lacking.

Sinfonia 1

Bar 6 (and analogously in bar 10):

Sources: all bracketed ornaments in small print, including the appoggiatura for soprano and alto in the last bar (notated as an "accent"), are later additions in C. Bar 6, 10: D has *tr* instead of ᴧᴧᴧ .

Sinfonia 2

Bar 1:

corresponding to the tone repetition e flat²-e flat² (3rd and 4th soprano notes) the repetition g²-g² should be observed. Therefore, the trill should begin with the principal note:  , or, in a faster

tempo,  (the same applies to the ornament in bar 3).

Bar 4:

execution as in bar 1, or else, if ᴧᴧᴧ is to be read as ᴧᴧᴧ:

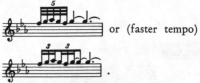 or (faster tempo)

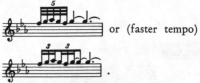 .

Bar 7 (and analogously in bar 30):

suggested execution:

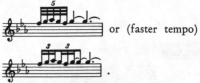

In bars 6, 28 and 29 (to match bar 5) a mordent should be played in the soprano on the 1st note of the 2nd beat.

Sources: all bracketed ornaments in small print are later additions in C. Bar 7, 15, 30: D, *tr* instead of ᴧᴧᴧ, the same in E, bar 15; no ornament in E, bar 30.

Sinfonia 3, embellished version

Bar 1/2:

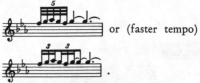 ; all appoggiaturas are executed as semiquavers here, despite the resultant parallel ninths in bars 3 and 4. These arise

logically from { 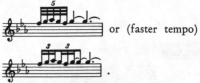 = } ,

a case of "telescoped" part writing. Like all suspensions, these, to have the proper effect, need definite and quite conscious stressing, "since every appoggiatura is played more loudly than the tone following it, and is joined to it whether there is a slur or not[22]." This, however, demands a considerably slower tempo (approx. $\mathbf{J} = 50$).

Bar 16:

 ; we recommend, however that because of the resultant parallel fifths, the appoggiatura should not be played.

Bar 24: to give even more variety to this expressive embellished version, the ornamentation of the motive — combined in bar 1, and separated at the later entrances (sometimes ♪♪♪♩, sometimes ♪♩♪♪) can be again joined together, throughout the whole last entrance:

 .

Sources: all ornaments in the embellished version are later additions in C.

Sinfonia 4, embellished version

Bar 2:

in conformity with the cadential function the longer

---

[22] C. P. E. Bach, *op. cit.*, II, 2, "Von den Vorschlägen", § 7.

form of the trill may be used here: [music]

(as in Invention 7, bar 6) or, corresponding to B ([music],

no trill marking): [music]. But it should

not be used on the 2nd beat of bar 16, for example, where the alto semiquavers and the bass mordent make a long trill in the soprano unadvisable.

Bar 17:

Bar 23:

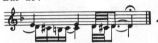

Sources: all ornaments in the embellished version are later additions in C. Bar 14: B, no ornament.

Sinfonia 5
Sources: bar 12: B, no ornament. For execution see below, Sinfonia 5, embellished version, bar 12.

Sinfonia 5, embellished version
In D the ornaments are written in Bach's hand, but in A presumably at a later date and surely independently of D. In this piece only, the origin of ornaments is shown differently: all ornaments contained in A (the subsequent ones and the only ornament present from the start — bar 12) appear in normal print; ornaments from D are in small print, while ornaments from C are — as usual — in small print in round brackets. Nearly equipollent ornaments from the MS. copies are given as footnotes in the musical text; other divergencies are mentioned below.
The principal problem here is the variable execution of appoggiaturas, all of which Bach writes as quavers.
A uniform execution of [music] and [music] as quaver appoggiaturas (according to the notated value, as C. P. E. Bach prescribes) would lead, for example (in bar 5/6, soprano) to [music],
i. e. to a result which surely could not have been intended. Bach himself puts us on the right track: in the soprano part at the beginning of bars 8, 22, 23, 34 and 35 he writes out the suspension as a crotchet — and we may assume that an appoggiatura appearing before a crotchet should be treated the same way — whether it is in fact a crotchet or somewhat shorter will be discussed below. Appoggiatures appearing before a dotted quaver, on the other hand, are short; but it should be kept in mind that a "short" appoggiatura does not mean only what has been notated by [music] since the 19th century — that is only its shortest possible value. "The upper boundary of the short appoggiatura is the long appoggiatura itself; the broad span of the former only stops where the latter begins[23]." For our part, we recommend at [music] an execution in semiquavers (*cf.* in this connection the written-out appoggiaturas in Sinfonia 4, bars 9 and 10, soprano and alto). The "leaping"

appoggiaturas (on the 3rd beat of bars 3, 5, 6, 7, 20, 22, 25, 31) could of course also be played as shorter notes — Landshoff even suggests hemidemisemiquavers! — but not the ones which approach the principal note stepwise (the 3rd beat of bars 4, 11, 15, 19, 23, 27, 32, 33, and the 2nd beat of 37), which apart from their harmonic value have an appreciable melodic value which cannot be brought out as a demisemiquaver, and even less as a hemidemisemiquaver.
As regards the long appoggiaturas on the 1st beat of the bar, the execution [music] = [music] has already been given above. However, Rudolf Steglich[24]) suggests what is, in our opinion, a much more satisfactory execution: the suspension is resolved on the least stressed part of the beat, namely the 4th semiquaver, *i. e.* [music].
The effect is extremely natural, for the simple reason that the same rhythmic motive is retained which forms the upbeat: [music] — a quite felicitious motivic unity. Moreover, the syncopation gives the melodic span its proper breadth, and this in turn gives the music that tendency towards large dimensions which is characteristic even of the unembellished version, and which ornamentation is meant to heighten, not diminish. Changing to a crotchet at the end of the first section (bar 9) lends the motive a last ounce of roundness. This kind of variability, which also includes the suspensions written out by Bach as crotchets, seems to us to match the required improvisatory aspect; therefore, we give preference to this suggested execution — although a few words must be said about the other possibilities.
The execution [music] does not seem to be quite in harmony with the dotted upbeat figure [music] — moreover, the dotted quaver in the upbeat figure would not seem to tolerate an appoggiatura of lesser duration than itself. Thus a value longer than that in the upbeat figure — that is, a crotchet — would in fact create a more favourable effect, were it not considerably lessened by the stereotyped repetition of the motive [music].
Bar 1, etc:
The embellished pattern [music] is also found in Inventions 7, 9 and 11. The reasons for which we recommended the rhythm [music] in bar 33 of Invention 9 and bar 10 of Invention 11 do not apply in this instance.

Much more to the point is the execution [music] suggested by Rudolf Steglich[25]) — which, however, can only be used at a tempo of ♩ = 40 (due to the subtle rhythmic differentiations). Since we find ♩ = 50 to be more suitable, the demisemiquaver sextuplet [music] already recommended in Invention 7 is probably the most convenient solution, although the rhythm [music] is also eminently Bachian (see Invention 14) and avoids shortening the final note, whereas the form we favour involves reducing it to a demisemiquaver. Whether or not a shortened final note should be retained consistently throughout the piece cannot be answered unequivocally; it can certainly not be retained when the concurrent semiquaver motion in the bass forbids it, as in bars 12,

[23]) Heinrich Schenker, *op. cit.*, p. 33.

[24]), [25]) Rudolf Steglich, *op. cit.*

16, 19, 20, 24, 28; in the figure [♪♩♪], on the other hand, shortening is quite possible ([♫♫]). The contradiction between semiquaver and demisemiquaver is in fact more theoretical than anything else, and the alternation of the two forms can be quite appealing, apart from having a beneficial effect on the free flow of the two concertante upper parts. In the tempo we recommend, the distinction will in any event scarcely be felt as awkward.

Bar 12:

according to the rule (see Bach's own table of ornaments) [ornament] — and [ornament] in bar 23 — could also be played

[musical example] Halving the principal note is recommended if the appoggiaturas on the first beat of the bar are played as quavers. In general, [ornament] or [ornament] probably indicate only the suspension itself, i. e. "that one stops on the 1st note of the trill[26]." [notation] in bar 7 means [notation]; likewise [notation] in bar 10: [notation]. [notation] in bar 35 means [notation]; but [notation] in bar 6 means [notation].

Further on we give — as an exception — a complete suggested execution (for the two upper parts, without fingering); we advise, however, that only Bach's musical text be used for study purposes; for a fixed rhythm would otherwise be "injurious to art," since "our notation is unable to express rhythmically free figures adequately, and the rhythmic sequence of the parts of an embellishment must remain flexible[27]."

In Sinfonia 5 the player has no lack of opportunity to bring in an improvisatory element that will spontaneously affect the way the piece is shaped, and can consciously oppose the "present-day ideal of perfectionist performance which produces the same result every time[28]."

Inveterate experimenters, who wish to leave nothing untried, might even "Frenchify" this Sinfonia, that is, play all the stressed semiquavers dotted, including those in the bass: [notation] and [notation] = [notation] and [notation].

Whatever lyricism may go by the board is made up for by the fascinating contrast between the cantabile melodic parts and the relentless "lash" of the bass rhythm. This manner of execution, however, requires a slower tempo ($\quarternote = 40$).

Sources: In A, several slurs from appoggiatura to principal note are lacking; they have been tacitly added in our text. In C and D, Sinfonia 5 was initially unembellished (except for [ornament] in bar 12); Landshoff conjectures that D could have been the source of the ornaments in C, and that C had already contained a few other ornaments ("the mordents below the alto part on the third beat of bars 4 and 21, and above the soprano on the 2nd beat of bar 36... since it is impossible to play them together with the embellishments later inserted from Gerber's manuscript."). This certainly

applies to bars 4 and 21, but not to bar 36, where the combination of the two ornaments (mordent followed by an "accent") is by no means unplayable — see below, and the footnote in the musical text. In both MSS. all appoggiaturas are notated as "accents."

Bar 2: C, no [ornament] . Bar 3: C, soprano appoggiatura to 1st beat reads e flat[2] rather than d flat[2], no appoggiatura to 1st beat in alto; D, no appoggiatura on 1st beat in soprano or alto. Bar 4: D, 3rd beat [musical example] (corresponding to bars 1 and 2; see footnote in musical text); the same in C, but with appoggiatura d[2] in soprano (as in A) and [ornament] on alto c[2] — not adopted in our text since the combination is hardly possible. Bar 5: C, D, no appoggiatura in alto; [ornament] (soprano, 3rd beat) from D, but that source lacks the appoggiatura present in A and C; the two ornaments, however (appoggiatura and [ornament]), do not exclude one another (cf. in the musical text the footnote to bars 34 and 35, which shows Bach's combination of the two ornaments in Gerber's manuscript); if [ornament] is played at this point, however, then [ornament] must also be played in bar 7, alto! Bar 6: C, D, no [ornament] . Bar 7: C, D, no [ornament] in soprano; [ornament] (alto, 3rd beat) from C, D, but C is again without an appoggiatura (see above, bar 5). Bar 9: C, D alto [musical example]; D, no appoggiatura in soprano. Bar 10: C, D soprano [musical example]; no [ornament] (alto). Bar 11: C, D no [ornament] ; [ornament] from C, D. Bar 12: C [musical example], D [musical example]. Bar 15: [ornament] from C, D. Bar 16: C, D, [musical example]. Bar 17, 18: C gives [ornament] instead of [ornament]. Bar 20: C, D, soprano appoggiatura before 3rd beat reads [♮] e[2] rather than c[2], Bar 21: C, penultimate alto note [ornament]. Bar 22: C, D [musical example] (no [ornament] in alto). Bar 23: C, D, [ornament] instead of [ornament]. Bar 25: C, D, no [ornament] or appoggiatura (alto); alto 3rd beat reads [musical example] in C, [musical example] in D. Bar 26: soprano 3rd beat reads [musical example] in C, [musical example] in D. Bar 28: C, D, soprano 2nd, 3rd beats read [musical example]. Bar 29: [ornament] from C, D. Bar 34: C, D, no [ornament] ; alto 3rd beat reads [musical example], but we find A's reading more convincing. Bar 35: C, D, no [ornament] ; alto 3rd beat reads [musical example]. Bar 36: C, D, soprano reads [musical example] (in C, moreover, [ornament] on g[2] — see footnote in musical text — and the "accent" is erroneously notated a second higher).

Bar 38: C, D, [musical example].

---

[26]) Hermann Keller, *op. cit.*, p. 34.
[27]), [28]) Georg von Dadelsen, *op. cit.*

*) Execution of Bach's ornamentation in Gerber's MS. copy:

Sinfonia 6

Sources: all bracketed ornaments in small print are later additions in C; the appoggiaturas in soprano, bar 34, and alto, bar 41, are not written as "accents" there, but appear as in our text, namely semiquaver and quaver respectively. Bar 18: B, no ornament.

Sinfonia 7, embellished version

Bar 1/2 (and analogously in bar 14/15 and 37/38):

Bar 7 (and analogously in bar 23):

; to avoid the parallel fifths between soprano and alto in bar 7, we suggest a slight rhythmic

shift: or .

Bar 8 (and analogously in bar 9 and 16):

"accent" = quaver appoggiatura. To soften the d sharp—D cross-relationship in bar 16, a semiquaver appoggiatura can be played, as at the beginning of bar 37

where there is no other choice: .

Bar 43/44:

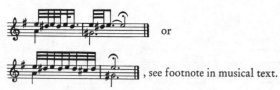

or

, see footnote in musical text.

Sources: all ornaments in the embellished version are later additions in C.

Sinfonia 8

A trill should be added in bar 15 ( ) and bar 23 ( ) as should a pralltriller in the principal motive at its reappearance in bars 8, 9, 10, 18, 19, 22 (soprano) and 12, 13, 19, 21 (bass).

in bar 2 means .

Sources: bar 2, 3: B, no ornament. Bar 10: D, no ⌣.

Sinfonia 9, embellished version

The execution of appoggiaturas and "slides" ("Schleifer" ⌣) needs sufficient time; therefore, the tempo cannot be much greater than ♩ = 44.

In D the ornamentation of the obbligato counterpoint

is lacking throughout; the player might also consider omitting it, to form a contrast to the embellished principal theme.

Bar 1, etc.:

=

Bar 2/3:

. The appoggiaturas, as we show at the beginning of bar 3, are played without exception as "sighing" semiquavers ("Seufzer,").

Pay special attention to the caesura when a phrase ending with a "Seufzer" is followed immediately by a new phrase in the same part (e. g. bars 13, 15, 23, soprano).

Bar 25:

the embellishment of the theme in D (see also below) includes a ⌣ on the 3rd bass note. We have not put this ornament into our text, because the same note (d flat¹) with the same ornament anticipates it by 2 quavers in the obbligato counterpoint which is embellished according to C. If the player does not embellish the counterpoint, however, the bass ornament should of course be played.

Bar 34/35:

In bar 19, alto, we recommend ⌣ instead of ⌣ (for execution see bar 2), likewise in bar 12 to avoid two

pralltrillers in immediate succession; in this case the fingering must be:

Sources: ornaments lacking in C appear in small print. In C and D, Sinfonia 9 was initially unembellished (except for ⌣ in soprano, bar 12). Landshoff surmises that in C the subsequently added ornaments "were obviously not all added at the same time or by the same hand[29]." It is thus conceivable that the ornaments appearing only in C are the last to have been entered. In D the form and placing of the "slide" are peculiar; ⌣ appears above the note rather than ⌣ before the note. This leads us to suspect that D served as the source of C's ornamentation: in bar 3, and in bars 11, 13, 23 (2nd half) and 33 (1st half) C writes ⌣ rather than ⌣ (as does D in bar 11); in bars 23 and 33 a "slide" is added to the pralltriller in C. In D the theme

is embellished

throughout; only in bar 1 are the two "slides" missing, compared to C. In the interludes (bars 5/6, 9/10, 15/17, 20/23, 28/30) D has ornaments only in bars 10 and 15, in bar 16 (bass), 23 (2nd half), 28/29 (bass) and 30 (soprano). The "accent" markings are taken from C; in D they can only be made out for certain in soprano, bar 5 (2nd beat) to bar 7 (all the later additions in D were made in green ink which is now badly faded). Bar 34: D has *tr* instead of ⌣ .

Sinfonia 11

Bar 9:

Sources: bar 9: the ornament in A is carelessly notated, and is most likely ⌣ ; B has *tr* instead. Bar 24, 28: B, no ornament.

Sinfonia 11, embellished version

The execution of the suspensions and appoggiaturas demands a tempo slower than that of the unembellished version. We suggest ♩. = 36—40.

The suspensions and appoggiaturas are best executed as semiquavers throughout, with the following exceptions:

in bars 6 and 70 as dotted quavers (i. e.), because of the alto voice-leading; in bar 8 as a crotchet, in bar 36 as a quaver, in bar 48 again as a crotchet (since all 3 bars end the cadence); in bar 48 a semiquaver appoggiatura might also be considered, because of the sequences which follow in bars 50 and 52.

We also suggest (for the sake of the desired assonance with the three-tone mordent) that pralltrillers begin as a rule with the principal tone, with the following exceptions: in bars 15 and 17 a short or long execution

beginning with the upper note, .

Bar 9:

[29] Ludwig Landshoff, *op. cit.*, p. 90.

Bar 38:
the appoggiatura is a flat[1], not a[1]!

Bar 69:
the unusual placement of the pralltriller (on e[1] rather than f sharp[1]) is probably due to the fact that a trill on f sharp[1] would weaken the effect both of the bass g[1] at the beginning of the next bar and the immediate sequence of alto tones (f sharp[1]—g[1]).

Sources: ornaments lacking in C appear in small print. Some of the ornaments in C seem to have been added at various times, and not in the same hand; in D only the three ornaments from A were present initially. The two MS. copies are probably interdependent as to ornamentation; bars 1—5 and their repetition (bars 65—69), for example, are embellished differently, but in precisely the same manner in both sources. Bar 5: C, "accent" marking (erroneously?) placed a third too low. In D, ⵁ is lacking in bars 1 and 46, and ⵡ in bars 7, 13, 18—22, 45.

Sinfonia 12

Bar 1:
either both appoggiaturas are played as semiquavers, or else the 1st is played as a semiquaver and the 2nd as a quaver.

In bar 31, soprano, a trill should by played on b[1] (beginning from above).

Sources: all bracketed ornaments in small print, including the appoggiaturas in bar 1 (written as "accents") are from C.

Sinfonia 13

We recommend that all trills contained in A and B begin without exception from above (even if preceded by the upper second) and be played short for the sake

of greater incisiveness: . It is left to the player to decide where and when (or whether) this trill should be added to the reappearances of the principal motive; to play it every time, and in the same way, would be overly pedantic. Comparison with the embellishments in C and D is especially instructive in this case.

Sources: bar 15, 35: ⵡ also present in B.

Sinfonia 13, embellished version

In this piece the execution of the ornaments does not make a slower tempo necessary since — except for the final bar — only bar 2 contains an appoggiatura.

Bar 1/3:
we recommend the following execution:

that is, the 2nd trill in bar 3 should be long and, as recommended in the unembellished version, should begin with the upper note, to distinguish it from the 1st trill (on c[2]) and give it more weight. An exception of a special kind is

Bar 7:
our fingering allows the execution of both trills; the trill in the alto will of course have to be short, although it is otherwise better long when it appears on that note of the principal motive. In principle, no objection can be made to the practice of altering ornamentation at motive repetitions (or even to embellishing other notes than were ornamented the first time — see Sinfonia 11, bars 67—71); the trill on the soprano leading tone is more important than the alto trill here, and could even be played as a long trill (see the semiquaver e[2] anti-

cipation): .

The trill in bar 31 should be played short (beginning from above) so that the suspension resolution in the alto (c sharp[2]) is audible; the same thing should perhaps be done in bars 23, 27, 35, 55, if the contrasting motive in the contrapuntal part cannot otherwise be brought out clearly enough.

Bar 11:
short trill beginning with the principal note.

Bar 15, 45:
short trill beginning with the upper note.

Bar 64:
if the appoggiatura is played, its resolution, in keeping with the character of the piece, should also be

embellished: for example 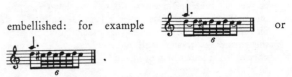 or

Sources: initially, C and D had only the ornaments in bars 15 and 35, which also appear in A and B; C further had the ornaments on the 2nd note of bar 3, soprano, and bar 7, alto (which likewise occur in B), and possibly the ornaments in bars 23 and 55 too. Bar 2/3: D, ⵥ and ⵡ (above c[2]) are lacking. Bar 7: D, no ⵡ in alto. Bar 45: D, no ⵡ.

Sinfonia 14

Bar 1:
the appoggiatura is played as a semiquaver.

Bar 2 (and analogously in bar 7):

ⵡ and *tr* mean the same thing:

C requires in bar 7 an execution beginning with the tone

below: , which for bar 7 is just as

good, if not better.

Bar 11:

Bar 15:

in C , *i. e.* ⵁ in addition. The 1st of the two "accent" markings is very difficult to see, because of the natural sign before b[1]; it is possible that the mordent was added because the "accent" marking was overlooked. We suggest playing either the mordent and 2nd appoggiatura, or the two appoggiaturas without the mordent.

Bar 17:

or .

Sources: all bracketed ornaments in small print, including the appoggiaturas in bars 1 and 15 (notated as "accents") are from C. Bar 2: B, no ornament.

Sinfonia 15

Bar 37:

or .

Sources: all bracketed ornaments in small print, including the appoggiatura in bar 32 (notated as an "accent"), are from C. Bar 37: in A, *tr* added later — not before 1725, since it is also lacking in D; B, C give ⵡ instead of *tr*.

Karl Heinz Füssl

THE FORMAL PRINCIPLES

(Translator's note: Many of the terms used by Erwin Ratz in this commentary derive from Schoenberg's teaching. Most of the English equivalents are found in Schoenberg's "Models for Beginners in Composition" and are used in the same sense here. Readers are advised to consult that book for the full definitions as given by Schoenberg. I have used "fugue theme" for "subject" in view of the fact that Erwin Ratz goes to some length to point out that while Bach often uses a fugal technique in the Sinfonias, what he is writing are not fugues; he treats the themes as themes and not subjects, i. e. they are varied in a number of ways.)

In his preface to the Inventions and Sinfonias Bach expressly states that one of their purposes is to lead the pupil "not only to be inspired with good inventions, but also to develop them properly ... and to gain a strong foretaste of composition." In previous editions little attention has been paid to this one of Bach's aims. It may not be out of place, then, to discuss ways of perceiving the formal principles which put Bach on a plane far above his contemporaries, and which had a decisive influence on the work of later composers, especially Beethoven.

In the following remarks, those pieces are singled out in which these new formal principles can be clearly recognized. In the other pieces Bach is more interested in demonstrating the art of carrying on an idea and its contrapuntal working-out.

I n v e n t i o n 1 already shows us with convincing clarity the goal Bach was driving at. The piece falls into four sections: 6 + 8 + 4 + 4. (To simplify matters, the structural disposition is given in whole bars; to be absolutely precise we would have to say bar 1 to 1st semiquaver of bar 7, 2nd semiquaver of bar 7 to 1st semiquaver of bar 15, etc., which is much too awkward and complicated.) The disposition is achieved by harmonic means (bars 6 and 14) and motivic means (bars 15—18, the tied minim motive). Looking at the sections individually, we notice at the start of the first six-bar structure a one-bar sub-phrase composed of a semiquaver motive plus a quaver motive (C: I—V), and its repetition which returns from the dominant to the tonic. We call such a relationship a "reply" (to distinguish it from the "answer" in a fugue; the German word for both is "Beantwortung." Translator's note). Both the literal repetition and the reply (especially the latter) serve to establish a "stable" situation, the stabilization of the tonic. Opposed to this is the sequence as the representative of the "loosened" condition, i. e. a state of motion. In bar 3 we see that the quaver motive in the right hand is dropped, the semiquaver motive being continued in the inversion. We call this procedure "elaboration" and describe the six-bar structure as a "sentence." After being interrupted by a new motive in bar 5 [musical example], which turns out to be a variation of the quaver motive in bar 2 [musical example], the reduction process is carried to the point of "liquidation" in bar 6 (Schoenberg: "liquidation ... is a method of getting rid of the obligations of the motive"). Now the scalar upbeat is dispensed with and only the "non-obligatory"

broken thirds remain, leading to the cadence in G major (C: V). Looking at the dotted motive in bars 5 and 13 — the only two places it occurs — we realize that its purpose is to emphasize the decisive harmonic turning-points.

It should be mentioned here that we apply the term "motive" solely to the element of rhythm, and that we denote as "thematic substance" everything that has to do with pitches. Only in this way can the two possible manners of variation be presented; either one retains the pitches and alters the rhythm (this is what happens in normal variations), or else one retains the rhythm and alters the pitches. Precisely this principle is of decisive importance in creating musical coherence, as we shall see on further investigation of the Inventions and Sinfonias. In simplified usage it often happens, of course, that definite pitches are imagined in connection with the term "motive."

As in many other Inventions, the second section begins with a transposed repetition of the first. Here bars 7 and 8 correspond to bars 1 and 2, transposed to G major and with the parts exchanged. Now the transposed elaboration to D major would have to follow. This, however, does not happen; an interpolation of two bars results in the elaboration leading not from G major to D major but from D minor to A minor — the harmonic goal of this Invention. Notice how closely the interpolation (bars 9 and 10) is related to the two bars preceding it. Motivically, bars 9/10 are identical to bars 7/8 (apart from the inversion); but their function is diametrically opposed. Bars 7/8 have a "reply" relationship and represent the "stable" situation; bars 9/10, on the other hand, have a sequence relationship and represent the "loosened" condition in the service of modulation, a state of motion. Thus we have two motivically identical segments with opposite functions; we will have occasion to discuss this point again in connection with Invention 5.

Now comes the return. In contrast to the interpolation (bars 9/10) which is only a part of the second section, the return (bars 15—18) is a section of the total form. The returning modulation is based on a two-bar model and its sequence; it is notable that the progressions of harmonic degrees, compared to the interpolation, are exchanged in pairs. The progression in bars 9/10 is C: V^7—I, VI^7—II; in bars 15—18 it is C: VI^7—II, V^7—I. The heightened importance of these four bars as a section of the form is derived from the new motive of the tied minim, and from the contrast of the original and inverted semiquaver motive within the two-bar model.

The fourth section is remarkable on many counts. We call it a recapitulation or coda. A complete recapitulation would make little sense, since the whole Invention is constructed from the motives in the first bar. Bach therefore chooses a form which has both recapitulatory and cadential features. Added to this is the "condensation" process in bar 19: thematically it is a recapitulation, but its structure is that of the "elaboration" in bar 3; these two presentations are, so to speak, superimposed. But there is something even more ingenious about this passage: bar 19 is the retrograde of bar 3 (compare bar 3, 2nd semiquaver to bar 4, 3rd semiquaver — and bar 19, 2nd semiquaver to bar 20, 3rd semiquaver). That the inversion of the inversion produces the original shape is obvious; but that it produces the retrograde at the same time is evidence of the art of musical invention in which Bach was one of the greatest masters.

This relatively detailed discussion of Invention 1 was necessary because, among other things, it sets up the guiding lines for our remarks on the other Inventions and Sinfonias.

One more important consideration: the student must be able to tell at all times what elements belong to homophonic presentation and what elements to polyphonic presentation. The cadences in bars 6 and 14, the sequences in bars 15—18, etc., are elements of homophonic presentation. The imitations in bars 1 and 2 are earmarks of polyphonic style, but they are too negligible here to have any influence on the form. Not until Invention 7 does imitation become a significant element of construction.

In I n v e n t i o n 2 we observe the same architectonic structure as in Invention 1: 10 + 10 + 2 + 5. The first section (bars 1—10) is constructed as a canon; thus a polyphonic principle follows as a contrast to the "sentence" structure in the first six bars of Invention 1 (which is in line with the homophonic principle). The canon leads from C minor to E flat major. The second section is an exact sequence of the first, with parts exchanged, and leads from G minor to B flat major. The return follows (bars 21/22). It takes up the motive from the upper part in bar 20, sequences it twice and thus reaches C minor. The fourth section is again a recapitulation or coda. It shows us quite clearly what classical composers meant by transformation of the material of the exposition for cadential (or closing-group) purposes. Now there is no sign of a canon. A two-bar phrase is formed from the material of bars 3 and 4; it leads to a cadence and is repeated with the parts exchanged. This five-bar group, then, has both the function of a recapitulation and of the closing group in a coda.

In this Invention the architectonic disposition is not easily perceived, but it is nevertheless operative if we are aware of it. Especially remarkable is the polyphonic interlacing in bars 11 and 12. The upper part makes a melodically quite distinct cadence in G minor, while the lower part has already begun the canon melody in bar 11, so that the caesura at the end of bar 12 seems much more forceful; even so, the resumption of the canon determines the structural disposition: 10 + 10 + 2 + 5.

The formal principles outlined in Invention 1 undergo a significant development in Invention 5. Its formal disposition is 11 + 11 + 4 + 6. Here again, only homophonic elements are decisive. We see at the beginning a four-bar phrase and its reply. We can consider these eight bars as a period. Motivically, the four-bar phrase is extremely plastically shaped: it begins with a one-bar sub-phrase and its sequence; a new motive appears in the third bar, and is extensively varied in the fourth. This constitutes the antecedent phrase, and leads from the tonic to the dominant; the consequent phrase leads from the dominant back to the tonic. In the next three bars the motive from bar 1 is repeated three times, rising stepwise, and leads to C minor.

Now comes the repetition of the eleven bars. Motivically, they are identical to the first section, but functionally they are diametrically opposed. What we observed in Invention 1 in the relationship of bars 9/10 to bars 7/8 is applied to the form of the whole Invention here. In the first section we noticed that the relationship is

one of "reply", of antecedent and consequent, i. e. a "stable" condition in the sense of a principal theme; now, however, the relationship is one of sequence, which gives the second section the function of a development, leading from C minor via F minor to B flat minor, with the next three bars returning — stepwise downwards — to F minor. The significance of bar 22 is especially emphasized by the only perfect cadence in the whole Invention. That the eleven bars are to be regarded as an architectonical unit is evident from the law which tells us that the independence of a structure is recognized by the structure being repeated.

A two-bar phrase and its sequence (bars 23—26) act as a return to the recapitulation or coda. The recapitulation begins like the first section, but after the third bar there is a sequence of the third bar; this interpolation brings about the transposition of the next bars and the cadence in the principal key of E flat major.

I n v e n t i o n 6 is the only one of the set that has a scherzo form with repeats of both the first section and the second and third (/:a:/:b + a′:/). The first section (the scherzo theme) is built as an expanded sixteen-bar sentence. We see a four-bar segment and its repetition, followed by an elaboration whose distinguishing characteristics are: acceleration of the presentation by reduction of the units, a quicker pace to the harmony, motivic liquidation. First a two-bar phrase is formed (bars 9/10) which combines the syncopation motive with the broken triad of the bar before (translator's note: Ratz calls this "Anschlußtechnik" which in this sense can be rendered as "affiliation technique"). We also find the demisemiquaver and semiquaver motive. Thus all the motives of the four-bar segment are used, but the space they occupy is reduced by half. After the sequence of this phrase a liquidation occurs: only the syncopation motive remains; at first, it is still combined with the broken triad, but in the next bar it is again joined to the scale. One extremely noteworthy point: the tones g sharp — f sharp — e (bar 14) are the highest tones of bars 9, 11 and 13; this creates a feeling of enormous acceleration, which is balanced by the expansion of the cadence and in the closing bars that follow.

In keeping with the scherzo form, the second section is constructed as a development. (Translator's note: Schoenberg calls the second section of the scherzo form the "elaboration" section; here, however, Ratz uses the word "Durchführung" as opposed to "Entwicklung", whose equivalent is elaboration. We must therefore depart from Schoenberg's terminology on this point.) In scherzo or sonata form, development involves two things: 1. the creation of a new organism, the so-called "model", which is formed of motives from the thematic material presented in the exposition and is constructed so as to modulate for the purpose of sequence; 2. the sequences of that model and the liquidation process which then sets in. The development of Invention 6 begins with the transposition of the four-bar segment and its repetition to B minor (E: V), the key in which the scherzo theme ended. We see how Bach constantly introduces new ideas in constructing the second section, proceeding each time from the transposed beginning of the first section but continuing it in new ways and functions. The four-bar segment and its repetition are followed by a modulatory group (bars 29—32) on the order of the introductory segment of the classical development. The elaboration in the first section took the broken triad of bar 8 as its point of departure; the modulatory group takes as its starting point the demisemiquaver motive of bar 8. The modulation leads from G sharp minor to C sharp minor (E: III—VI). The two-bar model that follows (bars 33/34) has a strong resemblance to the two-bar phrase of the elaboration group in the first section, but there are substantial differences all the same: first, the syncopation motive remains allied with stepwise progression. Second, we observe an important change in the harmonic conception: in the elaboration group the order was triad — seventh-chord (E: VI—II⁷), while now, to effect the return, the order is seventh-chord — triad (C sharp minor: V⁷—I). The two-bar model is sequenced twice, leading to the Neapolitan sixth of G sharp minor and preparing the end of the development (bar 42).

Since the first section (the scherzo theme) ended on the dominant, the recapitulation must be "adjusted." This occurs here by transposing the elaboration group a fifth lower. But we must not be led to confuse this transposition with that of a subsidiary theme in an adagio or sonata form, for bars 1—20 are a closed theme of sentence-like structure and not a principal theme plus a subsidiary theme.

Invention 7 consciously takes Invention 1 as its point of departure. Bach now shows how imitation affects the construction, whereas in Invention 1 it was of no significance for the structure of the theme. As in Invention 1, we find a one-bar unit consisting of two motives and followed by its "reply". Here too, the semiquaver motive is imitated in the lower part. Now comes the elaboration. This time the unit is not reduced in the upper part; it remains one bar long and the one-bar unit is sequenced. The acceleration of the presentation is achieved here by a contrapuntal principle: the imitation occurs at the fifth, thus leading to half-bar changes of harmony (E minor: I—IV, VII—III). Further liquidation takes place in the lower part in bar 5 (in half-bars) and leads to the cadence in the parallel key of G major. We see that the elaboration is not limited to one part as in homophonic presentation, but that both parts have a share in it.

Before continuing with the further progress of this Invention, let us look at its structure. It is highly

original: 6 + 2½ + 2 + [2] + 2 + 2½ + 6

Moreover, the parts grouped symmetrically about the middle axis correspond to one another in function. But the form can also be defined as four-part (the disposition which is normally valid for the Inventions): 1st section = bars 1—6; 2nd section = bars 6 to middle of 13; return = middle of 13—17; recapitulation = 18—23. A three-part division can likewise be made: theme (bars 1—6), development (bars 7—17), recapitulation (bars 18—23), in which case we divide the middle section into five subsections and thus come closest to doing justice to the dramatic occurrences it has in store. The first sub-section begins with the initial motive in G major, but then breaks off immediately and leads to a cadence on the dominant of G major (bar 9). The next sub-section also begins with the initial motive and leads to the dominant of B minor (bar 11). The expansion of the leap of a fifth in bar 1 to a sixth in bar 3 and finally to a seventh at the beginning of bar 10 is also an intensification of thematic substance. The absolute climax follows (middle of bar 11 to middle of bar 13). All the means available in two-part writing are mustered to achieve this dramatic point of culmination: stretto at

the fifth, seventh-chord with minor third, two tritones. The next sub-section (bars 13—15) leads to a pedal point on V of E minor with a further variation of the initial motive. In bar 7 the nucleus of the initial motive remained unchanged and only the upbeat was altered: the G is reached from below rather from above. As the passage continues, the upbeat is expanded to three semiquavers. In bar 13 the nucleus itself is altered. Just as in bar 2 the leap of a fifth was replaced by the octave (the fifth following only afterward), the fifth and octave are exchanged here too: instead of g — f sharp — g — e — b the motive now reads g — f sharp — g — b — e.

The biggest surprise awaits us in the recapitulation. At first, the new semiquaver motive evolved above the pedal-point B seems to provide the only connection. But if we look more closely at the motive which appears for the first time at this point we will notice that the tones b — a — g — f sharp (with which the motive and its repetitions start) are the first four tones of the initial motive in bar 1. The f sharp (middle of bar 19) must be imagined as sustained until the 3rd beat of bar 20. With the tones g — e — c, the initial motive is resumed — after a broad ritardando, so to speak. Thus we can in fact regard this section as a free recapitulation whose cadential function is strengthened even more by the deceptive cadence in bar 22.

It is extremely interesting to note that bars 18 and 19 do not appear in the first version of this Invention (written for the "Klavierbüchlein"), and that only the final version contains this ingenious treatment of the recapitulation.

Invention 8 divides into three sections. The first is constructed as a canon, at the octave until bar 7 and 1st beat of bar 8 respectively, and at the ninth from the 3rd beat of those bars until bar 10 and the 4th semiquaver of bar 11 respectively. A cadence in C major (F: V) ends the first section.

The structure of the second section is unusually significant: it is built as a development. To be sure, it begins as a transposition of the first section (we encounter this over and over again in the Inventions), but Bach uses only the first three bars, adding a new fourth bar which brings about a modulation to G minor; this creates a modulatory four-bar model for sequence purposes. A sequence of the model occurs; this time the upper part begins and the lower part follows in imitation. To comprehend this technique (which was of such great importance for Beethoven) it is advisable to imagine the bass from the 2nd quaver of bar 16 to the 1st quaver of bar 17 as not being there, for it disguises the structure. It is absolutely necessary to visualize exactly the connection between bars 16/17 (minus the bass figure in bar 16!) and bars 12/13, for here the decisive step is taken in the evolution of the musical presentation. Bars 20—25 are concerned with "liquidating" the model; the units become smaller — two bars at first, then one bar.

In bar 26, without any caesura, the recapitulation begins, in the subdominant and minus the first three bars. Bar 26 = bar 4; in this way the recapitulation is "adjusted", that is, designed to end on the tonic.

In the original version of the Invention (in the "Klavierbüchlein"), bars 17—20 are lacking. Not until the final version, then, did Bach insert the sequence of the model, which is so characteristic of the nature of the development; and only in this way do bars 12—15 come to have the significance of a developmental model at all.

In Invention 9 Bach goes one step further in the systematic build-up of his compositional method. He begins by writing a four-bar segment and its repetition with parts exchanged.

This is followed by the construction of a developmental model. Again Bach takes the first three bars of the Invention. This time, however, the modulation is not brought about by adding a fourth bar, but by changing the size of an interval: instead of the sixth in bar 1, we find in bar 9 a leap of a tenth, by which the change of harmony to the dominant of C minor is achieved. This procedure is a more refined artistic principle than the mechanical addition of a fourth bar. A sequence of the three-bar model follows. The harmony of bar 14 leads us to expect G minor in bar 15; instead, the dominant of C minor appears. The harmonic motion thus swings back, as it were. A cadence in C minor brings the first section of this two-section Invention to an end.

The second section starts by quoting the four-bar segment (in C minor) with which the Invention began. Then Bach goes on to a higher plane in setting up the developmental model: he takes two distant motives from the four-bar segment, the 1st bar (changing the leap of a sixth to a seventh) and the 4th bar. The tie-up of these two motives creates a new organism which functions as the developmental model of the second section. The model is sequenced with parts exchanged. The ensuing liquidation process leads to the dominant of F minor (bar 28), after which the opening four-bar segment reappears as a recapitulation and is followed by a cadence in F minor.

Our next example is Invention 14, in which new principles can be observed. The first section comprises 3 + 2 + 3 bars. The second section is again constructed as a development. The introductory part of the development (bars 9—11) carries out the modulation from F major to C minor. Until now the presentation was purely homophonic (melody + accompaniment); with the creation of the model, the contrapuntal element of imitation makes its appearance. Furthermore, the model ist distinguished by a new dotted quaver-semiquaver motive (bar 12). The liquidation process leads back to B flat major — and now we again see a new and decisive idea: the recapitulation does not match the exposition, but is enriched by the imitation which first occurred in the development. In this way the recapitulation undergoes a far-reaching alteration which we perceive as a substantial advance over its initial presentation.

The presence of a third part in the Sinfonias makes possible a further development of the formal principles evolved in the Inventions. There the construction principle of a section was the canon; in the Sinfonias the idea of a three-part fugue exposition appears in manifold variants as the principle basic to the form of a section. But we also encounter in the Sinfonias homophonic construction principles such as sentence, period, development, etc. The first section of Sinfonia 2, for example, is built as an eight-bar sentence: a two-bar phrase, its repetition, and a $4^1/_2$-bar elaboration. Again we find the typical features of accelerated presentation: reduction of the units, quicker harmonic motion, liquidation. It is remarkable how, in bar 5, bar 2 (in reduction) is worked into the one-bar sequential model. The acceleration can be seen very clearly in the descending bass line: it begins by moving in full bars (c^1, b flat), then in half-bars (a flat, g, f, e flat, d^1). The elaboration

heads first in the direction of E flat major (the parallel major key) and then turns towards the minor form of degree V. The repetition of this section occurs in G minor; it does not lead to D minor, however, but remains in G minor, extending the cadence in that key by an extra bar. The third section is constructed as a development (bars 19—27). A two-bar model, its sequential repetition and the ensuing liquidation process lead to the dominant of C minor. In bar 28 the recapitulation of the first section enters, minus the two-bar phrase and its repetition. The "adjustment" occurs in bar 30: in place of C minor: VI—III there is now C minor: IV—I, which makes possible the final cadence on the tonic of C minor.

Sinfonia 3 shows us the new formal principles in full flower. That this is not a three-part fugue is abundantly clear from the accompanying bass at the beginning, and especially from the way in the "fugue" theme is answered. The theme itself consits of a principal segment of two bars which merely expresses the tonic, plus a half-bar "appendix" which turns to the dominant. In the answer, the nucleus of the theme appears in the dominant (which would correspond to a real answer in a fugue), but the appendix turns back to the tonic, at which the third entrance of the "fugue" theme follows in the original manner. Incidentally, we must not overlook the contrasting part which appears at the second entrance of the theme and is retained at the third entrance.

Before the bass has finished its statement of the theme, a new one-bar motive enters in the soprano (bar 8), combining a dotted rhythm with the appendix of the theme; this new motive is sequenced in half-bars and accomplishes the modulation to B minor, the theme in B minor entering on the six-four chord (bar 10). The appendix now turns to the dominant of F sharp minor, and a liquidation process sets in which seemingly consists only of a four-tone scalar line repeated several times in upward and downward motion. If we observe it closely, however, we will find that this passage contains the complete theme in F sharp minor, divided between the upper two parts:

With a cadence in F sharp minor, the first section of the Sinfonia is finished. In behaviour and expression it has very much the air of the exposition of a sonata form: the three entrances in D major serve as a principal theme, the transition provides a modulation to the region of the subsidiary theme, which with thematic entrances in B minor and F sharp minor definitely presents a "loosened" condition.

Again, the second section is built as a development (middle of bar 14—bar 18). The systematic presentation of model construction in Inventions 8 and 9 reaches a climax here. The model begins with the initial motive of the theme; this is combined with the end of the theme nucleus (bar 2, 2nd half) which, however, is transposed by one step. The middle part imitates the initial motive. The bass brings the appendix of the theme and goes on to a variant of the initial motive. We have here, then, a consummate construction of a model which unites various motives into a new organism. As we advised in Invention 8, the soprano figure in bar 16 of this Sinfonia

(2nd semiquaver to 5th quaver) should be imagined as not being there, so that the strict sequence can be properly visualized. Here the middle part leads, the soprano imitates the initial motive, the bass remains unchanged (apart from the transposition). A short liquidation process over the pedal-point D, the dominant of G major, ends the development. A subdominant recapitulation follows, which, so to speak, copies the subdominant inclination of the theme. One notable point about the recapitulation is that it is one bar shorter than the corresponding exposition section. The reason is the appendix motive of the theme. Here Bach shows that it exists only for the purpose of reaching another harmonic region. The moment this need disappears, the appendix disappears with it. The penultimate entrance is in D major; so is the last entrance; the tonic reached in the penultimate entrance is not left, and so the appendix can be omitted both times.

Other formal aspects are demonstrated in S i n f o n i a 7, one of Bach's most significant creations. It is likewise constructed in three sections (bars 1—14, 14—37, 37—44). The first section begins like the exposition of a three-part fugue. Entrances of the theme in the soprano and alto are followed by two intervening bars, after which the bass presents the theme in bar 7. A six-bar continuation leads to a cadence in B minor (E minor: V). The striking thing about the beginning of the second section is that it does not enter on the degree reached at the end of the first section (B minor), but on the tonic. The theme acquires a new semiquaver counterpoint derived from the counterpoint in the first bar. No change from the exposition can be noticed in the first two entrances. But then a wide-ranging two-bar model is set up; it is followed by a sequence and a two-bar liquidation process which brings about a modulation to D major.

Seen formally, what happens now is the construction of a four-bar model in D major and its sequence in B minor. Much more important, however, is the fascinating idea of contrasting to the serious character of the E minor section a climax in brilliant D major, with the inversion of the semiquaver counterpoint emphasizing even more the triumphant nature of this passage. A grandiose conception. In the second half of the model the counterpoint again appears in its downward form, and the two forms maintain a balance until the end of the development. The liquidation process leads to the dominant of E minor, after which the recapitulation or coda follows.

S i n f o n i a 8 is utterly different in character. The first section begins with three entrances of the "fugue" theme, dux, comes and dux in tonal answers; then comes a transition which modulates to C major, after which two entrances of the dux follow in C major, ending with a cadence in that key. If we listen to these 7½ bars without preconceived formal notions, they will definitely give the impression of a tiny sonata exposition: the three entrances of the theme in F major have the role of principal theme, the two entrances of the dux in C major correspond to the subsidiary theme, to which the principal theme is joined by a transition. This impression is strengthened by the fact that the subdominant recapitulation has the same layout, except that the first entrance of the dux is in sixths and the comes is therefore omitted. From the middle of bar 18 on, that is, from the third entrance of the theme, what we have is a literal transposition of the exposition. These features are new ideas which cannot be derived

from the nature of the fugue. The middle section (middle of bar 7 to middle of bar 17) comes closest to matching the second exposition of a fugue, although what happens musically here also deviates greatly from the normal course a fugue takes. First the theme appears in stretto at the lower fifth, and then the pair of parts is sequenced twice. The entry tones g, e, a, are the first three tones of the theme with which the first section ends and the second section begins. The further progress of the Sinfonia leads to G minor and on to D minor, the cadential effect intensified by the deceptive cadence in bar 14. What follows is to be understood as a return which leads first to F major and then (overshooting the mark, as it were) to B flat major, after which — in bar 17 — the subdominant recapitulation begins over the sustained b flat. We observe the degree of freedom with which Bach handles formal elements to suit the expression he is striving for.

Bach reaches a new peak in S i n f o n i a 9. This piece is based on three themes invented in triple counterpoint, and they are used in all possible combinations. The formal structure is quite original: the first section (bars 1—8) is arranged like the exposition of a fugue — one entrance in F minor (dux), one in C minor (comes), two intervening bars whose motives do not appear again anywhere in the piece, and a further entrance in F minor (dux). An interlude follows, modulating to A flat major. Now comes a group of nine bars which can best be designated as a subsidiary theme: one entrance in A flat major, one in E flat major, three intervening bars which modulate to C minor, and a cadence in that key. The next section — the climax of the Sinfonia — is a development in which a two-bar model is constructed from the material of the interlude (bars 9/10); its sequence leads to D flat major. Following the development comes the transposition (at the lower fifth) of bars 11—19, which strengthens the impression of a subsidiary theme function. After this group reaches F minor (bars 31/32, as the transposition of the C minor entrance in bars 18/19), the concluding F minor entrance follows as a recapitulation or coda corresponding to the first section (bars 1—8). The location of the nine-bar "subsidiary theme" group on both sides of the development gives the piece a symmetrical (or one could say retrograde) form: principal theme, transition, subsidiary theme, development, subsidiary theme (transposed), principal theme (coda). The severity of this form is closely bound up with the character of Passion music, which is present in all three themes.

S i n f o n i a 11 has a special charm. It is in two sections, each of which divides into three sub-sections (a-b-a'). Sub-section a can be thought of as a sixteen-bar period whose antecedent phrase is again influenced by the exposition of a three-part fugue: bar 1 = dux, bar 2 = comes, bar 3 = intervening bar which introduces the dotted motive, bar 4 = dux, followed by a cadence in G minor. The seemingly motley order of motives is held together by the descending G minor scale. The consequent phrase turns towards the parallel major key of B flat. The character of the middle sub-section is determined by the omission of the dotted motive. The pedal point on a prepares the return of the antecedent phrase in D minor. It is striking that the third sub-section of this (in effect) three-part song form begins on the dominant (bar 29), since we normally think of the middle section as ending only when the dominant has been left. This somewhat eccentric formal disposition (we can call it a kind of interlacing) is straightened out, so to speak, at the end of the second section (bar 64) where the customary formal disposition can be observed.

The second section begins with a return (bars 36 ff.) consisting of a two-bar phrase and its sequence, after which the adjusted recapitulation of the first section follows. Of the first sub-section, only the antecedent appears, in greatly altered shape; the middle sub-section is expanded by four bars (55, 56, 63, 64) after which — as the third sub-section — comes the antecedent again, now in G minor and in the same guise with which this capricious piece began.

How successful Bach is in presenting the most varied musical characters can be briefly demonstrated on S i n f o n i a 13. The form divides into three sections: exposition (bars 1—16), development (bars 17—48), recapitulation (bars 49—64). Again the exposition has the traits of a three-part fugue: dux, comes, intervening bars, dux. The next four bars bring about a modulation to C major. With a new motive in the bass, an eight-bar model is set up which is constructed so as to modulate for the purpose of sequence, the eighth bar turning towards D minor. After the sequence (bars 29—36) comes the liquidation process, which again introduces a new motive. In the return, the theme also appears in stretto.

The recapitulation is enriched by the addition of the new motive which entered in the development. It is remarkable that all three entrances are the dux; instead of the comes the theme appears in tenths, so that both shapes of the theme (A minor and C major) are heard at the same time. The upbeat motive of the liquidation (bars 36 and 56 respectively) allows the last entrance of the theme to come one bar sooner; this in turn permits the final bar to fit in, without the listener being aware of the shift.

This piece has a structure which we also find in Beethoven: the first and third sections together have the same length as the middle section (16 + 32 + 16). The strongly emphasized four-bar units, together with the peculiar nature of the melody, are responsible for the folksong character of this Sinfonia.

In S i n f o n i a 14 Bach's point is to achieve a richness of melodic expression by altering the intervals of the theme. The melodic alterations have a close connection with modulatory processes in the harmony. Both elements contribute to the intensity of the heightened expression that marks this piece. The first section begins with three entrances of the theme in tonal answers (dux, comes, intervening bars, dux) on the order of a three-part fugue exposition. The motive [musical notation] is varied in the second bar to form a contrast to the comes [musical notation]. In bar 3 it appears in yet another shape: [musical notation]. We see the same rhythm each time, but filled with new thematic substance. This kind of variation (retaining the rhythm and altering the pitches) creates a particularly tight connection despite the strong melodic contrasts.

In bar 7 comes the first entrance of the altered theme. As the piece progresses the student must keep in mind the differences in expression the altered themes create in comparison to the original shape (dux or comes). A further entrance follows in bar 8 in the soprano part, circumscribing the dominant of C minor. In bar 10 the theme appears as dux in F major, but here too the leap to A is felt as a special accentuation. The first section ends with a cadence in F major. In the second section the entrances of the theme (with intervals altered) appear in a number of strettos, thus achieving a further heightening of expression. Notice the many variations of the basic thematic shape in bar 12 (soprano and alto), bar 14 (soprano) and bar 15, 3rd beat (middle part). This extremely lively section ends in a cadence in E flat major (bar 17). A short return leads to strettos between dux, comes (bar 20) and dux (bar 21). Then a short coda concludes a piece which, in a way that is again new, demonstrates an amazing liveliness of musical invention. What is new here is that the alterations made in the theme are not possible within the confines of the fugue, since a fugue subject is not supposed to be varied. In the fugue, the subject remains constant, while the other parts are responsible for the various harmonic "interpretations" of it; here, however, the theme itself is, so to speak, the source of the expressive alterations that occur.

This brings our brief survey of characteristic formal principles to an end. We hope that it may give the player an attentive awareness of the expressive content of Bach's Inventions and Sinfonias. The student will discover how the form itself comes to be the source of expression — and that in the work of great masters form and content are identical. For those masters found, for every intended expression, the formal structure equal to it.

Erwin Ratz
(Translated by Eugene Hartzell)

PREFACE

In the autumn of 1726 Johann Sebastian Bach published Partita No.1 (BWV 825), under his own imprint, as a single work under the general title *Clavier Ubung / bestehend in Praeludien, Allemanden, Couranten, Sarabanden, Giquen, Menuetten, und anderen Galanterien* [Keyboard Practice consisting of Preludes, Allemandes, Courantes, Sarabandes, Gigues, Minuets and other Galanteries]. In doing so he was following the example of his predecessor as Thomaskantor in Leipzig, Johann Kuhnau (1660–1722), who in 1689 and 1692 had puplished two volumes of a *Clavier Übung*, each consisting of seven *Partien* or suites (the second volume also containing a *Sonate aus dem B* [Sonata in B flat]). It is no accident that the first appearance in print of a keyboard work of Bach's should have occured in the year 1726. Since being appointed Thomaskantor in the early summer of 1723, Bach had composed church cantatas on a regular weekly basis for Sunday services in the Thomaskirche and Nikolaikirche, thereby assembling three 'annual cycles' of cantatas which he was able to fall back on repeatedly in later years. Towards the end of his third year in the post he had performed a number of works by other composers – several cantatas by his distant cousin Johann Ludwig Bach (1677–1741) and, on Good Friday 1726, the St Mark Passion of Reinhard Keiser (1674–1739), the prolific Hamburg opera composer – and his fourth year was to yield only about twenty newly composed works. Given that about sixty pieces of church music were required in the course of a year, this suggests – even though we must assume that some of the works that were performed have since been lost – that Bach's interests had begun to shift in the course of the year 1726. It is possible that Bach's taking over of a student collegium musicum in the spring of 1729 was closely connected with the cessation of regular cantata composition. And indeed it is during this period, between 1727 and 1730, that the subsequent Partitas Nos. 2 – 6 (BWV 826–830) were published as single works at the rate of one or two a year. In 1731, finally, Bach assembled all six partitas in one volume, using the plates of the original editions (but with continuous pagination added); this volume was designated *Opus 1*. In view of the fact that by this time he had already composed the greater part of his surviving œuvre – for example, the two- and three-part *Inventions*, the first part of the *Well-tempered Clavier*, the organ works, the chamber music, the violin concertos, the orchestral suites, the *Brandenburg Concertos*, the cantatas already mentioned and, not least, the two Passions – this use of the term 'Opus 1' may seem hard to fathom. It was, however, the custom of the period to give opus numbers only to printed works; and among printed works only to instrumental music. Except for this second condition, in fact, Bach would have designated as his Opus 1 and 2 the two cantatas he wrote for the change of town council in Mühlhausen in 1708 and 1709, both of which were published, although unfortunately only the first of them (*Gott ist mein König*, BWV 71) has survived.

The sale of the partitas may have encouraged Bach to continue the *Clavier-Übung* series. He had now even found a publisher, which also indicates that *Opus 1* had achieved some circulation, and in the spring of 1735 Christoph Weigel in Nuremberg brought out a collection entitled *Zweyter Theil der Clavier Ubung bestehend in einem Concerto nach Italiaenischen Gusto und einer Overture nach Französischer Art vor ein Clavicymbel mit zweyen Manualen* [Second Part of the Keyboard Practice consisting of a Concerto according to the Italian Taste and an Overture in the French Manner for a Clavicymbal with two Manuals].

Four years later, in 1739, there followed a *Dritter Theil der Clavier Übung bestehend in verschiedenen Vorspielen über Catechismus- und andere Gesaenge vor die Orgel* [Third Part of the Keyboard Practice consisting of different Preludes on the Catechismal and other Hymns for the Organ]. It may seem surprising that organ pieces should figure in a 'Clavier-Übung', but in this period the term 'Clavier' was primarily taken to refer to keyboard instruments in general. This is apparent from the fact that the expression *2 Claviere und Pedal* was often used with reference to the organ, the term 'Clavier' corresponding to our term 'manual'. Apart from the organ chorale preludes mentioned in the title (BWV 669–689), this third part of the *Clavier-Übung* also contained a Prelude and Fugue in E flat major *pro Organo pleno* (BWV 552) and four duets, in the style of the two-part *Inventions,* for organ or harpsichord (BWV 802–805).

Finally, the fourth part of the *Clavier-Übung* (not so numbered when published, in 1741 or slightly later) consisted of the *Aria mit verschiedenen Veränderungen vors Clavicimbal mit 2 Manualen* [Aria with divers Variations for the Clavicymbal with 2 Manuals]: the so-called Goldberg Variations (BWV 988).

Unfortunately, no full autograph of the first part of the *Clavier-Übung* survives to supplement the printed version. Only Partitas No. 3 and 6 (BWV 827 and 830) have come down to us in Bach's hand, included in the second *Clavier-büchlein* for Anna Magdalena Bach in 1725, and these are early versions that were later re-worked and expanded for publication. Naturally, at one time there must have been manuscript versions, by Bach himself, of each of these partitas in their revised form, to serve as copies for the engraver. Similar engraver's copies must also have existed for Partitas Nos. 1, 2, 4 and 5. In 1879 an autograph of Partita No. 1 (BWV 825) came briefly to light,[1] containing the following dedicatory poem on the verso of the title page and the succeeding blank page:[2]

Dem Durchlauchtigsten Fürsten und Herrn
Herrn Emanuel Ludewig,
Erb-Printzen zu Anhalt, Hertzogen zu Sachßen,
Engern und Westphalen, Grafen zu Ascanien,
Herrn zu Bernburg und Zerbst, etc. etc.
    Widmete diese geringe Musicalische Erst-
    linge aus unterthänigster Devotion
        Johann Sebastian Bach.

Durchlauchtigst
    Zarter Prinz
        den zwar die Windeln decken
Doch Dein Fürsten Blick mehr als erwachsen zeigt,
Verzeihe, wenn ich Dich im Schlaffe sollte wecken
Indem mein spielend Blatt vor Dir sich nieder beugt.
Es ist die Erste Frucht, die meine Saiten bringen;
    Du bist der erste Printz den Deine Fürstin Küst
Dir soll sie auch zuerst zu Deinen Ehren singen,
    Weil Du, wie dieses Blatt, der Welt ein Erstling bist,
Die Weisen dieser Zeit erschrecken uns und sagen:
    Wir kämen auf die Welt, mit wünzeln und Geschrey
Gleichsam als wolten wir zum vorauß schon be Klagen,
    Daß dieses Kurtze Ziel betrübt und Kläglich sey.

---

[1] The owner gave an account of the document in the *Magdeburgische Zeitung* of 19 February 1879, No. 83, *Morning Edition* (cf. *NBA*, Krit. Bericht, p. 49).
[2] Quoted from *Bach-Dokumente*, Vol. I, No. 155, Kassel etc., 1963, p. 223.

Doch dieses Kehr ich um, und sage, das Gethöne,
  Das Deine Kindheit macht, ist lieblich, Klar und rein,
Drum wird Dein Lebens Lauff vergnügt, beglückt und
                                             schöne,
  Und eine Harmonie von eitel Freude seyn.
So Hoffnungs-Voller Prinz will ich Dir ferner spielen
  Wenn Dein Ergözungen noch mehr als tausendfach.
Nur fleh ich, allezeit, wie iezt, den Trieb zu fühlen
        Ich sey
              Durchlauchter Prinz
                    Dein
                        tieffster Diener
                              Bach.

[To His Most Serene Highness and Lord, Emanuel Ludewig, Hereditary Prince of Anhalt, Duke of Saxony, Engern and Westphalia, Count of Ascania, Lord of Bernburg and Zerbst, etc., etc., these modest musical first-fruits are dedicated in humblest devotion by Johann Sebastian Bach.

Most Serene tender Prince, still in swaddling clothes, whose sovereign gaze yet shows you grown beyond your years, forgive me if you should be woken from your sleep as these pages of my music take their bow before you. They are the first-fruits to be plucked upon my strings; you are the first prince to receive your sovereign mother's kiss; and she shall be the first to sing your praises, since you, like these pages, are first-born in this world. Wise men are apt to frighten us by saying that we enter this world with cries and whimpers, as if we are lamenting from the first that our brief span is wretched and full of woe. But I declare the contrary, and pronounce your infant sounds sweet, pleasant and pure; and hence your life's course will be blithe and blessed with happiness, a harmony of unmingled joy. I shall, O Prince of hope, play for you henceforth, may your delights be multiplied a thousand times or more. I pray that I shall always, as now, be impelled to do so, and remain, Serenest Prince, your humblest servant, Bach.]

Bach's description of this partita as his 'musical first-fruits' is, again, fully in line with contemporary practice, in the sense that it was the first printed edition of an instrumental work that was regarded as first-born. Prince Emanuel Ludewig was the first son of Bach's former employer, Prince Leopold of Anhalt-Cöthen. He was born on 12 September 1726, and it has been suggested that Bach added these dedicatory lines into his manuscript copy of Partita No. 1 after it had served its purpose as the engraver's copy.[3] We should note, however, that the engraving process, lasting weeks or even months, would inevitably have left its traces on the manuscript, and Bach would more probably have prepared a new fair copy for dedicatory purposes. Unfortunately, it is impossible to draw any inferences from the handwriting itself, since the copy is no longer extant.

On 1 November 1726 the following announcement appeared in the 'Selection of news received in the XLIVth week of the year 1726' in the *Leipziger Postzeitungen:*

Da der Hochfl. Anhalt-Cöthensche Capell-Meister und Director Chori Musici Lipsiensis, Herr Johann Sebastian Bach ein Opus Clavier Sviten zu ediren willens, auch bereits mit der ersteren Partitœ den Anfang gemachet hat, und solches nach und nach, bis das Opus fertig, zu continuiren gesonnen; so wird solches denen Liebhabern des Claviers wissend gemacht. Wobey denn zur Nach-richt dienet, daß der Autor von diesem Wercke selbst Verleger sey.[4]

[It is drawn to the notice of amateurs of the *Clavier* that the Capell-Meister of His Highness the Prince of Anhalt-Cöthen and *Director Chori Musici Lipsiensis*, Herr Johann Sebastian Bach, who proposes to publish an *opus* of *Clavier Suites*, has begun the same with the first *Partitae*, and intends to *continue* in such manner until the *opus* is complete. It is also announced that the *Author* of this work is himself the publisher.]

The first edition must accordingly have been prepared shortly before this date.

As far as the dates of composition of the individual partitas are concerned, we can do no more than offer conjectures. It is quite possible that Partitas Nos. 1, 2, 4 and 5 were not composed until shortly before they were published; equally, however, they may derive (at least in part) from works written earlier. According to Georg von Dadelsen[5] Partitas Nos. 3 and 6, published respectively in 1727 and, probably, 1731 (no printed copy of Partita No. 6 as a single work is extant), were transcribed into Anna Magdalena Bach's *Clavierbüchlein* in 1725 on the basis of a pre-existing copy. It is clear from the nature of the handwriting that the version in the *Clavierbüchlein* is not the compositional draft. It is possible, therefore, that these two partitas were composed even earlier, and indeed there exist early versions, in Bach's hand, of two movements Partita No. 6, the Corrente and the Tempo di Gavotta. They belong to a specific phase of evolution of the Sonata No. 6 in G major (BWV 1019) for violin and obbligato harpsichord, which itself has survived in three different versions. This work may be assumed to have originated during the period when Bach was Kapellmeister at Cöthen, between 1717 and 1723.

Klaus Engler

We are grateful to the following libraries for making available the sources we have used: the British Library, London; Library of Congress, Music Division, Washington, DC; Musikbibliothek der Stadt Leipzig; Österreichische Nationalbibliothek Vienna; Staatsbibliothek zu Berlin – Preußischer Kulturbesitz, Music Division; University of Illinois Library, Music Department, Urbana, Ill. I also wish to thank Professor Paul Badura-Skoda for information and advice.

Klaus Engler
Edith Picht-Axenfeld

---

[3] *Bach-Dokumente*, Vol. I, p. 224, note C
[4] Quoted from *Bach-Dokumente*, Vol. II, No. 214, Kassel, etc., 1969, pp. 160f.
[5] *NBA*, V/5, Krit. Bericht, pp. 73 und 76

NOTES ON PERFORMANCE

I.

Ideally I should like to be able to present the player of Bach's Partitas with a complete facsimile of the original engraving. My brief, however, is to suggest fingerings and to offer some remarks on performance. And yet if I were to fulfil even this task conscientiously, I should need a whole book. Bach's Partitas represent the crowning synthesis of a history of the suite extending over centuries, and it would be necessary to deal with the European ramifications of that history as fully as Bach knew them himself.

The performer of Baroque music is faced with an art form that is strictly bound by conventions. At the same time, he is required to exercise, within those limits, a degree of freedom whereby the work is re-created in performance. *Executio*, in other words, is part and parcel of *compositio*. The player should have an intimate feeling for Baroque rhythm, should be familiar with the characters of the various dances, should have a mastery of the standard forms of articulation and the fingerings appropriate to them, and should be able to execute *Manieren* and free ornamentation with refinement and taste. On all these matters, however, the notated text of the music is silent. Such skills were transmitted by living tradition; instruction in instrumental playing during the Baroque period was simultaneously instruction in composition.

There is a further reason why the notated text is reticent. Metrical notation cannot represent the gestural quality of a dance. It cannot even reproduce the pattern of tensions of different metres, nor the danced structure of, for example, four-bar units in the minuet, which later became so important in shaping the periodic organization of music in the Classical era. All Baroque rhythm is governed by a polarity between tension and release, viewed in physical, gestural and rhetorical terms: this polarity can be defined by means of the three related pairs of oppositions: long/short, heavy/light and stressed/unstressed. It is difficult to illustrate these oppositions in isolation, and indeed they can replace each other in the living process of music-making. The character and capacity of different instruments also plays a part here. A sound or a note can be given prominence in very different ways: by its duration, its preparation, accentuation, its fullness of sound, or by ornamentation.

Baroque rhythm poses many conundrums for the performer. The sources of information on performance practice – François Couperin's *L'Art de toucher le clavecin* is a characteristic example – describe methods of playing which often deviate considerably from the notation, and it is difficult to know what to infer from them. The authors of these accounts, in attempting to pin down living, articulate rhythms, constantly met with an insoluble problem: the essential properties of a rich tradition of performance practice cannot be captured in words or in written symbols. The living quality of actual music-making can be recorded only approximately and in coarsened form. This is the reason why many of the written sources are confusing and unclear, or apparently inconsistent. They point to a lost world of living musical language and practice that is far removed from the over-mechanical, 'motoric' approach to rhythm which predominates today. Once this is understood, however, the notated text can be read in a different light, and the performer's rhythmic habits will be challenged and transformed.

As has been mentioned in the Critical Notes (p. 66 above), the present edition adheres as faithfully as possible to the visual appearance of the notation of the original engraving and thus, it is hoped, mirrors closely the form of the lost autograph as it was originally written. It should be noted in this connection that the handling of ligatures, or note-beams, including the now obsolete use of so-called cross-beams (e. g. ♫), often serves as an indication of the articulation which the composer intended. I strongly urge the reader to make as thorough a study of Bach's own notation as possible, using the facsimile edition of the original engraving (Leipzig, 1984). Something of the character of this first edition may be seen in the illustrations on p. 2 of either volume of the present edition.

* * *

The partita cycle forms a set, representing the characters of six different keys:

key	G major	A minor	B flat major	C minor	D major	E minor
No.	5	3	1	2	4	6

To these, Part II of the *Clavierübung* adds the keys of F major und B minor. In keeping with tradition, the composer of *The Well-tempered Clavier* has endowed each key with its distinctive meaning and expressive character. Comparing the Partitas with other works in the same keys helps to bring out these distinctive features and to illuminate the wider context within which they belong.

Unfortunately, space does not permit us to discuss the nature of the different dance forms included in the Partitas. Nor can we describe their origins, their lengthy evolution and the ways in which they gradually became stylized. I would urge the player to become immersed, body and soul, in the world of the dance: walking, running and striding in duple time, turning, jumping and skipping in the many forms of triple time. The latter is always potentially ambiguous; instead of presenting groups of three, beats may be grouped in pairs over two bars in the manner of a hemiola. Dance for celebration and rejoicing; gracefully stylized – popular and powerful: always flowing and light. The reader is referred to the writings of Hermann Beck, Walter Salmen and Karl Heinz Taubert.[1]

Bach intended the *Clavierübung*, like his other keyboard cycles – *The Well-tempered Clavier* and the *Inventions* – to be exemplary in nature. This is evident, for example, from the fact that the six partitas open with six different kinds of introductory movement, and that in each of the partitas a different prototype underlies the four dances – allemande, courante, sarabande and gigue – so that all of the historical traditions from which the suite drew are combined into a grand synthesis.

II. Rhythm

Various rhythmic conventions not apparent from the notation

a) Different ways of realizing the notation ♫
   i. French ouverture style i.e., pronounced dotting, full of suspense although the exact and powerful gestural quality cannot be captured in notation. Approximating to ♫ or ♫.
   Examples: Partita No. 1, *Sarabande*; Partita No. 2, *Sinfonia*, opening; Partita No. 4, *Ouverture*; Partita No. 6, *Toccata* and *Sarabande*.

---

[1] Hermann Beck, *Die Suite*, Cologne, 1964 (*Das Musikwerk*, vol. 26); Walter Salmen, *Tanz im 17. und 18. Jahrhundert*, Leipzig, 1988 (*Musikgeschichte in Bildern*, vol. IV/4); Karl Heinz Taubert, *Höfische Tänze. Ihre Geschichte und Choreographie*, Mainz, 1968.

    ii. ♫ : rhythm as notated, but with gentle cantabile articulation.
Examples: Partita No. 5, *Sarabande*; Partita No. 6, *Allemanda*.

    iii. ♫ in quick tempo, articulated ♫.
Example: Partita No. 3, *Corrente*.

    iv. Assimilated ♫ (binary notation for ternary) in rapid tempo, articulated ♪̣♪.
Example: Partita No. 1, *Corrente*.

    v. In slow tempos ♫ considered as ♬, i.e. ♪♪.
Example: Partita No. 5, *Allemande*.

b) Assimilation

    i. ♩ ♪.♫♩ = ♩ ♪.♫♩ Articulation: ♪ detached and forcefully declaimed.
Example: Partita No. 2, *Sinfonia*.

    ii. ♫♬ often ♪♬ ; ♩♫ = ♩.♪ or ♩.♪ ; ♩.♫ = ♩.♩

    iii. Other forms of assimilation are explained in the Detailed Comments below.

c) *Inégalité*

It was surely not the intention of François Couperin and others who described the style of playing known as *jeu inégal* to urge that *one* single mechanical rhythmic pattern should be replaced by another equally schematic one (e. g., ♫ by ♪.♪). Rather, *inégalité* should arise as a sensitive response, in the appropriate context, to the gestural and metrical character of the rhythm of a piece. The presence in the Partitas of broad cantabile passages and elaborate written-out ornamentation, and the influence of Italian coloraturas and violinistic virtuosity, suggest that the use of *inégales* should be very sparing. Nevertheless, the gestural and metrical rhythmic impulse below the surface is the prime source of movement in the music, and should find expression in subtle rhythmic inequalities, the use of *couler* on two-note slurs and the occasional use of gentle lombardic rhythms.

III. The dances: character, movement and tempo

Each dance has its distinctive, fundamental character. From this character springs its specific form of movement, and both together determine the tempo, serving to articulate and comprehend both character and movement. In order to establish the appropriate tempo it is advisable to compare other suites and to play through the corresponding movements a number of times: this will bring out the central point, namely how the dance 'goes'. It is also important to distinguish between the harmonic and linear aspects of the dance movements. The player should always read through the dances establishing the underlying figured-bass structure: this will make it easier to recognize the simple melodic lines beneath the rich and often ornamented figuration, and to develop a feeling for improvised ornamentation expected from every musicians of the time. The tempo is always to be determined by the bass line and the harmonic progressions built upon it. Even the slowest, most highly stylized sarabande still moves in crotchet steps. The sign ¢, on the other hand, does not denote a fast tempo: movements prefaced by this time signature (e.g., Partita No. 2, *Allemande*; Partita No. 4, *Ouverture*) employ half-bar motivic units and the musical flow is determined accordingly.

Mensural thinking, in the sense of proportional tempo relationships, is an active presence throughout Bach's music.[2] We should not, however, rush to be too systematic here. Baroque dances are very varied in origin, and some of them do not spring from the mensural tradition. The *integer valor* of the first of the two-part *Inventions* and of many of the preludes and fugues is a slower pulse than the crotchets of an Italian concerto movement. But the proportions – including 2 : 3 and 3 : 4 (or the inverse) – should be borne in mind so that those dance movements which do not belong within the proportional framework are not forced into a scheme that is alien to them. An example of simple proportions is the Sinfonia of Partita No. 2: *Grave adagio – andante* – fugato, ♪ = ♪ = ♩.

IV. Articulation

a) Bach taught his pupils to 'cultivate, above all, a cantabile style of playing' (cf. the preface to the *Inventions*). This 'cantabile style' is often taken, falsely, to mean simply legato, but in fact it encompasses all the qualities of well-articulated declamatory singing. Like vocal music, music for the keyboard should be 'communication in sound' (Klang-Rede). The Partitas represent a grand synthesis, at the highest degree of virtuosity, of the polyphonic with the French and Italian styles, and this synthesis calls for 'an extraordinary degree of sensitivity and versatility in musical expression and enunciation'.[3] The many levels and types of cantabile legato, the sustaining and separation of notes are indicated only sporadically in the original text, by means of dots, ties and slurs. The Baroque method of sustaining notes in order to create 'parts' and a quasi-polyphonic texture is a case in point: this technique can be used with single-voiced passages whenever appropriate. In the *Clavierbüchlein* for Anna Magdalena Bach, for example, Bach notates this passage from François Couperin's *Les Bergeries (6e Ordre)*

 as follows:

The player can explore the consequences of this approach for himself in the *Allemande* and *Menuet* 1 of Partita No. 1 and in numerous other movements.

b) The concertante movements and the correntes and Italian gigues bring violin forms of articulation to the keyboard, e.g.:

Choice of articulation will depend on the intervallic pattern of the figure, on the metre and on the harmonic structure. In general, the fingers are responsible for articulation with the arm lightly suspended, guided by the wrist as if drawing a bow. Articulation should always relate to the large-scale musical flow and is not to be confused with phrasing, which is the thematic, declamatory structuring of more extended passages.

c) The phrasing and articulation of the bass parts, corresponding to the basso continuo, should be as rich in nuance as they would be if these parts were being performed by a cello or viola da gamba. The purpose should be to clarify the cadential patterns and the sub-division of the piece into larger and smaller units and, generally, make the 'musical discourse' comprehensible. The bass generates the dance's movement, and because it provides the harmonic foundation, it functions as 'conductor' – governing the tempo.

d) Baroque non-legato allows each note the freedom to 'live and breathe' encompassing a wide range of nuance, including tenuto, portato and staccato. On the organ and

[2] cf. Walter Gerstenberg, *Die Zeitmaße und ihre Ordnungen in Bachs Musik, Freunde der Bachwoche Ansbach*, Einbeck, 1952, and other pertinent studies.
[3] cf. Rudolf Steglich, Preface to the Henle edition, Munich [1970], p. 4

the harpsichord such contrasting nuances are the means whereby the expressive character of different intervals can be brought out and the metrical pattern is given shape. Notes that are held longer endow strong beats with their appropriate weight. Equally important, however, strong beats can be prepared by a looser articulation and the progressive shortening of weak beats in approaching the end of a bar. A sprung, lightly played upbeat strengthens the following downbeat without the need for extra accentuation.

V. Fingering

Baroque keyboard music proceeds by means of motifs and figuration. Whenever possible, the five fingers of the hand span the figure as an organic unit; in sequences, the hand moves to the new position at the relevant moment. Non-legato is the prime and natural method of enabling the hearer to perceive each interval as a distinct motion in musical space. Important intervals – large ones in particular – as well as syncopations and cadential steps in the bass should thus be played portato. Fingering should always 'speak', in other words create coherence and structure. The original fingering of the *Praeambulum* in G minor (BWV 930) and the *Applicatio* from the *Clavier-Büchlein* for Wilhelm Friedemann (BWV 994) show Bach's intentions very clearly:

Reproduced by permission of Yale Music Library, New Haven, Conn.

In bar 33 of the *Praeambulum* the thumb plays the black note, since the whole hand is shaped accordingly; in bar 23 the thumb avoids the black note. The question of avoiding the use of the thumb in early keyboard music, and resultant problems of hand position, can be understood and sensibly discussed only with reference to the clavichord. Because of the simple lever system of sound production on the clavichord, and the short length of the keys, finger contact should take place as near to the edge of the key as possible. The sound is impaired with every millimetre by which the finger approaches the centre of the keyboard. The *Applicatio* shows that the 'old' fingering was by no means obsolete

as far as Bach was concerned. Its distinctive feature is that it makes for natural articulation.[4]

I have been extremely reluctant to provide suggestions for fingering in the score. Each player should work out his own fingerings for himself: I have spent a lifetime working on mine, and I keep changing them as I return to the music and study surviving, historical fingerings. Those suggestions I do make are meant to serve merely as a spur to further thought. A specific fingering – each represents only one interpretation – is a way of emphasizing certain aspects of a passage at the expense of others; possibilities left unmentioned may be of equal significance. Repeats provide an opportunity for presenting contrasting versions of the same passage. A fingering should not be used, however, until it has been appraised in context.

With the modern grand piano in mind, I have sometimes suggested fingerings derived from François Couperin. If an ornament begins on the note that has just been played, a new finger is needed in order to produce clear articulation within the cantabile texture. This technique is not appropriate on the clavichord and is not found in Bach's own fingerings.

VI. Manieren

In the Partitas *Manieren*, or embellishments, are often written out, but Bach also uses the conventional symbols. Ornaments should always be played in light but well-rounded fashion, spontaneously and quasi improvvisato, and yet in keeping with the wider musical context. With trills in slow

---

[4] I recommend as an instructive study the excellent essay by Bradford Tracey, *Fingersätze für J. S. Bachs Tastenmusik*, in: *Musica*, 1984, Vol. 4, pp. 353–60, which also discusses in detail the other examples of original fingering. Three-note figures in Baroque music are generally assigned to fingers 2, 3 and 4.

tempos the Baroque era favoured a gradual build-up (increase in speed) at the start of the ornament and a corresponding easing-off (decrease in speed) at the end. Reaching greatest speed at the mid-point of the trill approximates to the dynamic effect <>.

Appoggiaturas should always be played with particular sensitivity and individuality, again quasi improvvisato. The vital factor here is always to retain a lively sense of the tension between dissonance and resolution. A certain degree of rhythmic freedom is appropriate, as befits the somewhat intuitive nature of such ornaments when performed by the human voice. All appoggiaturas should be played on the beat.[5] The duration of appoggiaturas is highly variable, depending on the musical context. The dissonance, however, must always be resolved before the bass proceeds to a new harmony.

Ornaments taken from a few reliable sources (or even a single one) have been included in the present edition (cf. the references in the notes on the individual pieces in the Critical Notes, pp. 66ff.). The performer may thus gain an impression of the practical implications of style (*Manieren*). Suggestions for realising *Manieren* are given in the Detailed Comments below (pp. 74ff.). Numerals set in circles are used to indicate examples corresponding to those in the *Explication* in the *Clavier-Büchlein* for Wilhelm Friedemann Bach. The suggestions are merely intended to stimulate each player to work out his own preferences, deciding, for example, whether a short or long trill sounds better and more fitting in a particular context.

The fact that different ornaments are found in the various surviving copies of the original edition demonstrates that *Manieren* were to be handled freely. Likewise, it was Baroque practice to add embellishments freely in repeats. We can study Bach's own example by examining the ornamented versions of the three-part *Inventions,* for instance (reproduced in the appendix to the Wiener Urtext Edition UT 50042), and the original *agréments de la même Sarabande* in the *English Suites* Nos. 2 and 3. As far as the Partitas are concerned, with their rich coloratura style, moderation and restraint are advisable, and florid realizations should be avoided.

5 The only exception is at the end of melodic phrases, a feature determined by the intonation of the French language. Cf. Kenneth Gilbert, Preface to François Couperin, *Pièces de clavecin 1ier livre,* Paris, 1972 (*Le Pupitre, 21*).

Reproduced by permission of Yale Music Library, New Haven, Conn.

Explication unterschiedlicher Zeichen, so gewiße *manieren* artig zu spielen, andeuten

34

VII. Detailed comments

Partita 1 in B flat major BWV 825

For the character and 'affect'(emotional quality) of the key of B flat major – cantabile and sweet, but also brilliant and animated – cf. the two- and three-part *Inventions* (BWV 785 and 800); *The Well-tempered Clavier* I and II (BWV 866 and 890); the duet *Mein Freund ist mein* from the cantata *Wachet auf* (BWV 140); the soprano aria *Ich folge dir gleichfalls mit freudigen Schritten* from the St John Passion (BWV 245); and *Brandenburg Concerto No. 6* (BWV 1051).

Praeludium

In three parts. Lively, rocking. Additional parts at close. The long final note must be sustained.

Ornaments:

If the trill occurs on a weak beat, a tie can be added (*tremblement lié*).

Allemande

Ascending opening line as variation of *Praeludium*. Upbeat gentle, strictly in tempo. The figurations tend to generate inner lines through held notes, see bars 17–18 (latent counterpoint); cf. *French Suite* No. 4 (BWV 815), *Allemande*.

Ornaments:

tremblement lié

Corrente

♪♪ to be assimilated throughout (duple for triple); ♪ detached. The movement is modelled on correntes for the violin. Ample articulation required, e.g. ♫♫♫♫. An effect of brilliance and virtuosity. Assimilated upbeat, flowing.

Ornaments:

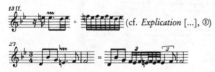

Sarabande

Example of the *sarabande grave*. Crotchet pace strictly in time, the figures given room to breathe. ♫♪ declamatory in the French style, approaching ♫♪.

Ornaments:

or trill throughout and fuse with the turn. The initial suspension can be expressively longer.

Written-out Anschwünge and Nachschläge (approach and termination figures) should be fused with the trill.

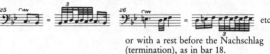

or with a rest before the Nachschlag (termination), as in bar 18.

Menuet

1: latent counterpoint. Lively and vigorous. Can be articulated in many different ways.
2: delicately melodious, galant.

Ornaments:

 Schneller or Schleifer (coulé)

The two *Menuets* are the only paired dances in the six partitas. The usual major-minor contrast is lacking. The fermata at the end of *Menuet* 2 seems to indicate that a *da capo* of *Menuet* 1 is optional.

Giga

In the original engraving (see facsimile p. 2) of this movement all the crotchets are given extended stems below the quavers: an indication that they are to be played by the right hand crossing over. This conflicts with what has been customary since Czerny.

Partita 2 in C minor BWV 826

For the character and 'affect' of the key of C minor – grand and passionate; but also intense, bordering on the mystical – cf. the two- and three-part *Inventions* (BWV 773 and 788); *The Well-tempered Clavier* I and II (BWV 847 and 871); *Jesu, meine Freude* from the *Orgel-Büchlein* (BWV 610); the closing choruses of the two Passions, and the tenor aria *Ich will bei meinem Jesu wachen* from the St Matthew Passion BWV 244).

Sinfonia

Grand opening movement in Italian orchestral style. Rhythm, bar 1ff.: ♩ ♪ ♫♫, dramatic articulation, ♪ detached. Bar 2: ♫♫♫♫; bar 5: ♩ ♫♫♫♫
Andante (bar 8), quasi solo (violin or oboe). Bars 28–30 in free recitative style. Allegro (bar 30), concertante fugato in orchestral style. Bars 90–91, expansive close of the three-section form as a whole.

Ornaments:

On the question of tempo relationships, see p. 71 above, *III. The dances: character, movement and tempo*, paragraph 2.

Allemande

Motivic upbeat. Preparation for the close begins, in the penultimate (not the final) bar, with its secondary dominant and gestural climax. The cadence bar itself can then be played without the need for further slowing down. This is typical of all Allemandes.

The time signature ¢ indicates the motivic structure, not a rapid tempo (cf. p. 71 above).

Ornaments:

Courante

Majestic, French style. Note the thematic relationship:

Courante:

Fugue theme, *Sinfonia:*

Fiery upbeat quavers can also be given additional impetus.

Bar 1: short appoggiatura

Ornaments:

; bars 4, 6, 10, 22 and 23 respectively. The duration of the suspension and the number of trill notes may vary.

It is possible that the appended ᵃ, bar 16, 2nd quaver in G 25 (e″ flat) is misplaced and should refer to the next quaver (d″); the present edition, however, follows the original.

Sarabande

Sarabande tendre, flowing but meditative. One should play the movement reduced to its harmonic outline to become aware of how the basic structure has been decorated. Compare the *Sarabande* from the *English Suite* No. 6 (BWV 811). The ornaments preserved only in G 25 in bars 4–9 are particularly suitable for the performance of the repeats. Appoggiatura bar 4: see p. 61, footnote 5.

Rondeaux

Elegant French character piece. The couplets to be played in virtuoso style, with ample articulation.

Ornaments:

Bar 1: not really suitable; cf. bar 33:

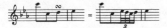

In bar 1, in order not to anticipate the e″ flat, perhaps also:

Bars 83, 85, 98 and 106: short appoggiaturas, stressed suspension.

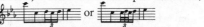

Capriccio

Instead of a gigue, almost a concerto movement for two violins. The fugal style, however, and the inversion of the theme in the second part are also characteristic of the gigue. Play with sprung upbeats.
Bar 47 short appoggiatura. ᵃ cf. *Explication* ③.

Partita 3 in A minor BWV 827

The key of A minor is commonly used for string writing. For the character and 'affect' of the key cf. the alto aria *Geist und Seele* from the cantata *Geist und Seele wird verwirret* (BWV 35); *The Well-tempered Clavier* I and II (BWV 865 and 889); *English Suite* No. 2 (BWV 807); and the aria *Bereite dich, Zion* from the *Christmas Oratorio* (BWV 248).

Fantasia

Extended two-part movement. Not a fantasia in the manner of other pieces with the same title; rather, Bach's title indicates an opening movement written in a free form and not based on existing models.

Ornaments:

Allemande

Allemande grave.

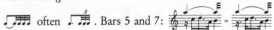

The basic metrical unit is a gently paced crotchet. Dramatic declamatory style.

Ornaments:

In the early autograph version H 4 (the *Clavierbüchlein* for Anna Magdalena Bach, 1725) the ornament is described as a 'trilled turn' ≋.

Corrente

Violin style. Lively articulation. ♪♪ rhythm to be played exactly as notated, the short note detached. Rapid springy tempo.

Ornaments:

Sarabande

Arioso type, somewhat *tendre*, very smooth-flowing, reflective. Long melodic spans. Bars 5ff., rocking bass figure. Fingerings in style of Couperin's *L'Art de toucher le clavecin.* very cantabile, legato and rounded; ornamental.

Ornaments:

Bar 8, first crotchet as in the version from *Clavierbüchlein* for Anna Magdalena Bach, 1725:

Burlesca

Galant; rhythmically very defined. Brilliant ornamentation. Bar 5 'sprung' crotchets. Articulation of principal motif:

Ornaments:

Bars 18 and 20: acciaccaturas also possible in l. h.

Scherzo

Very rapid tempo. Note the upbeat structure of the phrasing. Possible variation in performance: use different tone colour in alternating phrases. Articulation: violin style.

Ornaments:

Gigue

Highly wrought thematic structure. Articulation: or or depending on context and figure. End of bar 2 and similarly bar 28ff. etc. Fingering governed by choice of articulation.

The performer may wish to create a contrast by playing each version of the second part of the *Gigue*, one for the first time and the other for the repeat.

Edith Picht-Axenfeld

NOTES ON PERFORMANCE

Detailed comments

Partita 4 in D major BWV 828

For the character and 'affect' of the key – trumpet key: grand and radiant, but also delicate and transparent – cf. *Et resurrexit* from the B minor Mass (BWV 232); opening chorus from the *Christmas Oratorio* (BWV 248); *The Well-tempered Clavier* I and II (BWV 850 and 874); Brandenburg Concerto No. 5 (BWV 1050); and opening chorus from the cantata *Unser Mund sei voll Lachens* (BWV 110) (corresponding *Ouverture*, Orchestral Suite No. 4, BWV 1069).

The opening movement is majestic and ceremonial. The dances, especially the *Allemande* and *Sarabande*, are distilled into highly individual solos with extended melodic spans.

Ouverture

Grand, elegant, French overture rhythm. The spring and tension of the dotted rhythms and ornamental flourishes cannot be exactly notated. Here are some model examples of the sorts of rhythmic assimilation that are required:

In bars 7 and 8 the placing of ornaments, which corresponds exactly to the original engraving, is rather imprecise in respect of their rhythmic alignment.

In bar 7 a ⌣ over the first note ♪♪ is doubtless intended; in bar 8 ♪♪ is likely, but a connecting turn should not be ruled out.

The concertante fugato, in a floating 9/8, is harpsichord music of the purest kind. Bars 33–48 and 74–104 more or less solo. Fugato-subject not ♪♪♪ but an anacrustic: ♪♪♪♪♪

Ornaments: Bar 2: appoggiatura ♪♪ (notated ♪♪. or ♩♩).

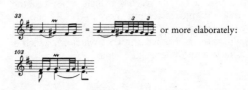 or more elaborately:

Allemande

Richly coloured solo. Gentle crotchet pace. Bar 21, assimilate ♪♪ to the rhythm ♪♪♪♪♪♪♪

Bar 35 similarly. Bar 37: ♪♪♪♪♪♪♪♪

or ♪♪♪♪♪♪♪

Ornaments:

Courante

Grand and spirited. Upbeat springy. Metrical interplay of characteristically alternating ♩♩♩ and ♩♩♩♩♩♩ subdivisions of the bar.

Ornaments:

Appoggiatura ♪♪ short, ♪♪., ♩♩ or ♩.♪

or bar 11, l. h. ⌣ as short appoggiatura only

Bar 18: appoggiatura (♪♪.) short.

Aria

Lively cantabile; sprung syncopations; *galant.*

Sarabande

Sarabande tendre. Elaborate violin-like solo over what can still be perceived as a dance rhythm. The first two bars of each section present the sarabande's basic gestures in highly expressive form.

Ornaments:

Menuet

Lively. Bar 6: ♪♪♪♪ slightly inégal; bars 10 and 12 similarly. Assimilate ♪♪ to ♪♪♪.

Ornaments:

Gigue

Fanfare-like main theme; the dotted-quaver rest adds tension. The $\frac{9}{16}$ time signature, uncommon with gigues, gives the movement added drive. Rich articulation. No closing ritardando; instead, tension reaches its highest point on the third-inversion dominant seventh chord in bars 46 and 94, before being released in the closing cadence. The second part presents a new theme (rather than the inversion), which is later combined with the opening theme.

Partita 5 in G major BWV 829

For the character and 'affect' of the key – bright and brilliant; joyful – cf. the 'Pastoral' Symphony and alto aria *Schlafe, mein Liebster* from the *Christmas Oratorio* (BWV 248); the soprano aria *Ich will dir mein Herze schenken* from the *St Matthew Passion* (BWV 244); two- and three-part *Inventions* in G major (BWV 781 and 796); *The Well-tempered Clavier* I and II (BWV 860 and 884); *French Suite* No. 5 (BWV 816); *Toccata* in G major (BWV 916); organ prelude and fugue in G major (BWV 541); and *Brandenburg Concerto* No. 3 (BWV 1048).

Praeambulum

Unlike the *Praeludium* of Partita No. 1, a freely composed harpsichord movement incorporating all of the elements of Scarlatti's style; concertante, virtuoso writing. Tempo correspondingly brisk. Dance-like rhythm.

Allemande

Highly stylised. Flowing ♫♫ against crotchet pulse. ♫♫ should be assimilated to a ♪♪ rhythm, and articulated ♪♪. Note the following model examples of rhythmic assimilation:

bar 17 as bar 4 or:

The metre is almost alla breve: cf. Partita No. 2, *Allemande*; Partita No. 4, *Ouverture*.

Ornaments: Bar 2: appoggiatura ♪, or resolution on sixth semiquaver. Bar 3: appoggiatura ♪ or resolution on third semiquaver.

Corrente

Violin-style virtuosity. Figuration latently contrapuntal. Bar 23: flow partially halted by staccato quavers, but then fully resumed. No ritardando. Rich articulation.

Ornaments:

Sarabande

Sarabande tendre; clavichordal and *empfindsam* (sentimental) in style. Upbeat unusual for a sarabande. Sensitive treatment of non-harmonic notes needed; cf. approximate model realizations as follows:

The use of thirds and sixths creates an effect of softness. The rhythm ♫ should be gently dotted, in accordance with the original articulation ♫♫. Rhythm of bar 4 like that of bar 8. Bar 6 and similar passages:

Ornaments:

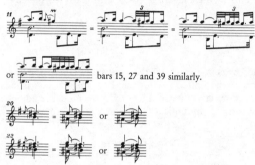

or ... bars 15, 27 and 39 similarly.

Tempo di Minuetta

Style luthé. Metrical ambivalence: $\frac{3}{4}$ rhythm in the background, which emerges strongly in cadential bars; hence the title. *Galant.*

Passepied

Strong upbeats, springy. Similar to a brisk minuet. Bar 21, articulation ♫♫♫ or ♫♫♫♫; appoggiaturas ♪ or shorter. Two bars more often joined as hemiolas: ♫♫♫ rather than ♫♫|♫♫.

Gigue

Well defined head-motif for the theme; new theme in the second part, later combined with the first. *Galant.* Eloquent quaver rest within main theme. Second theme opens questioningly and then answers after extended rest; brilliant trill. Big final climax. Articulation: bar 1, ♪|♫♫♫♫ ♩; bar 2, ♫♫♫♫♫; bars 9ff., ♫♫♫♫ or ♫♫♫♫ or ♫♫♫♫.

The ornament bars 33 ff.:

the ♫ to be played without rhythmic distortion, as approach to the trill. The long initial stems of the trills are copied from the original engraving in order to remind the performer of the *galant* impetus from the upper note. (Here they do not signify a longer upper note in the sense of an appoggiatura.)

Partita 6 in E minor BWV 830

For the character and 'affect' of the key – universal power – cf. the opening chorus, choral entry, from the *St Matthew Passion* (BWV 244); prelude and fugue for organ (BWV 548); *Duet* No. 1 (BWV 802); *The Well-tempered Clavier* I and II (BWV 855 and 879); and *English Suite* No. 5 (BWV 810). In E minor Bach often uses themes which shoot up, flame-like, from the tonic to the octave above, stretching from earth towards heaven.

Toccata

Upward-sweeping arpeggio, dramatic French-style dotted rhythm, protracted suspension: from this grows the fugal theme, with its sighing motif. A free toccata and fugue, then, but all of a piece. The quiet flowing passage in bars 9–12 and 21–24 also returns in the fugue so, for this reason alone, a single overall tempo is suggested.

In bars 34–35 and 40–41 ornaments need to be added. (cf. the fughetta in the *Goldberg Variations*, where Bach included ornaments in soprano and bass in his personal copy, but not for the middle part.) Bar 85 implies latent counterpoint in bars 9–12 and 21–24. The slurs for the bass part in bars 9 and 21 are not necessarily identical with the slurs for the upper part in parts 11 and 23 ff. in the original engraving. It is possible that the bass, which carries more harmonies, has a more structural function (cf. Critical Notes, p. 76).

Ornaments:

Allemanda

Allemande grave. It is impossible to capture the rhythms of the decorative part-writing in notation. Dottings, in my opinion, should not be over-pronounced (in the French style) but neither should they be inflexible. The articulation of ♪♪ tends towards ♪♪. Rhythmic assimilation in bar 13, for example, can be along the following lines:

Ornaments:

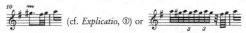

Appoggiaturas in bars 2 and 15 ♪ or shorter.

Corrente

Originally a harpsichord solo in the early version of the Sonata No. 5 for harpsichord and violin (BWV 1019a). Virtuoso violin-style figuration. The quaver bass must underpin the syncopation (cf. E major two-part *Invention*): the corrente rhythm should be fiery and clearly defined against the passionately resisting syncopes.

Air

Introduced by a gavotte upbeat. Quiet, cantabile and flowing. The second phrase of the theme of this *galant* piece is the retrograde of the first half, transposed up by a fourth.

Ornaments:

Bar 3: trill with grace notes (Nachschlag).

Sarabande

Sarabande grave, grand and highly intense. The unusual upbeat is a quotation from the *Toccata*. Pronounced dotting. Notation is incapable of capturing the nuances of the declamatory style here. The tempo and characteristic sarabande motion must be maintained throughout, providing a stable basis for the free decoration above it.

Ornaments:

Bar 31 and 32: tenor part, short trill, tied to previous note, also possible; similarly in bar 34. Bar 18, r. h., last chord; in the *Clavierbüchlein* for Anna Magdalena Bach of 1725, the last chord is marked with acciaccaturas:

Bar 19: second crotchet, alto, g′ with ♪.

40

There are various possible realizations of the appoggiaturas. Their power to convince is a question of declamatory style.

Rich articulation, commonly ♫ ♫ , Bars 11 and 31 ♫ ♫ ♫.♫|♩; ♫ should be assimilated to the triplets and articulated ♪.

Tempo di Gavotta

Characteristic ♩ ♩ |♩ upbeat. *Galant*. In my judgement ♫ is not ♫, but is thematically a written-out 'Schneller' ∿. For bar 22 and similar passages use the following rhythmic model:

Gigue

Strict fugal treatment; the main theme is inverted in the second section. The notated rhythm is out of the question in a gigue. The solution is to be found in the *Gigue* from Suite No. 7 by Froberger, which is notated in duple, but recast in Suite No. 23 in triple metre:[2]

Ornaments: Bar 2, trill without Nachschlag, for the duration of a crotchet, pause on f sharp; or, with Nachschlag as inversion of bar 26:

Edith Picht-Axenfeld

The latter version gives the following rhythmic models for Bach's gigue:[3]

[2] Howard Ferguson, *Keyboard Interpretation from the 14th to the 19th century*, London 1975, p. 92
[3] Ibid., p. 96f.

Johann Sebastian Bach: Small Preludes and Fughettas

INDEX

I Kleine Präludien aus dem Klavierbüchlein für Wilhelm Friedemann Bach
Small Preludes from the Klavierbüchlein for Wilhelm Friedemann Bach

Präludium C-Dur / C major BWV 924

Präludium g-Moll / G minor BWV 930

Präludium d-Moll / D minor BWV 926

Präludium F-Dur / F major BWV 928

Präludium F-Dur / F major BWV 927

Präludium D-Dur / D major BWV 925

BWV = Bach-Werke-Verzeichnis. Wolfgang Schmieder: *Thematisch-systematisches Verzeichnis der musikalischen Werke von Johann Sebastian Bach.* Breitkopf & Härtel, Leipzig, 1950

II Sechs kleine Präludien aus der Sammlung Johann Peter Kellners
Six small Preludes from Johann Peter Kellner's Collection

Präludium C-Dur / C major BWV 939

Präludium a-Moll / A minor BWV 942

Präludium d-Moll / D minor BWV 940

Präludium C-Dur / C major BWV 943

Präludium e-Moll / E minor BWV 941

Präludium c-Moll / C minor BWV 999

III Sechs kleine Präludien für Anfänger auf dem Klavier
Six small Preludes for Beginners on the Clavier

Präludium C-Dur / C major BWV 933

Präludium D-Dur / D major BWV 936

Präludium c-Moll / C minor BWV 934

Präludium E-Dur / E major BWV 937

Präludium d-Moll / D minor BWV 935

Präludium e-Moll / E minor BWV 938

IV Kleine Fugen
Small Fugues

Fuge C-Dur / C major BWV 953

Fuge C-Dur / C major BWV 952

Fughetta c-Moll / C minor BWV 961

V Kleine Präludien mit Fughetten
Small Preludes with Fughettas

Präludium G-Dur / G major aus BWV 902

Präludium und Fughetta d-Moll / D minor BWV 899

Präludium G-Dur / G major BWV 902 a, Fughetta aus BWV 902

Präludium und Fuge e-Moll / E minor BWV 900

Präludium und Fuge a-Moll / A minor BWV 895

PREFACE

The Preludes and Fugues in this edition were not grouped together by Bach himself. Some of them are to be found scattered among collective manuscripts of differing contents, while others have survived as individual manuscript copies. Later copyists, including, most recently, the editors of the Bach Complete Edition, have been responsible for gathering them together and for arranging them in a more or less random order. The time has now come for a new edition of the pieces, based on a critical evaluation of all the sources available.

The first group of six Preludes (I, 1—6) comes from the *Klavierbüchlein* for Wilhelm Friedemann Bach, which was begun on 22nd January, 1720. They appear as Nos. 2, 4, 8, 9, 10 and 27 in this little musical notebook. As the autograph Preludes Nos. 2, 4, 9 and 10 (= I, 1, 2, 4, 5) are among the first insertions in the *Klavierbüchlein* and are partly first drafts, there is no doubt about their authorship and time of composition: they are original Bach works, composed on or soon after 22nd January, 1720. I, 3 and I, 6, which were later inserted by Wilhelm Friedemann — in 1722/23 and 1726 — on pages that had been left blank, were perhaps also his own compositions, undertaken with the guidance of his father.

Six other Preludes (II, 1—6) have been taken from the 57 manuscripts or fascicles which make up the collection of Johann Peter Kellner (1705 until 1772); they exist only in this edition. Preludes II, 1—4 join I, 3 in Fascicle 53, but in the sequence II, 2, 3, 1, I, 3, II, 4 and without numbering and specification of author and title. The combination with *Klavierbüchlein* I, 3 and the stylistic similarity between I, 1 and II, 1 provide sufficient proof that II, 1—4 also have their origin in Bach's teaching; in view of the inferior quality of the compositions, however, it is doubtful whether Bach was solely responsible for them. We consider them to be the work of one of Bach's pupils (Wilhelm Friedemann or Carl Philipp Emanuel?), who composed them under the supervision (and certainly not without the assistance) of his teacher. II, 5, an early work, perhaps an organ prelude from the Arnstadt period, and II, 6, a prelude for lute, are undoubtedly by Bach. Both appear as single compositions in Kellner's manuscripts.

The third group of Preludes (III, 1—6) were collected together under the title "Six Preludes pour les Commençants" in 1781 at the latest. They appear in another sequence in an older source (without title).

The small three-part fugues (IV, 1, 2) can be described as teaching examples of fugal composition. IV, 1 appears as No. 31 in Wilhelm Friedemann's *Klavierbüchlein* and was inserted by Bach c. 1726. It provides a natural conclusion to the course of instruction followed in the *Klavierbüchlein*, cf. W. Plath in the Neue Bach-Ausgabe, Serie V, Band V (NBA V, 5), Critical Report, p. 70 f. The charming two-part fughetta IV, 3 is an early work; Bach's authorship is often disputed, but without much justification.

The Preludes and Fugues V, 1—4 point to the "Well-tempered Clavier". Kellner's copy in Fascicle 38 already bears the title which Bach employed for the 1st of the "48":

"Praeludia, und Fugen. Zum Nutzen und Gebrauch der Lehrbegiergen Musicalischen Jugend, als auch derer in diesem Studio schon habil seyenden Besondern Zeit Vertreib aufgesetzet und verfertiget Von Johann Sebastian Bachen." *

"Das wohl temperirte Clavier, oder Praeludia, und Fugen … Zum Nutzen und Gebrauch der Lehr-begierigen Musicalischen Jugend, als auch derer in diesem studio schon habil seyenden besonderem Zeitvertreib aufgesetzet und verfertiget von Johann Sebastian Bach … 1722."

This ambitious title refers not only to the three Preludes and Fugues in C major, D minor and E minor (BWV 870 a, 899, 900), which are to be found in Kellner's Fascicle 38, but also to other compositions. The series can be continued with BWV 901, 902 a and 895 (in the key sequence of F major, G major and A minor) from other manuscripts, although it is open to question whether such an order is authentic. As Bach made further use of BWV 870 a and 901 (as Prelude und Fugue in C major and as Fugue in A flat major) in Part II of the "Well-tempered Clavier", they do not appear in our edition. The player is referred to the final versions: BWV 870 and 886. We have included only the Fugue in G major (BWV 902) together with the Preludes V, 1 a and V, 1 b; not only can it stand on its own beside the late version BWV 884 as an independent composition, but it also enriches our collection with an additional Prelude (V, 1 a). Although it was combined with V, 1 b originally, this fugue appears with V, 1 a in another source. The Prelude V, 1 a was composed in Leipzig and was perhaps intended for inclusion in Part II of

---

* "Preludes and Fugues. Composed and prepared by Johann Sebastian Bach to meet the requirements of the young musician eager for instruction and to provide particular diversion for those already at an advanced stage in the study of music."

the "Well-tempered Clavier", where it was eventually replaced by another Prelude (BWV 884). It is given its proper place in this volume.

The small Preludes and Fugues, as they are not unjustly entitled, reveal with their various differences of quality and origin the didactic side of Bach. Both the early works, i. e. Bach's own studies, and also the later compositional models and individual pieces written ad hoc for purposes of instruction (including, as documents of this teaching, the "student works") point the real way to Bach's great works.

The Critical Notes provide the necessary information about textual criticism. Equivocal readings, particularly those which present two conflicting versions from sources of equal importance, can be investigated there. Editorial additions, for which there is no supporting evidence in the sources, have been indicated by means of brackets, and obvious writing mistakes, forgotten ligatures and missing rests have been rectified without commentary.

The notation of ornaments in the sources often defies the logic of textual criticism. Quite understandably, therefore, freedom in the interpretation of embellishments is also noticeable in the manuscript copies. Sometimes the oldest surviving reading (the archetype) requires ornamental elaboration (which is provided by a more recent manuscript), and sometimes the ornamentation of the older sources does not find its way into the more recent sources. And so, in order to do justice both to the performance practice of the early 18th century and to the music itself, almost all the ornaments present in the sources have been retained in our text, even those which, according to the rules of textual criticism, should have been omitted.

A table of Bach's ornaments, which appears below, gives guidance as to the interpretation of the various signs. The compositions are best suited to performance on the harpsichord, on which it is much easier to provide a convincing realization of the polyphonic network and to execute the ornaments. A more discreet use of ornaments is advisable when a modern piano or clavichord is used in performance.

We wish to thank *Berlin, Staatsbibliothek Preuß-ischer Kulturbesitz, Musikabteilung* and the *Deutsche Staatsbibliothek,* and the *Stadtbibliothek* in Leipzig for allowing us to consult the sources.

Walther Dehnhard

NOTES ON ORNAMENTATION

Bach's table of ornaments from the *Klavierbüchlein für Wilhelm Friedemann Bach* ("Explication unterschied-licher Zeichen, so gewisse manieren artig zu spielen, andeuten")*:

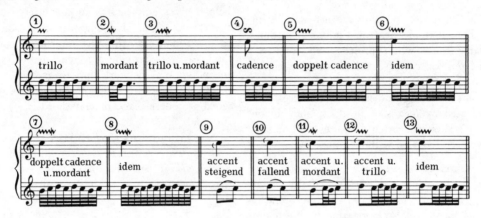

The embellishments are formed with the upper/lower diatonic auxiliary note. They begin — apart from ②— with the auxiliary note, but exactly on the beat. Whether a trill is to be made with the semitone or tone is determined by the harmonic-melodic context. The modulation to G major in I, 1, bars 7—9, 1 and in II, 1, bars 9—11, for example, calls for the mordent g, f♯, g, even when f' sounds in another part at the same time. In the same way, the tonic of a minor key forms a mordent with the leading note. In III, 6, bars 1, 3, 10, 20, 21, 23, 32, 48, there is a sharp above the mordent in the more recent sources H and S (cf. Critical Notes).

If the note before a trill happens to be the auxiliary note, it must be repeated at the beginning of the trill. J. S. Bach's table includes (in ⑫ and ⑬) an example of the exceptional case in which the auxiliary note is not repeated. These signs do not appear in the pieces printed in our edition. They are replaced by ♪ ∿ in more recent sources — cf. ⑭ and ⑮. The trills in III, 6, bars 11, 13, 15, 22, 24, 41, 43 are to be executed as in ⑫ or ⑬. Embellishments which appear in our edition, but which are missing from Bach's table:

The trill ≈ , which is described as a "prallender Doppelschlag" by C. Ph. E. Bach and which is to be found frequently in the works of Couperin and Johann Gottfried Walther, makes only one appearance in Bach's autographs, namely in the *Klavierbüchlein für Anna Magdalena Bach* of 1725 (Partita in A minor BWV 827, Allemande, NBA V, 4, p. 50, bars 6, 9 and KB p. 74). Bach, however, replaced it with ⑦ in the first print of 1727. The executing of III, 1, bar 4, 7 and III, 3, bar 23 is illustrated in ⑭ and ⑮. The slide ∿ in IV, 3, bar 26, 8 (see ⑯) begins on the beat like all the ornaments.

* "Explanation of various signs, showing how to play certain ornaments properly"

Johann Sebastian Bach: The Well Tempered Clavier I BWV 846-869

INDEX

PREFACE

Only one autograph score of Bach's Welltempered Clavier, a fair copy dating from 1722, has survived. It has been preserved in the Deutsche Staatsbibliothek, Berlin (catalogue number Mus. Ms. P 415). The search for autograph entries in the other sources has proved more or less fruitless.[1] So the text of the present edition is based mainly on this one source, which made the business of textual criticism easier, and favoured reliable results. Despite the numerous, and no doubt authentic corrections made in the meticulous fair copy, one can always clearly recognise one version that corresponds to the composer's intentions: the final amendment is always the valid one. Apart from this, all obtainable copies and early printings were compared. Comparison with the autograph makes it clear that Bach made his corrections bit by bit; the copies indicate the stage Bach's amendments had reached at the time the copy was made. These copies enable one to clearly identify four distinct phases in the correction of the autograph. Detailed information about this is given in the Critical Notes at the end of this volume. This apart, no deviations were found in the secondary sources that might be regarded as authentic variants.

If there are no doubts about the valid final text in a philological sense, some questions still remain open. For example, Bach often subsequently altered thematic shapes at certain points, to make them sound better. Here one must consider carefully whether to follow the composer's later correction, or whether to retain the original version, which accords better with the composition's inner logic. This problem arises in the C major fugue, for example. All passages of this kind have been commented on in detail, so that the user of this edition will have the possibility of drawing conclusions different to those of the editor.

Obvious slips of the pen on Bach's part, already amended by the copyists, required no comment; nor did the added or omitted pauses that result from the exigencies of printing, or simply make the text easier to read. A few final fermatae were also tacitly added.

The distribution of notes between the staves is not determined by performance considerations. The fingering-orientated distribution – notes for the right hand in the upper stave, notes for the left hand in the lower one – may facilitate sight-reading, but it can only hinder one's visual grasp of the individual voices. The notation should really clarify the voice-leading, a pedagogic-theoretical requirement, since the optical effect of the notation demands a grasp of the polyphonic structure.

What left and right hands play is made clear enough in our edition by the fingerings and stems; deliberately, the change between hands (which is only meant as a recommendation anyway) is not laid down in all cases.

Accidentals apply to the bar and the part; 'safety signs' were used sparingly. The markings in the autograph to indicate voice-leading are reproduced only exceptionally, since the method of printing already shows this clearly. But sometimes supplementary voice-leading markings are shown with dotted lines, the original ones having unbroken lines.

Supplementary ornaments not found in the autograph, but justified by contemporary sources, are identified by square brackets. In addition, one will need to add trills at parallel moments in the music. Further ornamental or textual additions or modifications, however justifiable they may appear in the light of the performance practice of the times, are inadmissible in view of the clear writing, multiple revisions, and the detailed corrections Johann Sebastian Bach made to his autograph fair copy.

The player is recommended to consult the readily accessible facsimile of the autograph and make comparisons.[2]

The editor is particularly grateful to the directors and staff of those libraries that gave him access to manuscripts of the Welltempered Clavier in their possession. Since these libraries are enumerated in the Critical Notes at the end of this volume, there's no need to mention them again at this point. Many thanks to Professor Detlef Kraus for his unflagging aid in drawing up the "Performance indications"; valuable encouragement came from Professor Maria Jäger and Dr. Herbert Anton Kellner. My thanks also to Dr. Magali Philippsborn, Professor Dr. Georg von Dadelsen and Dr. Alfred Dürr for help in locating and classifying the numerous sources.

Walther Dehnhard

[1] Apart from amendments in the Klavierbüchlein für Wilhelm Friedemann Bach, there are just a few headings in copy P 202 which are in the composer's hand.
[2] Johann Sebastian Bach, *Das Wohltemperirte Clavier* (Facsimile Edition) Leipzig 1971, VEB Deutscher Verlag für Musik (Agents: B. Schott's Söhne, Mainz).

PERFORMANCE INDICATIONS

Welltempered Tuning

The title of the work alludes to the art of *"How the tuning of a Clavier may be well tempered, so that all Modi ficti* (= tonalities) *may be brought into a pleasant and tolerable Harmonia".*[1] Numerous attempts were made in this direction; the equal temperament which is in standard use today is only one of them. What method did Bach use?

Certainly Bach knew about equal temperament; but whether that is what he intended in the Welltempered Clavier, is questionable. For the present day piano, it is the traditional and appropriate tuning. But the harpsichord player prefers a graded tuning, which is not only easier to carry out, but also creates audible differences between the different keys, i.e. precisely the key characteristics that are appropriate to older music. It seems suitable to mention the tuning methods of Andreas Werckmeister or Johann Philipp Kirnberger. But one should also note the tuning scheme described by Herbert Anton Kellner,[2] which is superior to the older methods: starting from C (with a C tuning fork!), one tunes six pure fifths downwards, and the rest (with the exception of the fifth E-B) are tempered. By this means one easily arrives at a C major triad whose fifth C-G has just as many beats below (narrow) as its third C-E has beats above (wide). Thanks to this equality of beats, the ear perceives the best of all possible triads, one which certainly isn't pure, but is, in the truest sense of the word, well tempered. As the remaining keys diverge from the centre of C major, the corresponding relationship between the beats of the thirds and fifths is systematically displaced, so that in passing through the cycle of fifths, an evenly graded series of key characteristics ensues; yet these are such that even the remotest keys are perfectly satisfactory to play in.

Tempo

The indications *Adagio, Largo, Andante, Allegro* and *Presto* that occur in the C minor, E minor and B minor pieces are more than mere tempo indications; they point to the 'affective' character of the piece. And it is this which, ultimately, determines the choice of tempo. "Here, some might perhaps seek to know: how may one recognise the true pace of a musical composition? Only, such knowledge goes beyond all words that might be used in this respect: it is the highest perfection in music, and it is only by much experience and great talent that it is gained."[3]

The idea that there must always be a simple numerical tempo relation between each prelude and fugue cannot be substantiated historically. It has, however, been verified that (for example) the duple beat of a prelude and triple beat of a fugue (or vice versa) are to be set in a *proportio tripla* ("two against three") relationship.[4]

Fingering, Phrasing and Articulation

Bach notated only a few staccato dots and legato slurs; these are not sufficient to reconstruct Bach's phrasing, nor can it be the task of this edition to do so: the player must work out the details for himself. Sometimes one finds that the articulation is implicit in the given fingerings; for the placing of the fingers, whose audible effect is often underrated, should be determined in detail by the sound the player is aiming for.

In general, manual movements should be adapted practically to match musical intentions. The fingerings worked out for this edition follow that basic precept, though they don't aim to impose obligatory phrasing and articulation on the player. They have been designed with the modern piano in mind, but may also be profitably used on historic instruments. Where the tempo permits it, experienced players will make greater use of the silent change of finger than we have been able to show here (in the interest of legibility). The frequent sliding of the finger from a black key (on the piano) to an adjacent white key may be unfamiliar to some. Like the consistent use of the thumb on black keys (indispensable since Bach!), it makes for smoother hand movements. The same end is served by the – partially new – distribution of voices between hands. However, that doesn't mean that one shouldn't try to avoid using the thumb.

---

[1] Andreas Werckmeister, *Musikalische Temperatur, oder deutlicher und warer Mathematischer Unterricht, Wie man durch Anweisung des Monochordi, Ein Clavier, sonderlich die Orgel-Wercke, Positive, Regale, Spinetten und dergleichen wol temperirt stimmen könne.* Frankfurt and Leipzig 1691.

[2] Herbert Anton Kellner, *Wie stimme ich selbst mein Cembalo?* (= The periodical *Das Musikinstrument*, Vol. 19), Frankfurt am Main 1976.

[3] Johann Mattheson, *Der vollkommene Capellmeister*, p. 173, § 27. Hamburg 1739. (Reprint: Kassel 1954.)

[4] Ulrich Siegele, *Zur Verbindung von Präludium und Fuge bei J. S. Bach*, in *Bericht über den Internationalen Musikwissenschaftlichen Kongreß Kassel 1962*, Kassel 1963, P. 164–167.

Ornamentation

For the execution of the signs for ornaments, see the Klavierbüchlein für Wilhelm Friedemann, which includes Bach's own table of ornaments. The rule of starting trills with the upper auxiliary note, even when this note has been anticipated, should only be disregarded in exceptional circumstances. The "Special Remarks" give further information in this respect.

In the preludes in E flat minor (Bar 36) and E minor (Bar 9), as also in the D major fugue (Bar 10), Bach uses the archaic form of notating an appoggiatura, namely an "accent" (see below). In our edition we have used the small quaver, but without seeking to imply anything about the length of the appoggiatura.

("Klavierbüchlein für Wilhelm Friedemann Bach")

SPECIAL REMARKS

Prelude in C major

Bar 35: like the analogous final bar of the E minor fugue, the triad in the right hand may be arpeggiated.

Prelude in C minor

The initial tempo (Bars 1–27) is the same as the Allegro of the closing bars. There is a widespread opinion that, apart from liberties at transitional moments, the basic pulse should be the same throughout the prelude, the crotchet being equal to the minim of the Presto and the quaver of the Adagio. But it is also reasonable to assume that Bach used his tempo indications to designate distinct tempi which shape the piece more vividly.

Prelude in C sharp minor

The arpeggios in Bars 2 and 4 should be played in the same way as those in Bars 1 and 3. – The appoggiaturas in Bars 11, 13 and 35 are of quaver length, those in the top part of bars 2 and 4 may be quavers or crotchets, and the remainder are short appoggiaturas.

Prelude in D major

Bar 33: many copyists wrote a B in the bass, instead of A, probably so as to make it easier to play. On the piano, using the pedal, one has the option of taking not only A-d-f-g♯ in the left hand, but d″ (upper voice) as well.

Fugue in D major

Bar 3: the correct notation of the first crotchet in the bass would be:

The same holds good for all similar passages. – Bar 10: The appoggiatura in the soprano part lasts a semiquaver, and may also be played in the following bar.

Fugue in D minor

The trill belonging to the theme (Bar 2) always begins with the main note, even in the inversion (Bar 24) and in the sequential passage (Bar 9–11).–In Bars 43–44 ties could be added in the soprano and bass.–The DEN HAAG copy shows an articulation deviating from that in the autograph:

Bar 3, unmarked there, is to be articulated like bar 4. DEN HAAG has a slur over the first two soprano notes in Bar 16.

Prelude in E flat major

The tempo of this three-section piece is maintained throughout.

Prelude in E flat minor

Bar 15: the slur over the gb'-f' is in the autograph; it means that the trill starts with f'.–In P 202, Wilhelm Friedemann Bach (?) has subsequently marked in these appoggiaturas in quavers: db' before the c' (Bar 15, 1st note), ab' before f'' (Bar 24), db' before cb' (Bar 38). It is possible that they stem from Johann Sebastian, or that he was heard playing them.–

It is also worth mentioning the legato slurs in bars 20–21, which likewise occur only in P 202:

Bar 36: the appoggiatura consists of double "accent" in the autograph; it could last a crotchet. The trill on the following note is marked in A 4 with the sign 𝄿, the meaning of which is not clear at this point.

Prelude in E minor

Bar 9: the suspension is an "accent" in the autograph; in the shorter, unembellished version in Friedemann's

Klavierbüchlein, it has the following format:

Analogously, the appoggiatura in A can be executed as a minim.

Prelude in G minor

The trills in bars, 1, 3, 7 and 11 begin on the main note.

Prelude in B flat major

The way the stems of the demisemiquavers point show Bach's changes of hand. Our fingerings – above or below the notes – consciously deviate from them.

Fugue in B flat minor

Bar 46: after the first crotchet, the tenor rests (till Bar 52); the second alto line re-enters with f'.–Bar 71: the first alto part leaps from bb' via bb (Bar 72) to g' (Bar 73); once this is clear, the leading of the other voices is easy to follow.

Johann Sebastian Bach: The Well Tempered Clavier II BWV 870-893

INDEX

PREFACE

Twenty years after the *Welltempered Clavier I* of 1722 Bach produced a second collection of preludes and fugues in all the keys. Since then it has been customary to refer to a first and a second part, which is not strictly accurate since each "part" is an entity in itself and does not need to be complemented by the other. However, Bach used the designation "part" himself. Having completed the second work, he drew up a title page which was designed to serve for both collections. The extant autograph manuscript (London, British Library. Add. MS. 35021) has no title page, but the manuscripts Berlin, Staatsbibliothek Preussischer Kulturbesitz, Mus. ms. Bach P 430 (Altnikol) and Hamburg, Staats- und Universitätsbibliothek MB 1974 reproduce what is undoubtedly the wording of the authentic title:

Des Wohltemperirten Claviers
Zweyter Theil
bestehend
in
Praeludien und Fugen
durch
alle
Tone und Semitonien
verfertiget
von
Johann Sebastian Bach
Königlich Pohlnisch und Churfürstlich. Sächsischen
Hoff Compositeur, Capellmeister
und Director Chori Musici
in Leipzig

The Hamburg manuscript, while giving the same wording, adds *Anno 1742*. This provides us with evidence – even if it is not in Bach's own hand – for the date of completion of the second *Welltempered Clavier*.

"Completion" in the context of a Bach composition does not mean that he simply put the work aside. Rather – as the source material indicates – he went back to the work, making a number of later modifications and corrections. On the basis of a critical comparative study of the textual sources anything up to four versions can be discerned. In most cases it is also possible to establish which is the latest and thus valid revised version: as a rule the more highly developed version proves to be the more recent, while the simpler version tends to be the older one. It should be added, however, that the evaluation of the sources is not as straightforward as this, because the "superior" reading is to be found now in the one source, now in the other. Neither the London autograph nor the manuscript copy which Altnikol made in Bach's house (P 430) constitute the final version of the complete work. We cannot even be sure whether Bach carried out a final revision of the score.

These questions are dealt with in the Critical Notes at the end of this volume, which explain the choice of textual readings in the present edition. Above all the Critical Notes provide information on those passages in which alternative and equally acceptable variant readings are available: cases in which a decision is difficult or even impossible. The attempt has been made to present those sources most closely related to the autograph – including lost manuscripts which can be hypothetically reconstructed – in their genealogical sequence in order not only to demonstrate the correlations between the evidence but also to shed some light on the occurrence of apparently contradictory readings. This presentation of source material gives the reader the opportunity to make a justifiable selection of readings other than those printed in the present score.

This edition sets out to meet the requirements of an "Urtext": on the basis of philological methods it aims to establish or reconstruct Bach's final version, but only insofar as this derives from Bach himself as attested by the sources. No attempt has been made to incorporate such modifications to the score as Bach might have made in a final revision and as have been made repeatedly in copies and printed editions. It might be of assistance to the performer to point out that not every variant reading which is extant is to be discarded, not every version is definitively established, not every trill is notated and not every note is attested by Bach's final statement of intent. The addition of ornamentation and a free selection of the variant readings offered are not merely permissible but recommendable. Readers are referred to the general "Performance Indications" in volume I (*The Welltempered Clavier I*, Urtext Edition, Mainz/Vienna, UT 50050, pp. VIIff.). The section "Special Remarks" has not been included in this edition.

The editor wishes to express his especial thanks to the head librarians and staff of those libraries which provided access to their manuscripts of the *Welltempered Clavier II*. Since these libraries are referred to by name in the Critical Notes at the end of the present volume, it is not necessary to list them here. Frau Anneliese Küch-Spitta made the manuscripts then in her possession available for scrutiny; these have now been incorporated in the collection of the Staatsbibliothek Preussischer Kulturbesitz, Berlin. I am grateful to the Johann Sebastian Bach Institute in Göttingen – specifically to Dr. Alfred Dürr and Dr. Klaus Hofmann – for much advice and assistance.

Walther Dehnhard

Ludwig van Beethoven: Bagatelles Op. 33, Op. 119, Op. 126

INDEX

7 Bagatellen, Opus 33

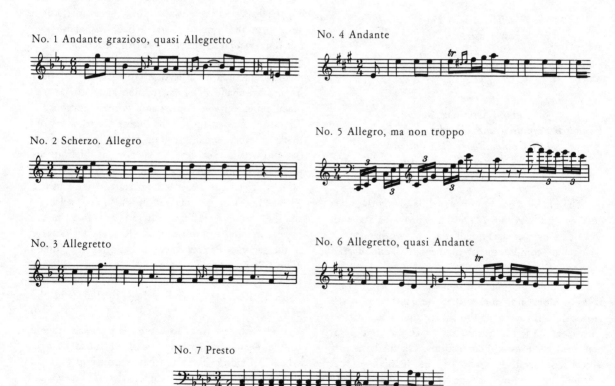

No. 1 Andante grazioso, quasi Allegretto

No. 2 Scherzo. Allegro

No. 3 Allegretto

No. 4 Andante

No. 5 Allegro, ma non troppo

No. 6 Allegretto, quasi Andante

No. 7 Presto

11 Bagatellen, Opus 119

6 Bagatellen, Opus 126

PREFACE

Since the 18th century, the title "Bagatelles" has been used for a set of short pieces which have no cyclic connection with one another.

At least some of the Bagatelles Op. 33 were probably written before 1802. The date on the manuscript is actually 1782 (the original second digit, an 8 (!), was corrected to 7), and this early date has been taken as referring to the first Bagatelle of the set. It is more likely, however, that Beethoven used ideas and sketches from his boyhood; he must, as was so often the case, have taken older material, or have revised finished pieces from an earlier period. Considering the style and mastery of the first Bagatelle it is unthinkable that, in the form we know it today, it could have been the work of a twelve-year-old.

The bagatelles that were grouped as Op. 119 fall into two parts which were written at different times. The first five, like Op. 33, are probably of rather early date (Nos. 2—5 between 1800 and 1804 according to Nottebohm who based his conclusions on preserved sketches, and some of them perhaps even earlier, namely Nos. 1, 2 and 4); only No. 6 can be said with some certainty to have been composed in 1822. The second part of the Bagatelles (Nos. 7—11) was written as a contribution to Ferdinand Starke's "Viennese Pianoforte School", in which they were published in the spring of 1821 as Nos. 28—32. Soon after that, Beethoven offered all 11 pieces to several publishers. Clementi published them in June 1823 in London. Contrary to the opinion of Georg Kinsky and Hans Halm, the London edition is the authentic original edition, and not the Paris edition by Schlesinger towards the end of 1823, which was later reprinted in Vienna (see the Critical Notes).

All of the Bagatelles Op. 126, which can be dated 1823 and 1824, are late works; they are both an epilogue to Beethoven's piano writing and the splendid climax of his compositions in small forms. In a letter to Schott, the publishers of the original edition, Beethoven wrote: "6 Bagatelles . . . some of which are a bit more expanded, and quite the best pieces of their kind that I have written . . ."

Our edition is based on the manuscripts (if extant), original editions and early printings. I am especially grateful to Alan Tyson, whose research work has proved that several London first editions are among the most important authentic sources. As regards the piano pieces, these are the London editions of Opp. 33 and 119. Tyson's book *The Authentic English Editions of Beethoven* (Faber & Faber, London 1963) and his article "The First Edition of Beethoven's Op. 119 Bagatelles" (*Musical Quarterly*, July 1963) were of great help to me in preparing this edition.

Additions in round brackets are by the editor. A differentiation has been made between staccato dots and strokes, so far as the sources permit. Expression or articulation markings added on the basis of analogous passages are mentioned in the Critical Notes. Where possible, however, the editor has refrained from making such additions, since he believes that overloading the musical text with superfluous markings makes reading more complicated, not easier. Even the first editions went rather too far in this respect, compared to the manuscripts. Several slurs in a row can mean a continuous legato, especially in the late pieces. At unmarked passages the articulation last in force continues "until further notice", or else the articulation is meant to be the same as that in similar passages. Only occasionally and with much hesitation did the editor decide to assimilate parallel passages. Apart from correcting obvious oversights and errors, Beethoven's markings, by no means always consistent or clear, should be retained even when they are contradictory.

Alfred Brendel

Ludwig van Beethoven: Grosse Fuge Op. 134 (Piano four hands)

PREFACE

The *Große Fuge* was the sixth movement of the String Quartet Op. 130 (completed in 1825 and first performed on 21 March 1826). On the insistence of his publisher, Beethoven replaced the outsize finale with a closing movement of far less weight, composed in 1826. The original finale, the fugue, was published in the following year as a separate work with the opus number 133, together with a piano reduction for four hands (in which the publisher had shown great interest) prepared by Beethoven himself; this was given the opus number 134.

The piano transcription of music written for strings poses a number of problems, especially in a fugal composition. A transcription by Anton Halm (1789–1872) was not approved by Beethoven, who thereupon decided to transcribe the quartet movement himself; ultimately only he possessed the artistic licence to rethink his composition in terms of another instrument.

The piano reduction differs from the version for string quartet mainly in the altered position of the voices and, consequently, their division between the two piano parts. There are occasional passages in which for a short time the setting of the voices is completely new – for example, bars 203, 212, 214, 372–78, 437 and 492. In bar 247 and its parallel, bar 543, there is a significant change in harmonic colouring.

Editorial conventions adopted for the volume I (UT 50160) also apply here. Square brackets indicate an addition by the editor; changes which are not specifically indicated in the music text are recorded in the Critical Notes except where they are based on parallel passages. Missing accidentals about which there is no doubt have been supplied without comment.

Vienna, Christmas 1991

Karl Heinz Füssl

FINGERING

The suggested fingerings were made with a number of considerations in mind. As these works are first and foremost intended for domestic music-making, ease of playing is the chief criterion for any decision on fingering. This is particularly pertinent where tricky passages can be made more playable through the choice of fingering, and also where the hand is held at an angle because of the close body positions of the two players. At the same time historical fingering practices were observed, for example the *Gleitfingersatz* used by Beethoven himself (see Volume I, UT 50106, p. 24, Variation VI, m.-7, left hand, where the same finger plays 2 adjacent notes) or the *Übersatz* described by Carl Philip Emanuel Bach (e.g. to put the 4th finger over the 5th).

The *Große Fuge* Op. 134 presents additional difficulties for the performers, such as the playing of semiquavers if they were triplets, or the both having to play within a narrow range, where one hand has to cross the partner's hand either from behind (near the piano lid) or from the front (at the edge of the keyboard). (How much easier it would be to use two instruments!) If Beethoven was dissatisfied with Halm's arrangement (see Preface, p. 4) for going too far in dividing the voices into first and second piano (A. W. Thayer, *Beethoven*, Vol. V, p. 299), in his own arrangement Beethoven strove to make the contrapuntal voice leading optically clear. While he made a few concessions to the performer, such as the occasional octave displacement or rewritten voice leading,

on the whole he was willing to accept that big leaps, crossing of hands, a shared narrow range and other technically awkward passages would impede easy sight-reading. It seems rather that Beethoven regarded the score as a study tool for musicians to be able to analyze the composition by playing it through. The present fingering tries to respect the intentions of the composer and rearranges the voicing only in extremely difficult passages.

The fingering for the right hand is always placed above the notes, for the left hand under the notes, regardless of whether the fingerings are printed in the upper or lower system. The following additional signs are also used:

⌞ to be played by the right hand
⌐ to be played by the left hand
→ hand position from above
← hand position from below
( ) Notes enclosed in round brackets are to be played by the other pianist, in whose music these same notes appear in smaller type.

Secondo

62

Primo

62

PREFACE

Next to nothing is known of the circumstances surrounding the composition of the Sonata in E flat major, Op. 7. We do not even know what prompted Beethoven to write it. Martin Gustav Nottebohm[1] points out that sketches of the sonata's third movement (*Allegro*) in the so-called *Kafka Sketchbook*[2] are in close proximity to various draft versions of bagatelles. Nottebohm concludes that the movement might originally have been conceived as a bagatelle itself before being appended to the Sonata Op. 7. Important though this evidence may be, it provides no hint as to the date of the sonata's composition. The only available conclusive evidence relating to the work's appearance in print is an announcement by the publisher Artaria in the *Wiener Zeitung* on 7 October 1797[3]. This advertisement for the first edition suggests that the date of composition would in all probability, have been the years 1796/97.

The other works which Beethoven composed during this period–between 1796 and 1798–include: the Sonata in D major for piano duet, Op. 6; the Serenade in D major for string trio, Op. 8; the Piano Rondo in C major, Op. 51/1; the Variations in C major for two oboes and cor anglais on the theme of *La ci darem la mano* from Mozart's *Don Giovanni*, WoO 28; the three String Trios Op. 9; the three Piano Sonatas Op. 10; and the three Sonatas for violin and piano Op. 12. By and large the above-mentioned compositions show Beethoven's output in his late twenties to have been prolific and to portend the scope of his later development while at the same time still to have been strongly influenced by Haydn and, especially, by Mozart.

A. W. Thayer[4] notes the sharply focused manifestation of this development in the Sonata Op. 7, calling it a *notable step forward in terms not only of Beethoven's piano music but also of the emergence of his musical personality.* Thayer continues in the same analysis: *The sonata is throughout a product of that so fertile epoch which revelled in its prolific creativity; yet the work's greater seriousness and profundity put it on an infinitely higher level than the output of Beethoven's contemporaries.* Thayer sees the culmination of the sonata in its second movement, *unanimously regarded as the most beautiful Adagio which Beethoven had composed to date.*

It is not the purpose of this Preface to consider any extra-musical allusions which Beethoven may have concealed in the sonata–and more particularly whether the key to such allusions might be found in the person of the work's dedicatee, Countess Anna Louise Barbara (Babette) Keglevics. The only fixed point of her biography which has come down to us is the date of her death: 2 April 1813. Oral tradition claims that Beethoven had given the Countess piano lessons in her youth. Carl Czerny is said to have recounted[5] that the composer was at the time infatuated with his pupil, who was by no means a beauty, and that he named the Sonata Op. 7, dedicated to the countess, *The Enamoured.* This claim is to some extent borne out by the testimony of the countess's nephew, who recalled[6] that Beethoven had composed the sonata for her *when she was still a girl and he was her teacher. Because he lived directly opposite her, he was in the habit– one of his many eccentricities– of going across the road in his nightgown, slippers and nightcap to give her lessons.* These somewhat anecdotal biographical links with the Sonata Op. 7 are strikingly corroborated by three further dedications through which Beethoven may have sought to convey his affection and reverence for the countess[7] (she had married Prince Innocenz d'Erba Odescalchi on 10 February 1801). She was the dedicatee of the later Variations in B flat major for piano, WoO 73 (1799) on *la stessa, la stessissima* from Salieri's opera *Falstaff*, of the Piano Concerto in C major, Op. 15 (the dedication dates from the year of the work's publication, 1801, although it had been composed six years previously), and of the Six Variations in F major for piano, Op. 34, composed in 1802 (published in the following year). Moreover, Thayer notes that Beethoven was a frequent visitor to the Odescalchi household in Pressburg (Bratislava) and took part in the distinguished musical soirées which the couple hosted. After 1803 the evidence of this friendship trails off. The later conversation notebooks[8] make only passing reference to the prince, who was Deputy President of the Vienna Philharmonic Society around the year 1819.

Unlike Beethoven's later works, the Piano Sonata Op. 7 was slow to achieve widespread popularity. Only eight years after the appearance of the first edition did leading publishing houses–the Bureau de Musique in Leipzig, Schott in Mainz, Nadermann in Paris, and others– begin reprinting the sonata; and it was the reprints which appeared after 1820 and then the new editions from 1830 onwards that led to the work's broad popularity[9].

Karl-Heinz Köhler

---

1 Martin Gustav Nottebohm, *Zweite Beethoveniana* (Leipzig 1887), p. 511

2 Named after the previous owner, the Viennese pianist Johann Nepomuk Kafka (1819 - 1886); since 1875 owned by the British Library, in London, Add. Ms. 29 801

3 Alexander Wheelock Thayer, *Ludwig van Beethovens Leben.* Nach dem Original-Manuskript deutsch bearbeitet und weitergeführt von Hermann Deiters. Mit Ergänzungen von Hugo Riemann, Volume II, 3rd edition (Leipzig 1922), p. 51

4 ibid. p. 51f.

5 Theodor von Frimmel, *Beethoven - Handbuch*, Volume I (Leipzig 1926), p. 256

6 ibid.

7 Thayer, Beethovens Leben, p. 135

8 Ed. K.H. Köhler and G. Herre, *Ludwig van Beethovens Konversationshefte*, Volume I (Leipzig 1972), pp. 295, 299 and note 682

9 Georg Kinsky, *Das Werk Beethovens. Thematisch-bibliographisches Verzeichnis seiner sämtlichen vollendeten Kompositionen.* Completed and edited by Hans Halm (Munich, Duisburg 1955), p. 16: notes on Opus 7

Slurs and Articulation

At the time this sonata was composed slurs primarily indicated a musical unit or a group of notes which were to be played *legato*. The end of the slur should not necessarily be interpreted as a caesura or a short pause. It is helpful to recall the original meaning of the slur, which linked notes to be played with a single up- or down-bow of a stringed instrument. In studying this work it is a good idea to imagine a change of bow between the last note of one slur and the first note of the next.

In many cases it will be clear that a break is necessary at the end of a slur: for example, when a slur connects only two or three short notes and the next note is marked staccato (1st movement bars 39-40, 67-78, 93-96, 109-110, etc.) or when a short slur is repeated (4th movement bars 34-35, 42-44, etc.).

Fingering

Depending on the shape and size of the player's hand, and technical preferences, the alternative fingerings may be found more appropriate (they are separated from the other fingering by an oblique stroke).

Pedal

Tying individual notes and chords through discriminating use of the pedal is often an essential factor in variety of tone.

1st movement: *Allegro molto e con brio*
Recommended tempo: ♩. 112-120

A faster tempo is often recommended (Hans von Bülow ♩. 126, Artur Schnabel ♩. 132); this can, however, be detrimental to the performance of this passionate movement. Furthermore, the tempo must not be too fast for performing the trills in bars 355-358, which are written out in semiquavers.

Bars 1-4, 137-140, etc.:
The pedal should be used sparingly to take the edge off the repeated notes; they should neither stand out nor be blurred. They can also be played *pp* (especially in bars 169-172) with one finger, preferably with the second.

Bars 51, 53, 231, 233:
A frequently used alternative fingering, in which the first quaver in the right hand (in bar 51: a') is played by the left hand, is not to be recommended: the tonal separation of the two hands is thereby lost. In addition the leap of the left hand which it necessitates (transition from bars 52 to 53 and from 232 to 233) creates a new difficulty, so that, all in all, this change does not make matters easier.

Bars 66 and 246:
The appoggiatura should be short, stressed, and sounded on the beat:

Bars 72 and 252:
The recommended fingering is applicable to both versions of the text (in bar 72: f' – e' flat – e' flat ⅄ e' flat – e' flat or f' – e' – e' ⅄ e' flat – e' flat).

Bars 109-110, 209-211, 289-290:
Realization of the upper mordents:

The first note in each of the semiquaver triplets should be stressed. They should be made to sound rhythmic, lively and sharply contoured.

2nd movement: *Largo, con gran espressione*
Recommended tempo: ♩ 42

Carl Czerny accurately described the character of this piece as 'sublime and profound'[1]. It is essential that the player should give the rests their full value.

Bars 9, 11, 59, 61:
At first glance the *cresc. – dim.* marking (< >) seems impossible to perform. However, it creates a psychological situation in which the player attempts to realize it, thus creating an otherwise unachievable tension between the chords on the second and third crotchets[2].

Bars 10, 12, 15, 43, 60, 62, 65:
The narrow width of the keys on instruments of the time certainly explains, to some extent, the frequent use of wide intervals within a single hand (e.g., bar 15, second crotchet: a tenth in the left hand). Individual solutions must be found for players with smaller hands.

In bar 10 the following is recommended for pianists with smaller hands:

The note d'' which both chords have in common should be sustained by the finger, so that there is no gap in the melody.

In bar 15 the following is recommended for players with smaller hands:

d should be played a little later very softly so as not to disrupt the musical flow.

Bars 25-36:
Here we might imagine a chorus of trombones accompanied by *pizzicato strings*. The right hand should be played as *legato* as possible with little pedal in order not to spoil the *pizzicato* effect in the left hand.

Bar 43, right hand, a solution for small hands:

The e'' flat in the right hand should be played simultaneously with the left-hand chord, followed immediately by f'''.

Bars 10, 12, 60, 62, 73:
Recommended performance of the turn:

Bar 73, second crotchet:
It is basically correct for the first note of the double appoggiatura (c') to be sounded together with the left-hand chord:

Bars 74-77:
The upper voice in the left hand can sound more colourful and lively if it is played exclusively by the thumb. In this case the fingering for the underlying chords must be changed accordingly.

Bar 89:
recommended realization:

3rd movement: *Allegro*
Recommended tempo: ♩. 72

The character of this movement could be called elegant (e.g., bars 1-4) and playful (e.g., bars 5-8). To bring out the playful element, the rests should be clearly observed.

Bars 19-24 and 80-86:
These bars are in charming contrast to the *legato* passage at the beginning. They are notated without slurs and should therefore be played *marcato* (imagining the constant change of bow on a violin).

Bar 33, recommended performance of the trill:

Bars 45-46:
It is impossible for a small hand to sustain the b flat in the upper voice of the left hand (see 2nd movement, bars 10, 12, etc.). The sound required may be achieved to some extent through the sensitive use of half-pedal.

Bars 96ff:
The middle section is like a surge of harmony. To achieve this effect a touch is required that does not quite reach the bed of the keys. A subtle but definite use of the pedal for *ffp* helps sustain the mood.

4th movement: *Rondo – Poco Allegretto e grazioso*
Recommended tempo: ♩ 58-60
for bars 64-91: ♩ 63-66

The elegant, narrative character of the principal Rondo section (bars 1-16, 50-61, etc.) is to be achieved by a singing melody, supple, elastic rhythm, and discriminating use of the pedal. The first episode, on the other hand (bars 16ff), should be played resolutely and almost without the pedal.

Bars 5, 55, 98, 143, 144:
Recommended realization:

Bars 11, 104:
Recommended realization:

Bars 15, 100, 108, 149:
Recommended realization:

Bars 34-36, 43, 44, 127-129, 136, 161-166:
Particular attention should be paid to shaping the slurs (see the remarks at the beginning of these notes).

Bars 36-42, 129-135:
Recommended performance of the trills:

(bar 36, second crotchet in the left hand)

Bar 43, 136:
Recommended realization:

Bars 62-63:
This calls for a *cresc.* between two double appoggiaturas leaping an octave. Similar situations have already occurred in the second movement (see 2nd movement, bars 9, 11, 59, 61)[3].

Bar 68ff:
Czerny's fingering has been modified somewhat. In spite of the greater range of movement in the key action of modern instruments, this fingering remains the best for expressing the tempestuous character of the middle section. The following fingering by Artur Schnabel is also worth considering:

Naoyuki Taneda

---

1 Carl Czerny, *Über den richtigen Vortrag der sämtlichen Beethoven'schen Klavierwerke*, Vienna, 1842 (new edition UE No. 13340, Vienna, 1963)
2 For a thorough discussion of this problem see: Heinrich Schenker, *Erläuterungsausgabe der Sonate op. 110 von Beethoven*, Vienna, 1914, p. 38 (new edition UE 26304, Vienna, 1972, p. 33-34)
3 cf. fn. 2

PREFACE

The three piano sonatas opus 10 were composed in Vienna between 1796 and 1798. Alexander Wheelock Thayer[1] and Gustav Nottebohm[2] assign preliminary sketches to the year 1796. Sketches dating from 1797 bear the following entries in Beethoven's hand: *For the new sonatas very short minuets. For that in C minor the presto also stays* and: *Intermezzo for the sonata in C minor.*

On the basis of this sparse autograph material Thayer notes that the sonata was originally to have had a further movement, an intermezzo, on which Beethoven embarked a number of times. Two of these attempts are published in the Supplement to the complete edition[3].

We possess no evidence to shed any light on the origins of the original edition, which the Viennese publisher advertised in the *Wiener Zeitung* on July 7th 1798: *Within six weeks we shall publish three very fine piano sonatas by Ludwig van Beethoven.* A further advertisement on September 26th 1798 announced the publication of the sonatas[4]. Since the autograph manuscript is not extant, the original edition — with all its errors — remains the only source (cf. Critical Notes).

The work's dedicatee, Anna Margarete von Vietinghoff-Scheel, was the wife of Count Georg von Browne-Camus (1767—1827), an officer in the service of the Russian Tsar; the count was one of Beethoven's aristocratic patrons during these years. It was to him that the composer dedicated the string trios opus 9, the piano sonata opus 22, the Lieder opus 48 and the variations for piano and cello WoO 46, while his wife was also the dedicatee of the variations on Wranitzky's ballet *Das Waldmädchen* WoO 71 and the trio *Tändeln und Scherzen* from Süssmayr's opera *Soliman II* WoO 76. Her early death (on May 13th 1803) prompted Beethoven to compose the six sacred Lieder after Gellert opus 48[5].

Karl-Heinz Köhler

---

[1] Alexander Wheelock Thayer, *Ludwig van Beethovens Leben*. Translated into German and expanded from the original manuscript by Hermann Deiters. With additions by Hugo Riemann, 2nd printing, vol. I—V Leipzig 1901—1911, vol II, p. 91 f.

[2] Martin Gustav Nottebohm, *Zweite Beethoveniana*. Leipzig 1887, pp. 32, 479

[3] Ludwig van Beethoven, Werke. Vollst. krit. durchgesehene, überall berichtigte Ausgabe, 24 series. Leipzig 1862/65, supplementary volume, Leipzig 1888, p. XXV, Nos. 295 and 299

[4] Quoted from: Georg Kinsky, *Das Werk Beethovens. Thematisch-bibliographisches Verzeichnis seiner sämtlichen vollendeten Kompositionen.* Completed and edited by Hans Halm. Munich, Duisburg 1955, p. 24: notes on opus 10

[5] Theodor von Frimmel, *Beethoven-Handbuch.* Vol. I, Leipzig 1926, pp. 70—72

Ludwig van Beethoven: Piano Sonata Op. 10/1

NOTES ON INTERPRETATION

The tempestuous, energetic character of the opening movement calls for a fairly fast tempo ($\downarrow$. = 76—84). The marking *Allegro molto e con brio* also implies the need for clear contours in the shaping of all the lines and absolute precision in rhythmic details. The dynamic markings must be observed exactly, especially in passages in which dynamic extremes are immediately juxtaposed. At this tempo the pedals should be used sparingly and with considerable caution: for example in the second subject from bar 56 onwards, where the bass line must not be blurred by full-bar pedalling. The same applies to bars 118 to 136 in the development and again to bar 233 onwards in the recapitulation. In these passages the *legato* in the right-hand octaves must be produced primarily by the fingers and not by the use of the right pedal. In the rising scale passages in bars 64/65 and 68/69 the quavers marked with strokes should be played *staccato* and *marcato,* thus clearly distinct from each other; a loose *non legato* would be very much easier to play but would run contrary to Beethoven's articulation markings.

The second movement, marked *Adagio molto,* is in complete contrast to the first with its rapid succession of events and is intended to radiate a mood of great tranquillity. I would suggest a very broad tempo here ($\flat$ = 60—66), which should be retained throughout the movement — thus also in the dreaded 'coloratura' passages (bars 28 ff. and 75 ff.). Great attention should be paid to the *cantabile* playing of the principal part and a more restrained, accompanying style in the secondary parts and chords. Embellishments like the turn in the very first bar must be incorporated in the *cantabile* flow of the melody and should not sound obtrusive or mannered. The player should avoid letting the right pedal blur left-hand figures in horizontal triads wherever these figures are soloistic in nature (for example, the quasi-cello solos in bars 10 and 12, particularly in bars 55 and 57/58 and also the figures in bars 40 and 42 which need to be played *marcato* — also the parallel passage). A clear distinction must be made between semiquaver and demisemiquaver dotting. Special care should be taken over the many-voiced writing in the coda (bars 91 ff.), which must sound perfectly transparent without overemphasis on any one part.

The next movement is extremely fast and strikingly exuberant. It is marked *Prestissimo* ($\downarrow$= 96—104). While the player should be careful to ensure clarity of articulation, the *piano* should be retained up to bar 12. The second subject (bars 16 ff.) is in the same tempo but brings a certain relaxation by virtue of its *scherzando* nature. Special emphasis may be given to the dialogue between the upper part and the bass part in bars 22 ff. Bars 43—45 are still *piano,* only the last chord being accented. The *ritardando* from bar 106 represents an unbroken transition to the very slow *Adagio* in bar 113 ($\flat$ = 72—80); the *arpeggio* should be played slowly and very quietly, in complete contrast to the incisive *arpeggio* in the following bar (114). The ending of the movement should take the listener by surprise, so it should not be anticipated by a *ritardando* in the closing bars. The *decrescendo* leads to a *pianissimo* chord which must be as quiet as possible and have exactly a crotchet value — the fermata is not over the last chord but over the rest.

Gerhard Oppitz

Ludwig van Beethoven: Piano Sonata Op. 10/2

NOTES ON INTERPRETATION

In the first movement (♩96–104) Beethoven contrasts playful elements with more expressive phrases – a musical parlance which clearly points forward to the Romantic age. In the two opening chords the staccato crotchet should sound slightly longer than the staccato quaver of the upbeat. The *legato* beginning at bar 18 cannot be realised with the fingers alone and needs the help of the right pedal (change pedals carefully!). For bars 77 and 94 I suggest a transparent sound making no use of the pedal at all. The transition from the recapitulation in bar 118 (in the "wrong" key) to the return of F major may be interpreted with a great deal of improvisational freedom.

For the second movement with its fundamentally elegiac mood I recommend thinking the musical progression in whole-bar terms (♩approx. 56). In the Trio section (beginning at bar 39) the *sforzati* and the *cresc.* and *decresc.* nuances should be seen in relation to the basic *pp* dynamic level.

The buoyant and energetic Finale (♩138–144) needs extremely precise delineation, especially of the semiquaver passages, in order to allow the quasi-polyphonic part writing to take on suitably sharp contours. The *piano* passages, which should be played with a loose and light touch, provide an attractive contrast to the sections of a *martellato* character.

Gerhard Oppitz

Ludwig van Beethoven: Piano Sonata Op. 10/3

NOTES ON INTERPRETATION

In order to establish a plausible correlation between the contrasting ideas of the first movement, I recommend selecting a tempo which can be gauged to all of the themes without noticeable changes (♩138-144). The opening bars, up to the *sforzato* in bar 4, remain *piano*, unlike the parallel *crescendo* passage from bar 16 onwards. The right-hand chords from bar 87 onwards should be sustained for their full duration where possible; the right pedal cannot be used here since the left-hand octaves have to continue *staccato*.

The second movement (♪approx. 60) requires, on the one hand, great inner composure if the extremely slow tempo is to be sustained right to the end and, on the other hand, the self-assurance to employ a high degree of expressivity and declamatory freedom in the quasi-recitative passages (e.g. from bar 9 onwards). In the 'Coda' from bar 65 onwards the *crescendo* from *pp* to *ff* should be judiciously apportioned, and at the same time the player should avoid any hint of *accelerando*.

For the *Menuetto* I recommend a moderate tempo (♩.60-66) to allow the marking *piano dolce* to come across and the theme to be played truly *cantabile*. The somewhat 'bucolic' character of the Trio is best conveyed if the articulation markings are scrupulously observed.

The capricious *Rondo* is a brilliant *tour de force* and can be played with wit, sophistication and spontaneity. Recommended tempo: ♩ 132-144. The opening bars and their recurrence at later points in the movement leave scope for a high degree of improvisational freedom. The energetic nature of the episode which begins at bar 33 should be in clear contrast with the surrounding passages.

Gerhard Oppitz

Dem Fürsten Carl von Lichnowsky gewidmet

KLAVIERSONATE
Grande Sonate pathétique
Opus 13
1798/99

PREFACE

With no more to go on than the chronology of the few identified sketches and the announcement of the impending publication of the first edition in the *Wiener Zeitung* of December 18th 1799, it is not possible to establish an exact date for the present work's composition beyond allocating it to the years 1798—99. There is no other documentary evidence — and above all no reference in the correspondence — to shed light on the date or the occasion of its composition. The autograph manuscript is not extant[1].

The piano sonata opus 13 thus belongs to a period which saw the composition of a number of works whose stylistic characteristics have their roots in the classical tradition of Haydn and Mozart: the C major piano concerto, opus 15; the B flat trio, opus 11; the cello variations on "Ein Mädchen oder Weibchen" from Mozart's *Magic Flute*, opus 66; and the piano sonatas opus 14 and opus 49.

It should be remembered, however, that opus 13 is also chronologically adjacent to many compositions which are conspicuous for their highly innovative, as it were "Beethovenian" language: the string quartets opus 18 (1798); the C minor piano concerto, opus 37 (1800); and the first symphony, opus 21 (1800). This juxtaposition poses the question: why did Beethoven evolve a style in his piano sonata opus 13 which differs markedly from that in the preceding sonatas? One answer which has been put forward cites the influence of certain compositions by Neefe, Haydn, Mozart and even F. W. Rust[2]. A more plausible explanation may be seen in the fact that the year 1798 brought two experiences which were to have a profound effect on Beethoven's life: the first realisation that he suffered from a hearing disorder, which gave rise to the characteristically Beethovenian concept of the triumph of the will[3]; and the composer's first real encounter with the music of the French revolution in the residence of the French Consul Bernadotte.

The innovative character of the present sonata, reflected in its title *Grande Sonate pathétique*, was accorded an enthusiastic welcome by the contemporary public. This is clear from a review which appeared on February 19th 1800, shortly after the publication of the first edition[4]: *This craftsmanlike sonata justifies its epithet pathétique, being of a distinctly passionate nature. Sublime melancholy is the keynote of the vivid, skilfully and smoothly modulated Grave in C minor which punctuates the highly emotional Allegro, itself an expression of the profound feelings of an earnest mind. The A flat major Adagio, not to be taken too slowly, contains beautiful flowing melody, modulation and a judicious sense of movement. Here the soul finds reassurance in the music's tranquillity and consolation but is reawakened — in both senses — by the first note of the Allegro. Thus, the sonata's underlying mood remains consistent, investing the work with homogeneity and inner life, in other words genuine aesthetic worth. To be able to make this claim on behalf of a sonata — provided that all the other requirements of the musical arts are complied with, is incontrovertible proof of its beauty. Beethoven is of course free to invent and to innovate as he wishes; but the present critic would raise one point, not so much in reproach as in the expression of a desire for even greater perfection: the subject of the Rondo is too strongly reminiscent of something. Of what the critic cannot say; but certainly the idea is not a new one.*

(Nottebohm and Thayer noted that the sketches contained evidence of the last movement having originally been conceived for several instruments but not for the keyboard[5].)

That the sonata opus 13 rapidly acquired an enthusiastic following is testified by the numerous contemporary reprints and copies as well as by the critical acclaim it was accorded. The *Wiener Zeitung*, for instance, on March 13th 1805 described the work as "*. . . outstanding, widely popular and well-known*".

For a long time the edition by Eder (VN 128), in fact a reissue under a new title, was thought to be the original edition. It was the Viennese bibliographer Alexander Weinmann and the two men who carried on his research where he left off, Richard S. Hill and Alan Tyson, who demonstrated that the first edition was brought out by Hoffmeister, who later sold the plates to Eder[6] (cf. Critical Notes).

The sonata's dedicatee, Prince Carl von Lichnowsky (1756—1814) had been a pupil and patron of Mozart. With his brother Moritz and other members of his family he was amongst the most important of Beethoven's patrons in Vienna. The composer lived in Lichnowsky's house during his first years in the Austrian capital, and in 1800 Lichnowsky provided Beethoven with an annuity of 600 guilders. Relations between the two men were not always untroubled, as is testified by the anecdote concerning Beethoven's refusal to play for French officers at the Prince's estate in Troppau, but also by the fact that the Mass in C major was performed in Lichnowsky's residence in 1811. The works which Beethoven dedicated to Prince Lichnowsky include the piano trios opus 1, the piano sonata opus 26 and the second symphony, opus 36[7].

Karl-Heinz Köhler

[1] On the dating of the work, cf. above all: Georg Kinsky, *Das Werk Beethovens. Thematisch-bibliographisches Verzeichnis seiner sämtlichen vollendeten Kompositionen.* Completed and edited by Hans Halm. Munich, Duisburg 1955, notes on opus 13
Beiträge zur Beethoven-Bibliographie. Studien und Materialien zum Werkverzeichnis von Kinsky-Halm, edited by Kurt Dorfmüller, Munich 1978, p. 297
[2] Theodor von Frimmel, *Beethoven-Handbuch*, vol. II, Leipzig 1926, p. 191
[3] Cf. amongst other documents Beethoven's letter to his friend Karl Amend dated June 1st 1800
[4] See *Allgemeine Musikalische Zeitung* of February 19th 1800
[5] Alexander Wheelock Thayer, *Ludwig van Beethovens Leben.* Translated into German from the original manuscript and enlarged by Hermann Deiters. With additional material by Hugo Riemann, vol. II, 3rd edition, Leipzig 1922, pp. 94/95
[6] Cf. above all: Richard S. Hill, *Wiener Musikverleger und Musikalienhändler von Mozarts Zeit bis gegen 1860.* In *Notes* 1958, p. 396. Alan Tyson, *Beethoven's Pathétique Sonata and its Publisher.* In: *Musical Times* 1963, p. 333f.
[7] Cf. above all: Theodor von Frimmel, *Beethoven-Handbuch*, vol. I, Leipzig 1926, p. 349

NOTES ON INTERPRETATION

Suggested relative tempi:
I. Grave ♪ = Allegro di molto e con brio 𝅝 =
II. Adagio cantabile ♪ = } 66—76
III. Allegro 𝅗𝅥 =

1st movement:
bars 51 ff.: the right hand always above the left. The leaps must be practised carefully, not only for the sake of accuracy but also to avoid rhythmic distortion.
bars 280, 284: the lower fingering is suitable only for a thoroughly practised right hand.

2nd movement:
bar 3: convenient fingering provided that the fourth finger is strong.
bar 21: begin the turn on the seventh semiquaver or slightly later.
bar 37: the legato in the upper parts will benefit from the left hand taking over some of the middle parts.
bars 55, 63: the penultimate demisemiquaver in the right hand should be played simultaneously with the last triplet semiquaver, which means slightly abbreviating the value of the last two notes in the upper part. In the original edition the passage concerned is notated ♪♪♪♪, which illustrates this principle of performance practice (See our facsimile).
bar 68: suggested realisation:

3rd movement:
bars 2, 3, etc.: the appoggiaturas should be very brief.
bars 5, 6, etc.: by contrast with the preceding semiquavers, which must retain their full value, the slides should likewise be very brief.
bars 58—60: the lower fingering is not that conventionally prescribed for the C minor scale but is here more convenient. The same applies to bars 209—210.
bars 167 ff.: divided between both hands for the sake of the legato.

Alexander Jenner

PREFACE

The December 21th 1799 issue of the *Wiener Zeitung* contains an advertisement by the Mollo publishing house of the impending publication of the two piano sonatas opus 14[1]. (On the original edition see Critical Notes.) This fact has led the authors of most of the copious secondary literature on Beethoven to deduce that the composition of or at least the sketches to these works roughly coincide with the *Sonate pathétique* opus 13 — dating them around 1798/99. The musical idiom of the present works is so utterly different from that of opus 13, however, that we must assume their origins to go back to a considerably earlier period. This supposition is borne out by the sketches to opus 14/1 (today in the Staatsbibliothek Preußischer Kulturbesitz, Mus. Ms. autogr. Beethoven 28) in that they precede the violin sonata opus 12/3 and follow the sketches to the piano concerto Op. 19[2]. This cannot, however, be accounted conclusive evidence, since Beethoven might merely have been using up blank pages in his sketch book. At best the origins and composition of the sonatas can be attributed to the years 1795–99, since no other documentary evidence has come to light and the autograph is not extant.

In the light of the above there appears to be little justification for speculating about influences on these works, as writers like Frimmel do[3]. Frimmel traces the principal subject of opus 14/1 back to a string quartet by Haydn No. 12 [?] and the Andante of opus 14/2 to an idea in a polonaise by Friedemann Bach or a Rondo by Johann Christian Bach. In the same way little new light is shed on the question of these sonatas' origins by investigating the chronological proximity to the *Pathétique*, as Deiters does when he states somewhat glibly that the sonatas opus 14 are *polished in their form, beautiful in their melodies and characteristic in their content,* features which — he claims — *convey a sense of relief after the oppressiveness of the Pathétique*[4].

On the other hand the secondary literature has tended to take an especial interest in the sonatas opus 14, on the strength of the claim made by Beethoven's close friend Anton Schindler in his biography of the composer (1840) that Beethoven himself described the two works as depicting the clash between two principles. According to Schindler, Beethoven termed them the imprecating and the opposing principles. Schindler went to far as to append to this supposed quotation of Beethoven's own words an analysis of passages from opus 14/2. This prompted the Berlin musicologist Adolf Bernhard Marx to an outburst of invective against Schindler, who omitted the analysis in the second edition of his Beethoven biography (1845). A. W. Thayer, whose approach was consistently sceptical, also noted that Beethoven had himself always resisted attempts to interpret his music in this way and had tended to be evasive and vague when asked to enlarge on the subject. Thayer argues that the reference to a dialogue between two contrasting principles is about as unspecific as it could be. In 1977 it was shown at the Beethoven Congress in East Berlin that Schindler's entries to this effect in Beethoven's conversation notebooks dating from 1823 and 1824 were interpolations, in the light of which the entire line of approach based on Schindler's claims must be regarded as devoid of the slightest documentary significance[5]. However that may be — whether Schindler was recording a genuine observation by the composer, putting forward his own views or merely inventing the whole story — the idea of the confrontation of two principles

as the scheme of the aesthetic structure is certainly applicable to other works besides the sonatas opus 14.

It is evident, however, that both works established themselves as amongst Beethoven's most popular compositions for piano soon after their first appearance in print. In 1804 and again four years later Mollo reissued them. During the composer's lifetime several other publishers brought out editions, not only in their original piano versions but also — as was customary at the time — in arrangements for other instruments. Of especial interest here is Beethoven's own arrangement of the sonata opus 14/1 for string quartet (transposed from E to F major). This version was published in May 1802 by the "Bureau d'Arts et d'Industrie" in Vienna. It is worth citing Beethoven's remarks on the difficulties of making such an arrangement. In a letter to Breitkopf & Härtel dated July 13th 1802 he writes[6]: *With regard to the arrangements, I am now thoroughly glad that you rejected them . . . I am convinced that only Mozart could arrange his own piano music for other instruments — and Haydn as well. Without wishing to place myself on the same level as these two great men I would say the same about my own piano sonatas. It is not just that whole passages have to be omitted altogether or completely rewritten; additions have to be made to the music, and herein lies the nub of the problem. To perform this task satisfactorily one either has to be the composer of the original or at least possess the same degree of skill and inventiveness. I have arranged but a single sonata of mine for string quartet, in response to pressing demands, and I know as an absolute certainty that my arrangement would be difficult to rival . . .*

Both the arrangement alluded to above and the two sonatas themselves are dedicated to Baroness Josepha von Braun (1765–1838), the wife of Baron Peter von Braun (1758–1819), who was Deputy Director of the Imperial & Royal Court Theatre in Vienna (1794–1806) at the time when the sonatas were composed. The secondary literature describes the dedicatee as a skilled pianist. The horn sonata opus 17 (1801) is also dedicated to her[7]. We possess no detailed historical evidence relating to Beethoven's connection with this influential couple — a connection which would undoubtedly shed considerable light on the origins of the two sonatas.

Karl-Heinz Köhler

---

[1] On the evidence relating to the composition of these works cf. above all Georg Kinsky: *Das Werk Beethovens. Thematisch-bibliographisches Verzeichnis seiner sämtlichen vollendeten Kompositionen.* Completed and edited by Hans Halm. Munich, Duisburg 1955, p. 32: notes on opus 14.

[2] In this connection cf. above all Alexander Wheelock Thayer: *Ludwig van Beethovens Leben.* Translated and expanded on the basis of the original English manuscript by Hermann Deiters, with additions by Hugo Riemann. Volume II, 3rd printing, Leipzig 1922, pp. 95–99.

[3] Cf. Theodor von Frimmel: *Beethoven-Handbuch*, volume II, Leipzig 1926, p. 191.

[4] See 2.

[5] Cf. Dagmar Beck and Grita Herre: *Einige Zweifel an der Überlieferung der Konversationshefte.* In: Bericht über den Internationalen Beethoven-Kongreß 20.–23. März 1977 in Berlin, Leipzig 1978, pp. 257f.

[6] Quoted from A. Ch. Kalischer: *Beethovens sämtliche Briefe.* Berlin and Leipzig 1906.

[7] On the dedication cf. Kinsky and Frimmel, op. cit. (notes 1 and 3).

Opus 14/1

Recommended tempi:
I. Allegro [♩ = 132—144]
II. Allegretto [♩. = 66—72]
III. Allegro Comodo [♩ = 66—72]

I. Bars 1 ff., 13 ff., 57 ff. etc.: the chord repetitions reminiscent of string quartet writing should not be played too short but with little or no pedal. The fingers always remain close to the keys.
Bars 5 f.: take care to keep the tempo consistent

($\sqcap\sqcap$ $\sqcap\sqcap$ = $\sqcap$ $\sqcap$).

Bars 50 ff.: the staccato in the upper part must on no account detract from the melodic intensity. Staccato dots are frequently used merely to countermand the legato generally required in the music of the Viennese classical period.
Bars 69/70: *crescendo* only up to *mf.*
Bars 81 ff.: full-toned *p*, so that the tone can be taken back in bars 89/90.

II. The numerous *sf* must not be allowed to disrupt the four-bar phrases; rather they should lend them shape. The *sf* in bar 3 (and bar 11 etc.) marks the upper third in the middle of the phrase; while the *sf* in bars 18 and 20 (as subsequently in bars 26 and 28 etc.) — metrically the „weak" second and fourth bars within the four-bar phrases — mark the same note as previously but at shorter intervals (two *sf* per four-bar phrase instead of just one). The *sf* in bars 18 and 20, like all the expression marks occurring in metrically "weak" bars or segments of bars, are "tenuto" in character. The *sf* on the second crotchet of bars 45 and 46 further reinforce the tendency towards greater compression and acceleration (now two *sf* within two bars).
In the maggiore section the phrase endings, now reduced to a single part, should deliberately be played *espressivo* (bars 69/70, 77/78, 87/88, 91/92, 95/96).

III. The upbeat of the theme (a "gavotte upbeat") should be played consistently "lightly".
Bars 3, 11: *crescendo* only up to *mf.*
Bar 13: *sf* signifies "tenuto"; i. e. do not lose the second ("weak") crotchet.
Bars 47 ff.: The notes with staccato dots (in the r. h.) are integral to the melody and should be made to stand out from the triplets by accentuation.

Opus 14/2

Recommended tempi:
I. Allegro [♩ = 80—88]
II. Andante [♩ = 44—50]
III. Allegro assai [♩. = 76—84]

I. Bars 1 ff., 64 ff., 99 ff., 125 ff., 187 ff.: even without the explicit marking *ligato* (r. h.) and the carefully written out "finger legato" or "harmonic legato"[1] (l. h.) there is a generally applicable principle which prescribes the use of legato[2]. The divergent notation for passages which are to be played identically is to be explained by the necessity to give a "visually" correct reproduction of the spread chords in the bass as a harmonic foundation:

instead of . Thus, the marking *ligato* at the beginning of the movement is intended merely to connote the same manner of playing as the "finger legato" written out here.
Bars 14—18: *crescendo* only up to *mf;* likewise bars 39—40, 56/57 etc.
Bars 15, 17 etc.: r. h. appoggiatura not anticipated (i. e. to be struck simultaneously with the first note in the l. h.).
Bars 41 ff.: The absence of slurs does not necessarily indicate staccato. When Beethoven intended a contrast in the articulation between legato and staccato he carefully notated the appropriate markings; cf. for instance l. h. bars 81 ff., slurs; bars 84 f., staccato dots, etc.

II. Czerny already noted the *allabreve* marking and described this movement as a *fairly lively Allegretto*, although he designated the tempo in crotchets (116). During the Viennese classical period "Andante" and "Allegretto" were regarded as virtually identical tempi.
Another point to note in this movement is its "instrumentation", achieved by the use of changing octaves which produced different sound qualities on the "Hammerklavier" of Beethoven's day. As the piano developed into the modern instrument we know today with its perfectly balanced sound, the variety of tonal colour which could be exploited by using the various octave "registers" gradually disappeared. In playing this movement we recommend bearing the tonal shading of the "Hammerklavier" in mind and taking account of the many different kinds of touch.

III. The hemiolic figure at the beginning of the theme must be brought out clearly as such; the 3/8 metre does not make itself felt until bars 3 and 7.

Hans Kann

---

[1] "The *legato*... means not just the linear connection of notes, but also the holding of all non-dissonant notes. This way of playing was used from the seventeenth century until well into the second half of the nineteenth (one still comes across it in Brahms); the editor of this volume terms it 'harmonic legato'". Jan Ekier, in Chopin: *Impromptus.* Mainz/Wien 1977, Urtext Edition No. 50058.

[2] Cf. Ex. 5 and Ex. 7 in J. B. Cramer: *21 Etüden für Klavier... nach dem Handexemplar Ludwig van Beethovens.* Edited by Hans Kann, Wien 1974, Universal Edition No. 13353.

PREFACE

The publication by Jean Cappi of Beethoven's Piano Sonata Op. 26, together with Op. 27 Nos. 1 and 2, was announced in the *Wiener Zeitung* of 3 March 1802. Drafts of this work are found in the sketchbook F 91 Landsberg 7 held by the Staatsbibliothek zu Berlin – Preussischer Kulturbesitz, after the sketches for the first movement of the Second Symphony, dating from 1801. Assuming that these notes were written in chronological order, Beethoven must have started work on the sonata in 1801, and not as early as 1800, as Nottebohm and, following him, Kinsky and Halm, assumed[1].

The autograph of the whole of Op. 26, written in Beethoven's own hand after the sketches, is the first autograph of his piano sonatas to have survived. Found among Beethoven's papers after his death, it was acquired by the Vienna publishing house Haslinger and bought by Ferdinand August Grasnick, a collector of autographs from Berlin, in 1842. Erich Prieger, a Bonn academic, rediscovered it in 1878 as part of Grasnick's estate, "in the midst of a pile of waste paper". Prieger published it in 1884 as the first facsimile edition of a Beethoven autograph[2]. Grasnick's heir sold the autograph to the Preußische Staatsbibliothek Berlin. Moved during the Second World War, the manuscript finally came to the Jagiellonian Library in Cracow.

In the opening movement of Op. 26 Beethoven dispensed for the first time with the sonata form typically used for the main movement in this genre. Instead, we find an expansive, song-like *Andante* theme with five variations. In this movement, even before the piano variations Op. 34 of 1802, Beethoven completes the transition from the older, figurative variation form to intensively expressive "character variations" which do not conform to any standard type. The theme of this movement reveals to us less Beethoven's fighting spirit, creating and overcoming conflicts, than his "inner world", filled with an endless intensity of experience. Above the first sketch of the theme for the variations, in which the melody is already fully matured, we find the dedication "Sonata pour M.", which to the present day has not been explained with any degree of certainty[3].

The *Marcia funebre*, in the A flat minor key of the third variation, relates directly to the first movement. It can to some extent be seen as a free-standing, final variation on the opening theme. In the continuous repeating of the e' flat anacrusis, the melody of the opening, reduced to an absolute tonal repetition, freezes in the presence of death, similarly evoked by Beethoven in 1803 in the shocking brass sounds of the *Marcia funebre* of his *Eroica* (bars 160ff.)[4]. Concerning the brighter major middle section, Frimmel notes sensitively: "It is natural that in the sunny parts with the major triad on the tonic, the major third should be emphasized a little."[5]

Thus the Sonata Op. 26 contains two *Andante* movements. If the impact of the second one was not to be diminished, they could not follow each other directly. Beethoven therefore placed the contrasting *Allegro molto* scherzo between them[6], and finally responded to the funeral march with the exuberant sonata rondo of the *Allegro* finale, whose thematic independence leaves behind, in every respect, all that has gone before.

The resulting irregular sequence of movements – the scherzo as second movement and the slow movement as the third – appears several times in Beethoven's work after 1810: in the String Quartet Op. 95, the Piano Trio Op. 97, the Piano Sonatas Opp. 101 and 106, the Ninth Symphony, and the String Quartet Op. 131.

Concerning the historical context of the work, it can be said that in the opening variation movement Beethoven was able refer back to at least one highly significant model, Mozart's A flat major Sonata K 331. Frimmel has investigated further Mozartian echoes in the variations[7]. On the other hand, Beethoven's pupils, Ferdinand Ries and Carl Czerny, report that the *Marcia funebre* was influenced by the funeral march in the heroic opera *Achilles* by the Italian composer and later musical director to Napoleon's court, Ferdinando Paer (successfully performed in Vienna on 6 June 1801)[8]. This presupposes, however, that the sonata was in fact begun at that time, for according to the sketches, the funeral march was written directly after the variation theme. This in turn suggests that it is less a case of specific influence, than of the general impact of French revolutionary music of fundamental significance to Beethoven's creative work whose "neoclassical" heroic cult also gave rise to a corresponding genre of funeral music. Carl Czerny reports that while writing the *perpetuum mobile*-like finale, Beethoven had in mind the "running style" of the finale of Johann Baptist Cramer's sonata in A flat major, which the composer had performed in Vienna at that time[9]. In addition, it should be emphasized that Beethoven, like all masters of their craft, necessarily absorbed all stimuli that suited his own purposes. In the creative process, he fused them in every case into an ultimately incomparable, logically consistent whole which set its own standards for future generations.

The first edition of the sonata, published in 1802, and the first reprints which appeared in the same year, were quickly followed by separate editions of the popular *Marcia funebre*[10], numerous transcriptions of the theme of the first movement for various instruments, and settings for voices, with words[11], as well as arrangements of the funeral march. As late as 1815, Beethoven used the funeral march again in a B minor orchestral version as the closing movement of his incidental music to Johann Friedrich Leopold Duncker's drama *Leonore Prohaska* (WoO 96).

Like the earlier Three Piano Trios Op. 1 and the Sonata Op. 13, and later the Second Symphony, Beethoven dedicated this sonata to Prince Carl Lichnowsky, "one of Beethoven's warmest friends and most self-sacrificing patrons" in those years[12].

Peter Hauschild
Translated by Angela Davies

---

[1] Sketchbook Landsberg 7, Staatsbibliothek zu Berlin – Preussischer Kulturbesitz, Music Section, ed. by Karl Lothar Mikulicz, *Ein Notierungsbuch von Beethoven aus dem Besitze der Preussischen Staatsbibliothek zu Berlin* (Leipzig, 1927). Gustav Nottebohm, *Zweite Beethoveniana. Nachgelassene Aufsätze* (Leipzig, 1887), pp. 236–43. Georg Kinsky, *Das Werk Beethovens. Thematisch-bibliographisches Verzeichnis seiner sämtlichen vollendeten Kompositionen*, completed and ed. by Hans Halm (Munich-Duisburg, 1955), p. 63.

[2] Erich Prieger, *As-dur Sonate op. 26 von Ludwig van Beethoven*, facsimile edition (Bonn 1895). Cf. also Kinsky/Halm, loc. cit.

[3] Nottebohm, loc. cit. p. 239, speculated that the "M." might perhaps refer to Count Moritz von Fries, to whom Beethoven later dedicated the Violin Sonatas Opp. 23 and 24. But would Beethoven have used his Christian name? Thayer, loc. cit., p. 250 (see footnote 8), suggested the Viennese publisher Mollo, which is not fully convincing either, given the early stage of the sketches for the work-in-progress. We would prefer to suppose that the dedication conceals one of Beethoven's more poetic secrets.

[4] The sketches, Mikulicz, loc. cit., pp. 56–7, suggest that the funeral march was directly related to the variation theme in conception. After it, Beethoven noted: *variée tutto a fatto poi Menuetto o qualche altro pezzo caracteristica come p. E. una Marcia in as moll e poi questo* (completely varied, thereafter a Menuetto or some other characteristic piece such as, for example, a March in A flat minor and thereafter this): An eight-bar finale opening which follows this appears later, in a minor version, in the third move-

ment of Op. 27 No. 2, bars 92/93; the definitive finale figuration appears earlier on p. 54. Of the *Marcia*, still on p. 56, we first find sketches of the A flat major middle section. On p. 57 the main part follows, at first concentrating exclusively on the tonal repetition of the upper voice as the sole harmonized "melody", and later again on p. 135:

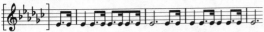

The independent middle voice with its anacrusis of an interval of a sixth which, as it were, comments on the action, was added only in the autograph. Tonal repetition as a symbol of death became extremely important for Franz Schubert, who was deeply fascinated by Beethoven. Among many examples, we can mention the *Lied* 'Der Tod und das Mädchen' (Death and the Maiden), and 'Wegweiser' from the *Winterreise*. In the year of Beethoven's death, Schubert may have cited the Sonata Op. 26 in yet another way, in his A flat major *Impromptu* Op. 142, No. 2, which can be seen as a "hommage" to the variation theme. Cf. Paul Badura-Skoda/Jörg Demus, *Die Klaviersonaten von Ludwig van Beethoven* (Wiesbaden, 1970), p. 82.

[5] Theodor Frimmel, *Beethoven-Handbuch*, Vol. II (Leipzig, 1926), p. 197.

[6] This movement, the *Menuetto*, contemplated at the beginning of the sketches, was the last movement to be drafted, on p. 158. It is labelled as *Scherzo* only in the autograph.

[7] Frimmel, loc. cit., p. 193.

[8] Franz Gerhard Wegeler and Ferdinand Ries, *Biographische Notizen über Beethoven* (Koblenz, 1838), p. 80, quoted by, among others, Frimmel, loc. cit., p. 196. Carl Czerny, quoted in Alexander Wheelock Thayer, *Ludwig van Beethovens Leben*, translated from the original manuscript into German and continued by Hermann Deiters, with additions by Hugo Riemann, Vol. II, 3rd edn (Leipzig, 1922), p. 249, note 1.

[9] Thayer, loc. cit.

[10] In the newly engraved first Title Edition by Cappi (see Critical Notes), the heading *Marcia funebre* was printed with spaced letters, and the composer's name was given again, so that no new plates had to be prepared for the first separate edition.

[11] Beethoven himself had asked Franz Gerhard Wegeler, a friend of his since the days of their youth, to provide a text for the *Andante* theme. Wegeler, however, gave the text neither to Beethoven nor to anyone else, as he himself was not satisfied with it. Wegeler-Ries, loc. cit., p. 48, quoted in Kinsky/Halm, p. 65.

[12] Kinsky/Halm, loc. cit., p. 6.

NOTES ON INTERPRETATION

Movement I: *Andante con Variazioni*

The song-like theme – which initially displays a serious and elevated character by doubling the melody at the octave – contains both lyrical and more playful features, evoked by shorter time values and dotted rhythms.

The first and second variations are largely based on those rhythmic figures which express the light-hearted, playful mood.

In the third variation, the seriousness of the opening changes to the sudden gloom of A minor, and a premonition of the later Funeral March, with passionate syncopation and frequent *sforzati* which catch the listener's attention.

The fourth variation, by contrast, strongly emphasizes the scherzando element, while the fifth and final variation, in which the theme returns richly ornamented (with the ornaments written out in full), provides a balanced finish. The final bars, from bar 205 onwards, echo the character of the theme.

Tempo:
More or less the same basic measure applies to the theme and all the variations, as Beethoven does not specify changes in tempo for individual variations. The theme should be played more calmly than the first variation. The lilting, lively staccato demisemiquavers in bars 57 to 59 (roughly *Andante con moto*) set the tempo of the first variation. The second variation is a little livelier than the first. The third variation relates to the theme in tempo, but should have a weighty, measured character. A quicker tempo expresses the light, bright nature of the fourth variation. A return to the tempo set at the beginning of the movement for the fifth and final variation closes the circle.

Further notes on Movement I:
The appoggiatura to the demisemiquaver motif which frequently appears in the Theme and in the first, second and fifth variations is to be played on the beat; it should be somewhat shorter than the following notes of the group. The temptation to play the figure as a quintuplet, produced by lazy execution, should be avoided.

For bars 23, 25 and 59 – in each case 3rd quaver, right hand, the following realization is recommended:

A quintuplet (see below) is also possible, however, especially in the first variation (bar 59), which should be played a little faster than the theme:

Since in Beethoven's autograph the trill in bar 25 is written with, in bars 23 and 59, however, without „Nachschlag", the following realizations of the trill may possibly express the composer's intention for bars 23 and 59:

or

For bars 180 and 198, the following fingering is recommended for smaller hands:

Movement II: *Scherzo/Allegro molto*

The significance of the light-hearted, playful mood which we have already encountered in three of the five variations in Movement I is reinforced here, where it is released from the constraints imposed by the Theme-and-Variations form of the first movement. From the second part onwards (bars 17ff.), the music becomes more and more gripping.

The Trio is to be played at the same basic tempo, but more calmly. It seems to anticipate some passages in Schubert's piano sonatas, in which the piano sounds like a purified choir, released from all earthly burdens.

Movement III: *Marcia funebre sulla morte d'un Eroe*

The third movement, marked *Marcia funebre sulla morte d'un Eroe* (Funeral March on the Death of a Hero) begins with an e' flat in the upper voice. This remains unchanged until the beginning of bar 7, giving the movement an extremely oppressive, sombre mood.

Playing a suitably restrained *fortissimo* from bar 19 on helps to express the inner emotional restlessness of the music.

The tremolo in bars 31, 32, 35 and 36 evokes a funeral procession accompanied by muffled drum rolls.

One way of executing the trill in bars 23 and 61, left hand:

Movement IV: *Allegro*

The final movement is cheerful and lively, presenting a clear contrast with the preceding Funeral March. Nevertheless, the drama of fate casts a shadow over the mood, veiling its brightness. Occasionally it intrudes into the foreground – for example, from bar 81.

Note should be taken of the following comments by Carl Czerny[1]: 'In bar 6 the two quavers in the left hand should be given some weight. The same applies wherever they appear as a cadence or an imperfect cadence, e. g., in bars 12, 20, 28, 30, 32, 34, etc. One often finds in the works of Beethoven that the tonal structure is built on individual, seemingly insignificant notes, and by emphasizing these notes (as Beethoven did himself) one gives the whole composition its proper character and unity.' This means that the two quavers mentioned, which recur frequently in this movement, should be regarded as a bridge between the phrase they are in and the one that follows, and that they should be played with a suitably light emphasis.

The characteristic rhythm of the triadic theme entering in the second half of bars 32 and 138 (subsequently answered by the bass), along with the surprisingly simple coda (from about bar 154) bring this sonata to an end.

Naoyuki Taneda
Translated by Angela Davies

Carl Czerny, *Über den richtigen Vortrag der sämtlichen Beethoven'schen Klavierwerke*, ed. by Paul Badura-Skoda (Vienna 1963, Universal Edition)

PREFACE

Unlike the majority of Beethoven's piano sonatas, the two *sonates faciles* opus 49 are unknown quantities in terms of the background to their composition, the way they have come down to us and the purpose for which they were written. Little documentary evidence has survived. The relatively high opus number is to be explained by the date of publication and – as with many of Beethoven's works – has no bearing on the date or purpose of composition. The standard Beethoven biographies generally devote little space to these two sonatas. Any discussion of the works tends to falter at the point at which the attempt is made to assign them to a particular stylistic category, and on the whole their pedagogic purpose has been misconstrued[1].

The complete autograph manuscripts of both sonatas are not extant. The so-called Kafka Sketchbook (named after the previous owner, the Viennese pianist Johann Nepomuk Kafka [1819–1886], and since 1875 in the possession of the British Museum, London, Add. Ms. 29801) contains sketches for both sonatas which date from no earlier than 1795/96[2]. A page of sketches for the scherzo of the string trio opus 9/3 contains seven bars from the opening of the G minor sonata with the heading *Sonatine par L. v. Beethoven*. Clearly this sheet was originally intended for the fair copy of the sonata but was subsequently used for sketches. This fact prompted G. Nottebohm to conclude that the sonata opus 49/1 was composed at the latest in 1798 but certainly before the completion of the string trio opus 9 and in chronological proximity to the sonata opus 13 (1799)[3]. On the basis of the existing sketches Nottebohm assigns the G major sonata opus 49/2 to the year 1796 and sees it as belonging to the period which saw the composition of the wind sextet opus 71 and the scene and aria *Ah, perfido!*[4]. Douglas Johnson has recently corroborated this hypotheses: on the basis of watermark analysis he links the paper Beethoven used for the sketches with the composer's stay in Prague during his trip to Berlin in 1796[5].

However that may be, the fact that both sonatas probably belong to the years 1796/98 – thus to a time which produced such major works as the piano concertos in B flat (1795) and C major (1798), the three sonatas opus 10 (1798) and the *Sonate pathétique* opus 13 – strongly suggests that they were intended only for relatively elementary teaching purposes and were regarded as little more than pleasing practice pieces. That they did in fact serve this purpose during Beethoven's lifetime is demonstrated by, for example, the inclusion with minor changes of the minuet from opus 49/2 in the *Übungs- und Unterhaltungsstücke* which formed a supplement to Joseph Czerny's piano method *Der Wiener Clavierlehrer*, published by Anton Strauss in Vienna in December 1825. Beethoven's friend Karl Holz indignantly alludes to this fact in a conversation recorded in one of the notebooks from early December 1825[6].

Almost certainly Beethoven did not originally contemplate publishing these works. This view is borne out by the absence of a dedication; the fact that both sonatas consist of only two movements, and these in a somewhat unusual sequence; and the recurrence of the minuet theme from opus 49/2 in his septet opus 20 (1800). It seems likely that pieces of this kind were not even written a particular pupil in mind but were intended for general teaching purposes. A. W. Thayer notes that both sonatas make only modest technical demands on the player and are appropriate vehicles for encouraging musical taste and an understanding of musical form[7]. It comes as no surprise that Beethoven's brother Kaspar Anton Karl – who was a cashier at the Austrian National Bank, had a keen eye for business propositions and had the composer's permission to conduct his own negotiations with publishers – sought to make some money out of having these sonatas published. On November 23rd 1802, several years after their date of composition, he offered them to the Offenbach publisher André for the sizeable sum of 280 guilders. This offer, like the one made to Breitkopf & Härtel in Leipzig on August 27th 1803, came to nothing[8]. Obviously both publishers were loath to add works clearly written for teaching purposes to their catalogues, particulary at the price being asked. As it turned out, they were the losers. When the Viennese "Bureau d'Arts et d'Industrie" published the sonatas as opus 49 in January 1805 (the publication was advertised in the *Wiener Zeitung* on 19th, 23rd and 30th January 1805) they turned out to be such best-sellers that they were immediately reprinted in Altona, Augsburg, Berlin, Amsterdam, Bonn, Leipzig, Mainz, Paris and London. Within a matter of 10 to 15 years after the appearance of the first edition the two sonatas had reached a huge public[9].

Karl-Heinz Köhler

---

[1] Cf. for example Adolph Bernhard Marx, *Ludwig van Beethoven – Leben und Schaffen*. Part One, 4th edition, Berlin 1884, pp. 74–75

[2] Joseph Kerman, *Beethoven's Early Sketches*. In: *The Musical Quarterly*, vol. LVI, No. 4, New York 1970, pp. 516–519

[3] Martin Gustav Nottebohm, *Zweite Beethoveniana*. Leipzig 1887, p. 44

[4] Nottebohm, *Beethoveniana*, Leipzig 1872, pp. 1/2

[5] Douglas Johnson, *Music for Prague and Berlin: Beethoven's Concert Tour of 1796*. In: *Beethoven, Performers and Critics – The International Beethoven Congress Detroit 1977*. Detroit 1980, p. 30

[6] *Ludwig van Beethovens Konversationshefte*, vol. 8, edited by K.-H. Köhler and G. Herre, Leipzig 1981, p. 208 and notes 560 and 560a

[7] Alexander Wheelock Thayer, *Ludwig van Beethovens Leben*, 3rd edition, Leipzig 1922, pp. 54f.

[8] On the documents and sources cf. above all Georg Kinsky, *Das Werk Beethovens. Thematisch-bibliographisches Verzeichnis seiner sämtlichen vollendeten Kompositionen*. Completed and edited by Hans Halm, Munich, Duisburg 1955, p. 117: notes on opus 49

[9] Ibid. p. 116

NOTES ON INTERPRETATION

I think the requirements for an adequate interpretation of the sonatas are the following:
1. a well-planned disposition of the various dynamic markings;
2. a sharp differentiation of the various touches: *legato, non-legato, portato* and *staccato*;
3. an extra-sensitive awareness of Beethoven's phrase lengths.

One should deal with these works as one would with sonatas of Haydn and Mozart, where the highlighting of short phrases is esthetically and stylistically more correct than an attempt to create long *legato* lines.

My fingerings may seem often to be unconventional and uncomfortable, but they are meant to serve the purpose of enabling the performer to fulfill the composer's whishes without undue reliance on the sustaining pedal. In many cases of *legato* slurs, I try, through my fingerings, to develop a "hand pedal". For example, in bar 1 of the first movement of op. 49/1, there should be an overlapping of fingers. This means specifically that the fourth finger should remain on b♭ until the third finger has depressed g, and so on with the next two notes under the slur, thus ensuring a smooth legato. The right foot need not supply the "glue".

Opus 49/1

1st movement: Andante, ²/₄, ♩ = 76—84
Observe very carefully the fact that the upbeat d′ is not connected to the four notes under the legato slur in bar 1.
Bar 14: The three grace notes are to be played before the beat.
Bar 16 onward: The bass line should be clearly delineated, so that the semiquavers have a melodic as well as a rhythmic function.
Bar 17: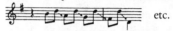

Bars 59—62: The changes between g♯ and g♮ in the left hand accompaniment figure should be strongly brought out, culminating in a strikingly arpeggiated chord in bar 63.
Bar 88:

I would say that the character of this movement — a bit melancholy — is very similar to the character of Mozart's song, *Das Veilchen*, despite that piece being composed in a major key. However, in that song, bars 27—30 are in minor and they carry us on to bars 35—37, which are so similar in theme and mood to bars 16—20 of the Beethoven movement. Perhaps an attempt to connect the thoughts of Goethe's *Veilchen* with the mood of op. 49/1 is too subjective, but I would try it.

2nd movement: Allegro, ⁶/₈, ♩. = 116—120
The quavers at the beginning are to be played *leggiero*, but with a hint of *marcato* — pointedly, not flabbily. These quavers remind me of incessant chattering, coming to a halt in a dominant seventh chord before chattering on again. Therefore in bar 12, there should be no pause after the fermata.
Bar 20 onward: The semiquavers in the left hand should be non-legato and sharply characterized.
Bar 32 onward: The quavers in the right hand should still be played *leggiero*, but more *cantabile* than *marcato*. The third and sixth left hand quavers should not be too soft in order to ensure rhythmic propulsion. Note fingering.
Bars 48—52 and 119—123: After a steady diet of quavers and semiquavers, we have here a deliberate slowing down — a short dramatic moment demanding a clear, careful articulation of the chromatic harmonization of a figure. And then we are off again.
Bar 148: Let the fermata tone die away. Then continue without a pause.
In this movement, the dramatic impulse depends much upon how one deals with the repetition of identical phrases, for example, bars 9—10, 20—21, 24—25 and 27—29. I would

suggest a dynamic intensification with each repetition and never an abatement of sound in the direction of an echo effect, which is not part of the musical language of the classical period.

Opus 49/2

1st movement: Allegro, ma non troppo, ₵, ♩ = 84
This is one of the simplest movements among the piano sonatas and does not profit from overdone dramatics or from too inflated contrasts. It relies far more on a direct "speaking" diction for its full effect.

Bar 4 and 8 resp.:

Bars 6—8: In the left hand figure, use the ostinato d in the thumb as a pivot to the next note:

etc.

The same applies to bars 54—58, 72—74, 88—91 and 96—99 to ensure a forward motion through inner phrasing.
Bars 15—20: The most important tones are the leading crotchets in the right hand. Do not make the left hand triplets too pointed and loud, so that the second theme can continue with the same speaking quality as before.
Bars 59—67: Try "orchestrating" and think of 2 oboes and bassoon.
Because this movement is basically so simple and does not warrant any extravagant interpretative gestures, I would arrange my set of dynamics and moments of tension and relaxation on the basic harmonic relationships inherent in every classical sonata form — the articulate movement from tonic to dominant and back. In bars 1—13, we have stable moments. In bar 21, the dominant wins, resulting in stable moments again. In bars 53 ff., we have the unsettling return to home base.

2nd movement: Tempo di Menuetto, ³/₄, ♩ = 126
The articulation of two-note legato slurs here is very important. One must take care that the semiquaver within the slur is neither shortened with an unintentional staccato nor given an inappropriate accent.
Throughout the movement, use the ostinato in the thumb of the left hand as a pivot (see movement 1, bars 6—8). For

example, bar 1:

bars 68—69:

One could make a case for giving a bit of an impulse to the second beat (third quaver) of each bar in bars 1—6 and all parallel places, in order to provide a more dancing character to this music without harming its classical proportions. This device could be carried over to the C major section (bars 68—85).
Bars 86—87: The *pp* is to be taken very seriously, as are the legato slurs over the two groups of four quavers.
Coda: Bars 107—111 can sustain minimal uneasiness in character due to the modulations into two neighboring keys before Beethoven arrives home in bars 112—113 and more certainly in bars 114—115, repeating himself harmonically in bars 116—118.
The movement ends with tho chords, which I would suggest to be played in time with good sustained tone — no prissy piano staccato and no agressive forte accents.

Ludwig van Beethoven: Piano Pieces

INDEX

„Für Elise", W o O 59

Poco moto

No. 8 Moderato cantabile

Polonaise, Opus 89

Alla Polacca, vivace

No. 9 Vivace moderato

Klavierstück B-Dur/B flat major, W o O 60

No. 10 Allegramente

No. 11 Andante, ma non troppo

11 Bagatellen, Opus 119

6 Bagatellen, Opus 126

No. 1 Allegretto

No. 1 Andante con moto

No. 2 Andante con moto

No. 2 Allegro

No. 3 à l'Allemande

No. 3 Andante

No. 4 Andante cantabile

No. 4 Presto

No. 5 Risoluto

No. 5 Quasi allegretto

No. 6 Andante

No. 6 Presto

No. 7 Allegro ma non troppo

WoO = Werke ohne Opuszahl / Works without opus number. Georg Kinsky:
Das Werk Beethovens. Thematisch-bibliographisches Verzeichnis.
G. Henle Verlag. München — Duisburg, 1955

PREFACE

Beethoven's piano pieces show how great the command was that the master of lange forms had in works of smaller dimensions, even though he composed only relatively rarely in small forms. He did not, however, always devote to them the conscientiousness that stamps every one of his Sonates as a masterpiece. Among the piano pieces are student exercises from the Bonn period, studies, sketches and unassuming little dance movements, all of which might interest the music historian or pedagogue. Such pieces have not been collected in the present volume; it includes, rather, all those pieces which have — or should have — lasting significance as a part of the living repertoire.

First, there are the three sets of *Bagatelles*, *Op. 33, 119* and *126,* the latter representing both the epilogue to Beethoven's piano works and the splendid climax of his endeavours in small forms. (From the 18th century onwards the title "Bagatelles" was given to sets of shorter pieces without any cyclic connection.) Next come the *Rondos*, *Op. 51* and *129,* both of which originale from the early Viennese period, despite their high opus numbers; the bizarre *Fantasia, Op. 77;* the sparkling *Polonaise, Op. 89;* the *Andante (favori) in F major* which had to relinquish its place as middle movement of the Waldstein Sonate Op. 53 to the marvellous Adagio introduction; an one more work originally intended for a Sonata, the *Allegretto WoO 53,* the more notable of the two pieces[1]) that Beethoven planned as an Intermezzo for the Sonata Op. 10 No. 1, and then rejected. Two *Albumblätter* are in the same class with the best of the Bagatelles: the Famous *"Für Elise"* (or "Therese"?), and one from a later period, the *Klavierstück in B Flat Major* from the estate of Marie Szymanowska. Finally, there are the *6 Ecossaises,* which I have not disdained to include, although it is possible that they are transcriptions of lost orchestra pieces, and although the only soucre — it comes from Nottebohm — leaves much to be desired. It is not for no reason that these pieces have often inspired virtuosos to their own adaptations.

In customary fashion, the edition is based on manuscripts (where they are extant), MS. copies, original editions and other early editions. I am particularly grateful to Alan Tyson, whose recent researches have proved that several London first editions are among the most important authentic sources; in connection with the piano pieces, these are the London first editions of Op. 33, 77 and 119. Tyson's book, *The Authentic English Editions of*

Beethoven (Faber and Faber, London, 1963), and his article, "The First Edition of Beethoven's Op. 119 Bagatelles" (Musical Quarterly, July 1963), were of great help to me in preparing the present edition.

A case of some peculiarity is that of the so-called *Rondo a capriccio 'Die Wuth über den verlornen Groschen ausgetobt in einer Kaprize'* ('The rage over the lost penny, given vent in a Caprice'). With this title a piano piece from Beethoven's estate was published in 1828. It was only in 1832 that it was given the opus number 129, which had remained vacant.

Bülow, in contrast to Czerny, Lenz and others, loudly proclaimed the Rondo to be a late work, condemning all doubts as "blasphemy worthy of the Kalmuk Oulibicheff". The autograph, which was rediscovered in 1945, refutes Bülow's and Riemann's view, for it also contains sketches to works from the years 1795/98. It is clear from the MS. that it was used as the basis for the OE (Orig. Edition). which version is the product of an unknown hand (Czerny? Schindler?) and is most certainly not by Beethoven. The title "Die Wuth...", is added to the MS. in another handwriting. In Beethoven's own handwriting are the heading "Alla ingharese quasi un Capriccio" and the title on the covering page, "Leichte Kaprice".

The MS. shows all the characteristics of a hasty first draft: passages are left blank, there are errors in voice leading and a total absence of dynamic and articulation marks. Additions and corrections made by the editor appear in small print. We have also noted those readings agreeing with the OE. The dynamic markings and articulation signs of the OE were not adopted, since only part of them seemed acceptable. The editor has refrained from making additions in this regard.

The MS., discovered by Otto E. Albrecht, is owned by Mrs. Eugene Allen Noble of Providence, Rhode Island, USA. Erich Hertzmann examined it in detail ("The newly discovered autograph of Beethoven's Rondo a capriccio", Musical Quarterly, Vol. XXXII, 1946). I cannot concur, however, in his opinion that the MS. served Beethoven as a preparation for an improvisation. In his edition of the Rondo (Schirmer, New York), Hertzmann's additions are not always clearly distinguishable from the original musical text. The edition by Henle Verlag is based more on the OE than on the MS.; no attempt was made to piece out the MS. in

---

[1]) The other is a Bagatelle in C minor, WoO 52.

a new and logical way. The editor has indicated the passages at which the MS. text given in the present edition differs substantially from the one published by Henle. I know from my own experience the confusion that besets the musician who attemps to find his way among several "Urtext" editions which diverge greatly from one another; I have often wished that editors and publishers would be less sparing in the matter of commentary. Errors should be exposed and decisions justified.

Our editorial principles follow by and large the custom of the "Wiener Urtext Edition". Additions in small print and round brackets are by the editor. Differentiation has been made between staccato dots and strokes, so far as the sources permitted. Expression and articulation markings added at analogous passages are mentioned in the Critical Notes. Whenever possible, however, the editor has avoided making such additions, since he finds that to overload the musical text with superfluous markings does not tend to facilitate reading but rather to complicate it. In this respect even the first editions did too much of a good thing in comparison to the manuscripts. Several slurs immediately following one another can mean a continuous legato, especially in the late pieces. At unmarked passages the articulation last in force usually remains valid "until further notice", or the articulation matches that of similar passages. Only occasionally and with much hesitation did the editor decide to "assimilate" parallel passages; the Critical Notes contain particulars. Apart from correcting obvious oversights and errors, Beethoven's by no means consistent or clear markings should be retained even when they seem contradictory. As is happens, the rights of a thoughtful and sensitive player are not limited to piously and phlegmatically reading off what the musical text contains.

This applies, of course, to an even greater degree to the editor's fingerings. (Fingering equally satisfactory for students, pedagogues and concert pianists, taking into account every hall and instrument, suiting the physiological characteristics of every player — such fingering is still waiting to be invented.) Two prerequisites will facilitate the use of the fingerings: utmost elasticity of the wrist and arm, and a refined treatment of the pedal. Without the help of a pedal technique that can enliven the sonority atmospherically and support the cantilena (particularly in the upper registers), certain fingerings will remain unintelligible. Fingerings below the notes apply to the left hand, those above the notes to the right hand. Beethoven's original fingerings are printed in italics.

I would like to thank Dr. Sydney Beck of The Lincoln Center Music Library, Special Collection, New York, for making available a film of the manuscript of the "Rondo alla ingharese"; the Beethoven-Archiv in Bonn, the Musiksammlung der Österreichischen Nationalbibliothek and the Bibliothek der Gesellschaft der Musikfreunde in Vienna, and the Bibliothèque du Conservatoire in Paris for their kind assistance in providing source materials; Karl Heinz Füssl and Paul Badura-Skoda for valuable advice; Prof. Franz Eibner for several suggestions regarding passages added by the editor in the Rondo Op. 129; and Hermann Nordberg for his patience and accuracy in proof-reading.

Alfred Brendel

Ludwig van Beethoven: Variations for Piano

INDEX

Band 1/Volume 1

WoO = Werke ohne Opuszahl / Works without opus number. Georg Kinsky:
Das Werk Beethovens. Thematisch-bibliographisches Verzeichnis.
G. Henle Verlag. München — Duisburg, 1955

INDEX

Band 2/ Volume 2

9 Variationen WoO 63
9 variations WoO 63
Maestoso

13 Variationen WoO 66
13 variations WoO 66
Allegretto

12 Variationen WoO 68
12 variations WoO 68
Allegretto

9 Variationen WoO 69
9 variations WoO 69
Allegretto

8 Variationen WoO 72
8 variations WoO 72
Allegretto

10 Variationen WoO 73
10 variations WoO 73
Andante con moto

7 Variationen WoO 75
7 variations WoO 75
Allegretto

8 Variationen WoO 76
8 variations WoO 76
Andante quasi Allegretto

7 Variationen WoO 78
7 variations WoO 78

5 Variationen WoO 79
5 variations WoO 79
Tempo moderato

WoO = Werke ohne Opuszahl / Works without opus number. Georg Kinsky:
Das Werk Beethovens. Thematisch-bibliographisches Verzeichnis.
G. Henle Verlag. München — Duisburg, 1955

PREFACE

Nowadays, there is a general desire, when reprinting old works, to provide as authentic a text as possible, free from any additions on the part of editor or publisher. This is usually difficult, for reasons that will be outlined below, and in most cases one can only attempt to find out what the composer really wanted. Moreover, the "Urtext" (original text) is not a final solution, since for correct interpretation one must also be conversant with the performing conventions of the period — thus an Urtext in fact increases the responsibility of the performer. Nineteenth-century editions tried to relieve the player of this responsibility, but were often based on insufficient knowledge of performing conventions, and on an excessively subjective approach, so that it was rarely possible to ascertain the composer's true intentions. Urtext editions were the answer to this evil, but they have to be supplemented by advice to interpreters and pupils as to how the Urtext is to be "read". Such advice should not be incorporated in the text, but should be left to textbooks based on specialist investigation; present-day views on this point differ from those prevalent at the beginning of the century.

Critical text-revision normally relies on four sources: the manuscript, or copies of it corrected by the composer; original printed editions, if the preparation of these was supervised by the composer; proof-sheets with the composer's corrections; and, where possible, printed copies subsequently corrected by the composer. Even very conscientious composers sometimes make improvements and alterations at the proof-stage, without entering these in the MS.; discrepancies between printed edition and MS. can not, therefore, automatically be taken to mean printing errors — this could often lead to serious mistakes. But, since proof-sheets of the printed edition have only very rarely been preserved, one has to use one's judgment in deciding whether differences are the result of alterations made by the composer himself, of faulty proof-reading or of alterations by engraver or publisher, accepted, if very reluctantly, by the composer. In the latter case, one has to see whether the MS. version is not preferable to that of the printed text; but one can not over-emphasise the dangers inherent in regarding the MS. as the sole criterion of authenticity — to do so could mean re-introducing mistakes that the composer himself removed in the proofs (but not in the MS.). Nevertheless, MSS. are the most important source; they often reveal subtleties that were lost even in the first edition. Owners of MSS. should be obliged by law to provide their national library with a photocopy, for manuscripts are the property of all mankind.

The layout of this edition has been based, in the main, on the MS., or, when this was not available, on the first edition, even when this meant breaking present-day rules of layout. Here, again, one should not be too rigid, but in most cases the composer knew the best way to make clear his musical content in such matters as the disposition of cross-beams, phrasing marks and performing indications, and also the division of the music between the two staves. Even some Urtext editions divide rigidly, writing on the upper stave the notes the right hand plays, and on the lower those of the left hand, but this practice, while facilitating performance, can obscure the musical content, and cannot be automatically recommended.

To what extent should one bring into line with each other passages which are basically similar but differ in detail? Sometimes these slight differences are deliberate and give life to the music — here any attempt at "ironing-out" would obviously be misguided. On the other hand, the composer may have improved the whole passage when he reached the repetition, and it would then be correct to alter the earlier one, too. One can only decide each case on its merits. This is also true of passages where a figure is repeated several times, and a performing indication is given only the first time. Here it could make the printed page too complicated if one wrote out all the indications, and this is only to be recommended where their omission could leave the performer in doubt.

The distinction between the markings dot (.), stroke (ı), and wedge (▾) is a problem that has been much discussed. In the second half of the 18th century each of these markings certainly had a different meaning, difficult though it may be to make out exactly what the difference was. Even Carl Czerny's "Vollständige Pianoforteschule", which appeared ca. 1840, makes an explicit distinction between "half-staccato" (⌢⌢), "staccato" (. . . .), and "marcato" or "staccatissimo" (▾▾▾▾), and even within these three categories there are further differentiations. Earlier sources distinguish between dot and stroke; usually the stroke shortens a note more than the dot. However, the stroke often has another meaning, which tends to be overlooked — it indicates the end of a phrase, where this is not self-evident (D. G. Türk, "Klavierschule", 1789). Some composers use the stroke not to shorten a note, but to indicate a kind of "comma" before the next note. However, in the early 19th century, the two markings were used indiscriminately as staccato-signs, so that it is often difficult for us to make out exactly what the composer wanted. This is true of Beethoven's MSS., which make it hard to tell when he specifically wanted a dot — at all events, he was content to see one or the other sign used exclusively throughout various works. There are, however, a number of works in which both signs are used (see Nottebohm's classic essay "Punkte und Striche" in "Beethoveniana", I, 107 et seq.). Even if there are only a few places where one may fairly regard the dot as a staccato-sign, one ought still to try to foster a feeling for these distinctions, not to iron them out. This is why the present edition uses both signs. The editor realises that this is done at the risk of making subjective decisions, but holds this to be a lesser evil than the general levelling-down that is customary nowadays. Perhaps when we know the contemporary sources better, we shall also find we have developed a feeling for the various subtleties with whose notation a musician of the period would have been familiar.

When one of the available versions could obviously be taken as authentic, this has been done without comment. Where there were major differences, they are mentioned in the *Kritische Anmerkungen*. Our text seems to the editor to be the most plausible; the variants listed in the following pages will, however, give interpreters the chance to decide for themselves.

Apart from the MSS. and first editions mentioned below, comparison has also been made with the most important of the other early printed editions (Peters, Simrock, Breitkopf, Artaria, Haslinger, André).

Where phrasing-marks, etc., were missing when a passage appeared for the second time, these have usually been added, unless there was reason to believe that their omission was intentional; but when definite performing indications were given only in the first few bars, they have been included only as far as the point where they ceased in the original, if their continuation is obvious.

One of the most difficult problems for any editor is whether alterations in later contemporary editions are to be ascribed to corrections on Beethoven's part or to additions by the publishers concerned (cf. the remarks above, on the differences between the MSS. and the first editions). Problems of this kind have been considered with particular care in the present edition, in an attempt to reconstruct a text that comes as near as possible to Beethoven's intentions (complete certainty is impossible).

Phrasing-marks are a specially difficult problem. One might be justified in assuming that a slur over part of a phrase is meant as a legato-indication for the entire phrase, but wherever phrase-marks have been altered, this has been mentioned, since in the MSS. it is often the phrasing-marks that give the most valuable information about the process of composition; often it is hard to decide what is the result of carelessness and what is intentional. Even in the earliest printed editions there are many distortions; however, there are cases where there is no MS., and where one does not feel sufficiently sure of oneself to deviate from the printed edition; in these cases, the latter must be relied upon.

Sextuplets in Beethoven can mean either 2×3 or 3×2; the decision rests with the performer in each case.

In works where Beethoven is known not to have corrected the first edition, but where the MSS. are available, grace-notes have been notated as Beethoven wrote them, so that performers may acquaint themselves with the subtler differentiations customary at the time. In the remaining cases, present-day notation has been used.

Two conventions of Beethoven's time have not been retained in our edition — the indication of a key-change at the beginning of the line, and indication of a change of time-signature at the end of the preceding line.

Obvious printing and engraving errors have been corrected without comment; only where there was some doubt have additions been indicated by smaller print or round brackets. Additions which are not mentioned in the *Kritische Anmerkungen* are by the editor.

In order to keep the printed page as simple as possible, fingering has only been indicated very sparingly, where it would simplify a first reading. Every pianist will have his own fingering.

Finally, the editor would like to thank all those who assisted his work by their ready help in making the many sources available, and in preparing photocopies of MSS. and early printed editions in their keeping: above all, the Director of the Musiksammlung der Österreichischen Nationalbibliothek, Dr. Leopold Nowak; Dr. Hedwig Kraus, Librarian of the Gesellschaft der Musikfreunde, Vienna, the Director of the Beethoven-Archiv in Bonn, Doctor Joseph Schmidt-Görg, and his assistant, Dr. Dagmar Weise. Valuable help and advice in revising the text was given by Dr. Ingrid Samson (Frankfurt), Franz Eibner, Karl Heinz Füssl and Bruno Seidlhofer (Vienna), Dr. Oswald Jonas (Chicago), Fritz Rothschild and Eduard Steuermann (New York).

The *Kritische Anmerkungen* select, from the wealth of problems arising in practically every bar, those passages where the reader might wish to know why a particular solution was chosen, and which sources were used.

Erwin Ratz

INDEX

1. Ballade

3. Ballade: Intermezzo

2. Ballade

4. Ballade

PREFACE

Brahms' *Balladen* opus 10 are generally thought to have been composed in the summer of 1854. Although an exact dating is not possible, the work must certainly have existed in more or less complete form before October 14th 1854 when Brahms travelled from Düsseldorf to Hamburg, from where he wrote to Clara Schumann one week later that his teacher Marxen had been very pleased with the *Balladen*. The wording of the letter implies that Clara Schumann must already have been aware of the work's existence. Two other passages in Brahms' correspondence indicate that the composition of the *Balladen* was closely bound up with Clara Schumann. On January 1st 1855 Brahms confided in his friend, the violinist and composer Joseph Joachim, that the pieces reminded him *so strongly of the hours of dusk* with Clara; and in February 1855 the composer Julius Otto Grimm, to whom Brahms intended to dedicate the *Balladen*, inquired whether Clara Schumann had given her consent to the dedication. Grimm continues: *For the Balladen actually belong to her — in terms of the true circumstances of their composition. But you will not have acted without her consent — and this lends the dedication to me a double sanctity* [...].

Brahms himself provided a hint as to the substance of the first *Ballade*, by stating explicitly in the heading that it is based on the Scottish ballad *Edward* from Herder's *Stimmen der Völker*. Brahms came across and was enthralled by this folksong anthology in Düsseldorf in 1854. We know from his friend, the composer Albert Dietrich, that at the time Brahms frequently had folksongs in mind while he was composing. Dietrich recalls Brahms saying to him that on such occasions the melodies occurred to him spontaneously. In the case of the first *Ballade* the opening four lines of the ballad *Edward* (Dein Schwert, wie ist's von Blut so roth,/Edward, Edward?/Dein Schwert, wie ist's von Blut so roth,/Und gehst so traurig her?) match the first section of the melody[1]. Brahms' great affection for this *Edward-Ballade* is also evident from the fact that he set it to music in 1878 as a duet for contralto and tenor with piano accompaniment (opus 75/1). At the time he wrote to Otto Dessoff: *I need barely mention how this fine poem persists in the mind, how one in a sense has to get rid of it.*

For Christmas 1854 Brahms sent a copy of the *Balladen* to Robert Schumann at Endenich. Schumann was

enthusiastic: *And the* Balladen *— how marvellous the first, how original; only I do not understand the* doppio movimento, *as in the second — does it not become too fast? The ending is beautiful = curious! How different the second, how diverse in the ways in which it appeals so richly to the imagination; it contains magical passages. The closing F sharp in the bass seems to introduce the third ballad. What is the word for it? Demonic, — absolutely magnificent; and the way it becomes more and more enigmatic and after the* pp. *in the Trio; the Trio itself transfigured, and the return and the ending. Did this ballad make the same impression on you, dear Clara? In the fourth ballad how beautiful that the first, curious note of the melody hovers between major and minor at the end and wistfully stays in the major. Now on to overtures and symphonies.* However, Brahms declined Schumann's offer to urge Breitkopf & Härtel to publish the work. He was not intending the *Balladen* for publication by themselves, Brahms replied, and had anyway promised them to the publisher Senff. He added that he *would prefer to give* [Härtels] *a larger-scale work at some stage.* Brahms' reluctance with regard to Breitkopf & Härtel probably reflected his pique at the fact that the same publishing house had only a short time previously turned down his arrangement for piano four hand of Schumann's piano quintet opus 44. In June 1855 Brahms, presumably for financial reasons, did after all offer Senff the *Balladen* on their own, but Senff turned them down. In October of the same year he decided to offer the work to Breitkopf & Härtel after all. Clara Schumann had acted as intermediary between the composer and the publisher. On February 29th 1856 the final printed copies were sent to Brahms.

I should like to express my gratitude to the Gesellschaft der Musikfreunde in Vienna for providing microfilms of Brahms' copies of the edition in their collection. I am also indebted to Breitkopf & Härtel in Wiesbaden for supplying me with a copy of the engraver's copy.

Hans Kohlhase

---

[1] For the text and an interpretation of the *Edward* ballad see *Gedichte und Interpretationen. Deutsche Balladen*, edited by Gunter E. Grimm, Stuttgart 1988 (*Reclam Universal-Bibliothek* No. 1857), pp. 57–68 (Gerhard Kaiser, *Zu Johann Gottfried Herders "Edward"*).

NOTES ON INTERPRETATON

1st Ballad

As the editor has pointed out in his Preface, the first Ballad was inspired by the *Edward* ballad in Herder's anthology *Stimmen der Völker*. It is, incidentally, one of the few romantic ballads which so closely follows its literary source. Thus, the completely new tonal colour which Brahms introduces here continues even after the first eight bars.

I suggest playing the first eight bars with less emphasis on the upper part in order to lend clarity to the empty fifths and octaves; but from the *Auftakt* to bar 9 the melody should be brought out subtly.

Play the *crescendo* in the major section (from bar 22) as late and slowly as possible, holding back something in reserve for the slip into the minor at the return of the principal theme.

From *Tempo I* (bar 59) right hand *legato,* left hand long notes sustained and allowed to sound fully, the middle part regular, without pedal, *non-legato* or *staccato*. In the closing bars regular *diminuendo*, no accent on the final chord.

2nd Ballad

Play the opening of this *notturno*-like piece *legatissimo,* the *arpeggios* soft, the melody brought out clearly.

Allegro non troppo: pick out the accents; at first pedal only on the minims.

Molto staccato e leggiero: no pedal as far as bar 68; allow the long notes to sound fully.

Bars 122ff.: a player with small hands will have to play the chords on the third crotchet as soft *arpeggios* (E major is harder to reach than the parallel part in G major in bar 5).

From bar 139 emphasize the middle part without accents, possibly vibrato pedal from bar 146.

3rd Ballad: Intermezzo

Left hand: the first two fifths as short as possible, follow the pedal markings.

From bar 9: pedal on all the chords or octaves not designated *staccato*.

Central section, bar 43: left hand as delicate as possible, otherwise the descant will not sound through on a modern instrument and the visionary character of the music will be lost.

From bar 93: as mercurial as the beginning, but play from the fingers with a lighter arm.

4th Ballad

I find the fourth *Ballad* more moving than almost any other of Brahms' piano compositions: comparable in its transparent longing for death, its abstractness and its transcendental mood with the slow movement of the second piano concerto. It is a key work in Brahms' œuvre.

This fourth *Ballad* resembles an étude in *legato* playing. A single wrong or unintentional accent can destroy the entire effect. Even at a slow tempo the slurs must not become disjointed (in the first four bars already, for example). The accompanying parts must be played quietly enough to allow the melody always to sound through.

Bars 27ff. very delicate.

Bar 34 very quiet, so that the *crescendo* from bar 38 grows, as it were, out of nothing.

Più lento: the middle parts without heaviness or accents, the outer parts all but inaudible.

From bars 57ff. the middle part is divided amongst both hands, so that both hands must play with an equally regular weightlessness.

Throughout the piece try to play as far as possible with "long fingers", always leaving them close to the keys to achieve the required "ethereal" sound quality.

From bar 73 the accompanying parts *leggierissimo,* dabbed, possibly vibrato pedal. Note the semiquaver rest in bar 93, and by analogy bars 98 und 103.

From bar 115 bring out the melody; a very gradual *ritardando* from bar 104 progressively until the *Adagio* is reached.

Justus Frantz

Nr. 1 Capriccio

Nr. 2 Intermezzo

Nr. 3 Capriccio

Nr. 4 Intermezzo

Nr. 5 Intermezzo

Nr. 6 Intermezzo

Nr. 7 Capriccio

PREFACE

Johannes Brahms composed the *Fantasias opus 116* during the summer of 1892 while on holiday in the Upper Austrian resort of Bad Ischl. In June he wrote to Eusebius Mandyczewski, the archivist of the Gesellschaft der Musikfreunde in Vienna, asking him to send music paper: *You might send me some 24–36 pages of broadside sheets for piano. You know that there are many ladies here who play the piano, and you will realise that they love to keep their mouths and fingers busy."*[1]

There is no evidence in the autograph manuscript to bear out Max Kalbeck's supposition that some of these piano pieces must have been written several years previously. The handwritten version, committed to paper quickly and sometimes, it seems, hurriedly, with a number of the readings crossed out again while writing, does not appear to have been based on an earlier version. There is also little evidence to support another view put forward by Kalbeck, Brahms' biographer: that *Intermezzo No. 6* and *Capriccio No. 7* were interpolated at a later date, shortly before the work was printed.

Some of the readings and fingering were added in pencil, clearly later when Brahms was working through the Fantasias at his own piano in Vienna. In November of the same year he played at least some of opus 116 to a small circle of guests at the house of the famous Viennese doctor Theodor Billroth.

The plates of the original edition were not engraved using the autograph manuscript as an engraver's copy. The whereabouts of this latter (the copyist's version) are not known. Before opus 116 was published, in late 1892, Clara Schumann and Hans von Bülow possessed copies of the Fantasias. *Frau Schumann for once has made no complaints about the difficulty of the music, she plays it with the greatest enthusiasm and is looking forward to performing it shortly for Joachim. Bülow discreetly returned it to me in Berlin; it was not until I was here that I noticed he had made a copy of it with the greatest neatness and care and had also included this"* (Brahms to Fritz Simrock, 20th October 1892).[2]

The present new edition is based on the original edition. Correlation with the autograph manuscript, which has been made use of here for the first time, did however require the correction of occasional inaccuracies. The divergent readings in the handwritten manuscript are referred to in the Critical Notes. Markings printed in round brackets are those given by Brahms, while the fingering printed in italics and the sparse pedal markings are also the composer's own. My thanks are due to the libraries which kindly allowed me to inspect the sources.

Bernhard Stockmann

[1] Johannes Brahms im Briefwechsel mit Eusebius Mandyczewski, mitgeteilt von Karl Geiringer. In: Zeitschrift für Musikwissenschaft, volume 15, 1933.

[2] Johannes Brahms: Briefe an Fritz Simrock, edited by Max Kalbeck, volume 4. Berlin 1919.

SUGGESTIONS FOR PERFORMANCE

No. 1 Capriccio

This Capriccio must be played with extremely intense feeling, observing the phrasing with great care. In the theme as in all the figures deriving from it the accentuation is on the third quaver in each case, reinforced by *sf* in bars 4, 5 and 6. By contrast, in bar 8 it is the first quaver which carries the metrical stress, and this must be conveyed with warmth of expression. The arpeggiated chords in the left hand in bars 9–12 should be played with the weight tending towards the thumb. From bar 21 onwards: consistent alternation of both hands in hemiolic rhythm; in bar 25 transfer the melody (which culminates in bar 28) from the left hand to the right hand. The first part of the phrase (bars 21–28) which begins at bar 21 retains *piano* as the overall dynamic level despite the expressive nuances implied by the *crescendo* and *decrescendo* markings, whereas in the second part (bars 29–36) the marked *crescendo* should reach its climax in bar 36. The octaves in bar 38 need to be practised with the thumb separately in order to achieve the required *legato* by keeping the weight evenly balanced. Before bar 56 a brief respite in order to land on the *sf* with the necessary weight (not hard!). From bar 86 onwards bring out clearly the "echoes" e–d sharp separated by an octave; similarly g flat–f in the left hand (bars 99/100 and 101/102). Begin bar 170 rather less strongly than *ff* and play through to bar 174 with intensity. Try as far as possible to keep up the *stringendo* of the coda without diminishing the strength of the passage, so that the piece ends with the crowning final chords.

No. 2 Intermezzo

The character of this piece is melancholy. It is full of resignation and longing. It has no great climax, yet it is satisfying. It requires a delicate touch, and in the Non-troppo-presto-section it requires not only a *legato*, but also a sense of freedom that gives the playing spontaneity. Please remember an important maxim: the softer the piece, the stronger the fingers. In bars 1/2, and 5/6 lean into the keyboard to achieve the swell. Bars 10/11: colour the repeat of the theme differently so as to bring it out with great tenderness. Non troppo presto: take special note of the tempo relationships indicated by the composer (♩. = ♩). I would suggest an alternative fingering for smaller hands for bars 19–21:

Rotate the hand so as to use the thumb as an extension of the hand, not as a finger motion. Bar 40: climax on a'''. Follow the line down to the low a. Save in bar 47 and begin the left hand in good *piano* so as to have a *decrescendo* to the double bar-line. Observe the *dolce* in bars 55/56. The editor plays the appogiatura on the beat. Bar 63: the phrase starts with both hands on the second quaver; suggested low point – D major chord (3rd quaver in bar 64); aim *stringendo* to D major (first quaver in bar 65) and maximum *ritardando* in the last two quavers of bar 65. Save most of the *diminuendo* for the last two notes in bar 86, in order to give the piece a sense of expiration.

No. 3 Capriccio

This is a fiery and driving piece which can be easily exaggerated, and is often played hard. I would like to suggest the use of a free arm and a supple wrist in order to do justice to the *sf*. Note that the piece is to be played *alla breve*. Vary the *sf* in bar 1. Bars 5 and 7: play the *sf* in the left hand as an intensification of the first outburst. Bars 9/10 etc.: bring out the skeleton e flat, f sharp, d. Build an organic *crescendo* from bar 24 to 28 (no *ritardando*). Let the *crescendo* continue through the rest so that the augmentation of the first bar comes like a heroic statement. Un poco meno Allegro: should be played like a chorale. Take care to be rhythmically exact in playing the two crotchets against the crotchet triplets. Join bar 42 to the *sf* in bar 43; do the same in joining bar 43 to the *sf* in bar 44. Bar 47: try to colour the G major chord in a special way. Bars 55/56: keep the interplay between the right hand and left hand triplets continuous. Start *crescendo* in bar 57, culminating, after the slightest wait, in the *sf* in bar 59. Bars 67–69: no *ritardando*. Brahms has indicated the *ritardando* by changing the triplets into crotchets. Whatever has been said about the first half applies with even greater intensity to the repeat. The ending, of course, has to sound grandiose. I suggest that one practice the piece by starting with the second half first in order to determine one's maximum strength, and then play the first half accordingly. Bar 101: start *crescendo* on D in left hand. Bar 103: play the right hand chord together with the g' in the left hand.

No. 4 Intermezzo

Here we have a most beautiful and sensitive piece, and in its economy, a truly perfect one. One has to practice and experiment in order to produce a variety of colours and textures as well as freedom which expresses itself in a most natural *rubato*. Up to the 36th bar the piece is a dialogue. The first bar should start with a full *p* in the left hand triplets, the low E in the second bar giving in a rich underpinning. The right hand response in *dolce* g sharp"-c sharp''', f sharp"-a' should be played like a singer calling a name. The fingers should be close to the keys, not striking, but pressing. Bar 10: hold the long note b' in right hand a fraction longer and make up for it by playing the triplets with a forward motion. Do something similar in the section starting with the triplet in bar 11 to bar 14. Bar 14: play the triplet figure in the left hand with full-sounding *p*, and wherever else it appears. Bar 21: practice right hand alone so as to balance the voices carefully, in the required dynamics, and lead to the climax in bar 25, in which the voices resolve (the top voice a sharp' to g sharp', and the second voice c sharp' to b). Then add the left hand triplets. Always be aware of the texture. Nothing must interfere with the quavers. Bar 36 *dolce, una corda:* again, keep fingers close to the keys, not hitting, but pressing down the keys to achieve a string-like sound. Bars 45 and 46 belong together. Observe the slight accent in the 3rd beat of bars 44 and 46 while the resolution in bars 45 and 47 has none. Bars 52–56: again work the voices separately. Pay attention to the *portamento* in both hands in bar 60, and to the beautiful *legato* weave in bars 61–63. Bar 64: the accent mark in the 3rd beat, but this time the response in bar 65 has a accent mark as well. Bar 69: play from the upbeat a to bar 70 through g sharp, f sharp, e with continuous *diminuendo* but without ever losing the line.

No. 5 *Intermezzo*

This short piece demands a finely tuned ear for balances. The rhythm, like a lullaby, should swing without a hint of heaviness. I would suggest that when first working on the piece one should follow the melodic line (b', c", b', a sharp', b', c", etc.). One will then be able to keep a large line in spite of the short phrases. I would also suggest a slight *crescendo* in the first ending – from the upbeat to the 12th bar – so as to give the repeat a sense of resolution and a true *dolce* sound. Bars 15–23: be careful not to give a false accent in the middle of the bar to the dotted crotchet, which is a part of the accompaniment. Bar 25: start with a full *p* so as to have enough *diminuendo* to come down to a real *pp* from the upbeat to the 29th bar. Notice the *dolcissimo* at the return of the theme a fourth higher. Play sensitively the slight *crescendo* in the final cadenza (bars 37/38). I would like to quote Florence May, a pupil of Brahms, who wrote: "He made very much of the well-known effect of two notes slurred together, whether in loud or soft tone, and I know from his insistence to me on this point that the mark has a special significance in his music."[*] For small hands I suggest re-arranging some of the larger stretches; for example, the opening chord could be played e', g' b' in right hand and e g b in the left hand. However, be careful to keep the correct balance.

No. 6 *Intermezzo*

This intermezzo of melancholic grace demands a keen ear for its harmonic refinement, and a loose arm to achieve a *ben legato*. As so often in Brahms, it is the transfer of the thumb that must be carefully practiced. Please observe that the piece is an andantino, and not slow and dragging, a common enough temptation. It should be played something like a "tempo di minuetto". The middle part, with its long melodic line, is beautifully set in different registers. In the accompaniment be aware of the continuous triplets that have to be even flowing without a trace of an accent. Take the g sharp" (upbeat to bar 9) with sufficient weight so that it will be sustained for two crotchets and be heard above the harmonic change. Beginning with bar 9, and throughout the piece, be careful with the triplets against two quavers. Bar 13: Save maximum *sostenuto* for bar 14.

Bar 22: bring the chord in right hand together with the B in the left hand. Bar 43: play the return *pp* and dreamily, in contrast to the singing *p* in the beginning. Bar 52: use last two quavers as upbeat. Bars 60–63: balance the top line (g sharp', f sharp', e) against alt line (c sharp', b, a, g sharp) with emphasis on the f sharp' in the top line so as to sustain 4 beats before resolving into e'.

No. 7 *Capriccio*

The character of this capriccio is fiery and the cross rhythm gives it a sense of restlessness which even the beautiful Schumannesque middle section cannot subdue. The cadenza-like section, which returns us to the beginning, should be built with inner tension so that the return to the beginning should sound like a climax. Have enough reserves for the last 3/8 section which must be wilder and leading up to the D major chords, the crowning chords of this piece as well as of the whole opus. Bars 1–6: be careful not to give the second beat a false accent. It would be advisable to practice the right hand and left hand interplay (crotchet to quaver: f", e" in the right hand, c sharp, d in left hand, etc.) leaving out the semiquavers. Bar 9: lean into the first chord. Bars 11–14: observe that the *sf* is only in the right hand. Bar 19: lean into the syncopated chord and feel and hear it resolve in the last two quavers in bar 20. Practice the middle section so that the triplets in the left hand are completed by the triplets in the right hand. Since Brahms indicated at the beginning of the theme (bar 21) two crotchets with staccato dots, I would suggest the same in bars 23, 25 and 27, in order to create a greater contrast with the *sempre ben legato* at the beginning of bar 29. Bar 36: bring out the d', c', b in the left hand. Please observe the two repeats in the middle section. Bar 47: start with a subdued *p*. Bar 48: hold f a full crotchet value and release to e. Do the same in bars 52–56 in order to give those fast-running semiquavers a melodic design. Bar 59: keep *crescendo* from second beat of 59 through bar 61; including the crotchet rest. Bar 74/75: give the notes full value in order to give the section starting in bar 76 greater excitement. Starting with bar 82 isolate the *sf* chords and play them as a *crescendo* series culminating in the D major chord in bar 90. After each *sf* chord start the four quavers *legato* without an accent, but with increasing intensity. The last time, in bar 86, start the four quavers after the *sf* with *mf* in order to achieve a rich *ff*. (Don't hit!) Bar 91: observe the arpeggiated chords in the left hand and the slightest hesitation before the final chord.

Menahem Pressler

---

[*] Florence May: The life of Johannes Brahms, William Reeves, Bookseller Ltd., London 1905 (new ed. 1948).

Johannes Brahms: Piano Pieces Op. 76

INDEX

Klavierstücke Op. 76

Heft I

1. Capriccio fis-Moll

Un poco agitato
Unruhig bewegt

2. Capriccio h-Moll

Allegretto non troppo

3. Intermezzo As-Dur

Grazioso
*Anmutig,
ausdrucksvoll*

4. Intermezzo B-Dur

Allegretto grazioso

Heft II

5. Capriccio cis-Moll

Agitato, ma non troppo presto
Sehr aufgeregt, doch nicht zu schnell

6. Intermezzo A-Dur

Andante con moto
Sanft bewegt

7. Intermezzo a-Moll

Moderato semplice

8. Capriccio C-Dur

Grazioso ed un poco vivace
Anmutig lebhaft

PREFACE

In 1877 Johannes Brahms agreed to assist in producing complete editions of the works of Robert Schumann and Frédéric Chopin for the publishing house Breitkopf & Härtel. Despite the rather unproductive and time-consuming nature of this work, it stimulated Brahms's creative powers, particularly in an area which he had neglected for fifteen years: the composition of original music for solo piano (two hands). The last piano music which he had written was the *Variations on a Theme of Paganini* in A minor, Op. 35, composed in Vienna in 1862-63. With the *Klavierstücke* Op. 76 of 1878 he revived his long interrupted production of works for piano.

The year 1878, however, marks only Brahms's resolve to publish works for solo piano, as some of the pieces in Op. 76 date from before 1878 (Nos 1, 3 and 4). On the other hand, in 1878 Brahms wrote more piano pieces than he actually published. In addition to those which went into the collection appearing as Op. 76 (Nos 2, 5, 6, 7 and 8), he composed a number of other pieces which he did not release for publication until much later, when the last piano pieces, Op. 116-119, were being collected.

Of the pieces brought together in Op. 76, Brahms placed the one which he had written first, the *Capriccio* in F sharp minor, at the beginning of the series. The reason for this privileged position was less the early date of its composition, however, than the particular occasion for which it had been composed. Brahms had written it for 12 September 1871, and had presented it to Clara Schumann to mark her wedding anniversary and to celebrate her birthday on 13 September. He had spent the summer of 1871 with Clara Schumann in Baden-Baden, and we can assume that the proximity of the woman he loved had produced the emotional state which finds highly personal expression in the 'agitated' piece in F sharp minor.

The original manuscript dedicated to Clara Schumann is still extant. It differs, in places, from the original printed version authorized by Brahms. None the less, even in its final version the F sharp minor *Capriccio* is inextricably connected with Clara Schumann. The whole of Op. 76, which was published without a dedication, and which opens with this *Capriccio*, may have been secretly intended for Clara Schumann.

The composition of the other pieces collected in Op. 76 was probably connected, as already suggested, with the close attention which Brahms had paid to the piano works of Schumann and Chopin. In making a selection from the sudden flood of piano music which he produced, Brahms

no doubt took publishing plans into account, and self-critical scruples also played a part. In addition, he clearly took care that the selected pieces should be connected, indeed, that they should form a two four-part 'cycles'.

Both 'cycles' are opened by *agitato* pieces in related keys (F sharp minor and C sharp minor) and with the same time signature (6/8), and both finish with pieces marked *grazioso*. Thus both cycles move from a tense to a more relaxed mood. The cyclical construction of the two groups is particularly apparent in the sequence of keys and harmonic transitions between the four pieces of which each is comprised. Thus the F sharp minor *Capriccio* No. 1 towards its conclusion in F sharp major makes a convincing dominant preparation for the following *Capriccio* No. 2 in B minor. The final bar of the piece in B minor ends in the major key. The D sharp, forming a major third here, re-appears enharmonically as the fifth (E flat) in the following A flat major *Intermezzo*. The transition from the A flat major *Intermezzo* to the *Intermezzo* No. 4 in B flat major is particularly well crafted. This begins with the following sequence of notes as an anacrusis: e'' flat - e' flat - c' - f, which at first seems to confirm the key of A flat major. Only when the a' natural falls on a stressed beat is the function of the chord as the dominant of the new key of B flat major revealed.

While the transition between the two cycles is abrupt (B flat major / C sharp minor), the beginning of each subsequent piece in the second cycle is harmonically related to the close of its predecessor. Thus the opening chord of No. 6 – A major with a doubled third in the bass – follows smoothly on from the C sharp minor chord of No. 5. The transitions from No. 6 to No. 7 (A major / A minor), and from No. 7 to No. 8 (A minor / C major) follow a clear logic, and the accented a' which opens the final piece echoes the tonic unison on which the previous piece ends.

The *Klavierstücke* Op. 76 can therefore legitimately be performed as two self-contained cycles of four pieces. The fact that Brahms sent them to the publisher in two separate parts, and that they were published in this form under Brahms's supervision, supports this view. On the other hand, it is true that the *Klavierstücke* were selected by Brahms from a larger number of individual compositions and can therefore, of course, also be performed individually. The F sharp minor *Capriccio*, in particular, is an exceptional piece which, in the original version available here for the first time, is inextricably connected with the circumstances of its composition in September 1871.

Peter Petersen

1 Intermezzo

4 Intermezzo

2 Intermezzo

5 Romanze

3 Ballade

6 Intermezzo

PREFACE

Brahms completed the six *Klavierstücke* compiling Op. 118 in Ischl, Upper Austria during the summer of 1892. Some of these compositions may well have been written earlier, perhaps the "Ballade" in G minor (Nᵒ· 3), although there is no definite proof of this. The title originally intended for this collection by the composer reads "Fantasien für Pianoforte", the same as that of the piano pieces Op. 116, after Brahms had declined terms such as "Pieces in the manner of a Fantasia" or "Character Pieces" to his publisher Fritz Simrock as "quite impossible" and declared titles such as "Monologues" or "Improvisations" unsuitable. He had originally considered entitling the "Ballade" as "Rhapsody".

After receiving the printed edition, published at the beginning of December 1893, at the same time as the four *Klavierstücke* Op. 119, the musicologist, Philipp Spitta, wrote the following to Brahms (22nd December, 1893): "Your *Klavierstücke* claim my attention continually. They are the most varied of all your piano pieces, and perhaps the most rich in content and depth of meaning among all the instrumental works of yours that I know. Ideally they are to be absorbed slowly in silence and solitude, and they are appropriate not only for meditative afterthought but also for contemplative forethought. I believe that I have understood you correctly when I suggest this is what you meant by the term 'Intermezzo'. 'Interludes' have antecedents and consequences, which, in this case, each player and listener has to supply himself."

We wish to thank the Musikabteilung Staatsbibliothek Preußischer Kulturbesitz, Berlin, the Library of Congress, Washington, the Sammlungen der Gesellschaft der Musikfreunde, Vienna and the Musiksammlung der Österreichischen Nationalbibliothek, Vienna for allowing access to the sources.

Imogen Fellinger

Johannes Brahms: Piano Pieces Op. 119

INDEX

1 Intermezzo

2 Intermezzo

3 Intermezzo

4 Rhapsodie

PREFACE

The four *Klavierstücke* Op. 119 are Brahms's last works for piano, apart from the "51 Exercises for the Pianoforte" published at the same time without opus number. Brahms completed them during his summer holiday in Ischl, Upper Austria in 1893. The "Intermezzo" in B minor (No. 1) was written in May and the following three pieces were composed in June. It is quite possible, although there is no definite proof, that some of these pieces were conceived at an earlier date.

In a letter written in May 1893, Brahms tells Clara Schumann: "I have been tempted to write you a little piano piece, well knowing how it will please you. It is seething with dissonances! . . . The little piece is exceptionally melancholic and 'to be played very slowly' is by no means an understatement. Every bar and every note must sound like a ritard., as though melancholy would be drawn in from each, with sensual pleasure from these dissonances!"

We wish to thank the British Museum, London, the Library of Congress, Washington, and the Sammlungen der Gesellschaft der Musikfreunde, Vienna for providing access to the sources.

Imogen Fellinger

Johannes Brahms: Three Intermezzi Op. 117

PREFACE

Concerning the Intermezzi Op. 117, which he composed during the summer of 1892 in Bad Ischl, Brahms was a first rather secretive towards his friends and his publisher, indulging merely in hints about the pieces. They were published at the end of 1892 by N. Simrock in Berlin, together with Op. 116. Simrock wanted to publish a separate edition of Op. 117/1 as a lullaby (Brahms had taken "*Schlaf sanft mein Kind*" from Herder's *Stimmen der Völker* as a basis for it), hoping that it would match the success of "*Guten Abend, gut' Nacht.*" Brahms, however, disposed of that suggestion with the facetious remark that in that case it could be called, at best, "*Lullaby of an Unhappy Mother (Herder's subtitle) or of an Inconsolable Bachelor,*" or, in graphic à la Klinger, "*Sing Ye My Sorrow Lullabies.*" In a conversation with his friend Rudolf van der Leyden, Brahms is supposed to have referred to the Intermezzi as "*Three Lullabies to My Sorrows,*" a name that is still encountered in the relevant literature. It is possible that the words of a folksong were Brahms' source of inspiration for the 3rd Intermezzo too, namely "*O weh! O weh, hinab ins Tal, und weh, und weh, den Berg hinan, den Berg hinan.*" In his copy of Herder's Folksongs Brahms marked the poem, whose rhythm fits the melody of the 3rd Intermezzo precisely.

As usual, Brahms sent an MS. copy of the work to his closest friends, Clara Schumann and Joseph Joachim, before publication, partly for their critical opinion. In her diary, Clara Schumann wrote about Opp. 116 and 117: "*A true source of delight; everything, poetry, passion, reverie, fervour, full of the most marvellous sounds . . . As to finger technique, Brahms' pieces, except for a few passages, are not difficult; but the intellectual technique in them demands a keen understanding, and one must be quite familiar with Brahms to play them the way he imagined them.*"

Hans-Christian Müller

Johannes Brahms: Two Rhapsodies Op. 79

PREFACE

Brahms composed the Rhapsodies Op. 79 in 1879, during his third summer sojourn in Pörtschach on the Wörthersee. The autograph is lost; however, a copyist's MS. prepared as engraver's copy for the original edition has been preserved. In many of his works, Brahms continued to make alterations even at such a late stage as the engraver's copy; Op. 79 is no exception, especially Rhapsody No. 1. That piece was entitled "Capriccio" in the engraver's copy, obviously because of its agitated character. Its original tempo marking in the autograph was "Presto agitato", and the marking of the second piece was "Molto passionato". But when Clara Schumann played the work at a private performance, she took the tempi substantially slower, which led Brahms to delete the "Presto" of the former and to qualify the "Molto passionato" of the latter by adding "ma non troppo Allegro" in the engraver's copy. Before publication, Brahms suggested to Elisabeth von Herzogenberg, to whom the work is dedicated, that the pieces be called "Two Rhapsodies for the Pianoforte". Frau von Herzogenberg (the wife of Heinrich von Herzogenberg, professor of music in Berlin, and herself an excellent pianist) often gave Brahms advice, which did not go unheeded. She replied on 3 May 1880: "*Concerning your question, I am always most in favour of the non-committal title 'Piano Pieces' precisely because it tells one nothing.*" The letter ends with the words, "*The title 'Rhapsodies' is probably the most suitable after all, even though the concise form of the pieces appears almost to contradict the meaning of the word 'rhapsodic'.*"

Apart from a few added dynamic markings and accents, Brahms made one substantial alteration in the first Rhapsody before publication. In the first version of the Rhapsody in B Minor the triplet passage which Brahms ultimately reserved for the coda (bar 219 ff.) appeared before the B major section ("Trio", bar 94 ff.). In place of the triplet passage Brahms inserted bars 89—93. He also cut one bar after 123. After the work had been published, Elisabeth von Herzogenberg wrote to Brahms about the alterations (23 July 1880): "*It was truly a curious surprise to see that the marvellous triplet passage, which was formerly used as a transition to the Trio too, has been reserved exclusively for the coda. Just imagine: when I first saw the piece, I immediately wanted to have this passage come only at the end, holding back its powering effect until the conclusion; this feeling was so strong that I almost wrote to you begging you to do it (what impudence), but my innate modesty kept me from doing so. And now I find that my feelings did not deceive me.*"

The engraver's copy for the original edition is now owned by Dr. Günter Henle, Duisburg. The editor and publishers wish to thank him for permitting a copy to be made.

Bernhard Stockmann

INDEX

Johannes Brahms: Waltzes for Piano Op. 39 (Piano four hands)

PREFACE

Brahms and the waltz: the two words seem to stare at each other in astonishment on the pretty title page. The solemn, silent Brahms . . . as a waltz composer? The key to the enigma is a single word: Vienna. The imperial city animated Beethoven, if not to dance, at least to write dance music; it inspired Schumann to compose his "Faschingsschwank"; and it might even have seduced Bach into perpetrating a heinous frivolity in three-four time. In Brahms' Waltzes his years in Vienna have born fruit — and fruit of the very sweetest kind. The beady, invigorating air of Austria was bound to leave its mark on his sensitive nature over so long a period of time, and the Waltzes bear witness to the fact . . . What delightful, ingratiating sounds! . . . They are pervaded by a simplicity and freshness such as even we would never have anticipated. The Waltzes, sixteen in number, are utterly unpretentious; they are invariably brief and dispense with both introduction and finale. The indi- vidual Waltzes vary in character, some being closer to the lilting Viennese waltz, many approximating to the more cumbersome gait of the 'Ländler', while every so often a reminiscence of Schubert or Schumann is heard in the distance. Towards the end of the volume the listener picks out the clinking of spurs; quietly and almost tentatively at first, then ever more distinctly and flamboyantly — there can be no doubt about it, we are on Hungarian soil . . . In their diaphanous eloquence these pieces as a whole must be accounted amongst those works of genuine craftsmanship which, while drawing nobody's attention to themselves, exert an irresistible appeal on everybody. Brahms' Waltzes do not require the slightest exertion or bravoura on the player's part, but they do address themselves to a discerning musical awareness . . .

It was with this highly perceptive review, published in August 1866, that Hanslick expressed his gratitude as dedicatee of the waltzes for four hands which, according to Kalbeck, had been composed in January of the previous year. Hanslick was an inveterate à quatre mains player and, moreover, prided himself on his waltz playing. In April 1866 Brahms had written to inform his friend of the planned dedication: I was just writing the title of four-handed waltzes due to be published soon when your name, as it were, intruded of its own accord. I don't know, I was thinking of Vienna, of the beautiful women with whom you sit at the piano, of you who enjoy such things, who are my good friend, and of much more besides. In a word, I realised there was nothing for it but to dedicate them to you.

Hanslick was likewise the dedicate of the later two-handed versions, which was published with the same opus number.

It is evident from the engraver's copy of the version for four hands that Brahms had originally intended to divide the Waltzes into two volumes but subsequently changed his mind. With only a few exceptions the metre of the closing bars of each waltz is such that it leads into the opening of the next piece; a feature which suggests that Brahms had a self-contained cycle in mind. What is more, the sequence of keys allows the pieces to be arranged in pairs or in lon- ger groups (e. g. Waltzes 1 and 2, 4 and 5, particularly clearly 9 and 10, 11 and 12, and finally 13 to 16), further evidence that Brahms envisaged these works being performed in sequence.

Hans Höpfel

INDEX

Ballade g-Moll / G minor, Opus 23

Ballade F-Dur / F major, Opus 38

Ballade As-Dur / A flat major, Opus 47

Ballade f-Moll / F minor, Opus 52

PREFACE

For more than one reason it is a daunting task to outline the history of that artistic genre which we know as the ballad within the limited space available. Its roots can be traced through many ages and many countries, and it has emerged in a bewildering number of distinct guises as a component of widely differing cultural and artistic traditions. It is thus no easy undertaking to give a concise account of how the ballad evolved over the centuries.

With a documented history going back no fewer than eight centuries – and evidence to suggest that its origins lie several hundred years earlier – the ballad is still a living art form today in European countries as far apart as Spain and Russia, Scotland and Greece. It belongs to the repertoire of the dance, of literature and of music, and it is equally at home in the realm of folk culture and in the context of the highest artistic aspirations. The difficulties entailed in establishing a satisfactory definition of the genre ballad are further aggravated by the fact that the term is applied to numerous different poetic and musical forms, while at the same time an equally large number of art forms, although referred to by other names, are closely related to or identical with the ballad[1].

For reasons which are evident from the above, the following historical account will deal with only those aspects which are of direct or indirect relevance to Chopin's ballads.

In 12th-century Provence we encounter the ballad in the guise of a folk-style dance song; that is, a dance accompanied by a song, or a song in dance rhythm, or alternatively a song with dance elements. (In Provençale, the verb 'balar' meant 'to dance'.) During the 13th century the ballad gradually discarded its connection with the dance and began to evolve in two fundamentally distinct poetic directions: the literary and the musical.

As a primarily literary genre the ballad developed from the rudimentary forms of folk poetry into a more sophisticated mould. The number of verses, of lines per verse and of syllables per line was strictly prescribed; a fixed rhyming scheme and a closing refrain became essential features. In this form the ballad continued as a living genre in France right into the 17th century. Perhaps the best known exponent of the French ballad was the 15th century poet François Villon ("Le Grand Testament"). The Italian "ballata" developed along similar lines, although not exactly contemporaneously. Here the most prominent exponents of the form were Dante, Petrarch and Boccaccio.

As a musical genre the ballad first emerged in the 13th century, undergoing a subsequent process of development at the hands of the 'trouvères' and troubadours. In the 14th century, during the period of "ars nova", it became a polyphonic composition (in between 2 and 4 parts) with an instrumental accompaniment. The vocal parts have come down to us in one or more voices. The most celebrated ballad composers were Guillaume de Machaut and Guillaume Dufay. A parallel development took place in Italy and Spain: in Italy the ballad emerged in the 15th century as a two-part choral piece; in 17th century Spain as a cantata for chorus and soloists. In England the origins of the ballad can be traced back as far as the 14th century. It became a verse form used for historical, narrative, satirical, political, religious, sentimental or similar subject matter. At the court of Henry VIII the recitation of ballads was a popular form of entertainment; while under Elizabeth I punitive meas-

ures were undertaken against the writers of ballads whose political implications gave offence. The most ambitious ballad form came into being in the 17th century with the ballad opera. This was the forerunner of the comic opera in which sung ballads were interspersed with spoken dialogue. The most notable example is John Gay's *The Beggar's Opera* of 1728, which paved the way for the later 'Singspiel' and the operetta.

The above outline, of necessity brief and far from exhaustive, covers the early history of the ballad. The period described roughly corresponds to the late Middle Ages. The most conspicuous feature of both the literary and the musical incarnations of the ballad up to this point was the great diversity of its subject matter.

The romantic age saw the second heyday of the ballad. The first stirrings of a new interest in early folk verse – including the ballad – emerged in 18th century England. This interest was reflected both in the collecting of existing folk ballads and in the writing of new ones. The poets who made use of the ballad form included Thomas Percy, Robert Burns, Sir Walter Scott and Thomas Moore. The fashion for folk verse spread to Germany, where Herder and Goethe were amongst the first to record the oral ballad tradition and the accompanying melodies. Goethe also termed several of his own poems 'ballads', setting a precedent for numerous other contemporary and later poets (Bürger, Schiller, Uhland, Heine). The German ballads of this period tended to be narrative poems involving epic, legendary, phantastic or fairy tale themes.

At this stage in its development the ballad as a musical genre meant a song based on its literary counterpart. The outstanding ballad composers were Zumsteeg, Loewe, Schubert, Schumann and Brahms. The overall structure of these works varied: some were strophic, others through-composed; and they were generally written for solo voice with piano accompaniment or for chorus with or without instrumental accompaniment. Whereas in the Middle Ages the ballad had been defined by its form, in the romantic period the term 'ballad' referred to its poetic content.

The ballad as a literary genre reached Poland in the early years of the 19th century. It found its finest advocate in Adam Mickiewicz, one of Poland's foremost poets, whose collection of poems published in 1822 under the title "Ballady i romanse" was the first programmatic work of Polish romanticism. (This collection includes a paraphrase of Schiller's famous ballad "Der Handschuh".)

It was Frédéric Chopin who composed the first purely instrumental ballads. The inspiration probably came from the poetry of Mickiewicz. Robert Schumann has recorded a passage of a conversation he held with Chopin: "He also ... mentioned that the idea for his ballads had come to him from some of Mickiewicz's poems"[2]. This theory appears to be corroborated by the fact that the composer's circle of friends referred to the first ballad as "The Polish"[3]. Chopin composed his four ballads as a mature artist, during his years in Paris. Their opus numbers bear witness to this: 23, 38, 47 and 52.

Liszt, Brahms and Grieg were later to entitle solo piano pieces 'ballads', as did Fauré and Frank Martin compositions for piano and orchestra. These are just a few of the names which might be mentioned in this context.

At this juncture one question needs to be answered:

in the light of the many different connotations of the term 'ballad', is there a common denominator? Are there elements shared by, for instance, the ballads of the 15th and the 19th century, the literary, the vocal and the instrumental ballad, the folk ballad and the ballad as a conscious artistic creation, the formally simple and the highly sophisticated ballad? Is there enough in common between the genre's various manifestations to justify the use of a single term to denote them all? The question needs to be answered because some specialists in the field have disputed the existence of any link between, for example, the medieval and the romantic ballad. I do not wish to discuss the fundamentals of this question here; but I should like to put forward my view that common features exist. Leaving aside marginal manifestations of the ballad form – those that were the product of adaptation to a prevailing fashion or convention, for instance –, we may say that the ballad is quintessentially a short poem depicting in compressed form great and significant events, unusual occurrences and powerful and sublime emotions. In the Middle Ages this meant in practice: the perfect and enduring love of womankind (in Middle High German 'minne'), unflinching satire, great deeds of chivalry, the tragedy and wistfulness of life's transitoriness, the horror of death, and the sublimity of religious sentiments. The romantic age, by contrast, infused the ballad with pathos and elements of the saga and the fairy tale, deriving its ethos from a sense of wonder at human existence and lending the whole a strongly narrative form.

The next question to be answered is: to what extent do Chopin's ballads conform with the definition given above? Before I attempt an answer, however, I should like to draw attention to a number of essential aspects of these works.

1) Chopin's ballads occupy a special place in his œuvre as a whole, each exemplifying a different idiosyncratic characteristic. In this connection it is worth quoting Schumann again: "I heard a new ballad by Chopin [that in G minor]. It seems to me to betray more genius than any other of his compositions (even if it is not his greatest work of genius). I told him that I liked it better than any of the others. After lengthy reflection he replied emphatically: 'I am pleased, it is also my favourite'"[4]. "I have not yet mentioned the ballad [in F major] – a remarkable work. Chopin has already written one composition with this title – one of his stormiest, most bizarre pieces. The new ballad is different, inferior to its predecessor as a work of art but no less phantastic and imaginative"[5]. "[...] A finer achievement than the Allegro [de concert, opus 46] is in our opinion the ballad [in A flat major], Chopin's third. It is markedly different from the earlier works in both form and character but must, like its predecessors, rank amongst his most distinctive compositions. The music principally reveals the delicate and imaginative Pole. Its poetic fragrance is not susceptible to more searching analysis"[6].

2) Although they were inspired by romantic poetry Chopin's ballads do not set out to illustrate any specific poetic subject-matter. Attempts to assign them to particular literary models have proved fruitless. On the other hand, documented critical response to the music has right from the start demonstrated how readily it evokes poetic associations. Schumann voiced the conviction that "a poet could easily invent a text to match his music"[7].

3) It is a widely recognised fact that Chopin's ballads do not comply with any fixed formal precepts. The composer borrows formal elements from various genres like the song, the rondo, the variation, the sonata, but he uses these elements freely and in a different way in each work, maintaining a structural homogeneity and a discursive logic from the first note to the last.

4) Finally, attention should be drawn to one intrinsic feature of Chopin's ballads: their dance-like manner, which derives from the $\frac{6}{4}$ or $\frac{6}{8}$ metre pervading all four works. While this dance-like manner is common to the ballads as a whole, it is most conspicuous in the first subject of the F major ballad, opus 38, and in the second subject of the A flat major ballad, opus 47. We do not know whether Chopin deliberately incorporated this dance element or whether he used it intuitively, sensing that the ballad's origins lie in the dance.

It is now time to return to the question posed above and, in answering it, to recapitulate a crucial aspect of the ballad's evolution. At two stages in its development the ballad lost an essential ingredient. Having begun life as a fusion of dance, word and music, it discarded its dance element – the most "mundane" of the three levels – in the course of the 13th century, although it never altogether lost its sublimated dance character, which was to determine the rhythmic nature of its poetic and its musical manifestations. In the 19th century the ballad again underwent a process of separation, this time becoming divorced from its "concrete" terms of reference in poetic meaning. This occurred first in Chopin's four ballads for piano without voice, which translate the entirety of the conceptual content into a purely musical expressive language. Thus, we sense the dance in Chopin's ballads without being able to identify the particular dance movements involved; and we become aware of lyrical, pastoral, dramatic, legendary, phantastic, heroic, wistful and epic themes without being able to identify them with specific situations, pictures, deeds or events. Yet at the same time the ballads constitute a complete, homogeneous and totally satisfying listening experience.

There can be only one answer to the question posed initially: in creating these four brief musical poems Chopin penetrated as far as any composer before or since into the central spirit of the ballad. Indeed, Chopin may be said to have rediscovered the source of an artistic genre which has richly contributed to many centuries of European culture in giving us the archetype of the ballad.

GENERAL COMMENTS ON THE EDITION

There are two respects in which the editing of Chopin's works poses special problems: one is the manner in which Chopin prepared his works for publication; the other is his attitude to notation.

It is often difficult to establish the independency, authenticity and precedence of the sources for Chopin, since the way he prepared pieces for publication was very strange, and varied considerably at different periods of his life. So for a while, the starting point for this process was a s i n g l e a u t o g r a p h, that served, directly or through the mediation of proof sheets, as the model for several editions. At other times this process revolved around a g r o u p o f m a n u s c r i p t s (autograph and copies), which were distributed among the publishers in various ways. In yet another period Chopin prepared s e v e r a l a u t o g r a p h s as printer's models for the various editions. Basically, Chopin had his works published — often simultaneously — in three editions: a

French one, a German one, and an English one. Further problems arise from the fact that Chopin showed a considerable aversion to proof-reading. He didn't correct all the copies, or all the editions, or all the works; he often did it in a great hurry and let mistakes pass. Sometimes he handed the proof-reading over to Fontana. Where there were several printer's models, Chopin didn't check to see whether they were exactly the same, and even during the process of engraving he made changes — usually in the French editions. When we also bear in mind that Chopin was in the habit of writing further variants into his pupils' copies, we get some idea of the difficulties involved in discovering the composer's ultimate intentions.

All these circumstances that arose prior to and during the process of printing, coupled with what happened to the works afterwards, permit us to assume that these variants are a characteristic feature of Chopin's creative thinking. This idiosyncracy of his should be reflected in an Urtext edition. Naturally it mustn't lead to a situation where the musical text is overladen with alternatives. Variants have only been shown in the music when they are really necessary, that is, when it is not possible to establish for certain what Chopin's final intentions were. If a variant is clearly meant as a correction, it is presented by itself as the definitive version, and its choice is vindicated in the Critical Commentary.

All the variants that are given as footnotes to the musical text are, accordingly, a u t h e n t i c and j u s t a s v a l i d as the main text, with regard both to their sources and their artistic worth.

But it is not just knowledge of the variants that is important in giving an adequate representation of Chopin's musical text. The present edition has attempted to retain the peculiarities of his method of notation. Chopin himself attached great importance to the way his compositions were notated. This is proved, for example, by a passage from a letter of 18. 10. 1841 to his friend Fontana, where he says of his manuscript "...I so love my irksome scrawl", and ends the paragraph with the words: "I don't want to hand this spider's web over to some coarse copyist." Exact inspection of Chopin's manuscripts shows that for him, the way a piece looked matched the way it sounded. Many of the amendments that at first sight seem to be largely cosmetic, but turn out to suggest a precise musical conception, prove that Chopin was concerned about the correct graphic impression of his music. For this reason, the following aspects of Chopin's notation have been faithfully reproduced:

D i v i s i o n o f t h e n o t e s between the two staves, wherever it has a significant effect on the voice-leading or distribution of notes between hands;

D i s t r i b u t i o n o f c r o s s - s t r o k e s in quaver and semiquaver pasages, where Chopin is always extremely methodical;

P o i n t i n g t h e s t e m s of the notes upwards or downwards, which doesn't always accord with the rules current nowadays;

P l a c i n g o f s l u r s, wherever observing them exactly can influence the layout and span of the musical conception behind what is being played.

Special mention should be made of the notation of a dotted rhythm in one part and a triplet rhythm in another. Chopin consistently uses this notation in the 18th century sense, i. e. the last notes in both figures are sounded simultaneously, e. g. or . In his fair copies, Chopin aligns the matching notes exactly over one another.[8] The present edition does the same.

A further characteristic of Chopin's notation that we have respected is the distinction between long and short accent signs. For Chopin, the short accent (>) denotes a louder dynamic, whereas the long accent ($\Longrightarrow$) implies an expressive stress.

The symbols for ornamentation have been left in their original form; it is only where Chopin uses several symbols for the same ornament that we have reduced them to a single form, to avoid misunderstandings, e. g. the symbols for arpeggio and turn.

Naturally, we have adhered to the range of the piano with which Chopin was familiar. In his piano works, Chopin never went outside the range C to f⁴. In a few cases where it is clear that the composer was hampered by the range of the piano at that time, the editor proposes variants which, however, never extend the compass of the work by more than a second above or below.

The original fingerings are given in italics, the editor's in normal type. The metronome markings are, without exception, the composer's. Additions and variants for matching passages (single notes, interpretation signs etc.) are set in round brackets; all editorial additions are in square brackets.[9]

It would be impossible to list here all the institutions and private owners who have made their sources available to us for this edition. So I take the liberty of expressing my general thanks here to the Chopin Society in Warsaw, the main centre for all Chopin sources, and to all the libraries and individuals who are mentioned in the Preface and Critical Notes as the owners of sources.

Jan Ekier

[1] For example, the ancient Ruthenian "bylina", the Ukrainian "duma", the French "virelai", the Spanish "villancico" and "romanza" and the later legends, rhapsodies etc.

[2] Robert Schumann, *Gesammelte Schriften über Musik und Musiker*, Leipzig 1888, Vol. III, p. 65.

[3] Cf. F. Mallepille's open letter in "Gazette Musicale" 1838, no. 36, reprinted in *Korespondencja Fryderyka Chopina* (Fryderyk Chopins Korrespondenz), Warszawa 1955, Vol. I, pp. 441–442.

[4] From the letter to Heinrich Dorn dated 14. 9. 1836, as above, Vol. I, p. 420.

[5] Robert Schumann, ibid., Vol. III, pp. 64–65. Schumann remarks on a further curiosity: "The passionate connecting passages appear to have been added at a later stage. I clearly recall Chopin playing the ballad here, when it ended in F major. Now it closes in A minor."

[6] Ibid., p. 128.

[7] Ibid., p. 65.

[8] There is only one exception to this rule: the Nocturne in C minor, Op. 48 no. 1, Bar 51.

[9] All the problems concerning the sources, their chronology and authenticity, and the way Chopin prepared his works for publication are discussed at length in Jan Ekier, Wstęp do Wydania Narodowego Dzieł Fryderyka Chopina, Cz. I. Zagadnienia edytorskie (introduction to the Fryderyk Chopin National Edition, First Part, Editorial Problems), Cracow 1974, at present only in Polish. Second part – Performance Problems – in preparation.

REMARKS ON INTERPRETATION

Ballade in G minor, Op. 23

Bar

25   l. h.: The first note of the appoggiatura should be played simultaneously with the g′ in the r. h.

92   Chopin's pedal change on the second crotchet is an example of "melodic pedalling" (the sustaining of the harmony is sacrificed by changing pedals to the clarity of the melody). On a modern instrument it is possible to hold the pedal down throughout the bar, in accordance with the preceding bars and the following bar; this would be an example of "harmonic pedalling" (which sustains the full harmony at the possible expense of slightly blurring the melody).

113   r. h.: The appoggiatura should be executed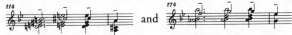

114–115,

174–175   r. h.: In order to bring out the melody of the second subject, the r. h. part should be played

 and

166   To facilitate the *fz* at the beginning of the bar, play

179   r. h.: *tr* = ～

179   The polyrhythmic figures in the second half of the bar should be played strictly according to Chopin's notation in the autograph:

246   l. h.: The top note of the arpeggio chord (g′) should be played simultaneously with the first note in the r. h. (e′′′′) ("anticipated arpeggio").

258–259   Chopin's characteristic use first of appoggiaturas and then of crossed note-stems on the octaves denotes gradually accelerated movement. The arpeggios should be played as prescribed by the markings *poco ritenuto – accelerando,* so that at the beginning of bar 260 they dovetail unobtrusively into what ought ideally to be a simultaneous and already quite fast movement.

Ballade in F major, Op. 38

Bar

18 and

analogous bars   r. h.:

164   l. h.: The first note of the appoggiatura should be played simultaneously with the first note in the r. h.

166–167   The trills should begin on the written note.

171, 175   r. h.: The following simplified versions are recommended:  (given by Chopin in one

of the first editions), or   (analogous in bar 175).

196   Beginning of the bar: a technically practicable and tonally satisfactory realisation would be:

202   r. h.: The g♯ should be played simultaneously with the l. h.

Ballade in A flat major, Op. 47

Bar

3, 39   l. h.: ～ or ♪ should be played simultaneously with the chord in the r. h.

98

11, 12 and analogous bars	r. h.: The quavers should be struck each time.
14	r. h.: The semiquaver octave figure can be simplified by sharing it out between both hands as long as it is not played too fast and sounds as though the octaves were being played by one hand (the upper part "legato", the lower part as it were "non legato").
22	r. h.: Execution of the second half of the bar:
26	r. h.: Execution of the trill with appoggiatura: (likewise bar 28 and analogous bars).
29 ff.	r. h.: The trills should begin on the written note. The most practicable realisation is as demisemiquaver quintuplets.
97–98	Alternative distribution of the chords amongst both hands, with the same broad arpeggio in the l. h. chords:
116, 118, 120, 122, 231, 233	In all of these bars Chopin himself indicated in a teaching copy the l. h. and r. h. notes to be played simultaneously.
134–135	r. h.: The trills should begin on the written note.
178	r. h.: A simplified alternative for smaller hands: (this reading is not authentic but is the only one given in many editions).
189–190 and analogous bars	Simplified version:
190, 198	r. h.: The appoggiatura note should be played simultaneously with the corresponding bass note.
235, 236	r. h.: Execution as in bars 26 and 28.

Ballade in F minor, Op. 52

Bar	
85, 93	r. h.: Execution as in *Ballade in F major, Op. 38,* bar 18.
99	r. h.: The lower note of the arpeggio chord should be played simultaneously with the bass note and should be picked up by the pedal.
112	l. h.: Execution of the trills: (likewise bar 114).
120	r. h.: The trill should begin on the written note.
131, 132	r. h.: Execution as in bar 99.
161	r. h.:
173	r. h.: Execution of the arpeggio with appoggiatura as in *Ballade in A flat major, Op. 47,* bars 190 and 198.
191 ff.	(cf. Preface, General Comments on the Edition).
223, 225	Simplified version, given in the editions by I. Friedman (Breitkopf & Härtel, Leipzig), A. Cortot (Salabert, Paris) and A. Casella (Curci, Milan):

INDEX

Frédéric Chopin: Etudes Op. 25

INDEX

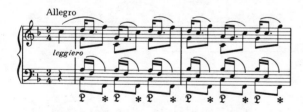

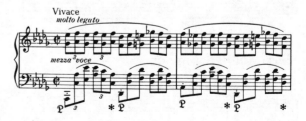

9 Ges-Dur/G flat major

10 h-Moll/B minor

11 a-Moll/A minor

12 c-Moll/C minor

Frédéric Chopin: Trois Nouvelles Etudes

1 f-Moll/F minor

2 As-Dur/A flat major

3 Des-Dur/D flat major

PREFACE

The editor of an Urtext edition of works by Chopin is faced with problems of more than ordinary thorniness; the reason is that Chopin never really stopped polishing away at his music, continuing to make this or that little alteration even after a piece was published. The principal stumbling block of Chopin's Urtext, then, lies in the fact that there is not just a single Urtext, but at least two, and sometimes even three or four different ones, all on a par with each other. This source situation has been responsible for the drawbacks of most Urtext editions so far; they have either tended to favour a single version, or — more frequently — have printed a mixture of several versions without enlightening the reader or player as to what readings come from what sources. In our edition an attempt has been made for the first time to present the equally authentic variants (identifying their origin) side by side as it were in the musical text[1]). Only in this way is it possible to do justice to Chopin's text. Banishing the (often highly important) variant readings to the Editor's Report or Critical Notes — as happened for instance in the Polish Paderewski edition — is tantamount to degrading them textually. All the more, since only very few musicians ever take the trouble to read things like Critical Notes. But would it not be logical to regard the last version in point of time as somehow definitive? This question, although perfectly justified, must be answered in the negative where Chopin is concerned. In this connection it is important to cast a glance at Chopin's way of working, as far as it can be reconstructed from biographies and from the source material. The large contours of a work were usually established in the first sketchy draft. It is amazing with what accuracy Chopin put his ideas down on paper and how very closely he kept to his basic concept at later stages of composition. His ceaseless polishing was limited to important formal junctures, to passages whose compositorial structure was problematic (e. g. due to parallel fifths or octaves in the first draft) or to passages for whose harmonic boldness there was no precedent. The variants, then, usually have to do with just a few, but important, places in a piece. Thus, each of the different original editions contains variants and corrections missing in other sources. Occasionally, Chopin made different autograph manuscripts of the same work.

---

[1]) In preparing the text of the Etude Op. 10/2 for this edition we were able to use, for the first time, a divergent autograph; the text of this Etude is thus a first publication.

In accordance with a publishers' agreement in force at the time, many of Chopin's works were published almost simultaneously in Leipzig and in Paris. For most of the original German editions an extremely painstaking copy was prepared (many of them by Chopin's friend and pupil Julian Fontana), in which Chopin — with the utmost accuracy — wrote in numerous changes of dynamics, pedalling, accidentals and embellishments. This corrected copy was — as in the case with several Etudes from Op. 25 — sent to the German publisher as the engraver's copy. For the original French edition, on the other hand, one of Chopin's own autographs (that of Op. 25 is now lost) seems to have served as the source. It is curious that Chopin neglected to put into the French edition many of the improvements he made for the German edition. One case in point is bars 37/38 of the Etude in G flat major, Op. 25/9; here Chopin made a correction in the copy intended for the German publisher, but allowed (probably an oversight) the uncorrected version to be printed in the French edition. But he also made alterations for the French edition which do not appear in the German one, for example in bar 21 of the Etude in A flat major, Op. 25/1, where the French version has a new bass line, obviously because Chopin wanted to eliminate the (not at all disturbing) "Schubertian" parallel octaves between the upper part and the bass in bars 20—21.

The textual situation in the Etudes Op. 10 is somewhat different. Here the original German and French editions agree exactly in the disposition of the staves and notes in Etudes 1—11. Since the French edition adheres to the autograph more closely in certain details (among other things it retains Chopin's notational errors), it is possible to conclude that either a set of proofs or an early copy of the French edition served as the source for the original German edition. The not inconsiderable number of little divergencies between the two editions, primarily as regards accidentals, can be explained either by the work of a very intelligent German publisher's reader or by a revision on the part of Chopin himself. Although we can assume that the former was more likely, there is no denying the curious circumstance that in the Etude Op. 10/3 the German version of bars 34—35 agrees exactly with a later correction made by Chopin in the French copy of his pupil Miss O'Meara (later Mme Dubois) at the parallel passage in bars 30—31. These holograph entries in his pupils' copies appear in round brackets in our edition (if they are not mentioned specially). In addition to the Dubois copy, there are also markings by Chopin in the copy of his pupil Jane Stirling. These are contained in the Oxford Edition by E. Ganche (the original is lost); that edition, however, is unfortunately not free from printing — and other — errors. Opinion may well be divided as to the definitiveness of alterations made in pupils' copies during lessons. Often the alterations in question are real improvements (e. g. in bar 46 of the Etude Op. 10/11), but in some instances they may equally well have been the result of a momentary whim.

The Chopin editorial problem is further complicated in that "Titelauflagen" (reprints with new title pages) und new engravings of both the French and German editions were printed until the late 19th century; these had the same publisher's numbers and almost identical title-page vignettes. Many a so-called first edition has proved to be a new engraving which was not published until after Chopin's death — yet another source of numerous errors. Even the Paderewski edition, which in most respects is extremely accurate, is not free from such mistaken judgements.

Chopin's Etudes present not only textual problems but pianistic problems of comparable magnitude, a discussion of which is certainly desirable. Unfortunately, it is not possible to go into these points in this edition. We have limited ourselves to printing the original text and most important variants in as concise a form as possible. Obvious errors in writing and printing, which are rather frequent in the original sources, cannot be mentioned singly. For example, in bar 15 of the Etude Op. 10/6 there is no ♭ before the 8th semiquaver in any source; in the autographs of Op. 25/1 there is no ♮ before the 1st note (d) in bar 16; in the German original edition of Op. 10/2 there is an E major harmony on the 2nd crotchet of bar 7 that could certainly not have been written by Chopin. A systematic list of errors of this kind will have to wait for a scholarly edition.

Particular care has been given to fingerings. Alternative fingerings often proved to be necessary, since the varying size, strength and extensibility of pianists' hands had to be taken into account. Chopin's own fingerings are of course directive, but we must bear in mind that the Chopin piano had a shallower touch than the modern one. Moreover, Chopin often varied his own fingerings, writing fingerings different from those of the original editions into the copies of his pupils. The good fingerings of the Paderewski editión and the editions of Cortot and Ignaz Friedman have been adopted in some instances.

When he wrote triplets, for example in Op. 10/12, bars 55, 60 and 62, Chopin put slurs over the three-note groups which cannot be distinguished from legato slurs. Here it is impossible to make a hard and fast decision as to whether these slurs are intended to mean legato as well. Like Schubert, Chopin often wrote his accent markings so big that they look like short diminuendo wedges. So far as possible, we have tried to reproduce this feature of his notation in print.

A crescendo extending over a long passage undoubtedly means that the passage should begin piano. This applies for example to Op. 10/4, bar 66; Op. 25/4, bar 23; and to Op. 25/12, bar 57.

Chopin's slurring perhaps needs some clarification: in the classical manner, Chopin often ends the slur at the bar line, although a legato to the next bar is undoubtedly intended. That is, ♪♪|♪ often means ♪♪|♪ .

Finally, we must mention an important but often disregarded rule: Chopin's appoggiaturas (whether they consist of one or more notes) are not played before the beat but on it, and usually unaccentuated.

The editor has made a very few additions which are not supported by the sources; these appear in square brackets.

For valuable information and advice, and for assistance in procuring source material, I wish especially to thank Dr. Ewald Zimmermann, Prof. Oswald Jonas, Dr. Georg Floersheim, and the late Arthur Hedley, as well as the Pierpont Morgan Library. I hope that this edition may contribute to a better knowledge and understanding of Chopin's unique genius.

Paul Badura-Skoda

INDEX

PREFACE

We don't know for certain by whom Chopin was inspired to give four of his works the title "Impromptu". Other composers had already used this description for piano pieces before Chopin, including Jan Vaclav Voříšek, Heinrich Marschner, Robert Schumann and Franz Liszt. It is possible that Chopin borrowed the "Impromptu" from Ignaz Moscheles. As Arthur Hedley[1] remarks, given the similarity between their themes, it is not inconceivable that Chopin's C sharp minor Impromptu was inspired by Moscheles' Impromptu in E flat Op. 89. The one thing these works, described by their various composers as "Impromptus", have in common is their improvisatory character (Latin: in promptu esse = to be on hand, to be ready).

In the present volume the four works are not placed in order of composition, but in order of appearance in print.

The Impromptu in A flat major Op. 29 was published in 1837. It is very probably later than the Impromptu in C sharp minor, and is thus likely to have been composed between 1834 and 1837. Schumann gave it an enthusiastic review: "Unimportant as it might appear in the context of his other works, there is scarcely another composition of Chopin's I could compare to it: it is so refined in form, its cantilena so full of attractive figuration from beginning to end, so authentically an Impromptu, that nothing among his other compositions may be set at its side."[2] – A few surviving printed copies with corrections and fingerings in Chopin's hand are proof that he often worked through the piece with his pupils.

The Impromptu in F sharp major Op. 36 is more free in form. It is probably the most appropriately named one, since the name suggests improvisation. It was written in 1839. On 8. 10. 1839 Chopin wrote to his friend Julian Fontana: "My manuscripts are in order, and well written. There are six of them [. . .], the seventh – Impromptu – isn't included: maybe it's weak; I don't know myself – it's too new."[3] It was published in 1840. A surviving concert programme shows that Chopin played this piece at his evening concert in Glasgow in 1848.[4]

The Impromptu in G flat major Op. 51 was composed by Chopin in 1842 and published in 1843. Even before its publication, Chopin had already played the piece at a piano recital in the Salle Pleyel at Paris in February 1842.

A printed copy of each of these Impromptus, with the corrections and annotations that Chopin made in the course of teaching, has likewise survived.

Of all the works that Chopin didn't have printed, the Impromptu in C sharp minor – called "Fantaisie-Impromptu" – is the most important. One can say with fair certainty that it is the earliest of the four compositions bearing this name. It was written in about 1834; the final version is dated 1835.

One can only speculate as to why Chopin didn't have the work published; Arthur Hedley[5], as mentioned above, detects a similarity between the main theme and that of Moschleles' Impromptu, which appeared in 1834, and concludes that Chopin, noticing this similarity, might have refrained from publishing his work. Another view is held by Arthur Rubinstein,[6] who concludes from the dedication of the work to the Baroness d'Este that Chopin had sold the work to the Baroness, and that is why he didn't publish it. The fact Chopin didn't plan to publish it is also confirmed by the inscription on an anonymous copy made in 1839: "[A] Mlle Marie Lichtenstein en la priant d'en faire usage p[ar] Elle seule."[7]

A hundred years ago, the Chopin biographer F. Niecks[8] had already remarked on the pleonasm of the title "Fantaisie-Impromptu", and doubted its authenticity. Neither the autograph nor the copy for Mademoiselle Lichtenstein have any title. Later, after Chopin had composed and published his other Impromptus, he may possibly have given the title "Impromptu" himself to his earliest work in this genre; this might be proven by the copy made by August Franchomme, a friend of Chopin's, in January 1849, that is, within Chopin's lifetime. One can assume that this copy was made with Chopin's consent, if not at his instigation. Since Franchomme is one of the reliable copyists of Chopin's works, it seems implausible that he would have taken it upon himself to add this title.

In the correspondence between Fontana, who had acquired the rights to the publication of Chopin's posthumous works, and Chopin's sister Ludwika Jędrzejewicz[9], we find a different description: "A Fantaisie for Mrs. d'Este", or simply "Fantaisie". It could be that within Chopin's circle of friends, among whom was Fontana, at that time living in Paris, the title "Fantaisie" became the standard name for this untitled piece (and it's not impossible that Fontana himself was responsible for this designation), possibly before Chopin, inclining towards the later Impromptus, decided on the title "Impromptu" for this piece as well.

---

[1] Arthur Hedley, Chopin, London 1963, p. 155–156.
[2] Robert Schumann, Gesammelte Schriften über Musik und Musiker, Leipzig 1888, Vol. II, p. 161 f.
[3] Selected Correspondence of Frederick Chopin, transl. and ed. by Arthur Hedley, London 1962.
[4] Reproduction of the programme in R. Bory, La Vie de Frédéric Chopin par l'image, Genève 1951, p. 189.

[5] Cf. note 1.
[6] Frederick Chopin, Fantaisie-Impromptu, Manuscript Edition from the Collection of Arthur Rubinstein, New York 1962.
[7] Deutsche Bücherei, Leipzig.
[8] F. Niecks, Frederick Chopin as a man and musician, London 1902, vol. 2, p. 260.
[9] One letter may have been written in 1853, another is dated 14. 3. 1854.

In 1841 Fontana journeyed to America, lived there till 1852, and didn't return to Paris until after Chopin's death; he would only have known the piece under the title of "Fantaisie", and when, amongst the manuscripts, he found the autograph or copy with the title "Impromptu", he dreamt up the combination "Fantaisie-Impromptu" for his edition of 1855.

Until 1962, when Arthur Rubinstein published his version based on the autograph he had discovered, the Impromptu in C sharp minor was known only in the version of Fontana's 1855 edition. Rubinstein regards the text of the newly discovered autograph as a definitive later version, and he is surely right to do so – the numerous, characteristically Chopinesque corrections of the accompaniment, the subtle harmonic inflections, and the precise expression marks all support this. – My cordial thanks to Arthur Rubinstein for placing a photocopy of this autograph at my disposal.

On the other hand, Franchomme's two copies and the copy for Mademoiselle Lichtenstein, which differ from one another only in small details, refer back to an earlier version, for which the autograph is lost. No doubt it is this earlier version that is presented in Fontana's edition, albeit with numerous deviations which are alien to Chopin's style and by no means tend in the direction of Chopin's final version; they are very much of a piece with the alterations which Fontana made in other posthumous works by Chopin. Moreover, when one bears in mind that many of these alterations occurred after the music had gone to press, then one has one more proof that Fontana is the author of these alterations.[10] But since the early version of the composition, which is one of Copin's most popular works, has built up its own editorial and performance tradition, it is printed in the Appendix to our edition in a cleaned-up version which matches the sources, and dispenses with Fontana's modifications.

Fontana provided the posthumous works of Chopin that he published in 1855 and 1859 with opus numbers from 66 to 74. The last authentic opus number is Op. 65. As the first of the works arbitrarily numbered by Fontana, the Impromptu in C sharp minor received the opus number 66. This numbering is pointless, firstly, because it covers barely more than half the posthumous works known today, and secondly, because the opus number 66 might suggest that this work was written later than the other Impromptus, whereas in all probability it was the first to be composed. For this reason, Fontana's numberings have been abandoned, and replaced by the designation "Op. post.".

GENERAL COMMENTS ON THE EDITION

There are two respects in which the editing of Chopin's works poses special problems: one is the manner in which Chopin prepared his works for publication; the other is his attitude to notation.

It is often difficult to establish the independency, authenticity and precedence of the sources for Chopin,

since the way he prepared pieces for publication was very strange, and varied considerably at different periods of his life. So for a while, the starting point for this process was a single autograph, that served, directly or through the mediation of proof sheets, as the model for several editions. At other times this process revolved around a group of manuscripts (autograph and copies), which were distributed among the publishers in various ways. In yet another period Chopin prepared several autographs as printer's models for the various editions. Basically, Chopin had his works published – often simultaneously – in three editions: a French one, a German one, and an English one. Further problems arise from the fact that Chopin showed a considerable aversion to proof-reading. He didn't correct all the copies, or all the editions, or all the works; he often did it in a great hurry and let mistakes pass. Sometimes he handed the proof-reading over to Fontana. Where there were several printer's models, Chopin didn't check to see whether they were exactly the same, and even during the process of engraving he made changes – usually in the French editions. When we also bear in mind that Chopin was in the habit of writing further variants into his pupils' copies, we get some idea of the difficulties involved in discovering the composer's ultimate intentions.

All these circumstances that arose prior to and during the process of printing, coupled with what happened to the works afterwards, permit us to assume that these variants were a characteristic feature of Chopin's creative thinking. This idiosyncracy of his should be reflected in an Urtext edition. Naturally it mustn't lead to a situation where the musical text is overladen with alternatives. Variants have only been shown in the music when they are really necessary, that is, when it is not possible to establish for certain what Chopin's final intentions were. If a variant is clearly meant as a correction, it is presented by itself as the definitive version, and its choice is vindicated in the Critical Commentary.

All the variants that are given as footnotes to the musical text are, accordingly, authentic and just as valid as the main text, with regard both to their sources and their artistic worth.

But it is not just a knowledge of the variants that is important in giving an adequate representation of Chopin's musical text. The present edition has attempted to retain the peculiarities of his method of notation. Chopin himself attached great importance to the way his compositions were notated. This is proved, for example, by a passage from a letter of 18. 10. 1841 to his friend Fontana, where he says of his manuscript ". . . I so love my irksome scrawl", and ends the paragraph with the words: "I don't want to hand this spider's web over to some coarse copyist." Exact inspection of Chopin's manuscripts shows that for him, the way a piece looked matched the way it sounded. Many of the amendments that at first sight seem to be largely cosmetic, but turn out to suggest a precise musical conception, prove that Chopin was concerned about the correct graphic impression of his music. For this reason, the following aspects of Chopin's notation have been faithfully reproduced:

Division of the notes between the two staves, wherever it has a significant effect on the voice-leading or distribution of notes between hands;

Distribution of cross-strokes in quaver and semiquaver passages, where Chopin is always extremely methodical;

---

[10] Although one is bound to take a critical attitude to Fontana's initiatives, as exemplified in the titling and preparation of the musical text, one shouldn't cast aspersions on the good faith of this devoted friend of Chopin's. Fontana's service in passing on Chopin's posthumous works is of great value. It's simply a matter of replacing those parts of Fontana's legacy which are of dubious value, wherever possible, with authentic sources.

Pointing the stems of the notes upwards or downwards, which doesn't always accord with the rules current nowadays;

Placing of slurs, wherever observing them exactly can influence the layout and span of the musical conception behind what is being played.

Special mention should be made of the notation of a dotted rhythm in one part and a triplet rhythm in another. Chopin consistently uses this notation in the 18th century sense, i. e. the last notes in both figures ara sounded simultaneously, e.g. or . In his fair copies, Chopin aligns the matching notes exactly over one another.[11] The present edition does the same.

A further characteristic of Chopin's notation that we have respected is the distinction between long and short accent signs. For Chopin, the short accent (>) denotes a louder dynamic, whereas the long accent (⪰) implies an expressive stress.

The symbols for ornamentation have been left in their original form; it is only where Chopin uses several symbols for the same ornament that we have reduced them to a single form, to avoid misunderstandings, e.g. the symbols for arpeggio and turn.

Naturally, we have adhered to the range of the piano with which Chopin was familiar. In his piano works, Chopin never went outside the range C to f⁴. In a few cases where it is clear that the composer was hampered by the range of the piano at that time, the editor proposes variants which, however, never extend the compass of the work by more than a second above or below.

The original fingerings are given in italics, the editor's in normal type. The metronome markings are, without exception, the composer's. Additions and variants for matching passages (single notes, interpretation signs etc.) are set in round brackets; all editorial additions are in square brackets.[12]

It would be impossible to list here all the institutions and private owners who have made their sources available to us for this edition. So I take the liberty of expressing my general thanks here to the Chopin Society in Warsaw, the main centre for all Chopin sources, and to all the libraries and individuals who are mentioned in the Preface and Critical Notes as the owners of sources.

Jan Ekier

---

[11] There is only one exception to this rule: the Nocturne in C minor, Op. 48 no. 1, Bar 51.

[12] All the problems concerning the sources, their chronology and authenticity, and the way Chopin prepared his works for publication are discussed at length in Jan Ekier, Wstęp do Wydania Narodowego Dzieł Fryderyka Chopina, Cz. I. Zagadnienia edytorskie (introduction to the Fryderyk Chopin National Edition, First Part, Editorial Problems), Cracow 1974, at present only in Polish. Second part – Performance Problems – in preparation.

REMARKS ON INTERPRETATION

Impromptu in A flat major, Op. 29

Bar

1, 2, 3, etc.　　It is more correct to execute the compact trill "on the beat", so that the first note coincides with the first note in the l. h. But in Chopin, an anticipation is also possible (i. e. the prinicipal note of the ornament coincides with the metric centre of gravity). In this context, the most important thing is to perform the melodic-figurative line in the upper voice cantabile. – The *legato* marking probably applies to the l. h. as well; it means not just the linear connection of notes, but also the holding of all non-dissonant notes. This way of playing was used from the seventeenth century until well into the second half of the nineteenth (one still comes across it in Brahms); the editor of this volume terms it "harmonic legato". Here it is to be

realised as follows:

This kind of playing actually requires great dexterity, precision and lightness in the left hand, the held notes being a sort of complement to the raised pedal on the weak beats of the bar.

41　　r. h.: suggestion for the performance of the appoggiatura:

45　　The following execution gives the right impression of calm and relaxation to the ornamental notes:

58, 74　　r. h.: in both bars in FE (OM), Chopin has indicated that the first note of the ornament should be struck together with the first note in the l. h. We find similar performing instructions in many of the copies of his works that were used for teaching. Although the accent signs in these two bars are differently placed, the same execution is probably intended for both: both the first note of the ornamental group c′ and the melody note c′′ are to be stressed.

62, 78　　Both ways of notating the beginning of the trill:　　and　　, mean the

same thing, namely:

62–63, 78–79　　In this context, the l. h. arpeggios sound better anticipated; for this reason, the notes g′′, b♭′′ and b′′ in the r. h. should be be struck simultaneously with the notes g♭′, f′, f′ in the l. h., so that the trills begin correctly on the strong beat.

81　　An easier way to play this run:

117–118　　The pedalling given by Chopin, which involves holding down the pedal throughout these two bars (cf. Detailed Comments), doesn't sound as satisfactory on the modern piano as it does on the piano of Chopin's day. To acheive a pedalling variant which manages to retain Chopin's intended effect of a soft mixture of tonic and dominant, one must push the pedal about halfway down, i. e. use so-called "half-pedal".

Impromptu in F sharp major, Op. 36

Bar

1　　The tempo *Andantino* in **C** metre (FE) is too slow; on the other hand, *Allegretto* in **¢** (DE) is too fast. It looks as though Chopin, who often changed both tempo and metrical indications (**C** for **¢**, and vice versa) in the engraver's copies, treated the categories of tempo and metre as being independent of one another. (A good proof for this assumption is the alteration of tempo and metre in the Studies Op. 10 and Op. 25). The solution which best accords with our present-day handling of these two categories would, in the editor's opinion, be *Allegretto* and **C**.

1, 2, etc.　　For hands with a narrow span, it is better to take the top note of the ninth in the r. h., rather than breaking the ninth (in the l. h.).

29–30   The clash of b′, a♯′ and g♯′ that results from the given pedalling can be softened by the following combination of pedalling and holding of the notes ("harmonic legato"):

47–57   The closeness of the parts in both hands in B. 48–49 and 52–53 yields the possibility of playing some of the upper octaves in the l. h. with the first finger of the r. h. One can make simplifications of the same kind in the remaining bars of this section.

57   The execution of the quintuplets in the right hand against the dotted rhythm in the l. h. is best realised as follows:

(one should avoid dividing the quintuplet into a quaver triplet and two quavers!)

58   l. h.: in FE (OM) Chopin has inserted vertical strokes (additional stems) over the second, third and fourth notes d′. This could mean: 1) that the appropriate notes d′ are to be taken in the r. h., 2) that the octaves d/d′ are to be taken in the r. h., 3) that these octaves are to be taken over and held for a crotchet.

75–78   r. h.: within the triplet figuration is concealed the theme that was begun in B. 73. Many of the thematically important notes were indicated by Chopin by additional stems in the opposite direction (crotchet value) and one note-head (minim value); one can gently underline the rest in performance as follows:

82–100   The dynamics in this section all come from FE. DE gives no indication of dynamics except *leggiero*. One could draw two possible conclusions from this: 1) that Chopin was undecided at first about the dynamic character, 2) that one shouldn't bring out the dynamic elements of this section in too exaggerated a manner: that the *f* at the beginning should not be too harsh (the marking *leggiero* is obligatory here!) and the crescendo and diminuendo in the scale-like passages should not be too overtly virtuosic.

Impromptu in G flat major, Op. 51

Bar

19   If making a diminuendo in this bar (cf. Detailed Comments), one should do so unobtrusively, leaving room for a reduction in loudness to *pp* in B. 21.

49–69   l. h.: ; cf. Detailed Comments and Preface, General Comments on the Edition.

74–75   *ritenuto* (probably added by Chopin during the proof-reading of DE) suggests no precise limits. No doubt one should get back into tempo at B. 76, perhaps even a little earlier – in the 2nd half of B. 75.

Impromptu in C sharp minor, Op. post.

Bar

41–42   From the graphic layout of these two bars one can assume that Chopin split this section between the hands (l. h. = stems downwards, r. h. = stems upwards.

43, 47, 51,   Here, the signs *tr* and ∿ seem to mean the same thing in terms of performance. With the use of great
55, 59, 67,   dexterity in executing the trills, the player can certainly observe the usual distinction – but it is rather
71, 75, 79   likely that, both here and in many other pieces, Chopin regarded *tr* as equivalent to ∿ when placed over short note values. (In his edition, Arthur Rubinstein has ∿ in all these bars; cf. also the corresponding passages in the first version given in the appendix.)

INDEX

TROIS NOCTURNES Opus 9

I   b-Moll / B flat minor

II   Es-Dur / E flat major

2ª   Fassung mit späteren authentischen Varianten
Version with later authentic variants

III   H-Dur / B major

DEUX NOCTURNES Opus 27

I   cis-Moll / C sharp minor

II   Des-Dur / D flat major

TROIS NOCTURNES Opus 15

I   F-Dur / F major

II   Fis-Dur / F sharp major

III   g-Moll / G minor

DEUX NOCTURNES Opus 32

I   H-Dur / B major

II   As-Dur / A flat major

DEUX NOCTURNES Opus 37

I g-Moll / G minor

DEUX NOCTURNES Opus 48

I c-Moll / C minor

II G-Dur / G major

II fis-Moll / F sharp minor

DEUX NOCTURNES Opus 55

I f-Moll / F minor

DEUX NOCTURNES Opus 62

I H-Dur / B major

II Es-Dur / E flat major

II E-Dur / E major

NOCTURNE Opus post.

e-Moll / E minor

LENTO CON GRAN ESPRESSIONE
[NOCTURNE] Opus post.

cis-Moll / C sharp minor

NOCTURNE Opus post.

c-Moll / C minor

PREFACE

The designation "nocturne" (from the Latin "nocturnus" = nocturnal) has its origins in the Middle Ages and was then applied to that part of the Mass celebrated at night or at dawn. In the 18th century "nocturne" ("notturno") was used to designate either short cyclical works for orchestra or chamber ensemble (Mozart, Haydn, Beethoven) or single-movement works for voice with instrumental accompaniment. While the former tended to be of a more concertante nature and had little in common with the later nocturne, the latter were clear predecessors of the romantic nocturne, their vocal writing anticipating the later form. The early 19th century saw the emergence of the nocturne for solo piano, which took its place beside the nocturne for orchestra or chamber ensemble (Gyrowetz, Schubert, Mendelssohn). The Irish composer John Field, who himself wrote 18 nocturnes for piano, is generally held to be the originator of this genre. During the first half of the 19th century – presumably in the wake of the publication of Field's first nocturnes – it became fashionable to compose piano miniatures of this kind. A multitude of such works appeared, by composers such as Cramer, Kalkbrenner, Czerny, Bertini, Dähler and the Polish composers J. F. Dobrzyński and Maria Szymanowska[1].

Chopin must have come across at least the earliest of Field's nocturnes during his childhood years in Warsaw. We know from his letters that Chopin had a particularly high regard for Field as a composer and considered any comparison of his own playing with that of Field to be a compliment. He wrote to a friend from Paris: ". . . complete artists have lessons from me and set my name next to Field's; and indeed, if I were a bigger fool than I am, I might imagine I had reached the peak of my career"[2]. Thus, Field's nocturnes inevitably exerted a certain influence on the younger man; not perhaps to the extent that Chopin's compositions in this genre may be called derivative, yet enough for us to detect slight similarities in some of them – in the melodic ornamentation, the left-hand accompaniment, the pianistic structure and even the harmonic atmosphere. This applies, however, only to Chopin's early nocturnes, and even here only to some. The majority of the Irish composer's 18 nocturnes are more similar in character to the music of Mozart, Beethoven, Schubert or Schumann.

Chopin's nocturnes represent a development of the genre as regards both its form and its expression and content. The majority of them comply with the form A–B–A, though the structure of some is based on rondo form (Nocturne in D flat major Op. 27 No. 2 or in G major Op. 37 No. 2) or figured variations (Nocturne in E minor Op. post. or in E flat major Op. 9 No. 2), while the Nocturne in E flat major Op. 55 No. 2 evinces the formal characteristics of an "unending melody". The range of expression in Chopin's nocturnes is extremely varied, far surpassing Field's music in opulence and profundity. It includes an infinite variety of nuances ranging from an extreme intimacy of musical statement (the opening of the Nocturne in F major Op. 15 No. 1, for instance) to strongly dramatic expression (Nocturne in C minor Op. 48 No. 1). It is the nocturnes which reveal Chopin at his most romantic. As Jan Kleczyński quite correctly pointed out in 1866: "By a thorough and correct comprehension of the nocturnes, one can acquire a key to unlock the mysteries of the other and more magnificent works of the master"[3].

Only few later composers were to devote their attention to this form of piano piece, amongst them G. Fauré (13 nocturnes) and F. Poulenc (7 nocturnes).

In accordance with the practice adopted in our previous Chopin editions we here print those nocturnes first which appeared in print during the composer's lifetime, while the posthumously published works follow in their order of composition.

It is not necessary to deal with each nocturne individually in detail. Two points relating to the nocturnes published during Chopin's lifetime are, however, worth mentioning, throwing considerable light as they do on the composer's musical thinking. In the course of his lessons Chopin wrote a number of variants for different passages at different times into his pupils' printed copies of the Nocturne in E flat major Op. 9 No. 2 – that which evinces the influence of Field most strongly and which was at the time most frequently played. Chopin's pupil Wilhelm von Lenz recounts that, while he was studying the piece with the composer, he asked Chopin to play it but that the latter was unwilling to do so: ". . . he did not play it to me. He wrote small, very important alterations into my score . . ."[4]; and Chopin's biographer Niecks, in discussing the same nocturne, remarks of another of Chopin's pupils: "Gutmann played the return of the principal subject in a way very different from that in which it is printed, with a great deal of ornamentation, and said that Chopin played it always in that way. Also the cadence at the end of the nocturne had a different form"[5]. The present edition gives all the authentic variants handed down by Chopin's pupils and attested in various sources. Although Chopin frequently wrote variants into the printed copies, nowhere else did he enter so many for one single work. How pianists today should proceed with regard to these variants is another matter which will be dealt with in the Remarks on Interpretation. – The Nocturne in G minor Op. 15 No. 3 was the only one of these works originally to have had a literary program. The well-known Polish ethnographer Oskar Kolberg recounted the following detail to M. A. Szulc, who was later to write a biography of Chopin: "[Chopin] is said to have composed the Nocturne Op. 15 No. 3 on the day after seeing a performance of 'Hamlet' and to have given it the heading 'In the Graveyard'. Before it went to the printers, however, he erased this heading, remarking: 'Let them guess for themselves'"[6]. This might serve as additional evidence for Chopin's reluctance to add programmatic titles to his compositions.

The three nocturnes published posthumously require a certain amount of comment:

The Nocturne in E minor must certainly be one of the earliest. It has come down to us in the printed version by Julius Fontana, who edited Chopin's posthumously published works. Fontana gives 1827 as the year of composition, which is possible though not indisputable. The musical text as published by Fontana is unclear in places, and the dynamics and pedal-markings are – at least in part – not authentic.

The "Lento con gran expressione" (C sharp minor) was not originally designated as a nocturne. It was Chopin's sister Ludwika, the dedicatee of the work, who added the subtitle "nocturne". Ludwika compiled a catalogue of the unpublished compositions and, under the heading "Lento przysłane mi z Wiednia 1830r." ("Lento sent to me from Vienna in 1830"), wrote "Lento w rodzaju Nokturna" ("Lento in the style of a nocturne"). Since then the piece has tended to be referred to as a nocturne, and the dedication – which is not given in the sources – has been reconstructed on the evidence of the remark cited above. In accordance with both traditional practice and the nature of the piece it has been included in the present edition. It is unique amongst Chopin's works in that the composer here quotes ideas from elsewhere in his oeuvre (piano concerto in F minor Op. 21 and "Girl's Wish"). So skilfully are these quotations woven into the texture of the piece, however, that they in no way detract from its homogeneity and melancholy beauty[7].

The first publisher of the Nocturne in C minor, L. Bronarski[8], considered it to have been composed in Warsaw, thus before 1830. All the objective evidence (paper, source, handwriting) suggests, however, that the piece was written in Paris, and internal evidence in fact points to Chopin's last years. The work's relatively low quality of invention clearly places it in that period when the ailing Chopin wrote to one of his friends: "I feel weaker – I cannot compose anything"[9]. Further evidence is provided by Liszt, who wrote: "From the winter of 1848 Chopin was unable to work fruitfully. From time to time he added the finishing touches to a number of sketches, but he failed to impose order on the musical thoughts contained therein . . . The only complete manuscripts which he left were the nocturne and the waltz . . ."[10].

The following table gives the date of composition of the various nocturnes:

Probable Order[11]	Published during Chopin's lifetime		Year of composition	Year of publication	Published after Chopin's death	Order in the present edition
1			1828–1830 (1827?)	1855	Nocturne E minor	19
2			1830	1875	Lento con gran espressione	20
3	3 Nocturnes Op. 9	Nr. 1	before 1832			1
4		Nr. 2	before 1832	1832		2
5		Nr. 3	before 1832			3
6	3 Nocturnes Op. 15	Nr. 1	before 1833			4
7		Nr. 2	before 1833	1833		5
8		Nr. 3	before 1833			6
9	2 Nocturnes Op. 27	Nr. 1	1833–1836	1836		7
10		Nr. 2	1833–1836			8
11	2 Nocturnes Op. 32	Nr. 1	1835–1837	1837		9
12		Nr. 2	1835–1837			10
13	2 Nocturnes Op. 37	Nr. 1	1837–1838	1840		11
14		Nr. 2	1839			12
15	2 Nocturnes Op. 48	Nr. 1	1841	1841		13
16		Nr. 2	1841			14
17	2 Nocturnes Op. 55	Nr. 1	1843	1844		15
18		Nr. 2	1843			16
19	2 Nocturnes Op. 62	Nr. 1	1845–1846	1846		17
20		Nr. 2	1845–1846			18
21			1847–1848	1938	Nocturne C minor	21

GENERAL COMMENTS ON THE EDITION

There are two respects in which the editing of Chopin's works poses special problems: one is the manner in which Chopin prepared his works for publication; the other is his attitude to notation.

It is often difficult to establish the independency, authenticity and precedence of the sources for Chopin, since the way he prepared pieces for publication was very strange, and varied considerably at different periods of his life. So for a while, the starting point for this process was a single autograph, that served, directly or through the mediation of proof sheets, as the model for several editions. At other times this process revolved around a group of manuscripts (autograph and copies), which were distributed among the publishers in various ways. In yet another period Chopin prepared several autographs as printer's models for the various editions. Basically, Chopin had his works published – often simultaneously – in three editions: a French one, a German one, and an English one. Further problems arise from the fact that Chopin showed a considerable aversion to proof-reading. He didn't correct all the copies, or all the editions, or all the works; he often did it in a great hurry and let mistakes pass. Sometimes he handed the proof-reading over to Fontana. Where there were several printer's models, Chopin didn't check to see whether they were exactly the same, and even during the process of engraving he made changes – usually in the French editions. When we also bear in mind that Chopin was in the habit of writing further variants into his pupil's copies, we get some idea of the difficulties involved in discovering the composer's ultimate intentions.

All these circumstances that arose prior to and during the process of printing, coupled with what happened to the works afterwards, permit us to assume that these variants were a characteristic feature of Chopin's creative thinking. This idiosyncracy of his should be reflected in an Urtext edition. Naturally it must not lead to a situation where the musical text is overladen with alternatives. Variants have only been shown in the music when they are really necessary, that is, when it is not possible to establish for certain what Chopin's final intentions were. If a variant is clearly meant as a correction, it is presented by itself as the definitive version, and its choice is vindicated in the Critical Commentary.

All the variants that are given as footnotes to the musical text are, accordingly, authentic and just as valid as the main text, with regard both to their sources and their artistic worth.

But it is not just a knowledge of the variants that is important in giving an adequate representation of Chopin's musical text. The present edition has attempted to retain the peculiarities of his method of notation. Chopin himself attached great importance to the way his compositions were notated. This is proved, for example, by a passage from a letter of 18.10.1841 to his friend Fontana, where he says of his manuscript "... I so love my irksome scrawl", and ends the paragraph with the words: "I don't want to hand this spider's web over to some coarse copyist." Exact inspection of Chopin's manuscripts shows that for him, the way a piece looked matched the way it sounded. Many of the amendments that at first sight seem to be largely cosmetic, but turn out to suggest a precise musical conception, prove that Chopin was concerned about the correct graphic impression of his music. For this reason, the following aspects of Chopin's notation have been faithfully reproduced:

Division of the notes between the two staves, wherever it has a significant effect on the voice-leading or distribution of notes between hands;

Distribution of cross-strokes in quaver and semiquaver passages, where Chopin is always extremely methodical;

Pointing the stems of the notes upwards or downwards, which does not always accord with the rules current nowadays;

Placing of slurs, wherever observing them exactly can influence the layout and span of the musical conception behind what is being played.

Special mention should be made of the notation of a dotted rhythm in one part and a triplet rhythm in another. Chopin consistently uses this notation in the 18th century sense, i.e. the last notes in both figures are sounded simultaneously, e.g. ♩ or ♩. In his fair copies, Chopin aligns the matching notes exactly over one another[12]. The present edition does the same.

A further characteristic of Chopin's notation that we have respected is the distinction between long and short accent signs. For Chopin, the short accent (>) denotes a louder dynamic, whereas the long accent (>>) implies an expressive stress.

The symbols for ornamentation have been left in their original form; it is only where Chopin uses several symbols for the same ornament that we have reduced them to a single form, to avoid misunderstandings, e. g. the symbols for arpeggio and turn.

Naturally, we have adhered to the range of the piano with which Chopin was familiar. In his piano works, Chopin never went outside the range $\underline{C}$ to f⁴. In a few cases where it is clear that the composer was hampered by the range of the piano at that time, the editor proposes variants which, however, never extend the compass of the work by more than a second above or below.

The original fingerings are given in italics, the editor's in normal type. The metronome markings are, without exception, the composer's. Additions and variants for matching passages (single notes, interpretation signs etc.) are set in round brackets; all editorial additions are in square brackets[13].

It is impossible to list here all the institutions and private owners who have made their sources available to us for this edition. So I take the liberty of expressing my general thanks here to the Chopin Society in Warsaw, the main centre for all Chopin sources, and to all the libraries and individuals who are mentioned in the Preface and Critical Notes as the owners of sources.

Jan Ekier

[1] Cf. B. Chmara: *Geneza nokturnu fortepianowego* (The Genesis of the Piano Nocturne, in Polish), *F. F. Chopin*, Warszawa 1960.

[2] *Selected Correspondence of Frederic Chopin*, transl. and edited by Arthur Hedley, London 1962, p. 115.

[3] J. Kleczyński, *Chopin's Greater Works*, transl. with additions by N. Janotha, London 1896, p. 25.

[4] W. von Lenz, *Die großen Pianoforte-Virtuosen, Chopin*, Berlin 1872, p. 42.

[5] F. Niecks, *F. Chopin as a Man and Musician*, London 1902, Vol. II, p. 263.

[6] O. Kolberg, *Korespondencja* (Correspondence, in Polish), Wrocław-Poznań 1966, Vol. II, p. 236.

[7] For further information on the composition of "Lento" and a detailed study of the piece see G. Belotti, *Un omaggio di Chopin alla sorella Ludwika: il "Lento con gran espressione"*, Rivista Italiana di Musicologia, Firenze 1968.

[8] *F. Chopin, Nokturn c-moll, Largo Es-Dur* (Dr. L. Bronarski), Towarzystwo Wydawnicze Muzyki Polskiej, Warszawa 1930.

[9] From the letter of 1.10.1948 to W. Grzymała, *Selected Correspondence* (see above), p. 344.

[10] F. Liszt, *F. Chopin* (in French), Leipzig 1890, pp. 294–295.

[11] The order of the chronological first five nocturnes, that of the Nocturnes Op. 27 and Op. 32 and of other opus numbers is not certain. Only the order of Op. 37 is established.

[12] There is only one exception to this rule: the Nocturne in C minor, Op. 48 No. 1, bar 51.

[13] All the problems concerning the sources, their chronology and authenticity, and the way Chopin prepared his works for publication are discussed at length in Jan Ekier, Wstęp do Wydania Narodowego Dzieł Fryderyka Chopina, Cz. I. Zagadnienia edytorskie (introduction to the Fryderyk Chopin National Edition, First Part, Editorial Problems), Cracow 1974, at present only in Polish. Second part – Performance Problems – in preparation.

REMARKS ON INTERPRETATION

For abbreviations see Critical Notes.

1 Nocturne in B flat minor Op.9 No.1

bar

3
The musically most satisfactory metrical distribution of this figure, according to Chopin's own instructions noted in FE(OM), would be:

This grouping should not, however, be discernible when the piece is played; in other words, the individual rhythmic figures should not be separated but rather give the impression of a free, irregular figure.

24, 32
For the significance of the reversed accent-marks ⊰ see Scherzo in B minor Op.20, UT 50061, Remarks on Interpretation, bar 330.

26
l. h.: Chopin's fingering assumes the use of the "harmonic legato":

(Cf. Impromptu in A flat major Op.29, UT 50058, Remarks on Interpretation, bars 1, 2, 3 etc.).

58
The pedal marking from bar 51 onwards can result in an unpleasant clash of the r. h. thirds on a modern instrument. We recommend a soft pedal change in the middle of the bar and then retaining the pedal until the A in the l. h. in bar 67.

73
r. h.: Recommended rhythmic distribution for the second half of the bar:

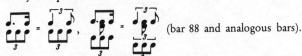 (Cf. note on bar 3.)

84
Last crotchet: a soft pedal change is advisable to obviate the clash g flat–f.

2a Nocturne in E flat major Op.9 No.2 (Version with later authentic variants)

Variants: A careful selection must be made from the Chopin variants which appear in different teaching copies; certainly they should not all be played in their entirety. The reading without additional variants (pp. 8ff. in the present edition) is strikingly simple and natural. The version which includes the variants (pp. 12ff.) is laid out in such a way that the musical text given in the principal staves is based on a moderate inclusion of the variants and accords with Chopin's own procedure in this respect in other compositions.

bar

7 (auxiliary stave),
15, 23
For the execution of the trill see Nocturne in F sharp major Op.15 No.2, bar 56.

3 Nocturne in B major Op.9 No.3

bar

88–128
(bar 88 and analogous bars).

4 Nocturne in F major Op.15 No.1

bar

3, 5 etc.
(also thus in the first editions).

27, 29, 39, 41
Simpler variant: At the beginning of the bar in the r. h. Chopin deleted the first chord in each case, replacing it with a semiquaver rest.

29ff.
The metrically correct manner of playing the dotted figure is included in the present text. In this connection see also the Detailed Comments.

5 Nocturne in F sharp major Op.15 No.2

bar

56
r. h.: As elsewhere in Chopin's compositions the first note of the appoggiatura always coincides with

the corresponding note in the bass:

116

7 Nocturne in C sharp minor Op. 27 No. 1

bar

1 ff.   l. h.: *legato* is intended not just horizontally but also vertically, in the sense of "harmonic legato", which avoids unclarity of the bass note before the change of pedal, as in bars 3–4, for instance:

The same applies in all cases when the bass note occurs before the change of pedal.

5, 9, 11 and analogous bars   Dotted rhythms against triplets: see Nocturne in F major Op. 15 No. 1, bars 3, 5 etc.

27–28   Chopin's distribution amongst the two hands (in two of the teaching copies):

37 and analogous bars

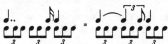

49–50   That the e flat' and a flat' should be played in the r. h. is a suggestion of the editor.

8 Nocturne in D flat major Op. 27 No. 2

bar

22   *sempre legatissimo* applies for the duration of four bars and should be understood as "harmonic legato". The quavers f–e (bar 23) graphically emphasized by Chopin should also be tonally emphasized.

51   According to FE(JS) the beginning of the run should coincide with the penultimate semiquaver c flat' in the l. h. This might, however, be an error in reading the manuscript, since the run played this way seems too thick in texture. It appears preferable to start the run one semiquaver earlier.

9 Nocturne in B major Op. 32 No. 1

bar

9   r. h.: ; a sharp' coincides with the first note in the l. h.

28, 49   First half of the bar:

30, 51   First half of the bar:

40   r. h.: For the execution of the trill see Nocturne in F sharp major Op. 15 No. 2, bar 56.

64–65   Execution of the last two bars:

10 Nocturne in A flat major Op. 32 No. 2

bar

4 and analogous bars   Dotted rhythms against triplets: see Nocturne in F major Op. 15 No. 1, bars 3, 5 etc.

8 and analogous bars   For the execution of the trill see Nocturne in F sharp major Op. 15 No. 2, bar 56.

27, 28, 32   (Cf. bar 27 with 39 and bar 32 with 44.)

30, 34, 42, 46   That the upper triplet note in the l. h. has been allotted to the r. h. is a suggestion of the editor.

11 *Nocturnes in G minor Op. 37 No. 1*

Appoggiaturas: Chopin's instructions on the placing of the appoggiaturas is binding for all similar passages.

bar

8, 24, 74   r. h.: For the execution of the trill see Nocturne in F sharp major Op. 15 No. 2, bar 56.

31   That the g′ has been allotted to the r. h. is a suggestion of the editor.

12 *Nocturne in G major Op. 37 No. 2*

bar

1 ff.   l. h.: *legato* is here certainly intended as "harmonic legato" (cf. Impromptu in A flat major Op. 29, UT 50058, Remarks on Interpretation, bars 1, 2, 3 etc.). Execution:

bars 1–2: 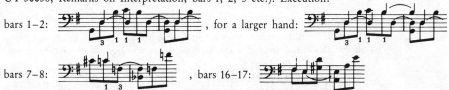 , for a larger hand:

bars 7–8:  , bars 16–17:

90   Execution: r. h. appoggiatura e to be played simultaneously with the fifth in the l. h. The arpeggio can also be seen as applying to the whole chord (see Detailed Comments):

118   Execution:

13 *Nocturne in C minor Op. 48 No. 1*

bar

10   r. h.: The fingering *1 1* which Chopin wrote into a teaching copy can also be understood as signifying that these notes are taken over by the l. h.

15, 16, 18   That the a flat′ is allotted to the r. h. is a suggestion of the editor.

45   For the execution of the trill see Nocturne in F sharp major Op. 15 No. 2, bar 56.

48   The entry noted by Chopin in a teaching copy (see Detailed Comments) suggests the following distribution:

51   r. h.: The second crotchet is the exception alluded to in the Preface, in which Chopin requires the semiquaver to be played after the third note of the triplet:

70   r. h., first half of the bar: Chopin entered the following simplified version in two teaching copies:

72–75   l. h.: The entry noted by Chopin in the teaching copies requires the bass line to be emphasized:

(the slurs have been added by the editor).

73–77   The pedal markings without brackets date from Chopin's later period (however, the pedal change marked in square brackets is obligatory). The pedal markings in round brackets were changed by Chopin in the FE.

14 *Nocturne in F sharp minor Op. 48 No. 2*

bar

44   r. h.: The slurred appoggiatura can be taken to signify either a conventional marking or an arpeggio. In the latter case the passage would be played:

66, 68, 82, 84   r. h.:  (bar 66); the remaining passages should be played by analogy with this.

69, 85   l. h.: For a smaller hand arpeggio in the 2nd quarter of the bar; likewise in the third quarter of the bar if this is not allotted to the r. h.

75, 91	The *pp* in bar 75 and the *p* in bar 91 were not entered by Chopin in one and the same teaching copy and should thus not be thought of as being related to each other. They should be used in only one of the given passages.
131–135	For the execution of the trill see Nocturne in F sharp major Op. 15 No. 2, bar 56.
136	The beginning of the scale passage is given variously in the sources: CFnt has it in the second quarter of the bar, DE not until after the fourth quarter. The former entry looks like a typical instruction for a less skilled pupil (approx. 2 notes to 1 triplet quaver). We suggest that the scale be played more or less at the same tempo as the preceding trill.

15 *Nocturne in F minor Op. 55 No. 1*

bar

14, 30, 46	For the execution of the trill see Nocturne in F sharp major Op. 15 No. 2, bar 56.
77–79, 81–84	*molto legato* here undoubtedly denotes "harmonic legato", that is, the holding of the notes as long as possible for the duration of this inherent two-part writing. Alternative fingering for bars 77–79:

99–101	The sources give the arpeggios for left and right hand separately, although this might signify no more than the distribution between the two hands – a is notated on the lower stave. The editor recommends that the arpeggio be played continuously (at least in the last chord).

16 *Nocturne in E flat major Op. 55 No. 2*

bar

1	For the execution of the trill see Nocturne in F sharp major Op. 15 No. 2, bar 56.
30, 32, 33, 41, 49	r. h.: The appoggiaturas should be played simultaneously with the quaver corresponding to the principal note.
52–53	The trills must in each case begin with the principal note (cf. the same part sequence in bars 44–45).
55	r. h.: The appoggiatura a flat' should coincide with E flat and e flat".

17 *Nocturne in B major Op. 62 No. 1*

bar

35	r. h.: In the first chord the d sharp' can be allotted to the l. h. (see also Detailed Comments, bars 31 ff.).
67 ff.	r. h.: The appoggiatura which anticipates the minim signifies that the trill begins with the principal note.
72	r. h.: The almost illegible variant at the beginning of the bar can also be read:

18 *Nocturne in E major Op. 62 No. 2*

bar

35, 73	The a in the lower stave is notated in all sources as two slurred minims instead of as one semibreve, like the a sharp in bars 34 and 72, for instance. This probably signifies a silent change from one hand to the other.
38	r. h.: [music example] : b sharp should be struck simultaneously with the G sharp in the l. h.
41	Where the two parts meet in one note (g sharp) this should be played only in the r. h. (the same applies to the b in bar 43, the c' and b in bar 50, and b and d' in bar 52).
52, 54	That these notes are allotted to the r. h. is a suggestion of the editor.
76	r. h.: [music example] : b should be struck simultaneously with the F sharp in the l. h.

19 *Nocturne in E minor Op. post.*

bar

3	Dotted rhythms against triplets: see Nocturne in F major Op. 15 No. 1, bars 3, 5 etc.
31, 32, 33, 35	*tr* above shorter time-values signifies in Chopin ⁓ . In bar 33 the trill can be played both on the c''' and on the c sharp'''.
37	r. h.: The c sharp''' trill should begin on the upper note (d''').

20 *Lento con gran espressione [Nocturne in C sharp minor] Op. post.*

bar

11, 56	For the execution of the trill see Nocturne in F sharp major Op. 15 No. 2, bar 56.

INDEX

1   C-Dur / C major

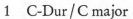

2   a-Moll / A minor

3   G-Dur / G major

4   e-Moll / E minor

5   D-Dur / D major

6   h-Moll / B minor

7   A-Dur / A major

8   fis-Moll / F sharp minor

9   E-Dur / E major

10   cis-Moll / C sharp minor

11   H-Dur / B major

12   gis-Moll / G sharp minor

120

13 Fis-Dur / F sharp major

14 es-Moll / E flat minor

15 Des-Dur / D flat major

16 b-Moll / B flat minor

17 As-Dur / A flat major

18 f-Moll / F minor

19 Es-Dur / E flat major

20 c-Moll / C minor

21 B-Dur / B flat major

22 g-Moll / G minor

23 F-Dur / F major

24 d-Moll / D minor

PREFACE

Chopin composed the *Préludes* at irregular intervals from 1836; the sketches for No. 2 and No. 24 date from the year 1831. No. 7 and No. 17 probably followed them chronologically; further *Préludes* (Nos. 4, 10, and 21) were conceived in Mallorca in November-December 1838; No. 1 was added, as the last one, probably in January 1839.

According to the title ("24 Préludes pour le piano forte dédiée à son ami J. C. Kehsler par F. Chopin"), Chopin dedicated the fair copy of the *Préludes* in the cyclical order (MS) to the pianist Joseph Christoph Kessler (1800—1872). The German first edition based on this manuscript was published by Breitkopf & Härtel, Leipzig, in September 1839. The French first edition (Catelin, Paris, June 1839) as well as the English first edition (Wessel, London, January 1840) is based on a copy made by the pianist Julian Fontana (1810—1869); both are dedicated to Camille Pleyel (1788—1855), the Parisian pianist, publisher, and instrument builder.

This copy of Fontana's was drawn upon extensively in the Complete Edition, which Breitkopf & Härtel published in 1878—1880 (*Friedrich Chopin's Werke. Erste kritisch durchgesehene Gesamtausgabe*, edited, among others, by Liszt and Brahms; *Préludes* as Volume VI). A synopsis of diverging readings, with an adaptation of the notation to the harmonic theory of the late 19th century, based on Hugo Riemann, is offered by the edition "*Fryderyk Chopin. The Complete Works*" of the Fryderyk-Chopin-Institute, Warsaw (Preludes, Vol. I, published 1949, with German commentary in 1956, edited by L. Bronarski and J. Turczyński). The present edition, on the contrary, is based on the very accurate MS.; alterations to this text are mentioned in the Critical Notes in each case.

The title *Prélude* has been generally adopted, since the late 18th century, for independent piano pieces. Like an *Intermezzo* or *Bagatelle*, it has no definite form, nor are its contents specified, in the sense of programme music or a character piece. Its particular suitability for cycles of free pieces of such a nature is supported by a history reaching back over centuries.

The task of preluding (or intonating) since the late Middle Ages was to lead into the mode of a (Gregorian) chorale, and, later, of a vocal or instrumental working of a chorale, or a fugue, on a keyboard instrument of fixed tuning. Ever since there has been an original manner of playing for keyboard instruments, independent keyboard formulae have been used for such Preludes (as first presented in Adam Ileborgh's organ tablature of 1448), similar to those of the Toccata, which the skilful player always had at his disposal for improvisation. Where collections of Preludes were designed for practical use, it was an obvious procedure to arrange them in the order of the usual keys. François Couperin places 8 Preludes together in his keyboard tutor "*L'art de toucher le Clavecin*" (1716), as an exercise ("*to make the fingers more nimble*") on the one hand, and to preface his suites in case the player does not want to improvise, on the other hand. The keys are C major, D minor, G minor, F major, A major, B minor, B flat major, and E minor. The arrangement according to keys passed from here into collections of non-functional chamber music; the most famous examples are the two parts of Johann Sebastian Bach's "*Well-tempered Clavier*" (1722 and 1744), each of which contains 24 Preludes and Fugues in all the major and minor keys. His 2- and 3-part *Inventions*, also called *Preludes* and *Fantasias* in the notebook for Wilhelm Friedemann, encompass as a preparatory exercise only the 15 most common keys.

As the technical exercise of fluency at the keyboard became more and more an independent, essential means of study from the last third of the 18th century, the *Etude* came into existence. Given names such as *Suite d'Etudes*, *Prélude*, or *Caprice*, it was likewise often led cyclically through all the keys; more frequently now in the order of the circle of fifths instead of the chromatic progression from C. Chopin's *Etudes* Op. 10 and Op. 25 also encompass the most important keys and are arranged in pairs with the major-minor contrast (e. g. Op. 10, Nos. 1—2, 3—4, 5—6, 9—10, 11—12).

Chopin's *Préludes* embrace characteristics of the study only in part, and, in their place, all the more intensively, those of the poetic, intimate character piece. The 'Mazurka' (No. 7), 'Song without Words' (Nos. 5 and 9), and 'Nocturne' (Nos. 13, 15 and 17) types are represented; the Biedermeier limits are exceeded by far, however, particularly in No. 18, which presents a dramatic scene, like the *Larghetto* of the F minor piano concerto. The relationship between individual Preludes and other piano works of Chopin, extending to similarity of "mood" and the type of figuration, is striking, e. g. between No. 3 and the "*Andante spianato*" *in G major* to the E flat major Polonaise, between No. 23 and the *Etude* Op. 10, No. 8, between No. 22 and the end of the G minor Ballade, between No. 10 and the figuration of the "chorale theme" in the C sharp minor Ballade, between No. 14 and the *Finale* of the B flat minor Sonata (fifth relationship).

If these connections are more amenable to sympathetic understanding than "demonstrations of proof", they add, nevertheless, to an understanding of the character of the pieces (as regards expression, tempo, and dynamics), and, moreover, to an appreciation of these cyclically connected miniatures as a microcosm of Chopin's works for piano.

Bernhard Hansen

CRITICAL NOTES
AND DIRECTIONS FOR PERFORMANCE

No. 1   C major   Agitato

To be slurred bar by bar basically. There are slurs over each bar throughout the piece, also in bars 29—31, in the MS., therefore. The slur is omitted in bar 1, because the triplets are marked off by means of group slurs.

A somewhat earlier raising of the pedal is recommended on the modern piano, thus departing from the original pedalling.

A 'crescendo' begins in bar 13, a 'stretto' is added at bar 17; both culminate in a 'ff' in bar 21, which is not present in the MS. By analogy, there should be a 'diminuendo' from that point, through the original 'piano' in bar 25 to a 'pianissimo' in the closing bar. — This dynamic course is to be planned according to the basic dynamic level, which is given as 'mezzo forte' in the MS., and as 'forte' in many editions.

No. 2   A minor   Lento

The MS. has pedalling only for bars 18—19. An impressionistic "half pedal" is most suitable for the delicate changing notes in the accompaniment. The necessary touch should be obtained by silent changes of fingering.

The slurs over the melody in bars 3—7 and 14—19 are obviously placed differently for a special purpose. In bar 17 the continuation of the slur, supported by the 'crescendo', must extend over the break, which results from the discontinuance of the accompaniment.

No. 3   G major   Vivace

The slurs over each bar in the l. h. are to be understood as signifying a continuous 'legato-leggiero', and not as a break between bars.

A clear "half pedal" is recommended again.

bars 7 and 9: As the semibreves in the r. h. are sustained by the pedal it is possible to play the f sharp[1] in the l. h. figuration with the r. h. thumb.

bar 17: Many editions make the e[2]-d sharp[2] of the melody correspond rhythmically to the other dottings and put ♩.. ♪ .

bar 26: By analogy with bar 24, the third b-d[1] in the r. h. must be quitted after a crotchet.

The MS. does not contain any dynamic marks in bar 31. Many editions have a 'crescendo' instead of a 'diminuendo'.

No. 4   E minor   Largo

The change of pedal occurs simultaneously with the change of harmony.

bars 8—10: There is a new slur after the tie g sharp[1] — g sharp[1] in the MS. The meaning of this "dovetailing slur" has been conveyed here in modern notation.

bars 17—18: It is not recognisable in the MS. whether a *decrescendo* wedge or a slur begun twice was written in bar 17.

No. 5   D major   Allegro molto

The pedalling is original, only ♌ and ✳ being added to the 3rd and 4th semiquavers of bar 30 to correspond with bars 29 and 31. Shorter pedalling in general is to be recommended today.

bars 1, 17, 33: Chopin's notation of the middle part is simplified: what is meant, of course, is the holding over of the final quaver into the following bar.

bar 16: Many editions give a sharp[2] as the final note in the r. h., but this is not likely, owing to the false relation with the tenor in bar 17.

No. 6   B minor   Lento assai

It is possible to play the note repetitions in the r. h. with the fingering 5⌢4, later 4⌢5, and 3⌢4 in the final bars — the so-called "finger slide".

No. 7   A major   Andantino

A light pedal change on the semiquaver each time is recommended.

No. 8   F sharp minor   Molto agitato

The MS. has slurs over the whole bar in bars 3 and 21; the slurring is split up in this edition, by analogy with bars 7/8.

bars 6 and 20: The highest note of the second group in the r. h. is a[2] in the MS., but is normally replaced by f sharp[2].

The ⸻ in bars 25—26 are to be understood as *espressivo-marcato* directions for the tenor.

bar 34: The e sharp[1] is to be played as a suspension, therefore long and with a *diminuendo* to the f sharp[1].

No. 9 E major Largo

On the question of the co-ordination of the semi-quavers and demisemiquavers with the triplet quavers: each semiquaver is notated above the third quaver of the triplet and should certainly be understood as part of the triplet. The same applies to the second quaver in the first beat of bar 8, although this is possibly meant to be interpreted as a rubato (Chopin deleted his original dot — cf. our facsimile frontispiece). There can be no doubt that the demisemiquavers in the bass should each be played after the triplet in question and very short, as should those in the melody from bar 9 onwards (that the first dotting in bar 11 is single in the MS is presumably an error).

From bar 9, a *crescendo* extending to the close is obviously intended. The dynamic wedge in bar 10 is to be interpreted as a continuation, not as a fresh beginning. The written-out *crescendo* in bar 11 can be conceived as an indication of intensification. The double indication in the MS. (by means of dynamic wedge and *crescendo*) is simplified both in this bar and in bar 8.

bar 12: It is recommended that the octaves in the l. h. be played unarpeggiated, so that the power of the *fortissimo* is not diminished.

No. 10 C sharp minor Allegro molto

Shorter pedalling are recommended throughout.

bar 8, 2nd crotchet: It is probably intended that, by analogy with bar 4, the G sharp be stressed as a minim and sustained.

No. 11 B major Vivace

bar 21: The MS. has

A change of pedal is recommended in bars 5—6, 9—12.

No. 12 G sharp minor Presto

The accents in the first three bars and in parallel passages should be applied to the l. h. in particular. Much more frequent changes of pedal, often on each crotchet, are necessary on modern pianos.

bar 23: c is usually played instead of c sharp in the r. h., originating from Mikuli etc. Perhaps an oversight on Chopin's part: cf. bars 24—26 as well as bars 3 and 43, where there are also no accidental marks.

bars 24—26: The natural sign at a¹ in the r. h. is missing in the MS.

bar 24: a¹ is notated as a crotchet in the MS. As no rests follow, it would appear that this was an oversight on Chopin's part. (cf. bars 21 and 28.)

bars 49—52: it is recommended that the bass octaves be played 'marcato'.

bar 70: The first octave in the l. h. is notated E-e instead of G sharp-g sharp in the MS. — surely an error.

bar 74: Fingering, with distribution of the two middle parts:

No. 13 F sharp major Lento

The time-signature is 3/2 in the MS.
The pedal should be used more frequently than is specified in the MS.

bar 7 and bar 9: The appoggiaturas should be short in spite of the crotchet notation often used summarily by Chopin.

bar 32: To correspond with bar 16, many editions have a sharp¹ instead of b¹ in the first chord, r. h.

No. 14 E flat minor Allegro

There are many differences of opinion among various interpreters and editions concerning the tempo of this Prelude. A few editions have **C** instead of **¢**. Chopin himself wrote the direction *LARGO* in a handwritten copy. There is a striking similarity to the Finale of the Sonata in B flat minor, however. The pedal must be used extremely carefully in a quick performance.

No. 15 D flat major Sostenuto

There was a double-stop originally, probably in the l. h. also, on the penultimate quaver, in bars 5 and 24; the passage is illegible in the MS.

bars 5, 6, 21, 24—26 and 77: The minims in the l. h. are without dots in the MS.

bars 33 and 49: The final crotchet in the l. h. is C sharp-c sharp in the MS. The deviation from the consecutive sixths is probably due to Chopin himself.

No. 16 B flat minor Presto con fuoco

The summary original pedallings must be supplemented by more frequent changes. The original fingerings are printed in italics. The arrangement of slurs in the r. h. is metrically disposed; irrespective of this, a continuous *legato* is intended in the very quick tempo, merging into a *leggiero* at, roughly, the *animato* in bar 34: The slurs in the l. h. have been adapted to the technical possibilities of stretch a) as in bars 2—7 with a leap between upbeat and accented quaver; b) as in bars 8, 9—16; c) as from bar 18 in octaves.

bar 23: The f flat^2 in the third semiquaver group is not included in the MS. and the first editions. The Breitkopf & Härtel Complete Edition includes it, however, to correspond with the figuration of the harmonically similar bar 22.

bar 41: The four semiquavers of the second beat can be taken by the l. h.

bar 45: The final note of the unison passage can be played as an octave by the r. h.

No. 17   A flat major   Allegretto

The directions *sopra* and *sotto* refer to the position of the left thumb.

bar 11: A g^1 can be added to the octave d flat^1 — d flat^2 in the fourth quaver, by analogy with bar 35.

A *crescendo* begins at bar 19, reaching a *forte* approximately at the beginning of bar 24.

Bars 30/31 are often interpreted as an echo of bars 28/29.

bars 44—45, 48—49: the absolutely necessary ties b^1-b^1, c sharp^1-c sharp^1 first appear in a copy of Fontana's and, also, in the English first edition.

bar 51: The *diminuendo* follows a *forte* approximately.

A *diminuendo* extending to the *pp* of the coda (bar 65) is recommended from bar 57, only increased somewhat by the dynamic wedge in bars 61—62.

bars 65/66: There is no slur in the MS.

The Prelude is presented in an essentially different, and certainly earlier form in a copy made by J. Fontana (Vienna, Library of the Gesellschaft der Musikfreunde, formerly in Brahms' possession). The tempo given is *Allegretto quasi andantino;* the copy contains no pedal markings, no large slurs, and the dynamic indications are less exact (they differ from those of the MS. in bar 24, for example: *p* after *crescendo* from bar 20). Bar 31 is extended to two bars, bar 83 is missing. The organ point in the bass throughout the final 7 bars is written in long notes; it can only be realised by means of the sustaining pedal. The ties in the melody are different in places (e. g. bar) 19 ff: [musical notation]. Crossing of hands is used extensively in the piano writing, moreover.

No. 18   F minor   Allegro molto

bar 9 ff: The distinction between wedges and dots for the *staccato* is problematical. In the MS. the wedges in bars 9, 10, 11, and 12 are clearly differentiated from the dots in bars 16 and 18. Intermediate forms occur at some of the other points, but dots both above and below the chords are to be read in bars 13 and 14, and there is a tendency towards the wedge in bar 15 (above the chords only). In this edition, the wedges are retained only at the *fz* chords between the rests. The same tendency is discernible in early 19th century editions viz. that wedges signify an accent with shortening of the note (chord) rather than a pointed *staccato*.

No. 19   E flat major   Vivace

In the MS., the slurs provided originally, from the second quaver of each triplet group to the first quaver of the following group, are deleted and replaced by the general direction *legato*. These slurs have remained only in bars 32 and 68. Fourth finger on the black keys is recommended — wherever possible — in the r. h.; it provides a better anchor in wide stretches.

bar 1: r. h. first triplet, third quaver e^1 flat in the MS.

bars 22—24: The MS. has a *decrescendo* wedge each time. It is open to question whether a *crescendo* is not meant in bar 23.

bar 49: l. h. second quaver of the triplet group g instead of b flat in the MS., an obvious oversight.

bars 62—63: The chromatic voice-leading of the tenor is underlined by crotchet stems in the MS. viz. bar 62, final quaver, bar 63, 6th and 9th quavers.

A more frequent change of pedal is recommended, particularly at the changing notes in bars 18—20 etc.

No. 20   C minor   Largo

bar 3: Chopin is reputed to have altered the e^1 in the final chord to e flat^1. As a natural sign is also missing in bars 8 and 12 and Chopin's own correction of the e to an e flat in his pupil Jane Stirling's copy appears authentic, there has been disagreement for a long time between one group of pianists and music scholars who advocate e flat^1 and another group who advocate e^1.

It emerges from a (facetious) remark in the MS. that Chopin inserted the repeat of bars 5—8 (= bars 9—12) on the advice of the publisher Pleyel.

bars 8 and 12: The natural sign before d^1 in the third beat, r. h., is missing in the MS., but the authenticity of d^1 natural is confirmed by other sources.

No. 21   B flat major   Cantabile

A crotchet appoggiatura before the last crotchet e flat^2 is not possible in the given time, but it was a custom of Chopin's to notate appoggiaturas as crotchets, without determining their rhythmical value thereby.

No. 22   G minor   Molto agitato

There is a change from the upbeat phrasing in bars 1—4 to slurs over each bar, probably the conventional manner of writing, in the MS. The bar slurs are not introduced until bar 13 in the present edition, however; the phrasing from bar 35 corresponds to that at the beginning. The shorter dynamic wedge in bar 17 ff. are not to be interpreted unequivocally. The editors prefer their interpretation as accents to their interpretation as *decrescendo* signs.

bar 41: There is a slur from the lower to the upper system in the MS.; it is reproduced as an arpeggio here.

No. 23   F major   Moderato

bar 1: The fingering is recommended on account of the fixed position of the thumb as a pivot.

bars 3, 7, 11, 19: The slurring in the l. h. is divided only in bar 19, probably because the motive is an octave lower. In the MS., a divided slur was also provided in bars 3 and 7 first of all, it would appear, but was then deleted in favour of the bar slur.

bar 14: The 6th and 14th semiquavers are already b^2 instead of g^2 in the English original edition.

No. 24   D minor   Allegro appassionato

The notation of the grace-notes has been standardised to semiquaver without slur. The modern notation (in bars 5 and 9, for example) would be ♩ ♩ ♪♪ instead of the original ♩ ♪♪ .

bar 50 ff: On account of the greater power, the fingering ⁵/₁ is recommended for all the octaves.

The summary pedalling — from bar 6 or so — must be made clear by frequent changes.

The freely negotiated trills (bars 16 and 34), as well as those preceded by the note a second higher (bars 12 and 30), should commence on the principal note, whereas the preceding appoggiatura in bars 10 and 28 indicates commencement on the upper auxiliary note.

Jörg Demus

Frédéric Chopin: Scherzi

INDEX

PREFACE

Considered as a genre, the piano scherzo has two historical aspects: firstly as part of cyclic sonata form, and secondly, as a self-sufficient work.

Two Chopin scherzi have come down to us as parts of sonatas: the second movements of the Piano Sonatas in B flat minor Op. 35, and B minor Op. 58. (It's not really relevant to consider the scherzi from Chopin's chamber compositions here, i. e. from the Trio Op. 8, and the Sonata for Violoncello and Piano Op. 65.) Robert Schumann gives a telling characterisation of the Chopin sonata scherzo when, writing about the B flat minor Sonata, he says: "The second movement simply extends this mood [of the first movement], bold, imaginative, fantastic, with a tender, dreamy trio, as is so typical of Chopin: like many of Beethoven's, it is a scherzo in name only." [1]

The four scherzi that Chopin created as pieces in their own right — in B minor Op. 20, B flat minor Op. 31, C sharp minor Op. 39, and E major Op. 54 — are without doubt the high point in the development of this genre. None of the scherzi by his contemporaries, the most notable being those by Schubert, Mendelssohn and Schumann, are comparable to Chopin's, either in terms of their content and dimensions, or in terms of their exploration of instrumental technique. Of later scherzi, only the Scherzo in E flat minor Op. 4 by Brahms, which shows many points of similarity to Chopin's scherzi (especially the Scherzo in B flat minor), invites direct comparison.

The features common to all four scherzi are: the 3/4 metre, the lively tempo of the outer sections, the basic A-B-A form (the Scherzo in B flat minor is based on first-movement sonata form, an the C sharp minor Scherzo is expanded to the form A-B-A-B-Coda), and the virtuoso character of the pieces — either largely or as a whole. Another characteristic of Chopin's Scherzi is the great emotional span between the dramatic and lyrical parts; and one should note that the dramatic sections are in the majority. This feature, which is etymologically at odds with the title (scherzo is Italian for joke, fun), was best highlighted by Schumann, in reference to the Scherzo in B minor Op. 20: "How will seriousness be clad, when even a 'joke' bears such sombre garments?" [2] The one exception in this respect is the Scherzo in E major Op. 54, whose outer sections have a character that matches the title.

Particular attention should be drawn to one significant characteristic which greatly affects the performance of the Chopin Scherzi: their fairly rigorous construction in four-bar periods. (The few exceptions to this rule are to be found only in the middle section of the B minor Scherzo, and the octaves passage of the C sharp minor Scherzo.) Awareness of this peculiarity will help the performer to get a proper grasp of the musical process.

The Scherzo in B minor Op. 20 was presumably written while Chopin was staying in Vienna or Stuttgart (1830—31), either as an expression of the lonely composer, living abroad, and longing to be back home with those he was closest to, or in despair at receiving reports of the outbreak of the Warsaw Uprising. (The incorporation of a Polish Christmas carol — "Lulajże Jezuniu": "Sleep, little Jesus" — at the beginning of the middle section argues in favour of Vienna, where Chopin spent Christmas, but the musical character of the outer section suggests Stuttgart.) Though there is reason enough to accept this assumption, there is no documentary proof for it. In any case, it is highly probable that the work was definitively completed only a short while before it went to press in 1835.

The Scherzo in B flat minor Op. 31 was composed from 1835—37, and published in 1837. Schumann wrote of this scherzo: "It remains an utterly compelling piece; one could compare it to a poem by Lord Byron: so tender, coquettish and affectionate — yet full of scorn." [3] The expressive contrasts in this piece result from the fairly frequent alternation of dramatic and lyrical themes, accompanied by changes of key and mode. (It is worth noting that the beginning is in B flat minor, and the ending in D flat major, a fact that underlines the bipolarity of this piece.) Chopin attached great important to the correct understanding of the opening triplet motive and its basic gesture. His pupil Wilhelm von Lenz writes: "It must be a question, Chopin taught us, and for him it could never be questioning enough, never piano enough, never tomb-like (tombé) enough, never significant enough. It must be the house of the dead, he once said." [4]

Chopin began work on the Scherzo in C sharp minor Op. 39 during his trip to Mallorca with George Sand (January 1839), and finished it at Nohant (August 1839). This work was published in 1840; somewhat earlier, at Chopin's wish, his pupil Adolf Gutmann (to whom the piece is dedicated) played it for Ignaz Moscheles, in the summer of 1839. [5] The Chopin pupil mentioned above, Wilhelm von Lenz, makes the following somewhat malicious comment: "The Scherzo in C sharp minor Op. 39 is dedicated to Gutmann, and the

---

[1] R. Schumann, *Gesammelte Schriften über Musik und Musiker* ("Collected Writings on Music and Musicians"), Leipzig 1888, Vol. III, p. 53.

[2] op. cit. Vol. I, p. 237.

[3] op. cit. Vol. II, p. 162.

[4] Quoted from F. Niecks, *F. Chopin als Mensch und als Musiker* ("F. Chopin: Man and Musician"), Leipzig 1890, Vol. II, p. 280.

[5] *Aus Moscheles' Leben, nach Briefen und Tagebüchern herausgegeben von seiner Frau* ("From the Life of Moscheles, edited by his wife from letters and diaries"), Leipzig 1872, Vol. II, p. 39, as well as B. Stavenov — an article on A. Gutmann —: *Der Lieblingsschüler Chopins* ("Chopin's favourite pupil"), Schöne Geister, No. 3, Bremen 1879.

chord in the bass is probably conceived in terms of his boxer's fist; no left hand can grasp it (d♯ — f♯ — b — d♯′ — f♯′, bar 6 f.), least of all Chopin's hand: even on his light-touched, narrow-keyed Pleyel, he used to arpeggiate it. But Gutmann could knock a hole in a table with it!" [6]

We know very little about the circumstances that gave rise to the Scherzo in E major Op. 54 (completed in 1842 and published in 1843). From Chopin's correspondence with his publishers, we find that he offered them this piece at the same time as the Ballade in F minor Op. 52 and the Polonaise in A flat major Op. 53.

We don't know whether Chopin himself ever played any of his scherzi in public, though there is possible evidence in relation to the C sharp minor Scherzo.[7] On the other, the copies of all four scherzi that Chopin used for teaching, containing his own handwritten annotations, have survived to this day.

GENERAL COMMENTS ON THE EDITION

There are two respects in which the editing of Chopin's works poses special problems: one is the manner in which Chopin prepared his works for publication; the other is his attitude to notation.

It is often difficult to establish the independency, authenticity and precedence of the sources for Chopin, since the way he prepared pieces for publication was very strange, and varied considerably at different periods of his life. So for a while, the starting point for this process was a single autograph, that served, directly or through the mediation of proof sheets, as the model for several editions. At other times this process revolved around a group of manuscripts (autograph and copies), which were distributed among the publishers in various ways. In yet another period Chopin prepared several autographs as printer's models for the various editions. Basically, Chopin had his works published — often simultaneously — in three editions: a French one, a German one, and an English one. Further problems arise from the fact that Chopin showed a considerable aversion to proof-reading. He didn't correct all the copies, or all the editions, or all the works; he often did it in a great hurry and let mistakes pass. Sometimes he handed the proof-reading over to Fontana. Where there were several printer's models, Chopin didn't check to see whether they were exactly the same, and even during the process of engraving he made changes — usually in the French editions. When we also bear in mind that Chopin was in the habit of writing further variants into his pupils' copies, we get some idea of the difficulties involved in discovering the composer's ultimate intentions.

All these circumstances that arose prior to and during the process of printing, coupled with what happened to the works afterwards, permit us to assume that these variants are a characteristic feature of Chopin's creative thinking. This idiosyncrasy of his should be reflected in an Urtext edition. Naturally it mustn't lead to a situation where the musical text is overladen with alternatives. Variants have only been shown in the music when they are really necessary, that is, when it is not possible to establish for certain what Chopin's final intentions were. If a variant is clearly meant as a correction, it is presented by itself as the definitive version, and its choice is vindicated in the Critical Commentary.

All the variants that are given as footnotes to the musical text are, accordingly, a u t h e n t i c and j u s t a s v a l i d as the main text, with regard both to their sources and their artistic worth.

But it is not just knowledge of the variants that is important in giving an adequate representation of Chopin's musical text. The present edition has attempted to retain the peculiarities of his method of notation. Chopin himself attached great importance to the way his compositions were notated. This is proved, for example, by a passage from a letter of 18. 10. 1841 to his friend Fontana, where he says of his manuscript "... I so love my irksome scrawl", and ends the paragraph with the words: "I don't want to hand this spider's web over to some coarse copyist." Exact inspection of Chopin's manuscripts shows that for him, the way a piece looked matched the way it sounded. Many of the amendments that at first sight seem to be largely cosmetic, but turn out to suggest a precise musical conception, prove that Chopin was concerned about the correct graphic impression of his music. For this reason, the following aspects of Chopin's notation have been faithfully reproduced:

D i v i s i o n o f t h e n o t e s between the two staves, wherever it has a significant effect on the voice-leading or distribution of notes between hands;

D i s t r i b u t i o n o f c r o s s - s t r o k e s in quaver and semiquaver pasages, where Chopin is always extremely methodical;

P o i n t i n g t h e s t e m s of the notes upwards or downwards, which doesn't always accord with the rules current nowadays;

P l a c i n g o f s l u r s, wherever observing them exactly can influence the layout and span of the musical conception behind what is being played.

Special mention should be made of the notation of a dotted rhythm in one part and a triplet rhythm in another. Chopin consistently uses this notation in the 18th century sense, i. e. the last notes in both figures are sounded simultaneously, e. g. or . In his fair copies, Chopin aligns the matching notes exactly over one another.[8] The present edition does the same.

A further characteristic of Chopin's notation that we have respected is the distinction between long and short accent signs. For Chopin, the short accent (>) denotes a louder dynamic, whereas the long accent (⟹) implies an expressive stress.

The symbols for ornamentation have been left in their original form; it is only where Chopin uses several symbols for the same ornament that we have reduced them to a single form, to avoid misunderstandings, e. g. the symbols for arpeggio and turn.

[6] Wilhelm von Lenz, *Die großen Pianoforte-Virtuosen* ("The Great Piano Virtuosi", *Chopin*, Berlin 1872, p. 47—48.

[7] E. Ganche, *Frédéric Chopin*, Paris 1921, p. 255.

[8] There is only one exception to this rule: the Nocturne in C minor, Op. 48 no. 1, Bar 51.

Naturally, we have adhered to the range of the piano with which Chopin was familiar. In his piano works, Chopin never went outside the range C to f⁴. In a few cases where it is clear that the composer was hampered by the range of the piano at that time, the editor proposes variants which, however, never extend the compass of the work by more than a second above or below.

The original fingerings are given in italics, the editor's in normal type. The metronome markings are, without exception, the composer's. Additions and variants for matching passages (single notes, interpretation signs etc.) are set in round brackets; all editorial additions are in square brackets.[9]

It would be impossible to list here all the institutions and private owners who have made their sources available to us for this edition. So I take the liberty of expressing my general thanks here to the Chopin Society in Warsaw, the main centre for all Chopin sources, and to all the libraries and individuals who are mentioned in the Preface and Critical Notes as the owners of sources.

Jan Ekier

All the problems concerning the sources, their chronology and authenticity, and the way Chopin prepared his works for publication are discussed at length in Jan Ekier, Wstęp do Wydania Narodowego Dzieł Fryderyka Chopina, Cz. I. Zagadnienia edytorskie (introduction to the Fryderyk Chopin National Edition, First Part, Editorial Problems), Cracow 1974, at present only in Polish. Second part — Performance Problems — in preparation.

REMARKS ON INTERPRETATION

Abbreviations: see Critical Notes

Scherzo in B minor Op. 20

Bar

31—32 and analogous passages
The slur between the e's, like the analogous slurs between the preceding bars, is not a tie, but an articulation slur; therefore e' should be repeated.

37—38, 41—42, and analogous passages
r. H.: Fingering for small hands:

however, one should be careful that the 1st finger doesn't accentuate the note d#'!

44—56 and analogous passages
ritenuto here doesn't mean an overall slowing-down; it merely implies the use of 'local' rubato.

56—57 and analogous passages
The fingering  aids the legato performance of the octaves.

57—64, 289—304, 553—568 and analogous passages
The four-bar structure is to be strictly observed, so as not to distort the metre.

65
It is permissible to regard the five-fold repetition (written out in what follows) that ends this part as optional, and not to observe the repeat marks.

305 ff.
With skilful pedalling, the pedal can be held to the end of each bar Using rather more modern pedalling, *ben legato* may also be realised as follows:

(= "harmonic legato": see Impromptu in A flat major Op. 29, Remarks on Interpretation)

322, 323, 324,
r. h.: According to Chopin's markings in several of the printed copies he used in teaching other

325 and anal-
ogous passages

pieces, ornaments of this kind should always begin 'on the beat'; e. g.

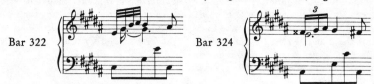

Bar 322   Bar 324

329, 361

r. h.: Here, the appoggiatura d♯'', could also be played as an anticipation, so as not to rob the crochet d♯'' in the previous bar of its accentuation.

330, 332,
362, 364

Chopin doesn't often use these reversed (long or short) accent-marks above (or below) single notes; their function is to emphasize whatever follows, and they may be intended as an analogy to instruments or ensembles that can make crescendi on single notes.

383—384

According to the original pedalling, the bass note C♯ should sound for two whole bars. On our modern piano, it is recommended that the pedal be changed when the harmony changes, and that the bass note be retaken silently. This measure allows one both to hold the bass note and to avoid the dissonance:

Scherzo in B flat minor Op. 31

Bar
73 and anal-
ogous passages

r. h.: Appoggiatura together with 1st note in l. h.

126—128

r. h.: some suggested ways of making this passage, which is awkward for small hands, easier:

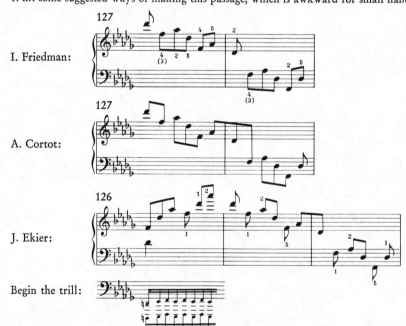

I. Friedman:

A. Cortot:

J. Ekier:

179, 630

Begin the trill:

281, 306, 383,
408

l. h. arpeggio: c♯ and c♯'' (r. h.) sound simultaneously, with both notes depalled; but an anticipatory arpeggio, with e♯' and c♯'' sounding together, is preferable at this point:

553—568	r. h.: Taking into account the rapid tempo and the sonority of the modern piano, the editor suggests that the chords be played unarpeggiated; apart from being much easier, this gives a more decisive effect.
744—755	On our present-day piano, one can get an excellent effect by holding the pedal on longer than Chopin requires, namely up to and including B. 754 (change in B. 755); a necessary condition for this is that the A♭ — A♭ — a♭ in B. 744 should be played with a full tone, and sufficiently loudly.

Scherzo in C sharp minor Op. 39

Bar

6—7, 14—15	l. h.: Smaller hands may arpeggiate the chords (Chopin himself is said to have done this); but they may also be simplified as follows:   If one uses the original pedal markings, and articulates the chords crisply in both hands, the difference between this and what was originally written is barely perceptible.
37—38, 54, 62, 75 ff. and analogous passages	r. h.: The middle voice in crotchets — formed from the material of the main theme in octaves, played staccato or non legato — should also be played staccato, so as to heighten the effect of the polyphonic structure; only in B. 54 and 396, which involve imitation of the melodic fragments in the preceding bar, should it be played legato. The long legato slurs above the line relate only to the top voice.
47, 129, 373, 389	Note that e i t h e r the principal text o r the variants for these four bars, drawn from FE and given in the footnote, must be used consistently at e a c h of these points. Cf. Critical Notes.
159 ff. and analogous passages	l. h.: Fingering for smaller hands (e. g. in B. 315—319): 
219	l. h.: Arpeggio signs in all sources, but only at this point. One can regard this as a purely technical matter (Chopin usually arpeggiated this, the widest tenth on the keyboard i. e. g♭ — b♭, or f♯ — a♯. A large hand can take all the notes at once).
374	The accents refer to the notes A—a′.
598	Begin the trill: 
629—633	Simplification for smaller hands:  or
637—643	The marking *stretto* applies only up to B. 642; i. e. B. 643 ff. are to be performed at *tempo primo*: the accelerating whole-bar octaves must come close to the length of the *tempo primo* crotchets!
645—end	✳ in B. 645 from FE it is missing at this point in CX. It is possible that ✳ is a mistake; we have put this marking in brackets, and suggest that the pedal should not be raised until after the last chord. (Cf. also the endings of the Scherzi in B flat minor and E major.)

Scherzo in E major Op. 54

Bar

56—57, 328—329, 656—657	Simplification: 

132

89, 689	Simplification for smaller hands, if the original pedalling is used:

117, 717	With smaller hands, the f♯ should be retaken; otherwise one should hold the f♯, and only arpeggiate the D♯—B.
165—168, 285—288, 765—768	l. h.: The unbracketed fingering gives the distribution between hands as written out in Aut; the fingering in brackets enables the top note of the l. h. to be taken over 'silently' by the r. h.
194, 762	It might be admissible to disregard the r. h. arpeggios found in Aut (by analogy with B. 93, 162, 693, 794, where Aut notates them in the l. h. only); EE gives l. h. arpeggios only in 3 of the 6 bars, while FE gives none at all.
308	r. h.: The appoggiatura d♯' is better played as an anticipation i. e. at the end of the preceding bar.
357—360	The final octave in each of the two-bar motives is to be played by the r. h.; ditto the last two octaves in each of the two-bar motives in B. 365—368.
375—376	The octaves in B. 375 split between the hands, the octaves at the beginning of B. 376 in the r. h.
400, 429, 440, 469, 520, 544, 552	Cf. Detailed Comments, Bar 89 and 400. Chopin's marking also applies to further analogous passages (in B. 440, 520, 544 and 552, also struck at the same time as the other voices in the r. h.).
419—422	To extract the fullest effect from the harmony of these 4 bars, and at the same time, to avoid the dissonance f✗' — g♯ in B. 422, the following use of 'harmonic legato' and pedal is recommended:

425	It is recommended that this bar be executed in accord with Chopin's pedalling for B. 461.
449, 529	r. h.: Play the appoggiatura b at the same time as the F♯ in the l. h. For hands with a broad stretch:

459	Execute the same way as B. 419.
477, 493	r. h.: The appoggiatura is to be played simultaneously with the 1st note in the bass.
478, 494	r. h.: The appoggiatura can be played either 'on the beat', or as an anticipation; the important thing is to execute the line in the lowest voice in a consistent manner.
480, 496	r. h.: Execution: . The lowest note of the arpeggio at the same time as the 1st note in the bass.
559—573	r. h.: The sequence in the lowest voice should be brought out clearly (cf. musical example in Detailed Comments on B. 567—568).
949	l. h.: The FE reading given as a footnote is recommended, because it expressly emphasizes the four-bar phrase that begins in this bar.
964	The pedal is to be held to the end, but it shouldn't be brought in until the final octave of the scales.

I. – Doctor Gradus ad Parnassum

II. – Jimbo's Lullaby

III. – Serenade for the Doll

IV. – The snow is dancing

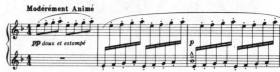

V. – The little Shepherd

VI. – Golliwogg's cake walk

PREFACE

In December 1898 Claude Debussy parted company with Gabrielle (Gaby) Dupont, who had for many years been his companion. On October 19th of the following year he married the milliner Rosalie (Lilly) Texier. The composer soon realised, however, that he had been deceived by his feelings. After protracted and unpleasant legal proceedings, which at times left Debussy unable to work, they were divorced on August 2nd 1905. *Madame Debussy has reverted to being Mademoiselle Lilly Texier, an identity which she should never have surrendered*[1]. Debussy had been all the more eager to obtain a divorce in view of the fact that his passionate involvement with Emma Moyse-Bardac, the wife of a Parisian banker and the mother of his pupil Raoul Bardac, was beginning to have practical implications. Madame Bardac had already left her husband in early 1905 to move into an apartment in the Avenue Alphand with Debussy. The couple subsequently took up residence in the adjoining Avenue du Bois-de-Boulogne, and it was here, on October 30th 1905, that Claude-Emma (Chouchou) was born. She was to survive her father by only a little over a year, dying of diphtheria in July 1919. Emma Bardac and Debussy were married on January 20th 1908[2], and a few months later he completed the six-part piano cycle *Children's Corner*. It was dedicated to *My dear little Chouchou, with tender apologies from her father for what follows* . . . For the first edition (Durand, D & F 7188) Debussy himself sketched a laconic title page. The work received its first public performance by the English pianist Harold Bauer at a concert of the Parisian Cercle Musical on December 18th 1908. In the orchestral arrangement by Debussy's friend André Caplet *Children's Corner* was first heard in New York in November 10th 1910.

As early as the spring of 1901 Debussy had come across Modest Mussorsky's song cycle *Nursery* and had reviewed it enthusiastically in the *Revue Blanche*: *Never has so fine a sensitivity been able to express itself with such simple means. It resembles the art of an inquisitive savage discovering music with every step which his feelings dictate. And there is no kind of form here, or if there is it is so* polymorphous that it could never be said to be related to conventional – one might also say 'legitimate' – forms. The entire work is made up of a succession of brush strokes which, thanks to his gift of commanding lucidity, are held together by an enigmatic thread[3]. Children's Corner owes not just its title to Debussy's enthusiasm for the Mussorgsky cycle: the parallels in the scenes evoked and their musical character – *Before Bedtime* – *Jimbo's Lullaby*, *With the Doll* – *Serenade for (of) the Doll* – amply testify to his admiration for the Russian work.

Of the first two pieces Debussy wrote to his friend and publisher Jacques Durand: *"Doctor Gradus ad Parnassum" is a kind of health-oriented, cumulative gymnastics: it should be played every morning before breakfast, beginning moderato and ending spiritoso. I hope that this graphic explanation will appeal to you. For "Jimbo's" moderato should be just right . . .*[4]. These lines should serve to substantiate the tempo marking *Assez modéré* for the second piece, which is not given in Debussy's manuscript.

In "Children's Corner" Debussy [. . .] portrays the enchanting and carefully supervised games, the secretive escapades and the tender gestures of a small girl from the city – more precisely, from Paris – who already has some attributes of womanhood and understands flirtatiousness, and whose high spirits and imagination are dampened by the presumed presence of a nanny[5].

Michael Stegemann

[1] Letter to Louis Laloy dated 28. 8. 1905.

[2] In the relevant secondary literature the date of Debussy's second marriage is often given incorrectly, between 1905 and 1915. In fact, the composer married Emmy Moyse on the afternoon of January 20th 1908 at the registry office of the Mairie du XVIe arrondissement.

[3] "La Chambre d'enfants" de Moussorgsky; in La Revue Blanche of 15. 4. 1901.

[4] Letter to Jacques Durand dated 15. 8. 1908.

[5] Alfred Cortot, La Musique française de piano I, Paris 41932, p. 33.

NOTES ON THE EDITION OF DEBUSSY'S PIANO MUSIC

In the case of the majority of Claude Debussy's piano compositions, textual research has two principal sources to draw on: the autograph manuscript, and the First Edition. Identifiable handwritten notes and the publisher's seal or stamp provide incontestable proof that the composer's manuscripts were used as engraver's copies. Consequently, it has hitherto been taken for granted that the First Edition of each work could be regarded as a definitive text and — in the case of compositions published during the composer's lifetime — as having been printed under Debussy's supervision.

A critical correlation of the two sources has, however, revealed numerous and in part significant divergences between the First Editions and the autograph manuscripts. The present editor raised this question with Editions Musicales Durand S. A. (Paris) — Jacques Durand had acquired the exclusive rights to Debussy's music in 1905. In response to an enquiry about the existence of *galley proofs, documentary material or letters which would establish that Debussy himself had made such changes or that they had been made with his consent*[1] the publisher stated that *all discrepancies between our editions and the manuscripts in the Bibliothèque Nationale were sanctioned by Claude Debussy*[2]. A subsequent enquiry to the same effect brought no additional information to light[3].

As it transpired, the appearance of the first volume of the *Œuvres complètes de Claude Debussy*[4] published jointly by Durand and Costallat showed that galley proofs corrected by Debussy himself did after all exist for the two volumes of the *Préludes* (and hence in all likelihood for other compositions)[5]. In many cases these proofs shed light on the origins and authenticity of the textual divergences. It is on the one hand highly regrettable that the present edition was not able to draw on this important source material. On the other hand, however, the Wiener Urtext Edition of the *Préludes I* (UT 50105), which appeared before the equivalent Durand/Costallat edition, succeeded on the basis of "circumstantial evidence" in reconstructing a textual reading which came close to that in Roy Howat's and Claude Helffer's volume of the complete edition, although the latter had been able to consult all the source material. It therefore seems reasonable to assume that subsequent volumes of the Wiener Urtext Edition of Debussy's piano music will be in a position to provide authoritative textual readings even without reference to the entire source material.

What is more, the galley proofs corrected by Debussy do not account for every discrepancy between the autograph manuscript and the First Edition. Some must presumably be attributed to errors on the part of the engraver or the publisher's proofreader which escaped the composer's attention, either because he overlooked them while he was correcting the galley proofs or because he never saw the proofs.

On source which sheds significant light on this question is Debussy's correspondence with his publisher[6], which tells us something about the procedure followed in the publication of his music.

After the manuscript had been sent to the publisher, it was engraved and corrected by the publisher's proofreader. A copy was then sent to Debussy for scrutiny. He appears to have found numerous errors which did not derive from the autograph manuscript: *Herewith the galley proofs of "La Mer". [...] I don't know who is responsible for the quite extraordinary alteration on page 30 of the "Jeux de vagues" (fi-*

gure 33), in the first bar of the bass "seconda". There is an e♯ there which would make interesting listening![7] And, in reference to the *Images* for orchestra: *Kindly find enclosed the corrected galley proofs. Monsieur Roques [the publisher's senior proofreader] has a bizarre habit of drawing attention to the "borderline cases" [...] by simply emending them — as though he knew exactly what he was doing!*[8] Other mistakes appear to have crept in as a result of negligence on the engraver's part. After looking through the proofs for the piano version of the *Images* Debussy wrote: *Be so kind as to implore your engraver not to alter the position of the performance markings. This is of the utmost pianistic significance.*[9] On other occasions Jacques Durand appears to have drawn the composer's attention to discrepancies: *I have returned the proofs of the "Images". They contained relatively few errors; one of your queries proved founded.*[10] It also happened the scruting of the proofs drew Debussy's attention to errors in his own manuscript: *You will see that a bar was omitted on page 8 of the "Jardins sous la pluie" [Estampes]. Incidentally, the mistake was mine; the bar was also missing in my manuscript.*[11] Galley proofs which had been corrected by the composer were stamped *Epreuve corrigée* and — if not submitted for further proofreading — then printed. The galley proofs of the *Préludes* bear the note *Le manuscrit original a été remis à l'auteur*, which indicates that after the engraving, proofreading and final printing the autograph manuscript was returned to the composer[12].

Despite repeated proofreading, however, it was impossible to eliminate errors altogether, particularly in the instrumental parts of the orchestral works, which Debussy may not have corrected: *Incidentally, the parts have been poorly proofread. [...] We [Debussy and the conductor Camille Chevillard] wasted a great deal of time hunting for missing naturals and overlooked slurs.*[13] And in a subsequent letter: *As you are probably aware, the orchestral parts for "Jeux" are full of mistakes. We owe a great dept of gratitude to Pierné, who went through the score with a fine toothcomb. It can safely be said that he didn't miss a thing. Incidentally, while I was writing the corrections into my own copy of the score I came across more mistakes by pure good fortune.*[14] In some instances, though, Debussy seems not have bothered with reading the galley proofs at all: *Since I have the utmost confidence in your sharp-sightedness, I think it is unneccessary for me to go through the proofs before the work is printed.*[15] In reply to Durand's query with regard to metronome markings, Debussy simply wrote: *Do as you think fit.*[16]

In the light of the above quotations it can be said beyond any doubt that, despite the assurances of the Editions Musicales Durand, the divergences between the autograph manuscripts and the First Edition cannot be assumed to derive from alterations *sanctioned by Claude Debussy.* Moreover, although the reprints which Durand has issued contain numerous additional emendations, so many inconsistencies remain that the First Edition and its subsequent reprints can no longer be regarded as definitive primary sources. The present new critical edition sets out to provide a reading of the text which accurately reflects the composer's intentions. Without consulting the galley proofs it is frequently not possible to establish the authenticity of the discrepancies between the First Edition and the autograph manuscript. In view of this, the manuscript and the First Edition have been accorded equal priority as primary sources. However, because Debussy appears generally to have transferred textual alterations which he made in the galley proofs to his own manuscript[17], in borderline cases the present edition follows the reading of the manuscript. This procedure is legitimized by two factors. First, Debussy's decorative but pedantically precise handwriting precludes any doubt about the reading of the manuscripts. Second, piano roll recordings exist of some of the piano music, made by Debussy himself for Welte-Mignon, and a comparison of these recordings with the manuscripts and the First Edition shows that in certain cases Debussy followed the reading of the manuscript rather than that of the First Edition.

There follows a list of the symbols used in the present edition and their connotations:

⟨⟩   All titles, tempo markings, metronome values, performance markings and accidentals which Debussy himself placed in round brackets.
     The composer's own fingering is printed in italics.

( )   All interpolations in the First Edition and subsequent reprints which
    a) are clearly additions or alterations made on the basis of analogy;
    b) are emendations of obvious mistakes or of inadvertent omissions in the autograph manuscript; this does not apply to accidentals, which have been added tacitly where necessary;
    c) were in all probability sanctioned by Debussy — in particular tempo and performance markings which are unlikely to have been arbitrary interpolations on the part of the publisher.
   For the reasons stated above it is not at present possible to establish which, if any, of these additions

were written into the galley proofs by Debussy himself.

[ ]   All additions made by the present editors. These have been inserted with extreme discretion and serve exclusively to clarify the musical text and facilitate its realisation. All staccato dots and note dots added by the editors are given in small print.

With the exception of obvious orthographic errors the orthography has been tacitly emended to comply with that of the autograph manuscript.

Michael Stegemann

[1] Editor's letter, January 4 1981
[2] Letter to the editor, January 19 1981
[3] Editor's letter, July 26 1983 / Letter to the editor, July 28 1983
[4] *Œuvres Complètes de Claude Debussy (Série I, Volume 5): Préludes (Edition de Roy Howat avec la collaboration de Claude Helffer)*, Durand-Costallat, Paris 1985
[5] Cf. ibid., p. 143f.
[6] *Lettres de Claude Debussy à son éditeur (publiées par Jacques Durand)*, Paris 1927
[7] Eastbourne, July 27 1905; loc. cit., p. 30
[8] December 25 1909; loc. cit., p. 81
[9] January 1907; loc. cit., p. 47
[10] September 29 1905; loc. cit., p. 34
[11] Bichain, August 1903; loc. cit., p. 10
[12] *Œuvres Complètes* etc.; loc. cit., p. 143
[13] October 10 1905; *Lettres* etc., loc. cit., p. 36
[14] January 4 1914; loc. cit., p. 119.
[15] Bichain, August 1902; loc. cit., p. 7
[16] Pourville, October 9 1915; loc. cit., p. 158
[17] Cf. *Œuvres Complètes* etc., loc. cit., p. 143

TEMPO INDICATIONS AND PERFORMANCE INSTRUCTIONS

animé	lebhaft	lively
animez	beleben	enliven
assez modéré	ziemlich mäßig	quite moderate
au mouvᵗ. (au mouvement)	im Tempo	in time
avec une grande émotion	mit großer Bewegung	with great feeling
cédez	nachgeben, langsamer werden	give way, become slower
délicatement	zart	delicately
dessus	übersetzen	put the finger over
doux	weich, sanft	soft, gentle
égal et sans sécheresse	gleichmäßig und ohne Härte	evenly and without asperity
en animant peu à peu	nach und nach belebend	enlivening gradually
en conservant le rythme	den Rhythmus beibehaltend	retaining the rhythm
en dehors	hervorgehoben	emphasised
estompé	verwischt	blurred
expressif	ausdrucksvoll	expressive
gauche	linkisch	clumsy
léger et gracieux	leicht und anmutig	light and graceful
léger mais marqué	leicht aber betont	light but emphatic
les 2 Ped.	beide Pedale	both pedals
m. d. (main droite)	rechte Hand	right hand
m. g. (main gauche)	linke Hand	left hand
marqué	betont	emphatic
modéré	mäßig	moderate
modérément animé	mäßig belebt	moderately lively
moins vite	weniger schnell	less fast
net	klar	clearly
plus mouvementé	bewegter	more animated
retenu	zurückgehalten	held back
sans retarder	ohne zu zögern	without hesitation
sans retenir	ohne zurückzuhalten	without holding back
sec	trocken	dry
toujours retenu	(noch) immer zurückgehalten	still held back
très	sehr	very
triste	traurig	sad
un peu	ein wenig	a little

NOTES ON INTERPRETATION

In selecting the fingering the prime consideration – assuming a hand of normal proportions – was to provide for a light and supple wrist which would to a great extent ensure freedom of touch. It seems to me that the technique of substitution is a preferable alternative to the use of the right (forte) pedal, allowing as it does real legato playing and in many cases a relaxation of the hand. If the present edition contains only few markings to this effect, then primarily to avoid typographic confusion.

These brief suggestions apart, one should never forget the precept which Debussy himself expounded in the Preface to the two books of his *Etudes* as the last word on the question: *Each person is his own best schoolmaster. Let us look for our fingering ourselves.* With considerable humour and more than a hint of real concern Debussy castigated the possible misuse of the forte pedal in his music: *It is perhaps quite simply a fact that the excessive use of the pedal serves only to disguise inadequate technique, and that a great deal of noise is necessary to prevent the music which is being massacred from being heard.*

For obvious reasons, then, the editor of the present edition has dispensed with pedal markings. The subtlety and precision required for the correct use of the pedals inevitably presuppose vague markings which would be detrimental to the tonal balance.

The use of the third (sostenuto) pedal – although admittedly tempting – also involves certain dangers: in the majority of cases the advantages gained in terms of clarity are outweighed by the impairment of the tonal beauty of the music.

A judicious and never excessive application of the three pedals should help to place Debussy somewhere between Monet, Seurat and Turner – at a considerable distance from that brand of "impressionism" which a distorted tradition has attempted to establish as the label for his musical world. This view is substantiated by Debussy's famous remark on Louis Leroy's "insight" as outlined above: *I try to create something different – in a sense realities – and these imbeciles call it "impressionism", a term which could not be used more inappropriately, especially by the art critics . . .*

Children's Corner is a work whose realisation is considerably more mature than its subject-matter would suggest. The most daunting problem for the performer must be the evocation of the child's psychological world with all its secrets and dreams. On the one hand the fantastic visions and emotional poignancy of this "fairytale world of the mind" need to be conveyed, while on the other hand any suggestion of tonal indulgence as called for in romantic piano music would be out of place in these miniatures.

Debussy attached great significance to the extreme simplicity of the means which Modest Mussorgsky used to evoke the brief scenes of childhood in his song-cycle *Nursery.* This same simplicity, combined with a complete and never self-conscious ingenuousness, is one of the keys to the interpretation of *Children's Corner.*

I. – Doctor Gradus ad Parnassum undoubtedly requires a far more controlled command of the keyboard than, say, the études of Czerny or Clementi. The marking *modérément animé* – which should of course be observed within reasonable subjective limits – demands a more complete technical mastery. The immensely precise markings anticipate the pointillism of the *Etudes.*

II. – Jimbo's Lullaby evokes an atmosphere of tenderness and intimacy. The dynamic range must not go beyond mezzoforte. Here again only the precise observation of the markings, the rhythmic values and the phrasing can lend the piece its true poignancy and lead plausibly to the ending which Debussy seems to have composed as a parallel to his comments on Mussorgsky's *With the Doll: The end of this lullaby is so gently soporific that the little narrator falls asleep over her own stories.*

III. – Serenade for (of) the Doll is clearly far removed from the vehemence of the *Sérénade interrompue* of the first book of *Préludes.* The graceful plucking of the guitar strings is obviously bound to pose problems of transparency which can be surmounted only by dispensing almost completely with the forte pedal and judiciously allocating the weight of the music. In the light of today's more brilliant instruments Debussy's instructions on the use of the left pedal are even more indispensable than they were in 1908.

IV. – The snow is dancing is much more a monotone and icy counterpart to *Jardins sous la pluie* (*Gardens in the Rain* from *Estampes*) than the "meteorological companion piece" to *Brouillards* (*Fog* from the second book of *Préludes*). In other words: no use of the forte pedal; at most the occasional tenuto note should be made to linger by slight pressure of the right foot. Half pedal is enough, otherwise the snowflakes turn into drizzle. The entire piece should be suffused with a gnawing yet dreamy and nostalgic monotony, with the exception of the tentative gesture of rebellion in bars 50 to 54. From bar 61 onwards I have recommended crossing the right hand over the left, which allows a greater fluency in bars 65 to 68.

V. – The little Shepherd reveals three psychological planes on which the shepherd delivers his simple song. Each transition naturally requires a new expressive mood. The first plane (bars 1 to 4) introduces the narration which is to follow. The second plane, considerably less personal, presents the song itself in all its simplicity and ingenuousness (bars 5 to 11 and 21 to 31, with bars 21 to 26 forming the expressive and emotional consequence of bars 12 to 20). The third plane, unquestionably the most moving and personal, shows us the shepherd boy becoming identified with the hero of his song. Its style is highly declamatory and keen-edged, with an inflated tone. Together with *Jimbo's Lullaby* this piece, by virtue of its poignancy, is without a doubt the most intense and emotionally charged of the whole cycle.

VI. – Golliwogg's cake walk poses few interpretative problems despite what Alfred Cortot called its *jerky and ungainly* manner. At the time jazz was just emerging, but today its rhythms and accentuation are part of the stock-in-trade of any young pianist whose mentors have been Igor Stravinsky and Duke Ellington. The irony of this observation is in keeping with Debussy's "hommage" to Wagner in the central section, where he juxtaposes and superimposes the opening bars of *Tristan* and a snappy humour typical of the *Minstrels* (from the first book of *Préludes*). The little black doll takes his revenge.

Michel Béroff

PREFACE

In terms of their dates of composition and of their musical diction the *Deux Arabesques* are roughly contemporary with a large number of other piano compositions by Debussy which still bear witness to the influence of their romantic antecedents: *Ballade slave, Danse, Fantaisie pour piano et orchestre, Mazurka, Nocturne, Rêverie, Suite bergamasque* (which contains the celebrated *Clair de lune*), *Tarentelle styrienne* and *Valse romantique*. Like these compositions, the *Arabesque* (whose manuscript is undated) belong to the end of the eighties or early nineties. The date 1888 given by some biographers is, however, probably too early; the signature *Cl. A. Debussy* (The *A* stand for the composer's second Christian name Achille) which also appears on the manuscript of the *Arabesques* does not occure before 1890[1].

As early as 1839 Robert Schumann entitled his piano piece opus 18 *Arabesque*. French usage invests the word with two meanings; on the one hand a decorative ornament in painting or sculpture, and on the other hand one of the positions in classical ballet[2]. Debussy will probably have had both connotations in mind; the ornamental device of the type found in the composition of the paintings by Antoine Watteau (which left their mark on other compositions dating from the same period; the *Ariettes oubliées*, the *Suite bergamasque* and above all *L'Isle joyeuse*), and the dance element – it is worth remembering that the second *Arabesque* was performed as a ballet on May 23 1894[3].

Durand & Schoenewerk published the *Deux Arabesques* in a small edition in October 1891. It was reprinted in 1904 (with some engraving errors emended; cf. Critical Notes). The pieces achieved such popularity that Durand commissioned one Henri Mouton to arrange them (and other piano pieces by Debussy) for chamber orchestra. Debussy himself appears to have entertained a poor opinion of Mouton's craftsmanship; certainly he had grave reservations about the latter's arrangement of *La plus que lente*, writing: *I am sure that Monsieur Mouton is a master of his craft, and I do not wish to cause him any distress, but their are several instances of ineptitude which could easily be remedied.*[4]

Debussy did not himself make a gramophone recording of the *Deux Arabesques*, but we do possess a recording (dating from 1930) by the French pianist Marguerite Long, who was acquainted with the composer and may therefore be regarded as an "authentic" interpreter of his music.

Michael Stegemann

© 1988 by Wiener Urtext Edition, Musikverlag Ges. m. b. H. & Co., K. G., Wien.

Used by Permission

[1] Cf. inter alia François Lesure: *Debussy – Iconographie musicale*, Geneva 1980, p.20f.
[2] *Grand Larousse encyclopédique I*, Paris 1960, entry entitled *Arabesque*
[3] Cf. Marcel Dietschy: *La Passion de Claude Debussy*, Neuchâtel 1962, p. 80
[4] Letter from Debussy to Jacques Durand, August 25 1910; in *Lettres de Claude Debussy à son éditeur (publiées par Jacques Durand)*, Paris 1927, p. 90

NOTES ON INTERPRETATION

In selecting the fingering the primary consideration – assuming a hand of normal proportions – was to provide for a light and supple wrist which would to a great extent ensure freedom of touch. It seems to me that the technique of substitution is a preferable alternative to the use of the right (forte) pedal, allowing as it does real legato playing and in many cases a relaxation of the hand. If the present edition contains only few markings to this effect, then primarily to avoid typographic confusion.

This brief suggestions apart, one should never forget the precept which Debussy himself expounded in the Preface to the two books of his *Etudes* as the last word on the question: *Each person is his own best instructor. Let us discover our fingering ourselves.* With considerable humour and more than a hint of genuine concern Debussy castigated the possible misuse of the forte pedal in his music: *It is perhaps quite simply a fact that the excessive use of the pedal serves only to disguise inadequate technique, and that a great deal of noise is necessary to cover up the sound of the music being massacred.*

For obvious reasons, then, the editor of the present edition has dispensed with pedal markings. The subtlety and precision required for the correct use of the pedals inevitably presuppose vague markings which would be detrimental to the tonal balance.

The use of the third (sostenuto) pedal – although admittedly tempting – also entails certain dangers: in the majority of cases the advantages gained in terms of clarity are outweighed by the impairment of the music's tonal beauty.

A judicious and discreet application of the three pedals should ensure that Debussy takes his places somewhere between Monet, Seurat and Turner – at all events at a considerable distance from that brand of "impressionism" which a distorted tradition has attempted to establish as the label for his musical world. This view is substantiated by Debussy's famous remark on Louis Leroy's "insight" as outlined above: *I try to create something different – realities in a sense – and these imbeciles call it "impressionism", a term which could hardly be more inappropriate, especially as it is used by the art critics...*

In performing these two *Arabesques* the player should seek to achieve an interplay of subtle emotions: on the one hand the delicate drawing of the melodic lines in the first piece; on the other hand the seemingly status quo dance character of the second. The "Divine Arabesque", which so accurately mirrors Debussy's subjective world, has its essence – like the ornamental devices of Arabic art – in the fusion of apparent freedom and geometrical regularity.

Première Arabesque

From the very first bars Debussy unravels the fine thread which will guide us to the heart of the labyrinth. Then in the manner of a troubadour he signs us his courtly lay (bars 39–71), first bashfully, then wistfully and finally with great intensity (bars 63–67). Finally he beckons us to retrace our steps, following the mythological thread back until we come in sight of the light-filled entrance.

The A-B-A structure which results from this sequence will also pervade the second *Arabesque*.

Even at this stage we find Debussy devoting minute attention to the details of his notation, so that even the most unobtrusive of markings is of demonstrable musical significance. For these reason the markings must be followed exactly if the fragile delicacy of these miniatures is to be conveyed. Soft-grained as the melodic contours may be, they need to be articulated with great clarity – avoiding excessive use of the pedal at all costs – to bring out the harmonic lines. In the same way the interplay of phrasing between the left and right hands must articulate the contrapuntal intricacies of the two voices.

Deuxiéme Arabesque

The dance-like character, the succession of feather-light pirouettes and the sardonic humour of the second *Arabesque* anticipate the world of such *Préludes* as *Minstrels* or *Général Lavine, eccentric*.

As in the preceding piece, Debussy exploits the piano's capacity for tone-colour and evokes a wide range of subtle orchestral sounds.

Even less use should be made of the pedal in this work than in the first *Arabesque*. Exceptions are the passages bars 50-58 (with their warmer, more earthy tone-colour), bars 82-90 (in which time seems to stand still), and finally the coda whose jovial good humour culminates in a tongue-in-cheek self-glorification bordering on kitsch.

The miniature pirouettes of semiquavers must be played with an exact regard for their rhythm so that they do not sound like accented mordents on the upbeat.

In bar 7 particular attention needs to be paid to the two crescendo forks, which will become a striking characteristic of Debussy's notation in his subsequent music.

The semibreve, minim and quaver rests are a vital component in the pulse and breathing of the music.

Michel Béroff

Claude Debussy: Préludes Book I

INDEX

PREFACE

Claude Debussy composed the first book of his *Préludes* for piano in a remarkably short space of time: between the beginning of December 1909 and the beginning of February 1910. They thus belong to a period in which the composer was principally preoccupied with two – albeit unfinished – stage works. One was the opera *La chute de la maison Usher*, for which Debussy had himself written the libretto based on Edgar Allan Poe's story *The Fall of the House of Usher* (or more precisely, on the French translation thereof by Charles Baudelaire, published in 1857). Debussy's preoccupation with this material goes back at least as far as January 1890, and even in the last months of his life he would still entertain hopes of being able to complete the work. With the second project, a ballet score which Serge de Diaghilev had commissioned from Debussy for his celebrated Ballets russes, he did not get beyond planning some of the titles (*Masques et bergamasques*, *L'Eternelle aventure* and *L'Amour masqué*) and sketching out his own scenario. Thus, the only major work, besides the *Préludes*, which dates from 1910 is the *Trois Ballades de François Villon*.

The dates given for nine of the twelve *Préludes* of the first book in Debussy's manuscript allow us to reconstruct a reasonably accurate chronological genesis. Although Durand published the pieces in one volume in 1910, Debussy does not appear to have conceived the *Préludes* necessarily as a continuous cycle. Certainly they were not intended for concert performance but for playing in private, as the composer once remarked; and they were first performed in groups and not in any strict chronological sequence. The following table lists the individual *Préludes* with, in each case, the date of composition and the date, location and pianist of the first performance.

– *I.* ⟨... *Danseuses de Delphes*⟩
7. 12. 1909 / 25. 5. 1910 – S.M.I.[1] – Claude Debussy

– *II.* ⟨... *Voiles*⟩
12. 12. 1909 / 25. 5. 1910 – S.M.I. – Claude Debussy

– *III.* ⟨... *Le Vent dans la plaine*⟩
11. 12. 1909 / 29. 3. 1911 – S.M.I. – Claude Debussy

– *IV.* ⟨... *"Les sons et les parfums tournent dans l'air du soir"*⟩
1. 1. 1910 / 29. 3. 1911 – S.M.I. – Claude Debussy

– *V.* ⟨... *Les Collines d'Anacapri*⟩
26. 12. 1909 / 14. 1. 1911 – S.N.[2] – Ricardo Viñes

– *VI.* ⟨... *Des pas sur la neige*⟩
27. 12. 1909 / 29. 3. 1911 – S.M.I. – Claude Debussy

– *VII.* ⟨... *Ce qu'a vu le vent d'Ouest*⟩
undated / first performance not ascertainable

– *VIII.* ⟨... *La Fille aux cheveux de lin*⟩
15.–16. 1. 1910 / 14. 1. 1911 – S.N. – Ricardo Viñes

– *IX.* ⟨... *La Sérénade interrompue*⟩
undated / 14. 1. 1911 – S.N. – Ricardo Viñes

– *X.* ⟨... *La Cathédrale engloutie*⟩
undated / 25. 5. 1910 – S.M.I. – Claude Debussy

– *XI.* ⟨... *La Danse de Puck*⟩
4. 2. 1910 / 25. 5. 1910 – S.M.I. – Claude Debussy

– *XII.* ⟨... *Minstrels*⟩
5. 1. 1910 / 29. 3. 1911 – S.M.I. – Claude Debussy

At first glance the two books of Debussy's 24 *Préludes* may appear to belong to that tradition of keyboard literature which can be traced back to Johann Sebastian Bach's *Wohltemperiertes Clavier* and was continued in, for instance, Frédéric Chopin's opus 28 (1836/39) and Alexander Scriabin's opus 11 (1888/96).

Certainly all of these cycles share a common numerical framework of 24 preludes which derives logically from the diatonic system (the only 19th century exception being the eccentric Charles-Valentin Alkan and his *25 Préludes* opus 31, dating from 1847). Yet the similarities relate only to the external features of the *Préludes*. Their number is not dictated by a superimposed harmonic scheme – they are in fact only sporadically tonal. Furthermore, Debussy's use of titles and his translation of these into sound and form place the *Préludes* more accurately in the genre of the character piece. It should be noted in this connection that Debussy deliberately put the titles at the end of the individual *Préludes* in order to avoid imposing a constraint on the performer by the immediate suggestive influence of the highly personal headings.

I feel that it is important at this juncture to give a brief account of the non-musical points of departure which Debussy wove into his *Préludes*.

The inspiration for the *Danseuses de Delphes* ("Delphic Dancers") will have been the photograph which the composer discovered in the Louvre depicting a section of a frieze from the temple of Apollo in Delphi. The photograph shows three female dancers. The French pianist Marguerite Long recalls Debussy himself playing this piece *slowly and with almost metronomic stringency,* an account which is corroborated by the composer's own recording for the Welte Music Rolls.

Voiles ("Sails" or "Veils") is a further hommage to the sea, written some five years after the symphonic triptych *La Mer.* The composer pointed out – in refutation of an "impressionist" (mis)interpretation – that *Voiles* is *not a seaside snapshot intended as a picture postcard for August 15th.*

Le Vent dans la plaine ("The Wind on the Plain") can be traced back to Debussy's first volume of *Ariettes oubliées,* composed in 1888. The first of the three poems by Paul Verlaine which Debussy set to music in this cycle – *C'est l'extase langoureuse* from the collection *Romances sans paroles* (1874) – is prefaced by two lines from the verse of Charles-Simon Favart: *Le vent dans la plaine / Suspend son haleine* ("The wind on the plain / Holds its breath").

It was a line from the poem *Harmonie du soir* from Charles Baudelaire's celebrated *Fleurs du mal* (1857) which provided the title of the fourth Prélude: *Les sons et les parfums tournent dans l'air du soir* ("Sounds and fragrances intertwine in the evening air"). Despite the piece's ⁵/₄ time signature there are perceptible traces of the waltz which derive from the Baudelaire line following that quoted in the title: *Valse mélancolique et langoureux vertige!* ("Melancholy waltz and languid dizziness").

Les Collines d'Anacapri ("The Hills of Anacapri") represent Italy. This is the only musical imprint which that country left on Debussy's work – hardly surprisingly when one considers that his stay in the Villa Medici as recipient of the Prix de Rome proved to be little short of a traumatic experience. The overall monotonal nature of the piece may well derive from Neapolitan folkmusic – although it is, of course, far removed from the tarantella form so dear to the romantic virtuosi.

The sixth Prélude, *Des pas sur la neige* ("Footprints in the Snow"), is perhaps the most personal piece in the set. Certainly such instructions to the performer as *ce rythme doit avoir la valeur sonore d'un fond de paysage triste et glacé* ("this rhythm should recapture the tonal quality of the background to a sad and frozen landscape") or *comme un tendre et triste regret* ("like a tender, sad sorrow") appear to constitute more than mere "stage directions". It

is plausible to surmise that the severe illness to which Debussy succumbed on March 25th 1918 and which first became apparent during the period in which he was writing the *Préludes* evoked a musical presentiment of death in the "footprints in the snow" – an intimation which was followed by many others in the composer's letters.

Ce qu'a vu le vent d'Ouest ("What the West Wind has Seen") is the pendant to *Voiles:* the light breeze in the second Prélude has grown into a gale which unleashes its inexorable strength in chromatic progressions and whole-tone scales. Then again, this piece is a logical heightening of the third Prélude, *Le Vent dans la plaine.*

La Fille aux cheveux de lin ("The Girl with the Flaxen Hair") also derives from a poetic source: the *Chanson écossaise* of the same name from Leconte de Lisle's collection *Poèmes antiques* (1845/62). Debussy had made use of this poem as early as 1882, setting it to music as a song which he dedicated to his patroness Marie-Blanche Vasnier. Whereas the song, composed at the age of twenty, was still entirely in the romantic tradition, the protagonist of the later Prélude emerges as a worthy companion in both words and music to the enigmatic Mélisande.

Debussy always kept a special place in his heart for Spain. After the three orchestral movements of *Ibéria* (1905/08, from *Images*) and *La Soirée dans Grénade,* the middle movement of the *Estampes* for piano which had been composed a few years previously, the sounds of the *Sérénade interrompue* ("The Interrupted Serenade") once again transport the listener to the country beyond the Pyrenees. Manuel de Falla gave the following account of the scenario of this piece: two singers are vying with their guitar playing for the favour of a beautiful lady who, concealed behind the flowered trellisses of her window, is attentively observing their amorous rivalry.

La Cathédrale engloutie ("The Submerged Cathedral") goes back to a Breton legend which Debussy chanced upon in Ernest Renan's *Souvenirs d'enfance et de jeunesse* (1883): according to the legend, at daybreak the cathedral of the submerged city of Ys occasionally rises from the waves of the sea of Douarnenez and the chiming of the cathedral bells is heard through the morning mist.

In William Shakespeare's *A Midsummer Night's Dream* Puck is an irrepressible sprite whose acrobatics and escapades are depicted in the brilliant scherzo of *La Danse de Puck* ("Puck's Dance"). This Prélude does not mark Debussy's first preoccupation with the work of the great English dramatist; but the earlier projects – incidental music for *As You Like It* (1902) and *True Chronicle History of the Life and Death of King Lear* (1904) did not progress beyond the initial stages.

Minstrels (here in the American music hall sense) is linked with *Golliwogg's cake walk* from the piano cycle *Children's Corner* (1908). The cakewalk, a traditional dance of the North American negro slaves in syncopated ²/₄ time, had made its European début around 1900 as a forerunner of jazz. It became associated with the atmosphere of the music hall which was in fashion in Paris around the turn of the century. This ensured the popular success of *Minstrels.*

Michael Stegemann

---

[1] The Société Musicale Indépendante, founded by Maurice Ravel and others. Its first concert was held on April 20th 1910 in the Salle Gaveau in Paris; the programme included the first performance of Debussy's piano composition *D'un cahier d'esquisses* (1903) played by Ravel.
[2] The Société Nationale de Musique, constituted on February 25th 1871 by Camille Saint-Saëns and others.

NOTES ON INTERPRETATION

In selecting the fingering the prime consideration – assuming a hand of normal proportions – was to provide for a light and supple wrist which would to a great extent ensure freedom of touch. It seems to me that the technique of substitution is a preferable alternative to the use of the right (forte) pedal, allowing as it does real legato playing and in many cases a relaxation of the hand. If the present edition contains only few markings to this effect, then primarily to avoid typographic confusion.

These brief suggestions apart, one should never forget the precept which Debussy himself expounded in the Preface to the two books of his *Etudes* as the last word on the question: *Each person is his own best schoolmaster. Let us look for our fingering ourselves.* With considerable humour and more than a hint of real concern Debussy castigated the possible misuse of the forte pedal in his music: *It is perhaps quite simply a fact that the excessive use of the pedal serves only to disguise inadequate technique, and that a great deal of noise is necessary to prevent the music which is being massacred from being heard.*

For obvious reasons, then, the editor of the present edition has dispensed with pedal marking. The subtlety and precision required for the correct use of the pedals inevitably presuppose vague markings which would be detrimental to the tonal balance.

The use of the third (sostenuto) pedal - although admittedly tempting – also involves certain dangers: in the majority of cases the advantages gained in terms of clarity are outweighed by the impairment of the tonal beauty of the music.

A judicious and never excessive application of the three pedals should help to place Debussy somewhere between Monet, Seurat and Turner – at a considerable distance from that brand of "impressionism" which a distorted tradition has attempted to establish as the label for his musical world. This view is substantiated by Debussy's famous remark on Louis Lerroy's "insight" as outlined above: *I try to create something different – in a sense realities – and these imbeciles call it "impressionism", a term which could not be used more inappropriately, especially by the art critics ...*

Debussy's comment that it is more important to see a sunrise than to hear the Pastoral Symphony provides a valuable key to the interpretation of his music. And when not with paper but with the ear in mind, that it is not a graphic abstraction but an audible reality, then there can be no mistake: Debussy's music is made up of sounds and colours, and only of those ingredients.

Yet despite their unique pictorial vividness the *Préludes* have nothing whatsoever to do with programme music. What Debussy does is to suggest, to give us access to a wide spectrum of sensory possibilities.

If I have outlined a particular approach to interpreting some of the *Préludes*, it goes without saying that this is only a personal view conditioned by an individual perception and a specific cultural background. After all, the titles of the pieces are intended to achieve their effect only in retrospect.

It is true that Debussy composed the first book of his *Préludes* in under two months and completed such disparate pieces as *Les Collines d'Anacapri* and *Des pas sur la neige* within the space of only two days. Yet this should not be taken as a reason for imbuing the interpretation of the music with an equivalent sense of haste and spontanei-

ty. Any performer who is aware of the metaphysical individuality of phenomena must realise that a time-consuming process of enlightenment lies ahead of him – the more so in a world in which not even "cloud" is necessarily synonymous with "blurred outlines".

– I. ⟨ ... *Danseuses de Delphes*⟩

Debussy opens the first volume of his *Préludes* with an evocation of ancient Greece.

The solemn tenor of the piece, suffused with archaic harmonies, requires that gravity and rhythmic stringency which Debussy himself prescribed. The passages echoing the finger cymbals (bars 8–9 and 16–17) should sound like a succession of concentric, resplendant waves. The final chord is a submissive obeisance, as after the disappointment of hope.

– II. ⟨ ... *Voiles*⟩

Like many symbolists, Debussy was fond of assuming a cloak of enigma and ambivalence. This Prélude is imbued with that kind of ambiguity. Its point of departure is a descending sequence of glissandi which could with equal plausibility evoke either sailing boats on the gentle swell of the ocean or a diaphanous fabric veiling the full voluptuousness of a symbolist painting.

It is extremely important here to achieve a judicious balance in the use of the two pedals, so that the sense of harmonic continuity produced by the insistent recurrence of the whole-tone scale (except bars 42–47) does not lapse into a monotonous and colourless wash of sound. (The first four bars, for instance, should be played with a degree of clarity and legato which suggests the use of two instruments distinguishable from each other.)

The sure path to a correct interpretation is to follow the notation and the dotting exactly, even when they appear to be "unnatural" (in bar 18, for example, which is typical of Debussy's idiosyncratic notation).

– III. ⟨ ... *Le Vent dans la plaine*⟩

This Prélude represents an intermediate stage between the gentle breeze in *Voiles* and the fully-fledged gale of *Ce qu'a vu le vent d'Ouest*. Thus, *Le Vent dans la plaine* must be imagined as a breath verging on incorporeality. The brief gust of wind in the central section should serve to remind us that this Prélude, while complying with Debussy's ideal of "not appearing to have been written down", is still of this world.

Throughout the piece the forte pedal must be used very sparingly so that the undulating movement is achieved solely by the seconds and sevenths. The exact observance of note durations is another ingredient which the aspiring apprentice of musical alchemy will find indispensable.

– IV. ⟨ ... "*Les sons et les parfums tournent dans l'air du soir*"⟩

This is perhaps the most profoundly ambivalent and the most ingenious of all 24 *Préludes;* a harmonic hybrid, toxic in the stupor it induces – *the sun has drowned in its own congealing blood.* Naïve, flaunting an affected modesty which conceals the abyss, the piece as a whole is offered like the forbidden fruit. Its repertoire of pianistic devices

142

is awesome: the music must proceed in figures which swirl and vibrate, the shading of the tone colour must avoid any hint of harshness, and the transitions should be as imperceptible as the dissolved fades of cinematic technique.

Paradoxical though it may seem, the tonal subtleties should exemplify an overtly materialist observation of Debussy's: *Music is the arithmetic of sound, just as optics is the geometry of light.*

– V. ⟨ . . . Les Collines d'Anacapri⟩

This Prélude inhabits a world diametrically opposed to that of the *Fleurs du mal*. The prevailing mood is playful and relaxed, sunny and carefree – an atmosphere which resists even the sombreness of the intruding folksong whose self-indulgent wistfulness will not deceive the player for long. The basic tempo chosen should be slow enough to allow the clearest possible articulation: each chord must be able to unfold its full "spectrum of sunlight" – thus, a maximum of upper partials. In the section marked *Modéré et expressif* the emphatic impact can be further enhanced by playing the appoggiaturas on the beat. Making the coda faster than the preceding music would weaken the effect created by the jubilant rising of the sap which lends the final outburst its vivid and explosive impact.

– VI. ⟨ . . . Des pas sur la neige⟩

Composed one day after *Les Collines d'Anacapri*, this Prélude is convincing testimony – if such were needed – to Debussy's phenomenally fertile flow of creative inspiration: a single being, a patch of snow, the desolation of a survivor in a world that has ended. Twice a glimmer of hope is fanned to life, each time to be stifled in a resurgence of inconsolable and inscrutable sorrow, reminiscent of Mélisande's past: timid, tender resignation in the face of the unknown, a final rearing up before death.

Despite the precautions which Debussy took to avoid an excessively descriptive interpretation of his music (by placing the titles after each Prélude for instance), the suggestive power of his invention proves irresistible.

The slight emphasis of the first bar (◁==▷) and the fading away of the second (==▷) underline the desolation and plaintiveness of the melody and should thus be closely observed. The final bars should convey the extinction of the last breath of life. Only optimists will then turn straight to the next Prélude.

– VII. ⟨ . . . Ce qu'a vu le vent d'Ouest⟩

As a depiction of a veritable hurricane, *Ce qu'a vu le vent d'Ouest* is fundamentally different from anything else which Debussy composed for the piano. Gales, whirlwinds and tornados rage in a world whose all-pervading horror is reminiscent of Edgar Allan Poe.

The turbulence, the sense of bracing for ever more violent onslaughts of the gale require the use of the entire range of dynamics, from pianissimo to fortissimo. The first arpeggios – *pp (animé et tumultueux)* – must be quite different from those at the end – *f (furieux et rapide)*. The crescendi in bars 15–23 (anticipated in *Voiles* and fully unfolded in *Le Vent dans la plaine*) should be played for all they are worth. Such markings as *commencer un peu au-dessus du mouvement, revenir progressivement au mouvement, animé, un peu retenu, en serrant et augmentant beaucoup* and so on should each have their own time scheme, until a fragment of the elf-like theme *(plaintif et lointain)*, which now makes its entry with deep-throated assertiveness, puts an abrupt end to the romantic nightmare.

– VIII. ⟨ . . . La Fille aux cheveux de lin⟩

The return to the unadulterated manner of seeing manifested in Europe's pre-Raphaelite art and advocated in Dante Gabriel Rossetti's *The Blessed Damozel* finds noble and resplendent sublimation in this Prélude. The subject inspired Debussy to create a melodic and harmonic timbre whose origins can be traced back to Celtic times.

Despite the emergent sensuality of some of the harmonic transitions, Leconte de Lisle's *Chanson écossaise* left little poetic imprint on the music. The marking *sans rigueur* on the first bar is to be understood as denoting rather a shy hesitancy than an invitation to indulge in excessive rubato.

To preserve the clarity and transparency of the texture, the performer should use his fingers to achieve legato wherever possible, leaving the pedal to follow the harmonic shifts as required.

– IX. ⟨ . . . La Sérénade interrompue⟩

In the travelogue of the 24 *Préludes*, *La Sérénade interrompue* is the first visit we make to Spain. This is the Spain of passions which are unleashed when two infatuated lovers find themselves courting the same woman: one timid, the other a self-assured ladies' man. The sudden, turbulent course of events is hardly registered by the two serenaders, and it is only when the object of their passion disappears that they lapse into resignation. Nothing short of a musical comedy, then, its humour growing out of repetition. The total demoralization of the closing 13 bars enters a bizarre alliance with something approaching dignity.

The tempo marking *Modérément animé* needs to be observed to allow each string its full resonance *(quasi guitarra)*. The accompanying figures of the serenade are muted – as is only appropriate for instruments of limited resonance – but they must always be absolutely regular. The element of surprise in the incidents – the first surreptitious, the other two tumultuous *(rageur)*; note the difference in the dotting by comparison with the first entry in bar 19 – should be achieved by a suddenness of both dynamics and gesture. The final rubato needs to be even more insipid and supplicating than before. The use of the pedal should likewise be "interrompue" throughout, except where Debussy specifies otherwise (bar 25).

– X. ⟨ . . . La Cathédrale engloutie⟩

Even before the first notes of this Prélude are heard, the typography anticipates its robust architecture and its varied arch forms, the rounded arch predominating. Beneath the vaults of sound the reverberations of mysticism and pagan ritual alternate in a pageant echoing the Breton legend of the submerged city of Ys.

The four major elements – water, air (the organ), stone and metal (the bells) – must each be represented by a specific basic timbre, while the play of light and shade (the cathedral rises from the waves at the first light of dawn) provides scope for nuances of tone colour.

A clear distinction needs to be made between the reverberations of bars 7–13 and the first shuddering of the submerged bells (the insistent E). From bar 16 onwards the first rays of the sun should be heard breaking through and glittering on the emergent arches. The left hand draws in mountains and valleys like a rolling wave, until the cathedral has fully appeared, triumphant and magical like the sword Excalibur which rises from the waters of the lake.

Bars 47–67 are pervaded by a feeling of religious penitence whose hope and plea for forgiveness are answered only by two sombre chimes of the death knell (bars 68–69). Right up to the final rays of light (the first chords of bars 85, 86 und 87) the left hand (*flottant et sourd*) should retain a largely transparent tone colour.

– XI. ⟨ . . . *La Danse de Puck*⟩

The virtuosity and inventiveness with which Debussy recreates the figure of Puck in no way falls short of Shakespeare's original, the humorous mischief-maker and spirit of the night.

The incandescence of this will-o'-the-wisp is brilliantly captured in the constantly rebounding dotted rhythms (as a careful scrutiny of the disparities in the first six bars will illustrate). The full effect of this can be achieved only by maintaining a moderate tempo and almost completely foregoing the use of the forte pedal.

The many detailed crescendi and decrescendi in this Prélude can be slightly overdrawn to reinforce the evanescent character of the music.

During the last ten bars, before Oberon's horn call, one might almost be tempted to feel sorry for Puck, if only his wistfulness were not just another form of whimsical humour presaging his disappearance into thin air.

– XII. ⟨ . . . *Minstrels*⟩

In *Hommage à Samuel Pickwick Esq., P.P.M.P.C.*, Debussy proved himself to be a great admirer and connoisseur of English humour. In *Minstrels*, which could have been inspired by the English theatrical clown tradition but more probably drew on the ensembles of black musicians in the days when jazz was being born, we hear the same wry humour flirting with the earliest manifestations of ragtime. This Prélude relies for its effect entirely upon pretence and make-believe. The necessary contrasts involve less the dynamics than the poise of the music-making.

In the opening bars the occasional flirtatiousness of the tempo may expose a preposterous affectation, but from bar 9 onwards only stringency will convey the real humour (the small trumpet in bars 16 and 17 must be clearly audible).

Having already assumed a derisory pose, Debussy becomes almost overbearing in bar 63, although the humour is markedly less caustic than in the *Tristan* quotation in *Golliwogg's cake walk.*

The "swinging" syncopations (bars 28–31) and the scene with the toy soldiers (bars 58–62 and later 81–84) demonstrate that *Minstrels*, while perhaps not the most inventive of the first twelve *Préludes*, is certainly the most childlike; and it is this quality which leaves the imprint of innocence on the whole volume.

Michel Béroff

TEMPO INDICATIONS AND PERFORMANCE INSTRUCTIONS

aérien	luftig	airy
allant	munter	lively
angoissé	ängstlich, erschreckt	anxious
animé	lebhaft	with animation
augmentant beaucoup	sehr viel stärker werdend (crescendo molto)	becoming much stronger
augmentez	stärker werden (crescendo)	becoming stronger
au mouvᵗ. (au mouvement)	im Tempo	in time
aussi légèrement que possible	so leicht wie möglich	as light as possible
avec la liberté d'une chanson populaire	mit der Freiheit eines Volksliedes	with the freedom of a popular song
calme	ruhig	calm
capricieux	launig	whimsical
cédez	nachgeben, langsamer werden	slow down
ce rythme doit avoir la valeur sonore d'un fond de paysage triste et glacé	dieser Rhythmus soll den Klangcharakter des Hintergrunds einer traurigen und vereisten Landschaft haben	this rhythm should have the tonal quality of the background of a sad and icebound landscape
comme en préludant	wie ein Vorspiel	like a prelude
commencer un peu au-dessous du mouvement	etwas unter dem Tempo beginnen	begin slightly slower than the prevailing tempo
comme un écho de la phrase entendue précédemment	wie ein Echo der vorher gehörten Phrase	like an echo of the preceding phrase
comme une lointaine sonnerie de cors	wie ein fernes Hornsignal	like a distant horn call
comme un tendre et triste regret	wie ein zärtliches und trauriges Bedauern	like a tender and wistful sadness
comme un très léger glissando	wie ein sehr leichtes Glissando	like a very delicate glissando
concentré	dicht, verdichtet	concentrated
dans la sonorité du début	im Klangcharakter des Anfangs	in the tone colour of the opening
dans le mouvᵗ.	im Tempo	in time
dans une brume doucement sonore	in einem weich klingenden Nebel	in a softly sonorous mist
dans une expression allant grandissant	mit immer stärker werdendem Ausdruck	with steadily increasing expression
dans un rythme sans rigueur et caressant	schmeichelnd und frei im Rhythmus	in an affectionate, flexible rhythm
détaché	abgestoßen (staccato)	staccato
doucement	leicht, ein wenig	softly
douloureux	schmerzlich	painful
doux	weich, sanft	soft
égal	gleichmäßig	evenly
emporté	aufbrausend	volatile
en animant	belebend	becoming more lively
en cédant	nachgebend, langsamer werdend	becoming slower
encore plus lointain	noch ferner	more distant
en dehors	hervorgehoben	stressed
en retenant	zurückgehalten	restrained
en s'éloignant	sich entfernend	becoming more distant
en serrant	schneller werdend	becoming faster
estompé et en suivant l'expression	verwischt und im Ausdruck angepaßt	blurred in outline and suited to the expression
expressif	ausdrucksvoll	expressive
flottant et sourd	fließend und dumpf	flowing and muffled
fluide	fließend	fluent
furieux	wütend	furious
fuyant	flüchtig, sich schnell entfernend	fleeting, rapidly receding
grave	schwer	heavy
harmonieux	klangvoll	sonorous
incisif	schneidend, grell	incisive
joyeux	fröhlich, lustig	joyful
la basse un peu appuyée et soutenue	der Baß leicht betont und tenuto	the bass slightly accented and sustained

French	German	English
laissez vibrer	(aus)klingen lassen	allow to fade
léger	leicht	light
lent	langsam	slow
les deux Pédales	beide Pedale	both pedals
les «gruppetti» sur le temps	die Vorschläge auf der Zählzeit	the appoggiaturas on the beat
librement	frei	freely
lointain	fern	distant
lumineux	strahlend	radiant
m.d. (main droite)	rechte Hand	right hand
m.g. (main gauche)	linke Hand	left hand
mais	aber	but
marqué	betont	accented, stressed
modéré	mäßig	moderate
modérément	mäßig	moderately
moqueur	spöttisch	derisive
mouv^t. (mouvement)	Tempo	tempo
murmuré	geflüstert	whispered
nerveux et avec humour	energisch und humorvoll	excitable and humorous
peu	wenig	a little, slightly
peu à peu	allmählich	gradually
plaintif	klagend	plaintive
plus	mehr	more
plus lent	langsamer	slower
presque	fast	almost
pressez	drängen, schneller werden	speed up
profondément	völlig	profoundly
progressivement	mehr und mehr	progressively
quittez, en laissant vibrer	(die Tasten) loslassen und (aus)klingen lassen	release and allow to fade
rageur	wütend	raging
rapide	schnell	fast
retenu	zurückgehalten	restrained
revenir au mouv^t.	zum Tempo zurückkehren	return to the tempo
sans nuances	ohne Abstufungen	without nuances
sans lourdeur	ohne Schwerfälligkeit	without heaviness
sans presser	ohne zu drängen	without rushing
sans rigueur	ohne Härte	without harshness
sec	trocken	dry
serrez	(das Tempo) anziehen, schneller werden	more compactly
sonore sans dureté	klangvoll ohne Härte	sonorous without harshness
sortant de la brume	aus dem Nebel auftauchend	emerging from the mist
souple	weich	pliant, lithe
soutenu	ausgehalten (tenuto)	tenuto, sustained
strident	grell	strident
suppliant	bittend	imploring
surtout dans l'expression	vor allem im Ausdruck	above all in the expression
tendre	zärtlich	tender
toujours	stets, weiterhin	still
tranquille et flottant	ruhig und schwebend	calm and weightless
très	sehr	very
très apaisé et très atténué jusqu'à la fin	bis zum Schluß sehr ruhig und sehr gemildert	very peaceful and subdued to the end
très peu	sehr wenig	very little
triste	traurig	sad
tumultuèux	wild	tumultuous
un peu	ein wenig	a little
un peu moins	etwas weniger	a little less
vif	lebhaft	lively

Claude Debussy: Préludes Book II

INDEX

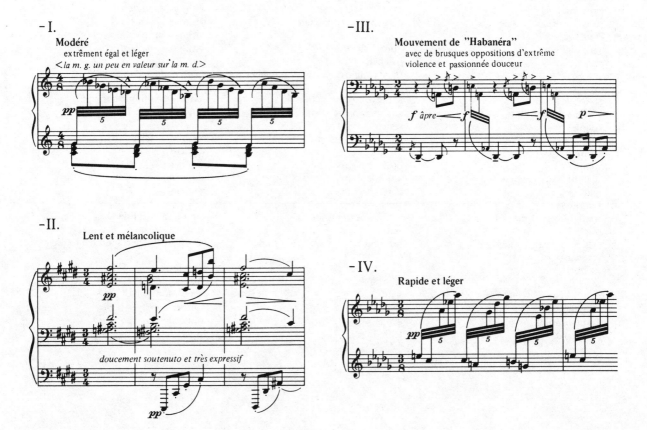

-V.

Calme - Doucement expressif $\langle \,\downarrow = 66 \rangle$

-VI.

Dans le style et le Mouvement d'un Cake - Walk

-VII.

Lent

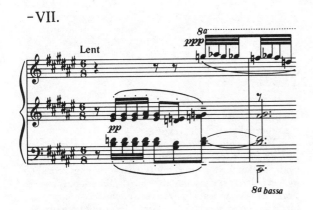

-VIII.

Scherzando

-IX.

Grave

-X.

Très calme et doucement triste

-XI.

Moderémént Animé

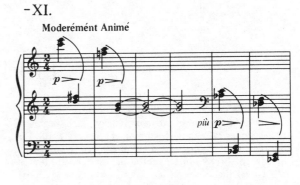

-XII.

Modérément animé

Léger, égal et lointain

PREFACE

The first volume of the *Préludes* was composed within the remarkably short time of two months (between the beginning of December 1909 an the beginning of February 1910). Debussy worked on the second volume, by contrast, for the best part of three years. Unlike the manuscript of the first set of *Préludes*, that of the second is not dated. It would appear, however, that Debussy began the sketches to the second volume soon after completing the first — in the spring of 1910. Partial autograph scores of *Brouillards* and *Feuilles mortes* (cf. Critical Notes) date from late (December) 1911 or early 1912. At the beginning of 1913 Debussy wrote to his publisher that he had in the meantime received *the two new Préludes*, and he adds: *I am working on the last two, but it is a dreadful amount of writing*[1]. This sentence might be an allusion to *Feux d'artifice*. Another letter to Durand followed on January 7th 1913: *My dear Jacques, you would have received the two missing Préludes long ago if I hadn't got my teeth into Tomai des Eléphants, which will never do as a Prélude! I have already started looking for a substitute, and the whole thing will be forwarded to you towards the end of this week*[2]. The piece which would *never do as a Prélude* (of which there is no trace) was clearly intended to be a musical setting of Rudyard Kipling's short story *Toomai of the Elephants*. Debussy possibly had *Les Tierces alternées* in mind as its *substitute*. This is the only *Prélude* in the second volume which does not bear a programmatic-evocative title. It also differs from the others slightly in its texture.

The seventh *Prélude La Terrasse des audiences du clair de lune*, poses specific problems. There is incontrovertible evidence that the manuscript was used as the engraver's copy, yet it diverges substantially from the final published version. Debussy appears to have revised the piece shortly before it appeared in print. Yet neither the proofs of the earlier version nor a manuscript of the revision have come to light.

Another unsolved puzzle relates to a note in Debussy's hand in an undated sketchbook: *Pour le 2d l*[ivre] *de Préludes, Paganini! (dans la technique du violon)*[3]. Not one of the twelve *Préludes* appears to represent the realisation of this plan.

Durand must have received the missing *Préludes* soon after Debussy's letter, because a de luxe edition of both volumes appeared in mid-March[4]. The bound edition of *Livre II* followed in mid-April. The pieces received their first performances one after the other in the course of 1913:

- I.   ... *Brouillards*
         5. 3. 1913 — Salle Érard — Claude Debussy
- II.   ... *Feuilles mortes*
         5. 3. 1913 — Salle Érard — Claude Debussy
- III. ... *La Puerta del vino*
         5. 3. 1913 — Salle Érard — Claude Debussy

— IV.   ... *"Les Fées sont d'exquises danseuses"*
          5. 4. 1913 — S.N.[5] — Ricardo Viñes
— V.   ... *Bruyères*
          8. 4. 1913 — Salle Érard — Norah Drewett
— VI.   ... *"General Lavine"⟨eccentric⟩*
          8. 4. 1913 — Salle Érard — Norah Drewett
— VII.   ... *La Terrasse des audiences du clair de lune*
          5. 4. 1913 — S. N. — Ricardo Viñes
— VIII.   ... *Ondine*
          5. 12. 1913 — Salle Pleyel — Jane Mortier
— IX.   ... *Hommage à S. Pickwick Esq. P.P.M.P.C.*
          19. 6. 1913 — "Gala Claude Debussy" — Claude Debussy
— X.   ... *Canope*
          19. 6. 1913 — "Gala Claude Debussy" — Claude Debussy
— XI.   ... *Les tierces alternées*
          unknown
— XII.   ... *Feux d'artifice*
          5. 4. 1913 — S. N. — Ricardo Viñes

It may seem at first sight as though the two volumes of Debussy's *Préludes* — 24 in all — were an extension of a tradition of keyboard composition which began with Johann Sebastian Bach's *Wohltemperiertes Clavier* and continued with Frédéric Chopin's Opus 28 (1836/39) and Alexander Scrjabin's Opus 11 (1888/96). All three works subscribe to the same numerical scheme of 24 dictated by the diatonic system. (The only exception in the nineteenth century was the eccentric Charles-Valentin Alkan and his *25 Préludes* Opus 31, dating from 1847.) The similarities are, however, purely superficial. In the first instance, Debussy's *Préludes* do not number 24 because they conform to a preconceived harmonic scheme — they are only occasionally tonal. Moreover, the fact that they have titles which they translate into tonal and formal terms assigns them more accurately to the genre of the character piece. It should also be noted that Debussy deliberately placed the titles after the *Préludes* in order to avoid exposing the performer to the immediate influence of these subjective headings.

In the second volume the range of Debussy's tonal articulation is by and large broader than in the first. This is reflected even in the notation. Whereas the *Préludes* of the first volume were generally notated on just two staves, Debussy distributes the pieces in the second volume over three staves almost throughout. (In the first three *Préludes* the bar lines even extend over four staves, although one was left blank.)

Another distinction between the two volumes is the influence of Igor Stravinsky on the second — most notably of Stravinsky's ballet scores *Petrushka* and *Le sacre du printemps*, which Debussy greatly admired[6]. Howat and Helffer have rightly noted the similarities between bars 11ff of *Les tierces alternées* and a section in Stravinsky's *Petrushka*, and bars 75—84 of the same *Prélude* are reminiscent of *Le sacre du printemps*[7]. All in all the second volume of *Préludes* constitutes the logical link between the middle-period piano compositions, the late triptych *En blanc et en noir* (for two pianos, June/July 1915) and the twelve *Etudes* (August/September 1915).

As with the twelve *Préludes* of the first volume, so too the second set of *Préludes* can be related to more or less precise non-musical models.

Brouillards ("Fog") is a bitonal and in some passages polytonal study in sound reminiscent of the natural mysticism of *Le vent dans la plaine*, *Les sons et les parfums tournent dans l'air du soir* and *Ce qu'a vu le vent d'Ouest* in the first volume — although in this case there is no objective correlative in the form of a line of verse.

Feuilles mortes ("Dead Leaves" or "Dead Sheets") might have been inspired by the volume of verse *Voix éparses: adagios, feuilles mortes, croquis rêvés* by the symbolist poet Gabriel Mourey (1883). On the other hand the title recalls *Cloches à travers les feuilles* from the second volume of the *Images* for piano: the "bell chords" seem to sound even through the withered foliage ...

It has long been established that *La Puerta del vino* was inspired by a picture postcard showing one of the Moorish gateways of the Alhambra in Granada. What remains unclear is whether the postcard in question was that sent to Debussy by Manuel de Falla (on which the monument, adorned with coloured reliefs and darkened by the shadows of tall trees, contrasts with a sunlit path whose perspective is extended on the other side of the arched gateway) or a different postcard — with a similar illustration — which the composer received from the pianist Ricardo Viñes[8]. Certainly, this *Prélude* is not (like *La sérénade interrompue* in the first volume) a genre piece focusing on movement but rather a static, as it were "architectural" documentation of Debussy's searing, unfulfilled longing for Spain.

At Christmas 1912 the composer's daughter Claude-Emma ("Chouchou"), then seven years old, received as a gift from the conductor Robert Godet an illustrated children's book: J. M. Barrie's *Peter Pan in Kensington Garden* (1906), containing the *art nouveau* illustrations by Arthur Rackham. One of the illustrations took its title from a line in the text: *Fairies are exquisite dancers*[9]. Debussy managed to capture the tiny 's balancing act perfectly in his music — with the right hand playing on the black keys, the left hand on the white keys. Shortly before the end of the piece (bars 117—120) we seem to hear the call of the magic horn from Weber's *Oberon* sounding from afar. Debussy knew the opera well enough to have quoted from it[10].

Bruyères ("Briars") is — like *Brouillards* and *Feuilles mortes* — a tonal study imbued with natural mysticism and, in the pentatonic shapes of its melodic structure, reminiscent of Breton (Celtic) folksong. No specific model has been identified for this *Prélude*.

In August 1910 (and again in 1912) the American clown Edward Lavine (who died in 1946) appeared at the Théâtre Marigny in Paris. The posters billed him as Général Ed Lavine, the man who spent his entire life as a soldier. Lavine's comedy act, in which he moved about the stage like a wooden doll, consisted of various episodes: a tightrope walk, playing the piano with his toes, a duel with himself and so on. The echo of these numbers is audible in Debussy's portrait of the "eccentric" comedian. The negro song *The Camptown Races*, which is quoted in bars 51/52 and 63/64, was probably part of Lavine's comedy routine. In an article in the *San Francisco Chronicle* in 1945 Alfred Frankenstein asserted that Debussy had actually been asked to compose a lengthy incidental score for Lavine's comedy act[11]. It is thus conceivable that this *Prélude* was part of (or a sketch for) a longer score, although no trace of it has come down to us.

In the case of *La Terrasse des audiences du clair de lune* ("The Terrace of the Moonlight Audiences") — the counterpart of *Et la lune descend sur le temple qui fut* from the second volume of the *Images* for piano — there are two possible sources. One is Pierre Loti's *L'Inde sans les Anglais* (1903), which contains a reference to *des terrasses pour tenir conseil au clair de lune* ("terraces for holding councils by moonlight"). The second possible source is the *Lettres des Indes* by René Puaux which appeared in the newspaper *Le Temps* in December 1912 and which contains an allusion to *la terrasse des audiences au* [sic!] *clair de lune* in the context of the festivities surrounding the coronation of King George V as Emperor of India. Kipling and *Toomai des Éléphants* also come to mind ... Yet Debussy's evocation of India is so devoid of specific exoticisms that it can even accommodate the French folksong *Au clair de la lune* and is in some phrases reminiscent of the setting of Paul Verlaine's *Clair de lune* (in the *Suite bergamasque* as a piano composition, in the *Fêtes galantes* as a song).

From de la Motte-Fouqué to Giraudoux, the Undine theme is one of the stock motifs of European fairytales. In the case of Debussy's *Prélude* of the same name it was once again Arthur Rackham who provided the immediate inspiration — *ce vieux Rackham* whom Chouchou rediscovered in a second illustrated volume (based on de la Motte-Fouqué's *Undine* set to music by E.T.A. Hoffmann).

Charles Dickens' satirical novel *The Posthumous Papers of the Pickwick Club* (1836/37) was one of Debussy's favourite books, and he paid musical tribute in the ninth *Prélude* of the second volume to the hilarious Samuel Pickwick Esquire, Perpetual President member of the Pickwick Club (P.P.M.P.C.). The appearance of *God save the King* is just one instance of Debussy's manner of incorporating quotations and allusions — a game which he plays in many of his compositions.

The two "Canopic jars" (Etruscan burial urns whose lids bear likenesses of the head of Osiris) which stood on Debussy's desk will presumably have inspired the title of the tenth *Prélude*. The origins of these urns go back to the death cult of ancient Egypt; and the parallel chord passages, the sometimes modal and sometimes chromatic progressions of *Canope* do seem to evoke the image of an archaic procession. This is the idiom which also determined the character of *Le Martyre de Saint Sébastien*, composed at roughly the same time.

Les tierces alternées ("The Alternating Thirds"), which is more of an *Etude* than a *Prélude*, requires no non-musical elucidation. Its title, however, recalls the *Pièces de Clavecin* by François Couperin and Jean-Philippe Rameau of which Debussy became increasingly fond in his later years.

What *God Save the King* is to the ninth *Prélude*, the *Marseillaise* is to the twelfth. It is the clue to deciphering the time and place of the musical setting: the "firework display" on July 14th, the French national holiday, which closes the set with a riot of colour and whirling sparks.

The inspiration of the twenty-four *Préludes* can be assigned with a high degree of accuracy to specific parameters: place and time (time of day, season or era), literary models and — depending on the thematic emphasis — people (P), nature (N) or depicted object (O).

Place	Time	Literature	
Danseuses de delphes			
Greece	Classical times		P
Voiles			
Sea	Summer		N
Le vent dans la plaine			
Unspecified	Unspecified	Ch. S. Favart / Paul Verlaine	N
"Les sons et les parfums tournent dans l'air du soir"			
Unspecified	Evening	Ch. Baudelaire	N
Les Collines d'Anacapri			
Italy	Unspecified		N
Des pas sur la neige			
Unspecified	Winter		P/N
Ce qu'a vu le vent d'Ouest			
Denmark/ England	Unspecified	H. Ch. Andersen/ P. B. Shelley	N
La Fille aux cheveux de lin			
Scotland	Unspecified	Leconte de Lisle	P
La Sérénade interrompue			
Spain	Evening		P

Place	Time	Literature	
La Cathédrale engloutie			
Brittany	Legendary	Ernest Renan	P/O
La Danse de Puck			
England	Legendary	Shakespeare	P
Minstrels			
America	20th cent.		P
Brouillards			
Unspecified	Autumn (?)		N
Feuilles mortes			
Unspecified	Autumn	Gabriel Mourey(?)	N
La Puerta del vino			
Spain	Summer (?)		N/O
"Les Fées sont d'exquises danseuses"			
England	Legendary	J. M. Barrie (A. Rackham)	P
Bruyères			
Brittany (?)	Unspecified		N
"General Lavine"⟨eccentric⟩			
America	20th cent.		P
La Terrasse des audiences du clair de lune			
India	Nighttime	Pierre Loti or René Puaux	N/O
Ondine			
Unspecified	Legendary	de La Motte-Fouqué (A. Rackham)	P/N
Hommage à Samuel Pickwick Esq. P.P.M.P.C.			
England	19th cent.	Charles Dickens	P
Canope			
Egypt	Classical times		P/O
Les tierces alternées			
Unspecified	Unspecified		Unspecified
Feux d'artifice			
France	20th cent. Nighttime		O
(Toomai des Éléphants)			
India	19th cent.	Rudyard Kipling	P/N
(Paganini)			
Italy	19th cent.		P

In this sense the twenty-four *Préludes* constitute a kind of musical journey round the world as well as a compendium of Debussy's aesthetics — ranging through every epoch, country and literary tradition.

Michael Stegemann

[1] Letter to Jacques Durand, quoted from Robert Orledge, *Debussy's Piano Music: Some Thoughts and Sources of Inspiration*, in: *The Musical Times* CXXII/1981, p. 27.

[2] Quoted from François Lesure (Ed.), *Claude Debussy — Lettres*, Paris 1980, p. 235.

[3] Bibliothèque Nationale Paris, Rés.Vmd.ms. 32.

[4] On 16. 3. 1913 Debussy thanked Jacques Durand for forwarding the edition; cf. Jacques Durand (Ed.), *Lettres de Claude Debussy à son éditeur*, Paris 1927, p. 113.

[5] The Société Nationale de Musique founded on 25. 2. 1871 by Camille Saint-Saëns and others.

[6] Cf. Debussy's letters to Stravinsky of 13. 4. 1912 and 5. 11. 1912 in: François Lesure, op. cit., pp. 223f. and p. 233.

[7] Roy Howat / Claude Helffer (Eds.), *Œuvres Complètes de Claude Debussy (Série I, Volume 5): Préludes*, Paris 1985, p. XII.

[8] Reproductions of both postcards are contained in: François Lesure, *Iconographie musicale Debussy*, Paris 1980, p. 180 (Manuel de Falla); E. Robert Schmitz, *The Piano Works of Claude Debussy*, New York 1950 (reissued 1966), p. 128 (Ricardo Viñes).

[9] Cf. Paul Hooreman, "... *Les fées sont d'exquises danseuses*", in: François Lesure (Ed.), *Claude Debussy 1862–1962*, Paris 1962, pp. 104ff.: Rackham's illustration is reproduced here and in *Iconographie musicale* (op. cit.), p. 179.

[10] Cf. Claude Debussy, *Titania* (*Gil Blas*, 26. 1. 1903), in: Claude Debussy, *Monsieur Croche et autres écrits*, Paris 1971, pp. 81ff.

[11] Cf. E. Robert Schmitz, op. cit., pp. 172f.

NOTES ON INTERPRETATION

In selecting the fingering the prime consideration — assuming a hand of normal proportions — was to provide for a light and supple wrist which would to a great extent ensure freedom of touch. It seems to me that the technique of substitution is a preferable alternative to the use of the right (forte) pedal, allowing as it does real legato playing and in many cases a relaxation of the hand. If the present edition contains only few markings to this effect, then primarily to avoid typographic confusion.

These brief suggestions apart, one should never forget the precept which Debussy himself expounded in the Preface to the two books of his *Etudes* as the last word on the question: *Each person is his own best schoolmaster. Let us look for our fingering ourselves.* With considerable humour and more than a hint of real concern Debussy castigated the possible misuse of the forte pedal in his music: *It is perhaps quite simply a fact that the excessive use of the pedal serves only to disguise inadequate technique, and that a great deal of noise is necessary to prevent the music which is being massacred from being heard.*

For obvious reasons, then, the editor of the present edition has dispensed with pedal marking. The subtlety and precision required for the correct use of the pedals inevitably presuppose vague markings which would be detrimental to the tonal balance.

The use of the third (sostenuto) pedal — although admittedly tempting — also involves certain dangers: in the majority of cases the advantages gained in terms of clarity are outweighed by the impairment of the tonal beauty of the music.

A judicious and never excessive application of the three pedals should help to place Debussy somewhere between Monet, Seurat and Turner — at a considerable distance from that brand of "impressionism" which a distorted tradition has attempted to establish as the label for his musical world. This view is substantiated by Debussy's famous remark on Louis Leroy's "insight" as outlined above: *I try to create something different — in a sense realities — and these imbeciles call it "impressionism", a term which could not be used more inappropriately, especially by the art critics ...*

Debussy's comment that it is more important to see a sunrise than to hear the Pastoral Symphony provides a valuable key to the interpretation of his music. And when not with paper but with the ear in mind, that it is not a graphic abstraction but an audible reality, then there can be no mistake: Debussy's music is made up of sounds and colours, and only of those ingredients.

Yet despite their unique pictorial vividness the *Préludes* have nothing whatsoever to do with programme music. What Debussy does is to suggest, to give us access to a wide spectrum of sensory possibilities.

If I have outlined a particular approach to interpreting some of the *Préludes*, it goes without saying that this is only a personal view conditioned by an individual perception and a specific cultural background. After all, the titles of the pieces are intended to achieve their effect only in retrospect.

— I. ⟨ ... *Brouillards*⟩

In the opening piece of the second volume of his *Préludes* Debussy emerges as an unsurpassed master of the alien, spreading a fine-meshed harmonic net which is neutralized by the guise of polytonality. The homogeneous density of this "fog" — a poem in pianissimo — is better evoked by the superimposition of layers of sound than by an unbridled vagueness. Bars 18—19 (and later 22—23) appear to pose unanswered questions, yet they require great precision of tonal contour. Throughout this *Prélude* the articulation must be clearly audible, rising and falling in volume almost to the point of violence (at bars 29 and 30, a reminiscence of the *Vent d'Ouest* from the first volume). The forte pedal should be changed frequently or used only as a half-pedal to avoid the irridescent fog becoming impenetrable.

— II. ⟨ ... *Feuilles mortes*⟩

This *Prélude* resembles the fourth piece in the first volume (*"Les sons et les parfums tournent dans l'air du soir"*) in its harmonic ambivalence; at the same time its tonal horizon is infinitely broader than that of *Brouillards*. *Feuilles mortes — this gentle decay* (Marguerite Long) occupies a very special place amongst the masterpieces of the "languor which penetrates my heart" (*langueur qui pénètre mon coeur*).

The piece, an apparition on the verge of evanescence, requires strict compliance with all the parameters upon which it is constructed: the typically Debussian *crescendi* (bars 23 and 24), the alchemical dynamics (bars 12—14), the note values, the harmonic *clarté*, the emancipation of the melodic line. (In bars 15, 16, 32, 34 and 41 the chords must be taken away but not restruck, with the forte pedal lifted.) In the final chord only the C sharp should linger.

— III. ⟨ ... *La Puerta del vino*⟩

In every fleeting moment I glimpse worlds in which a shimmering, iridescent game is being played out ... This sentence by the poet Konstantin Balmont which inspired Sergei Prokofiev to compose his *Visions fugitives* might well serve as a heading for this *Prélude*. It is a succession of moments *of abrupt shifts from extreme intensity to passionate finesse.* A warm, suggestive, lascivious sensuality contrasts with this violent, ironic provocation, the complete absence of shade typical of noon.

When Debussy received the picture postcard from Manuel de Falla and remarked that he would "do something with it" (*Je ferai quelque chose avec ça*), he might equally have said "I shall do the same thing with something or other (*Je ferai ça ... avec quelque chose*), so completely do his conviction and his sensitivity enable him to articulate the quintessence of the Spanish soul with utter mastery.

Regardless of its omnipresent, superficially perceptible seductiveness, this *Prélude* emanates a sense of solitude and wistful longing for the Spain which the composer was never to visit.

It is important to maintain the rhythmic pliability of the Habañera throughout — even when the tempo relaxes temporarily. Observe minutely the extremely precise dynamic markings and the dotting in order to achieve the greatest possible degree of characterization and prevent the piece becoming a caricature. Each and every exaggeration is exactly defined in the score.

— IV. ⟨ ... *"Les Fées sont d'exquises danseuses"*⟩

Debussy's "physics" captures the material world on the brink of dematerialization. In the same way the swaying equilibrium of an "exquisite dancer" balancing on the threads of a cobweb engenders a playful knowledge of and trust in the delicate magic being ... before the fairy (like *Ondine* later) wraps herself in her filigree veil and vanishes from sight.

The point of balance is to be sought somewhere between the white and the black keys — but on no account in the forte pedal, which remains virtually unused during the two stages of the tightrope act (beginning and end of the piece). Like all true artists, we should be working without a net! The trills need to sound like evanescent vibrations of sound and should be quite distinct from the *Rubato, sans rigueur* — much more sensual and fleeting.

— V. ⟨... Bruyères⟩

The spellbinding lay which this Celtic shepherd plays on his shawm irresistibly evokes the image of a wide, silent heath. The melody's sequence of triads epitomizes bucolic wisdom. Closely related to *La Fille aux cheveux de lin* from the first volume, this timid, archaic *Prélude* is like a fond recollection — but not a recollection of that small, porcelain-coloured blossom which Debussy loathed but rather of the sea between dawn and noon whose coastline is fringed with fragrant shrubs.

The section marked *Un peu animé* is joyous, slightly exuberant and intoxicated, followed by brief moments of the perfect equilibrium of full-sounding harmonies. Then, after an abandoned attempt to shift into the minor, Debussy returns to the gentle wistfulness of the opening: the five-note melody reappears, this time transposed up an octave, as a harbinger of farewell, as an echo, the "song of the young man". In this *Prélude* again, undue use of the right pedal would have a disastrous effect on the cantilene, since the musical phrase unfolds only through an uninterrupted manual legato.

In the fourth-last bar (47/48) the low E flat must be taken away but not struck again, so that the breath of the quaver rest can make its point.

— VI. ⟨... "General Lavine" ⟨eccentric⟩⟩

... or alternatively, the comedy routine of a magnificent American comic and juggler who conceals his painful sensitivity behind a mask of exaggeration and coyness. The clowns enters the stage to the accompaniment of brief fanfares whose strident sound will later signify his spectacular physical mishaps. The mood changes incessantly: witty and understated (the casual juggling in the left hand in bars 14, 15, 22—27 and so on), a hint of mockery, a suggestion of exaggeration, a brief pirouette before the juggling continues. Then a burst of emotion (the only true legato in this *Prélude*), and we are back to the original mechanical, "wooden" austerity. After the number has been repeated comes the inevitable teardrop, self-commiseration and finally the release of anger, an "eccentric" twinkle in the eye. All of this is to be achieved with very little use of the pedal, carefully observing the subtle dotting, and with a nuance of bad taste (in bars 22 and 81).

— VII. ⟨... La Terrasse des audiences du clair de lune⟩

This was the last of the twenty-four *Préludes* which Debussy composed, and it is at the same time the most esoteric of the series. It matters very little whether the piece was inspired by Pierre Loti's *L'Inde sans les Anglais* or by one of the *Lettres des Indes* which René Puaux wrote to the newspaper *Le Temps*. The music conjures up with the ritual power of a mantra the magical atmosphere of an India sleepwalking in the alien light of the moon. As in a dream, the incantations and episodes seem to pass, sometimes in slow motion, then intruding on the frontiers of reality in their sensual energy.

Without employing quasi-exotic devices as such,

Debussy uses a dense chromatic texture to evoke a mystical atmosphere in which wisdom and knowledge appear in the guise of discreet sensuality.

The gentle irony of the opening recalls the first notes of a metaphysically lingering *Au clair de la lune,* while the close of the piece is bathed in a cold light, a world permeated by the music of the spheres penetrated by the milky-white radiance of stray moonbeams (third and fourthlast bars).

The descending chromatic scales must be executed with the precision of an atomic timepiece. In general the sublime diction of the piece requires the greatest metric stringency — except for bars 10—13 in which the musical line permits a slight rubato towards the end of the bar. The appoggiaturas in the penultimate bar are to be played on the beat. In the final bar only the low F sharp should linger.

— VIII. ⟨... Ondine⟩

This *Prélude* is a far cry from the *Ondine* in Ravel's *Gaspard de la nuit.* What makes it so fascinating is the endless succession of musical invention. Each new section depicts with extraordinary vividness the various stages of the playful nymph's brief appearances in the mortal world. After the sirens' calls of the beginning, we follow Undine to the first seduction scene (bars 11—31) and the coy sensuality of her words, punctuated by pirouettes in the water. Bars 32—38 evoke the sound of a hushed, tentative lament. After a final appeal to reason and a repeated rejection the seduction grows ever more insistent and imploring — brief moments of dismay sow the bitter seeds of doubt in her heart. Then, because she does not know anger, she vanishes after a final hesitation into the depths of her realm — with (paradoxical though it may seem) an "airy" grace.

In bars 16—17 (and analogous passages) resist playing rubato, however tempting it may be. The impression of calm breathing can be created only by the regularity of the tied pairs of semiquavers. In bar 11 (and parallel bars) do not let the pedal blur the demisemiquaver arpeggios; the musical curve must be drawn sharply. The pliability and smoothness of waves are features of the whole piece, and any angularity of the accents or excessive use of the pedal must be avoided.

— IX. ⟨... Hommage à Samuel Pickwick Esq. P.P.M.P.C.⟩

As Marguerite Long noted, the epithet *Esquire* is as intrinsic to Pickwick as *eccentric* is to Lavine. On the other hand, Debussy with his great fondness for Anglo-Saxon humour once again proves that he himself combines both qualities. The opening *God Save the King* with its pompous complacency sets the tone for the adventures of the club President (as Pickwick in his immodesty terms himself) and its three members, who have set themselves the daunting task of conducting exacting research into the origins of the ponds of Hampstead.

In a pageant of bland courtesy and bumptious nonchalance, of belligerent assertiveness and cowering timidity, Debussy portrays his hero's make-believe world. Pickwick is so unassailably convinced of his own superiority that he stumbles from the sublime to the ridiculous. A hint of superciliousness, a measure of impertinence abruptly give way to diffidence which is in its turn dispelled by a royal bow.

The insipid and somewhat ponderous motif marked *Aimable* in bar 9, the forte in bars 21—22 and the fortissimo in bars 24—25 must sound like the hollow pretentiousness of crude organ registration. Do not hesitate to exaggerate the nuances and the dotting: don't worry, ridicule has already found a different victim.

— X. (... *Canope*)

This *Prélude*, imbued with the mystery of the unfamiliar, articulates the apprehension which everybody feels in the face of death. With great austerity in the musical means employed Debussy leads us along a metaphysical path on which lie both man's rebellion against divine injustice and the muted lamentation of an anachronistic remorse.

Debussy himself owned two "Canopic jars" — Etruscan burial urns surmounted by the animal heads of the gods. But the scene which he appears to be evoking here with the procession of triads is more probably an archaic ceremony in the ancient Egyptian city of Canope.

Throughout the piece the dotting must be minutely observed. Play the sequence of chords as legato as possible, without the audible use of the right pedal. The notes marked with staccato dots in bars 7, 9 etc. should not be made too distinct. In the final bar the chord should be taken away without being restruck, to allow a ray of hope to shine through the grim determination.

— XI. ⟨... *Les tierces alternées*⟩

These "alternating thirds" are the only instance of purely pianistic "divertissement" in the entire set of twenty-four *Préludes*. With its concentration on a single technical facet, the piece would appear to belong more naturally to the two volumes of *Etudes* composed three years later.

Once again Debussy seeks to limit the risk of "betrayal" of his music by adding an immense quantity of markings: the performer has no choice but to play "strictly in time". After the opening bars (with bars 7—9 sounding like a hesitant questioning) a perpetuum mobile sets in. With the exception of bars 40—65 the left hand takes the lead. The sparing use of the forte pedal (on the cautiously accentuated and cautiously pedalled notes marked with portato strokes) is permissible here. From bar 71 onwards the warmer harmonies may be brought out by somewhat more prominent use of the pedal, but never at the expense of the *clarté* of the change. (From bar 69 on it is advisable to cross over the right hand.) The central section, a development of the thirds in the opening passage, should in turns be sinuous, graceful, languorous and even slightly "precious" (in the sense implied by the "good French taste" which Debussy shared with the *clavecinistes* ...). Then comes a whimsical transition before the perpetuum mobile returns, this time played virtually without pedal right to the end and with special attention paid to the transparency of the chromatic bars.

Except for bars 40—60 the dynamics range from piano to pianissimo. As André Suarès remarked, *With Debussy music learnt to play the piano again.*

— XII. ⟨... *Feux d'artifices*⟩

The tightrope act with which Debussy concludes his two volumes of *Préludes* is remarkable not so much for its pyrotechnic innovations as for its anticipation of the composition styles of the future.

Feux d'artifices ranks as a completely atonal composition, because its harmonic structure lacks any consistent point of reference. The impression of novelty is further enhanced by the extremely fragmented and amorphous nature of its form and thematic material. This is not to say, however, that the piece does not evoke specific images: *The slumbering smoke of Bengal candles emitting single sparks, the crackling of rockets, the gradual parabolic descent of stars, the whirring of Catherine wheels, the blinding radiance of brightly-coloured bouquets, everything that sparkles and shines in the night, the entire magic of light is contained in this music* (Alfred Cortot).

The fragment of the *Marseillaise* with which the piece closes suggests that the firework display marked the July 14th holiday — a corroboration of Debussy's poetic formulation: *I wish for a freedom in music which is perhaps more intrinsic to it than to any other art form, since music is not confined to the more or less faithful representation of nature but is capable of conveying the enigmatic correspondences between nature and the imagination.*

The entire opening section of this piece must be played without pedal and absolutely evenly. From bar 25 the use of the pedal becomes increasingly necessary to allow the long note values *(très en dehors)* to resonate. In bars 33—35 the small crescendi need to be carefully gradated to their culmination.

Between bars 58 and 63 the right pedal may be allowed to highlight the dreamy, poetic character of this episode. After that great harmonic clarity is required. In bars 67 (and the following bars) the G sharp must be allowed to resonate in the pedal as long as prescribed each time. Bars 73—80 resemble a defiant suspension before the final explosion, dry but legato. The *Marseillaise* needs to sound as bright as a distant trumpet, the last D flat clearly distinct from the tremolo.

Michel Béroff

Georg Friedrich Händel: Keyboard Works I (Misc. Suites)

154

INDEX

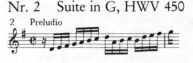

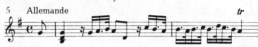

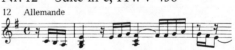

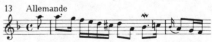

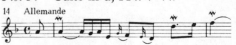
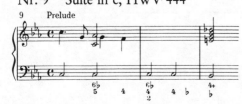

PREFACE

General

While it is generally known that Handel became a master of particular musical idioms, it seems that his keyboard music has received less recognition. Yet considered as the results of an immensely talented composer's response to idioms or style around him, Handel's keyboard music has both a distinct voice and a quality quite as startling, in its way, as his grander œuvre. Just as the vocal, choral and instrumental music draws on the composer's first-hand knowledge of particular Italian idioms — evidently grasped quickly by him and developed to a scale and a level of melodic inspiration beyond his 'models' — so the keyboard music draws on his first-hand knowledge of particular German idioms and works them to a similar end. In a key essay on the composer[1], Terence Best put it well when he wrote: *The boy Handel received his early training from the organist Zachow in Halle, so he must have studied the keyboard music of seventeenth-century German composers such as Froberger, Buxtehude, Pachelbel and Kuhnau, and their influence is detectable in several works which must be among his earliest surviving compositions.* To the list of names here one could usefully add Krieger, Zachow himself and the young Böhm[2]; and to their influence can be attributed not only certain characteristics of Handel's earlier keyboard music but so many characteristics of almost all the music in the present volume, as well as that in subsequent volumes in this edition.

This influence is less a question of Handel 'adopting' the various 'styles' and 'forms' of older music — these terms are often too vague to be useful — than naturally following along a route laid down by conventions. That is to say, German keyboard music before about 1720 (in particular before J. S. Bach's bold exploration of new techniques in composing and playing) had common qualities based on technical assumptions — such as that the hands were used and fingered in certain ways, that certain kinds of motifs or note-patterns (*figurae*) were the basis of the texture (whether fugues or dances, toccatas or suites), that specific Italian or French idioms might be imitated from time to time, and so on. Not as sensual as French music at its best nor as capricious as Italian at its best, the German keyboard music could nevertheless achieve other qualities: a kind of reliability and sound sense of how to develop motifs themselves, evidently beyond the French or Italian composer. At its best, that is to say in the work of Handel, the German styles were not only melodious — one can see lesser composers such as Kuhnau and Mattheson striving for the same quality — but had a gift for thematic development of a kind that was later to become the hallmark of German music in general, still very much a Cinderella in c1700, though not for long.

A further point of great importance is that despite first appearances the German keyboard styles are related closely to the harpsichord of the day. The kinds of note-patterns (*figurae*), the kinds of fingering and the kinds of harpsichord were not isolated phenomena: and this edition has been made on the assumption that all of Handel's keyboard music — not merely the obvious masterpieces — springs to life when these phenomena are understood. Some remarks on the 'correct' kind of harpsichord are made below ('Fingering'), and here it can be generally remarked that this instrument still had an 'old' sound, and that in any German city around 1700 there would have been little hint of the large, less precise, more 'public' harpsichords now so familiar in concert-halls and recordings based on copies of late harpsichords (i. e. those made in London, Paris, Dresden, Hamburg from the 1730s onwards). Handel is a master of 'figural idioms', creating music from particular note-patterns which can ultimately be understood and expressed only by certain fingerings, preferably on certain kinds of instrument. Though such music is playable by pianists in the more recent and conventional manner of fingering, this edition acknowledges the advances made in the understanding of old music and tries, by means of fingerings in the Text and comments in the 'Notes on Interpretation', to create a new kind of edition that alerts the player to details in the music as an original performer might have understood them.

The volumes of our edition are:

Vol. I Miscellaneous Suites (including six from the 1733 Collection (Walsh 1733); commonly called *the Second Set*)

Vol. II 1720 Collection of Suites (Cluer, commonly called *Eight Great Suites*)

Vol. III Selected miscellaneous Pieces (including the *Six Fugues* and remaining pieces from Walsh 1733)

We are aware that while certain suites in Vol. I seem to be incomplete (or not completed), certain movements in Vol. III seem to belong to other suites, and that accordingly the line of distinction between suite and non-suite is far from absolute. Nevertheless, the editor has not thought it useful to preserve the Collection Walsh 1733 as a set, since not only are three of its so-called suites pieces of a different kind, but it is not certain that their inclusion reflects the composer's wishes or his understanding of the term 'suite'.

Division of labour and responsibility is as follows: Terence Best has prepared data on the mss, the printed editions, the chronology and status of the pieces, and on the relevant background in the composer's life and works; Peter Williams has prepared the final text in its entirety (the music, the commentary and the fingering) and is responsible for any decision that had to be made on the basis of opinion.

Sources

In addition to various autograph copies of individual works or movements, several albums or collections of Handel's keyboard music exist in the hand of English-based copyists of the 1716–1721 period, as they do in the hand of German copyists of perhaps an earlier period. Around 1719–1721, a printed edition of selected pieces appeared in Amsterdam, probably engraved in London and certainly without the composer's authorization; he responded with a collection of suites, the *First Set* in 1720 (Roger). Thereafter, with one or two exceptions such as the two suites for George II's daughter (Nos. 14 and 15 of the present volume), he composed very little solo keyboard music. Some much earlier pieces were collected and published in the *Second Set* (Walsh 1733), having appeared earlier in different format in 1727 (Walsh 1727) and c1730; other publications include the *Six Fugues* (composed c1717, published 1735).

For further details on the sources of each suite, see the Critical Notes.

Peter Williams, Edinburgh

Georg Friedrich Händel: Keyboard Works II (Eight Great Suites) HWV 426-433

INDEX

PREFACE

General

Of his talents in composing for a single instrument, we need no better proofs than are given us in his Harpsichord-lessons. The first sett which were printed by his own order, will always be held in the highest esteem, notwithstanding those real improvements in the style for lessons which some Masters have since hit upon. HANDEL'S have one disadvantage, owing entirely to their peculiar excellence. The surprising fulness and activity of the inner parts, increases the difficulty of playing them to so great a degree, that few persons are capable of doing them justice. Indeed there appears to be more work in them than any one instrument should seem capable of dispatching.
John Mainwaring, *Memoirs of the Life of the late George Frederic Handel*, London 1760, p. 203.

It is probably true that *The Eight Great Suites* (Collection Cluer 1720 – see below) include movements more difficult to play either than was customary in 1720 or than is often found to be the case in the rest of their composer's œuvre. Judging by remarks made by Mattheson a few years later *(Grosse General-Bass-Schule*, Hamburg 1731, pp. 344–345), this was a period in which German composers were beginning to distinguish difficult 'hand-pieces' *(Hand-Sachen)* that needed to be practised from the more usual keyboard arias etc. that were for a simple playing-through. Mattheson instances the partitas of Graupner and J. S. Bach. English keyboard music remained relatively simple to play, despite the more exotic elements introduced by Thomas Roseingrave's edition of *XLII Suites & Pieces* of Domenico Scarlatti (London, 1739) and by his own piece added to them. By 1760, Mainwaring was reflecting a changed taste towards the thinner styles of 'galant' keyboard music, but it is doubtful if either changed tastes in general or the technical difficulties of the 'Collection Cluer 1720' in particular ever affected their popularity. For a century and more, there can have been no comparison between the sales-figures for Handel's *Suites* and Bach's neglected *Partitas*.

Some general points about Handel's style were made in the Preface to Volume I of our edition and further comparisons are made in the present volume to music contemporary with him and which can be supposed to have influenced him. While it is tempting with Handel, as with J. S. Bach, to seek from the works of his better contemporaries music that exercised influence on him, it could often be the case that less talented, even poor, composers were influential. On J. S. Bach, the influence of J. G. Walther must often have been far stronger than the qualities of his own music may lead one to expect; in the case of Handel, a major influence must have been the garrulous Hamburger Johann Mattheson. Not only did Mattheson publish in London in 1714 what amounts to the first major collection of suites (in an 'international' style) engraved there and to which one can suppose the c1719 and 1720 Collections of Handel (Roger; Cluer 1720) to be in some measure a response, but even the prefaces have a 'note of gratitude' in common:
Nothing, but an earnest Desire of acknowledging the many Favours I have received in this Nation, could have prompted me to this Undertaking... (I. D. Fletcher, publisher of Mattheson's *Pièces de Clavecin*, 1714)

...reckoning it my duty with my Small talent to Serve a Nation from which I have receiv'd so Generous a protection (Handel, *Suites de Pieces de Clavecin*, 1720)
The English Nation was very well served with published keyboard music between c1710 and c1740: it was a question not only of Mattheson and Handel (including the *Six Fugues*

of 1735), but of William Babell's collections, the Scarlatti editions, Walsh's versions of Italian sonatas published in Amsterdam (Zipoli, Pasquini etc., 1710, 1719, 1722) and reprints of such French music as Dieupart's suites.
The three volumes of our edition are:
Vol. I a and b Miscellaneous Suites (including six from Walsh 1733, commonly called the *Second Set)*
Vol. II the *Eight Great Suites* ('Cluer 1720')
Vol. III Selected miscellaneous pieces (including the *Six Fugues* and remaining pieces from Walsh 1733)
We are aware that while certain suites in Vol I seem to be incomplete (or not completed), certain movements in Vol III seem to belong to other suites, and that accordingly the line of distinction between suite and non-suite is only one of convenience.

Division of labour and responsibility is as follows: Terence Best has prepared data on the mss, the printed editions, the chronology and status of the pieces, and on the relevant background in the composer's life and works; Peter Williams has prepared the final text in its entirety (edition of music, commentary and fingering) and is responsible for any decision of whatever kind that had to be based on opinion.

The original Editions

Both the original composition and purpose of the movements first collected into the suites now published in this volume are obscure, although it can be assumed that some of them go back several, even many, years and that pupils or acquaintances copied (or had copied) suites or individual movements that were in some kind of 'composition portfolio'. 'Portfolio' ('Sammelband') is a general term for groups of pieces being composed or revised or compiled (or any combination of these), without any assumption that the composer necessarily had a 'collection' in mind, possible or even likely though this must often have been. One such collection was made by an unknown compiler and published some time between 1719 and 1721, probably while the composer was away from London:
Pieces / à un & Deux Clavecins / Composées / Par Mr. Hendel / A Amsterdam / Chez Jeanne Roger No. 490 (here called 'Roger')
The plates were probably prepared in London by John Walsh. On June 14 1720, the composer himself applied for a 14-year privilege to publish his own work, and in November 1720 J. Cluer published for him the definitive edition:
Suites de Pieces / pour le Clavecin / Composées / par / G. F. Handel / Premier Volume / J. Cole Sculp. / London printed for the Author, / And are only to be had at Christopher Smith's in Coventry Street the Sign of ye Hand & Musick book ye upper end of the / Hay Market and by Richard Mear's Musical Instrumentmaker in St. Pauls Church Yard. (here called 'Cluer 1720')
Sixteen of the movements appear in Roger, seven others (III 1, 3, 4, 6 and the preludes of V, VI and VIII) seem to have been specially composed for the making up of the very varied suites (including certain preludes replacing older ones); most of those in Roger but unused were taken into the *Second Set of Suites* (Walsh 1733; see our edition Vols I and III). Further editions of Cluer 1720 appeared in c1722, c1725 (corrections, formerly written in by hand in previous issues, now engraved), c1736 (re-engraved, with further mistakes and corrections, here called 'Walsh 1736') and two

of c1734/c1736 abroad (the first in Amsterdam, the second in Paris, the latter a copy of the former and here called 'Paris 1736'). A few pieces exist in autograph, but no complete suite.

Fingering

Compared to e. g. J. S. Bach's *Partitas*, Handel's keyboard music is on the whole not difficult to play, except that a certain virtuosity may be required for particular moments in a set of variations or (as in Scarlatti) for occasional bars in an otherwise not taxing movement. Such moments of difficulty are not only rather isolated but in any case require less an ingeniously agile hand or fingering-technique than an ability to play very fast such standard *formulae* as scales and arpeggios[1]. Occasionally, as for example in the F minor *Gigue* or the various fugues of the volume, keyboard technique is stretched more in the manner of J. S. Bach, though even there the counterpoint does not produce the complex and kaleidoscopic textures that demand such versatility from the fingers in the *Well-tempered Clavier I* or *Three-part Inventions*.

Fingerings are suggested in the present edition, therefore, not because the reasonably proficient player needs advice or suggestions if he is to play the notes at all but because the time has come when players are more willing to be alerted to the composer's own assumptions. Fingerings affect the end-result of a performance since they are part of the understanding of a piece, particularly when it is not immensely difficult to play; and instead of suggesting to the player a fingering by means of which he can make the music easier to play *per se*, our edition aims rather to help the player understand the music as it was composed. This is not to offer conjectures on Handel's compositional processes – 'how his mind worked' – but to show that without exception this music is composed of lines and motifs which have been associated with (produced by) certain usages of the hand – usages not only in the fingering itself but in touch, articulation, phrasing, tempo and 'style'. Thus a fingering system has been erected here on certain principles, as follows:

(1) the expected instrument was not only harpsichord but a harpsichord of certain kinds: rather narrow compass, single manual, perhaps of distinctly Italianate character (with a dry, immediate sound), and certainly rather modest in comparison to the high-baroque creations from the 1730s onwards. Of course, such later instruments – as conventional pianofortes too – can play such music, but it is a question of understanding the contexts in which Handel worked and contributed to German traditions;

(2) many of the fingerings that one can imagine to have been *lingua franca* in the period around 1700 require very well regulated harpsichords; this is especially so for trills and mordents fingered 5 4 or 4 3;

(3) the player fingers in such a way as to identify, preserve and convey the note-patterns (motifs, cells, *figurae*) of the lines;

(4) to play with a smooth, easy fluency is a far less important aim than (3), i. e. it would be an anachronism for such music and reduce its potential interest as well as misrepresent the composer. Thus, skill in hand-shifting – so familiar to such string-players as Handel and J. S. Bach – is more relevant than skill in 'thumb-under fluency' practised by every keyboard-player since Czerny's period;

(5) throughout the fingering suggested here there is great emphasis on the beats, i. e. the first note of a pattern or bar. This is not to say that in a 4/4 bar there are four strong beats – on the contrary, part of the player's skill should be devoted to preventing too square and repetitious an emphasis on all beats; but I have often left passages between beats unfingered on the grounds that it does not much matter how they are played so long as the *next* note or pattern is clear. In particular, the r. h. thumb has been placed on strong beats when this is amenable to the note-pattern concerned;

(6) very often – perhaps more often than not – a suggested fingering supposes that a break of phrasing is implied, i. e. fingering is not worked out on the grounds of continuity but on the grounds of phrase-structure;

(7) since the conveying of Handel's 'figural invention' is the aim of such fingering, sequences and other repetitive or insistent note-patterns have the same or very similar fingering. This is so irrespective of the precise layout of the naturals and sharps that change in the course of the sequence;

(8) it often happens that the same finger is used on adjacent notes: again in aiming to preserve the identity of Handel's note-patterns, this seems more 'in style' than the technique of finger-changing on the same note. Apparently typical of the *Well-tempered Clavier* and certainly characteristic of later *cantabile* styles[2], finger-changing essentially belongs to other, mostly later, techniques;

(9) by the standards of modern convenience, many fingerings suggested here are decidedly awkward, and ultimately players must do as they wish. But players should remember that those fingerings have been suggested as a means of pointing out Handel's note-patterns, in relation to a characteristic harpsichord touch.

Fingering of the present Volume

Since the fingerings in our Handel edition are a new attempt to return to some original conventions, there are bound to be moments of pure conjecture. It would be misleading to claim to understand the assumptions about fingering held by either the young or the maturing Handel, or to assume that his fingering-method remained unchanged. The player today needs to rethink his techniques in the light of what might be imagined to have been the priorities in the mind of players who were themselves composers. He could begin to teach himself the point of 'figural fingering' by taking a not too difficult piece, such as the *Allegro* or the *Passacaille* from the G minor Suite and fingering it himself, (a) avoiding thumbs under/over and any fluency contrived in this manner, (b) concentrating on fingers 2 3 4 of the r. h. in particular, and (c) looking for any distinct phrasing and articulation he thinks Handel intended or expected. When he has understood the principles outlined above, he could not claim to have 'recreated Handel's original fingering'; but he will certainly find the music spring to life in a way that pianistic fingerings could not help him achieve.

Particular doubts that must remain are whether Handel still understood r. h. scale-figures to be fingered descending 3232 and ascending 3434, and l. h. descending 4545 and ascending 2121. In fact, the fingering of scales and scale-figures is still one of the most uncertain areas, particularly as it affects free preludes.

Hand-distribution and crossing

Free preludes are found chiefly in our edition Vol III but are also represented in Vols I and II. According to the contemporary conventions that can be grasped from carefully engraved music (e. g. that of J. K. F. Fischer, 1715 etc.) and from the better ms traditions (e. g. for the organ-music of J. S. Bach), it was customary to divide between the hands any lively solo lines – scales, arpeggios, turning figures – in the preludes and toccatas of German composers in the earlier eighteenth century. Some Handel sources show this clearly, others do not, presumably either because the copyists did not understand and so reproduce the putative original or because the composer himself did not always trouble to be specific[3]. Precisely where each hand took over from the other can not always be known with certainty, nor perhaps was there meant to be only one possible solution; but in the case of the rather modest *Prelude* to Suite No. 3 (one of several similar D minor preludes by Handel – see also Vols I and III), the following assumptions operate:

(1) in turning figures (bar 6), one hand takes over from the other as the actual tessitura makes it comfortable; the change comes after the beat not on it;

(2) in descending scale-passages (bars 14, 19), r. h. begins the run and l. h. closes it; whichever hand conveniently takes any group of notes, the changeover comes after the beat not on it;

(3) in smooth arpeggios (bar 7ff) the hands can alternate the triplets; there can be a good deal of crossing, i. e. neither hand relies on thumb-under arpeggio-playing in the Czerny manner but alternates with the other hand even, from time to time, for single notes – thus,

(4) in broken arpeggios (bar 17), hands alternate in the chopping manner;

(5) the original notation gives some hints (bars 8, 14, 17, 18) but it is unlikely to give a totally clear direction. Even if the composer had been consistent, the engraver or copyist may not have followed exactly.

One result of these assumptions is that hands alternate more than later conventions would have prescribed; another result is that although the engraver put in an occasional triplet sign (*3*), in fact it is unlikely that the composer meant a triplet, his notation merely subgrouping the seven notes (4 + 3) of the diatonic scale, like the septuplet (*7*) of a later generation.

Ornamentation

Although most treatments of harpsichord ornamentation, both in the period of the original composers concerned and in books and tables published since, centre on the *notation* of ornaments – how the symbols are written, what they mean, how they are to be realised – in practice the player of Handel's keyboard music has rather to bear in mind three crucial factors. The first is that over a long period neither Handel nor any of his copyists is totally consistent in his notation; the second is that neither composer nor copyist will always notate an ornament when they can be presumed to expect one (e. g. at many cadences); the third is that in any case the 'feel' of ornaments is not to be grasped from any notation whatever but requires experience of the instrument concerned.

In view of these three factors, the following table is given only as a starting-point for the player able to develop his own response to a good harpsichord action. Some general points are the following:

(1) ornaments are more than 'ornamental' and are part of the rhetoric of the movement concerned, aiding its effect (*affetto*) by giving character to the lines, such as sharp mordents in a gavotte or languid *appoggiature* in an allemande;

(2) players can therefore learn to respond to and 'aid the effect' of movements by improvising ornaments above what the composer or even any imaginative copyist notated;

(3) while the 'sharper' ornaments speak for themselves, it is often forgotten by keyboardists – though not by good singers, gamba-players, violinists or flautists – that the basic and most sensitive ornament is the *appoggiatura*, both rising and falling. The small note is the harpsichordist's single most expressive device, for by definition it introduces a temporary discord into the harmony and is therefore a strong-weak gesture. The player should work out for himself how to play it – how it is to be slurred, how long it is to be in any given context, how the following note is to fade.

Moreover, *appoggiature* can be, and in so many cases ought to be, a part of the other ornaments: trills should often begin not only on an upper note but on an upper note long and leaned-upon (*appoggiato*);

(4) although the tempo and 'style' of a movement affect the nature of the ornament, whatever its family-type, the precise relationship between tempo and ornament cannot be notated. For example many a trill or mordent will have more repercussions in a slower tempo; but one could not claim this to be a fixed rule. Slower tempi seem to 'bring out' longer *appoggiature* (whether alone or as part of a longer ornament), but the same proviso holds. Even the French composers and theorists, anxious to standardize performance *à la parisienne* in a disparate country with a rather new musical culture, did not clarify these issues, nor even make clear such important details as whether by nature a trill involves acceleration;

(5) just as the beginning of an ornament is frequently notated imprecisely – e. g. *tr* can mean with or without *appoggiatura* – so often are the ends of ornaments, in particular whether or not the trill has a closing turn. When the trill is long, or the trill/mordent is at a cadence, it is unlikely that a turn will alter the harmonic implications, and players should not forbear simply on the grounds that the composer or copyist did not give a turn;

(6) while the on-beat, strong-weak *appoggiatura* is a vital ornament, there could well be places in Handel's keyboard music, as in Parisian, that make *tierces coulées* particularly appropriate, i. e. little notes gliding in between those main notes that outline a major or minor 3rd. The notation is often ambiguous (as it is in Couperin etc.). It could be argued that *tierces coulées* are 'too French' for Handel, but a reverse case could as easily be made out: that Handel and Böhm (to name two composers of *c*1705 very much alerted to stylistic niceties) understood the *coulée* principle and could well have applied it from time to time;

(7) although commentaries written since the period, from e. g. C. P. E. Bach's *Versuch* (II, 1762) to e. g. *HHA* III (1970), usually assume that all later appearances of a theme or motif should be ornamented like the first, in fact early eighteenth-century sources rarely support the assumption. Whether in keyboard or other kinds of music, for example, there is a general discrepancy between the treble and the bass parts; but if two parts are specifically producing a duo counterpoint (e. g. two voices or two violins above a bass), then one can reasonably assume the parts to be embellishing similarly to each other, in the interests of close imitation. Players must decide for themselves whether a given keyboard texture or movement-type is of this kind and whether the awkward fingering that can result from ornamenting imitative motifs in the same way (no matter what voice they may appear in) leads to an anachronism.

(8) In the case of the present volume, ornaments have not always been added editiorially to cadences (e. g. the close of the *Fugue* in Suite No. 2) on the grounds that it would add to the complexity of the fingering, i. e. occasions an unfamiliar placing of the fingers. Perhaps this factor alone suggests that a blanket adding of ornaments at perfect cadences is not appropriate to Handel, whatever the

assumptions of editors and authors have been during the period of the 'baroque revival'. Or perhaps in the simpler binary dance-movements, cadential trills are more automatically appropriate than in fugues, preludes etc.?

(9) Despite what was said under (3) above, some ornaments could well be meant to begin on the main (not upper) note. A motif characteristic of two particular movements in the present volume but also found in Vols I and III seems from its context to require a sustained or slurred articulation aided by a main-beat trill:

Table of Ornaments

moderate tempo   livelier tempo

very lively tempo   moderate tempo

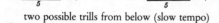

two possible trills from below (slow tempo)

fast tempo   slow tempo

as a tierce coulée

as a tierce coulée

moderate tempo   fast tempo

Editorial Note

Titles and numbering as in Cluer 1720, and *HWV* = Bernd Baselt, *Thematisch systematisches Verzeichnis: Instrumentalmusik, Pasticci und Fragmente.* Kassel, Basel, London: Bärenreiter 1986 *(Händel-Handbuch,* Vol 3), pp. 212–228, except spellings in the former have been regularized.

Abbreviations:
HWV = *Händel-Handbuch,* Vol 3, see above

HG 48 = *G. F. Händels Werke: Ausgabe der deutschen Händelgesellschaft,* Vol 48, ed. F. Chrysander, Leipzig 1894

HHA = *Hallische Händel-Ausgabe im Auftrage der Georg Friedrich Händelgesellschaft,* Leipzig–Kassel, from 1955. In the present edition, the references are as follows:
HHA I = *HHA* series IV, *Instrumentalmusik* Vol 1, *Klavierwerke I*
HHA II = *HHA* series IV, *Instrumentalmusik* Vol 5, *Klavierwerke II*
HHA III = *HHA* series IV, *Instrumentalmusik* Vol 6, *Klavierwerke III*
HHA IV = *HHA* series IV, *Instrumentalmusik* Vol 17, *Klavierwerke IV*

Editorial additions:
— notes, accidentals and rests in square brackets (editorial rests have been more systematically added in the fugues than in the dance-movements)
— ties and slurs as dotted lines
— all words in square brackets

Editorial suggestions:
— all fingering
— hand-distribution signs (⌐⌐)
— rhythmic signs above the stave, interpreting the notation as given by the sources. Such rhythms as (a) have been left in the main text on the grounds that they may not necessarily mean (b) but (c) or even (d):

— the small accidentals under/above all ornaments
— arpeggio signs under/above the staves, indicating a relatively marked spreading of the chord upwards or (if the arrow shows it) downwards.

Fingering conventions adopted:
— 5 4 (etc.) above or below an ornament fingered by 5 and 4 (etc.) in alternation
— 5 4 (etc.) above or below a note for changed-finger fingering
— alternative fingerings (those of a kind more familiar to pianists) are shown as the lower of two rows separated by a line, thus $\frac{1\ 4\ 3\ 2\ 1}{1\ 3\ 4\ 1\ 2}$

Ornaments:
In the present volume, the ornaments as left by the engraver of Cluer 1720 have been kept; perhaps Handel intended only 'single' mordents. See the Ornament Table above.

Peter Williams, Edinburgh

[1] In the case of Scarlatti, certain moments of difficulty arise because later periods than his may wrongly give too much emphasis to continuity, i.e. difficulties can often disappear when the music is more cut up and the hands are not compelled to play a *quasi perpetuum mobile.*

[2] The technique, described by F. Couperin in *L'Art de toucher* and perhaps not very familiar to his buyers, was clearly a factor in French *legato.*

[3] A similar situation can be found with some of J. S. Bach's fair copies: that for the G major *Prelude* BWV 541, for example, does not specify the distribution.

INDEX

162

Nr. 30 Chaconne in g, HWV 486

Nr. 31 Chaconne in G, HWV 435

Nr. 32 Fuge in F, HWV 611

Nr. 33 Fuge in g, HWV 605

Nr. 34 Fuge in G, HWV 606

Nr. 35 Fuge in B, HWV 607

Nr. 36 Fuge in h, HWV 608

Nr. 37 Fuge in a, HWV 609

Nr. 38 Fuge in c, HWV 610

PREFACE

General

Volume III of the Wiener Urtext Edition, Händel's Keyboard Works, contains a set of free preludes, various kinds of movement not part of completed suites (as far as sources suggest), several sets of variations, and a group of fugues including the *Six Fugues* of 1735. Other works found in *HHA* and certain other editions but not included are those of questionable authenticity, those that seem to be arrangements for keyboard and those that have the nature of sketches or drafts. One or two pieces included in the present volume may well belong to one or other of these categories but have been edited here either on the subjective grounds of effectiveness or on the objective grounds of being a *genre* familiar to English keyboardists of the time. Every editor of Handel, however, recognizes that this is an area into which opinion has to enter and for which every edition will have a different answer.

Some general points about Handel's style were made in the Prefaces to our Vols I and II, including those elements he can be supposed to have found in the music of his contemporaries and elders. It is also an aim of the present edition to describe 'the Handel harpsichord' and to suggest fingerings suitable for it, thus making hypotheses on Handel's own fingering. A summary of the reasoning behind the fingerings in our edition is given below, under 'Fingering'.

In the present volume, works are grouped by *genre* and ordered according to a chronology suggested partly by the sources, partly by the musical content. Such chronologies are, of course, only conjectural, and we are aware that, for example, the *Prelude* given here first already contains so much of the substance of the 'later' preludes. As to the different genres, the *Preludes* include those more or less fully written out, those comprising *arpeggiato* chord-progressions and those sharing both elements; in three cases, the sources suggest (in part or altogether) that one or more movements follow the preludes concerned. From the player's point of view the preludes have special points of interest and difficulty, and deserve particular attention; see below, under 'Fingering'. The Suite-movements are distinguished here from the Miscellaneous Pieces only as a means of conveniently grouping the French dances separately; we are aware that Handel's broad view of what a suite might contain would have allowed him to take any movement from either of these groups into a given suite. (Considered from this point of view, J. S. Bach's regular plans for his *English Suites, French Suites* and *Partitas* were old-fashioned and, as it were, pre-Handel.) A particularly unusual movement is the *Sonata for Two Manuals*: a ritornello movement rather like the concerto-arrangements being made by German composers of the period (e.g. J. G. Walther in Weimar *c*1715), in which the upper manual is used as the *concertino*, the lower as the *ripieno*. The *Chaconnes* and *Fugues* too could have found their way into suites; two chaconnes were indeed published as if they were suites (in Walsh 1733), and the fugues are often grouped in the mss along with other fugues that were published as parts of suites (in Cluer 1720).

The present Volume

Since the fingerings in our Handel edition are a new attempt to return to some original conventions, there are bound to be moments of pure conjecture. It would be misleading to claim to understand the assumptions about fingering held by either the young or the maturing Handel, or to assume that his fingering-method remained unchanged. The player today needs to rethink his techniques in the light of what might be imagined to have been the priorities in the mind of players who were themselves composers. He could begin to teach himself the point of 'figural fingering' by taking a not too difficult piece, such as the second of the two G major *Chaconnes* (No. 31) and fingering it himself by (a) avoiding the fluency of thumb-under fingering, (b) concentrating on fingers 2 3 4 of the r. h. in particular, and (c) looking for any distinct phrasing and articulation he thinks Handel intended or expected. The second *Chaconne* in G major is a particularly good starting-point for the player (even a beginner) trying to understand possible fingerings of the period: its note-patterns (*figurae*) are clear. I have often chosen fingerings for the purposes of exercise although they may appear at first unnecessarily awkward by modern conventions (e.g. the *Preludio* to the other G major *Chaconne*; our No. 28).

Peter Williams, Edinburgh

Capriccio G-Dur
Capriccio G major
Hob. XVII/1

Moderato

Fantasia C-Dur
Fantasia C major
Hob. XVII/4

Presto

20 Variationen G-Dur
20 variations G major
Hob. XVII/2

Arietta No. 1 Es-Dur
Arietta No. 1 E flat major
Hob. XVII/3

Arietta No. 2 A-Dur
Arietta No. 2 A major
Hob. XVII/2

6 leichte Variationen C-Dur
6 easy variations C major
Hob. XVII/5

Andante

Andante con variazioni f-Moll
Andante con variazioni F minor
Hob. XVII/6

Andante

Variationen über „Gott erhalte"
Variations on "Gott erhalte"
nach/after Hob. III/77[II]

Poco Adagio
Cantabile

Adagio F-Dur
Adagio F major
Hob. XVII/9*

Adagio G-Dur
Adagio G major
Hob. XV/22[II]

Allegretto G-Dur
Allegretto G major
Hob. XVII/10

Allegretto G-Dur
Allegretto G major
nach/after Hob. III/41[IV]

Il Maestro e lo Scolare
Sonata a quattro mani
Hob. XVII a/1

Andante

Anhang/Appendix
„Gott erhalte"
Klavierfassung des Liedes / Piano setting
of the song
Hob. XXVI a/43

Poco Adagio
Cantabile

PREFACE

In the first edition of his dictionary (1790/92), E. L. Gerber writes: "In naming Joseph Haydn, we call to mind one of our greatest men; great in small things, and yet greater in great ones; the glory of our age. Ever rich and inexhaustible; for ever new and striking; ever great and sublime, even when he seems to be smiling. He has brought a degree of perfection to our instrumental music, namely to our quartets and symphonies, that was unheard of before him."

Although Beethoven's output long had the effect of obscuring the unique significance of Haydn's work, so that by 1819 C. F. Zelter already had to report to Goethe from Vienna: "Beethoven is praised to the skies, because he takes great pains over his work, and because he is living; but the one who conveys their national character like an unadulterated stream that admits no tributary, that one is H a y d n, who lives in them, because he stems from them. Each day they seem to forget him, yet daily he is reanimated in them", Gerber's evaluation remains true to this day, for all that one can no longer compare our era with his.

Brahms' assertion (to Heuberger in 1896) is also frankly thoughtprovoking: "Today people hardly understand Haydn any more. The fact that we are living at a time where — a hundred years earlier — Haydn created our entire music, where he brought one symphony after another into the world, occurs to no-one. I have been celebrating these things for years! In a few years' time, when the 'Creation' and the 'Seasons' will be a hundred years old, a few festivals will be organised for business purposes — and no-one will even think of the many other pieces. At this time Haydn evolved for a second time to incomparable stature, having earlier seen the world and achieved so much."

And we are not yet generally aware of what Casals, who had achieved the utmost maturity, once wrote: "Simplicity in formal expression has never harmed the real creative artist, who well knows that originality is primarily a gift of nature. I could probably say that during my long life I have heard a great deal of music. Well, when I hear Haydn, I have the impression of discovering something new. If interpreted the way it deserves, great music really is rich enough to retain its 'novel' character and to let desire grow in us to hear it again and again." —

Even on the basis of the piano pieces, which are not very extensive, either in themselves or in relation to other groups of works in Haydn's œuvre, one can recognise his unique achievement; for this reason we have not arranged the pieces in our volume in a chronological-linear manner, but have grouped them according to genre.

The actual piano piece in the modern sense was only the creation of the 19th century masters. The great masters of the Viennese classical school entrusted their piano output almost exclusively to the sonata; which admittedly includes — particularly in Haydn's case! — the "accompanied piano sonata" (chamber music for piano). But even so, there are already a certain number of particularly significant pieces dating from this period. Within Haydn's output this means, in addition to the famous *Andante con variazioni* and the *Variations on the anthem*, whose authentic piano version is published here for the first time with the relevant arrangement of the theme, above all the *Capriccio* and the *Fantasia*. The *Capriccio* represents Haydn's personal engagement with the monothematic rondo created by C. Ph. E. Bach; the *Fantasia,* originally called "quite new Capriccio" by Haydn, transforms the idea of the rondo in a unique manner. One should also add the great *Adagio in G major* as it was originally conceived, before being subsequently incorporated into the Piano Trio Hob. XV/22.

To be sure, these works are not isolated ones, but are surrounded by other creations equally worthy of closer inspection. In our case, the reason for this is one particularly characteristic of Haydn, since of all the great composers, none made such relatively modest demands of the player as he. It is true that the intellectual force of his work was sometimes underrated for this very reason, but on the other hand it enabled him to win over a great number of practising musical amateurs. It has also been a special aim of the editor's to serve these latter. The wealth of fingerings added to this end are mainly the work of Gerschon Jarecki.

ON THE INDIVIDUAL WORKS

Capriccio in G major "Acht Sauschneider müssen seyn", Hob. XVII/1

Gerber, in his dictionary (1812), quotes the following assertion by Haydn: "Whoever knows me well must realise that I owe very much to Emanuel Bach, that I have industriously studied and comprehended him. And I recognise only him as my model." This relationship between the two masters is really a very concealed one, since Haydn copies none of the external features of his model! Such is the case with our *Capriccio,* the only piece in which Haydn adopts the characteristic Ph. E. Bach rondo, evolved from a single theme, and how personally he does it! The folksong on which the construction of the main and subsidiary sections is based, is one of those songs in which one person drops out in each verse. It begins (quoted from K. M. Klier, periodical *Das deutsche Volkslied* Nr. 34) "Eana achte müaßns sein, wanns an Saubärn wolln schneidn. Zwa vorn und zwa hintn, zwa haltn, oana bindtn / und oana schneidt drein: Eana achte müaßn sein!" and ends: " A glei oana brauchts sein... Is vorn und is hintn / Tuat haltn und bindtn / und nacha schneidt er drein / A glei oana muaß schon sein!" Note that the main and subsidiary sections each have the song twice, sometimes slightly shortened and altered, and the last main section actually quotes it three times (b. 265, 297 and 341); so the frequent repetitions of the song demanded by the text are comfortably exceeded by the musical bases that Haydn establishes here for his rondo!

Fantasia in C major, Hob. XVII/4

A year after the publication of the *Capriccio*, on the 29. III. 1789, Haydn worte to Artaria concerning the *Fantasia:* "In a moment of most excellent good humour, I have written a quite new Capriccio for the fortepiano, whose tastefulness, originality and special construction must win applause from connoisseurs and amateurs alike. It is just a single piece, rather long, but not really at all hard; since you have always given special regard to my earnings" ("Erwerben"; but could read "meinen Werken" — "to my works"), I am offering it to you for 24 ducats: the price is quite high, but I can guarantee you will make a profit from it..." One shouldn't regard these words simply as evidence of Haydn's business acumen, aimed at securing the highest possible price for his work. The piece really is unique. Reference to the older *Capriccio* makes it clear that here, once again, rondo form has been transformed in a "special" manner, as is expressed by the original title *Fantasia*. The certainty with which Haydn predicted the "applause of conoisseurs and amateurs alike", shows an overestimation of both, then as now. But we can well believe that with it he was able to charm his audience in "Estoras" (Eszterháza), where he composed the piece, and probably performed it himself.

20 Variations in G major, Hob. XVII/2

The work has come down to us in G major and A major. The fact that the only palpably complete version of this work would not, of itself, be sufficient reason to print it in this key: for the anthology in which it has survived contains many transpositions, such as that of our *E flat major Arietta* — transposed to C major. One should bear in mind that in Haydn's "draft catalogue" (see our pictorial supplement) the A major theme is a correction of a copy which has been begun in G major; even Elssler, in preparing the catalogue (known to scholars as the "Haydn-Verzeichnis" of 1805) Haydn commissioned from him, has mechanically adopted the G major key signature! We know of another two manuscript copies, one in G major, the other in A major, and containing only 11 and 17 out of the 20 variations respectively. In its complete version, Haydn's work lies firmly within the tradition of the chaconne, which at that time had the same objectives as later led, under utterly different technical conditions, to the composition of etudes. Great as the demand for variations was in Haydn's day, the market for this kind of variation had probably already declined. So it is not surprising that a revision was made later; even the copyists of the original works had displayed no interest in it as an entity. Yet today this work seems interesting precisely because of what was, at the time, its all too conservative character, since it gives a demonstration of Haydn's specific treatment of the piano during the sixties. The "broad stretches" (see below) are part and parcel of the attitude Haydn had developed at that time on encountering the "Hammerflügel". Although the only surviving complete copy seeks to avoid notes lower than C, it enables us to see that these low bass notes must have been present in the sources; the same is demonstrated by the second source, which gives us the work in the key of G major.

Arietta No. 1 in E flat major, con 12 variazioni. Hob. XVII/3

There are any number of manuscript copies of this work, so it must have enjoyed enormous popularity in its time. On the one hand, this is because what we have here is a typical set of variations of the kind desired by the many "amateurs of the clavier" at that time, on the other hand, it is due to the exceptional poise of the theme, which was used for the main section of the minuet in the String Quartet Op. 9 no. 2. Both parts are constructed over the same bass. Across this span, the melody spreads a broken chord from b flat^1 (b. 1 f.) via e flat ^{2} (b, 3, 6) to g^2, which opens the second part, putting the repetition of b. 5—10 in b. 15—20 is a new tonal perspective. The present-day player may regret that the last variation doesn't bear the clear imprint of a final variation. But perhaps Haydn had actually thought that after the XIIth variation the theme would be played once more, as is suggested by the anthology copy (Gesellschaft der Musikfreunde, Vienna, see Critical Notes) where the theme is written out again in full after the last variation!

Arietta No. 2 in A major, con 12 variazioni, Hob. XVII/2

It must have been around 1788 that the plan was laid to have a group of as yet unpublished works for piano issued by Artaria. It is not surprising that this plan led to the original version of the 20 Variations being reworked so that it could be produced as a sister work alongside the favorite E flat Arietta. Only 11 variations were retained, the whole was regrouped, and a capricious, newly composed variation was put in the tenth position. So the old piece has been made to pay lip service to the new taste. But the work, not least because of the light-weight theme, remains a very modest sister, and it is only as such that its charms are unfolded. It may be particularly useful to the present-day player to acquire a feeling for the expressive nuances of the playing technique of that period on his instrument. The strict two-part writing assumes that crotchets in the right hand that match the harmony or make suspensions of the notes of the harmony will be held overlong, whether forming middle voices below or above the notes to be struck next. It is this way of playing that our fingerings in the theme

aim to suggest. It is obvious that such continual treatment of individual voices, resting on the natural decay of piano notes, is implicit wherever legato effects are aimed at, and that such a way of playing presupposes its own special fingerings. In this respect the Arietta could prove very stimulating. Here too, one should bear in mind the possibility of ending the work with a repetition of the theme.

6 Easy Variations, Hob. XVII/5

This composition for amateur players was written by Haydn — still for Artaria — shortly before his first journey to London. It is a typical sequence of 6 variations on a major-key theme, the 5th variation being in the minor, and thus giving the last one a final character without any need of lengthening it. Here it would be senseless to perform the theme once more at the end. What strikes one is the extremely high register, as well as the purely figurative character of the whole. A comparison of corresponding bars shows the joy and art with which Haydn sets off various registers against one another.

Andante con variazioni in F minor, Hob. XVII/6

In this most celebrated of Haydn's piano pieces, which consists of a form he frequently used, that of the double variation, the combination of variations on two different themes evolved from the basic shape of the first, and whose content is immediately gripping in a way little other music is, — in this piano piece the form in which the composition has come down to us raised many questions which we report on in detail in the Critical Notes. If one can't always arrive at completely unambiguous solutions, then at least the wealth of variants shows the inner richness of this work, thereby opening it up to our deeper understanding. Despite the length of the work, we recommend the performer to play all the repeats.

Variations on the anthem "Gott erhalte"

In the Haydn Yearbook VII, Universal Edition 1970, I was able to prove the authenticity of this version. This is the first complete printing of this version with Haydn's own arrangement of the theme based on the movement for string quartet. In the first variation, the arrangement of the two violin parts for the piano can only be solved by complete recomposition. This alone is sufficient to make the arrangement extremely interesting, all the more so since this version contains all sorts of tiny features not found elsewhere. We know that Haydn's preoccupation with this song lasted into his last days.

The Adagio in F major, Hob. XVII/9*, whether an abbreviated version of a longer movement or an original work, is a self-contained and self-explanatory piece.

The large-scale Adagio in G major, Hob. XV/22^{11} may be played or heard with pleasure in this its o r i g i n a l version as a solo piano piece.

The Allegretto after a piece for Mechanical Clock, Hob. XVII/10 shows its artistic merit by not being determined to demand everything of ten fingers that the pegs of a mechanical clock can manage. Expressive playing enables man to do things that clockwork cannot. Since people nowadays like to play Haydn's mechanical clock pieces — particularly on suitable positive organs —, the study of this arrangement may be recommended in such a context.

The *Allegretto after Hob. III/41ᴵⱽ* is an authentic, shortened version of the finale of a string quartet. At the time, such arrangements helped to circulate music in the way a gramophone record does today. Everything has its advantages and disadvantages, and the advantage of shortened versions such as this is that the player could become actively involved in the music concerned.

Active involvement with music is central to the playing of piano duets, still too little cultivated today. It seemed sensible to end our volume with Haydn's only duet composition. Being a work in two movements, the *Sonata "Il Maestro e lo Scolare" Hob. XVII a/1* does not, strictly speaking, belong among the piano pieces. The first edition is an English engraving whose title ("Favorite Duetto . . .") and text fail to convince. Almost simultaneously there appeared an edition by Hummel, whose subtitle "Sonata con variazioni" has the correct meaning: namely a work in several movements, the first of which is variation form. This is a type of sonata which Mozart and Beethoven also cultivated, though not so assiduously as Haydn. Such a sonata, moreover, does not necessarily have to include a movement in sonata form. The variation movement, which seems rather simplistic at first sight — the master always plays first, and then the pupil — actually fulfills a pedagogic aim. The imponderables of interpretation should be directly taught and learnt by means of the living example afforded by the "maestro". For this reason we have deliberately avoided printing the duet writing 'in score', as is nowadays quite rightly recommended, lest the primo-player be distracted from concentrating on the evidence of his ears. In the closing minuet, the pupil is finally free to take over the lead.

SOME NOTES FOR INTERPRETATION

The end of our *Capriccio* and the last variation of the *20 Variations Hob/XVII,2* have s t r i k i n g s t r e t c h e s o f a t e n t h i n t h e l e f t h a n d. In addition, in b. 25/26 of A, as well as b. 36/37 of our *Capriccio* and Var. IX of the above-mentioned *Variations* (a variation that actually wasn't transferred to the shorter version, designated *Arietta No. 2)*, there are stretches of up to a twelfth. Since the notes G and A are always bottom keys, there is no question here of the "short octave" on older keyboard instruments. But these stretches seem to prove something else. Haydn wrote these earliest piano pieces not for the harpsichord but, already, for the H a m m e r k l a v i e r. That means: even when the pedal is depressed during a change of harmony (or on old instruments, when the general raising of the dampers is effected by hand, or by raising the knees). This slightly resonant blurring of the harmonies had at that time the special charm of a new effect. If nothing of the sort is to be found in the 1788 editions, then that amounts to a renunciation of the element of sheer novelty in this attraction, but not of the "registration pedal" itself, as I should like to call pedalling through a change of harmony, something that Beethoven frequently prescribes (e. g. in the Sonata Op. 31, No. 2).

How should Haydn's text be a r t i c u l a t e d ? B. 2 and 3 of the *Fantasia*, where no articulation is given, are certainly not meant to be executed *non legato*. In b. 2 the two semiquavers are legato, and b. 3 should probably be executed *legato* from the second to the last semiquaver. Obviously we haven't written this into the edition, since it is only when I know the original markings made by Haydn that I have a firm basis for my articulation.   According to C. Ph. E. Bach it is the "basic progression" of a piece that lends expression to its "affects". It is precisely in this sense that Haydn's music is to be interpreted; its relation to the basic progressions within which the diminutions are unfolded, needs to be properly understood and simply put across. An extremely concise example of this: the head motive of Haydn's *Fantasia*, whose meaning is rooted in absolute music, is a diminution of a "rising" basic progression from c² via d² to e²

;

but if one accentuates on the b a r here, the notes c²—b¹—c² are stressed and all the refinement of Haydn's declamation goes to the wall;

While talking of slurs, our sources also raise the q u e s t i o n o f t i e d n o t e s. Tied dissonances are of particular significance in classical composition, whose rhythm is given a profiled "light and shade" by these means. In the Critical Notes we have clearly described the situation with regard to the sources in b. 54—61 of the *Sauschneider-Capriccio*. If A, by the subtle tying of a note from the semiquaver run to form a middle voice forming the lower third to the dissonant cambiata note c³ which enters on the downbeat (b. 54), intends a certain "tender" (as one might say) articulatory effect, then Haydn may have regarded further markings at this point as dispensable when making the basic copy. Now if FE actually ignores the subtle notation of A, but unmistakeably marks the simpler ties from the upbeat to b. 55 onwards (not always exactly, but they are present), then it is drawing consequences which are more appropriate to Haydn's subtle marking than would be the slavish adherence to what is written in the autograph.

Haydn's d y n a m i c m a r k i n g s must also be understood as having various meanings. Fundamentally, one has to distinguish between two kinds of intention is writing out these signes. Firstly there are those which are concerned with revealing the articulation of formal components, then there are those which are concerned with the portrayal of detail, i. e. relate to "light and shade". In this sense, one could talk of general or formal dynamics on the one hand, and detailed or linear dynamics on the other. The *Fantasia* contains a relatively large number of dynamic markings, though the first of these is found only in b. 45. Since the *Fantasia* is one of the Artaria engravings referred to in a letter by Haydn: ". . . only I regret that here and there a few mistakes have slipped in, which it is now too late to change, since they have already been distributed and put on sale; it is always distressing for me that not a single work issued under your auspices is free of mistakes . . .", we cannot regard its dynamic markings as being completely reliable. But the dynamic superstructure can be reconstructed on the basis of what is present. Formally,

168

the *Fantasia* subdivides into a seven-part rondo. The main sections (b. 1—69, 124—192, 255—302, and b. 356 to the end) are basically *forte,* and b. 255 is expressly so marked. The first main section develops two themes, the second of which (b. 29 ff.) also has a *forte* character; the final main section actually begins with the second theme transposed into the tonic (b. 356). The subsidiary sections (b. 70—123, 193—254 and 303—355) always begin with the theme which is marked *p* at its very first entry (b. 70); the first and third subsidiary sections also contain passages veering to *forte* (the broken chords at b. 88 ff. and 324 ff.), the second subsidiary section has no such broken chords, and the *forte* beginning at b. 214 can scarcely apply to the entire remainder of the section (see Critical Notes). All these dynamic markings, whether actually present or merely inferred, are to be considered as general dynamics. The remaining markings indicate variations of whatever dynamic happens to be prevalent. That these markings too, like the articulation given by Haydn, are simply the basis for a much more varied interpretation of detail, should be obvious.

The *Sauschneider-Capriccio* may also be regarded as a rondo. Neither the autograph of 1765 nor the first edition of 1788 contain dynamic markings. Since in this case a single theme — the Sauschneider song — dominates both main and subsidiary sections, it is particularly recommended here that the variety of formal components should be brought into sharper relief by means of contrasted dynamics; the main sections in *forte,* the subsidiary sections in *piano: f* b. 1—61, *p* b. 62—132, *f* b. 133—189 (actually *diminuendo* from b. 162, in order to give consonance and dissonance "light and shade" in the subsequent modulatory passage), *p* b. 190 to 246, in b. 247 *f subito,* aiming towards b. 265 ff., followed by minor key "shading" *p* at b. 274, so as to prepare for a *crescendo* when the theme enters at b. 296; from then on, *forte* dominates to the end! These, of course, are only general indications. The whole should use a variety of shadings; e. g. the premature entry in b. 114, whose *pianissimo* colouring lays the basis for a big *crescendo* up to the next entry (b. 133). Each of these components once again requires a highly varied portrayal of "its own progress". It should be noted in this context that "light and shade" are particularly dependent on the absolute separation of consonance and dissonance, always inherent in classical music from the very start, with the result that their meaningful representation is essential if the interpretation of such works is to express their true content.

In achieving this end, an important part is also played by o r n a m e n t s, particularly the appoggiatura, trill and turn.

To start with, there is the b r o a d s u b j e c t o f a p p o g i a t u r a s. For their standardisation in modern editions, something which the editors of this volume also had to strive for, awakens in the user the false supposition that the way the appoggiaturas are written is completely unambiguous. In practise this wasn't so. So long as appoggiaturas were indicated not by notes, but by means of tiny slurs, there were certain rules, and also a certain possibility of different solutions. With the introduction of notes written very small, certainty was almost achieved, but not entirely, since there was no special sign for the short appoggiatura. Usually it was written as a semiquaver, but a semiquaver could equally well indicate a long appoggiatura. So there is a rule for appoggiaturas that small crotchet notes or longer values mean long appoggiaturas, but small quaver notes and shorter values can mean either long or short appoggiaturas! Here the principle applies that a long appoggiatura cannot be longer than its notated value. This freedom of interpretation from the quaver appoggiatura downwards then becomes a problem on account of the inconsistency of the notation. Since short appoggiaturas were usually notated as (single) semiquavers, a note length that was often not just written but even engraved in short form as a quaver with a stroke through it, during the 19th century this kind of semiquaver became the symbol for a short appoggiatura. To remove misunderstandings nowadays, one gets rid of this short form and engraves regular semiquavers in every case, as if the abbreviated notation and its frequent use for the short appoggiatura hadn't already graphically brought that relation to light! So to start with, one must establish that from the quaver note downwards, there is, in principle, freedom in the interpretation of appoggiaturas. In addition, it should be stressed that one or more small notes may not, in principle, be taken in advance, but must be subtracted from the length of the note they precede; the dissonant suspensions that result should be exploited to the full by the player. Yet

With trills, the first thing to remember is that the basic stipulation, that one must begin with the upper auxiliary note, is subject to exceptions depending on context, although this is not actually mentioned in the *Essay.* It seems important to me to decide in each case whether the trill is, in effect, a suspension repeated several times, or a repeated movement to an auxiliary note, since it can express either. If a dotted note has a trill, then usually the trill shouldn't end at the point where the dot comes into force, which is what one almost always hears, but extends a little further, meaning that the entry of the next note is slightly delayed, and the note thereby shortened. An example of this will be found in the footnote to b. 2 of the *Allegretto in G major Hob. XVII/10.* The fact that in secondary sources one may surmise the existence of a turn behind the sign for a trill, is shown by the following quotation from C. Ph. E. Bach, which is taken from the explanations of this embellishment:

There one reads (Vol. 1, p. 89, § 17): "Away from the keyboard, the sign for the turn is as little known as the ornament itself is necessary to music: so one indicates it with the normal sign for a trill, or even with the sign for a mordent, which is sometimes used to imply a trill." So what has since become known as the "Haydn ornament", a sign for a turn with a mordentlike stroke through it (cf. *Capriccio* b. 20) is not a completely isolated phenomenon! In the Critical Notes on b. 3 and b. 15 of the first of the *Variations on the Anthem,* we have elucidated the execution of the turn, and in particular the law of "spacing" — which is also specially applicable to undotted notes — with reference to Haydn's notation.

Franz Eibner

INDEX

Band 1a / Volume 1a

Hob. = Anthony van Hoboken: *Joseph Haydn. Thematisch-bibliographisches Werkverzeichnis.* B. Schott's Söhne, Mainz, 1957

INDEX
Band 1b / Volume 1b

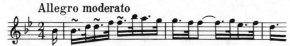

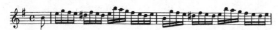

PREFACE

PREFACE

"I acknowledge with pleasure the desire of many music lovers to own a complete edition of my piano compositions, which is, I feel, a flattering indication of their approval, and I shall see to it that in this collection no work which wrongly bears my name will be included." So begins the foreword, drafted by Gottfried Christoph Härtel and signed by Haydn on December 20th, 1799, which appeared in *Cahier I* of the so-called *Oeuvres complettes* of Haydn, issued by Breitkopf & Härtel between 1800 and 1806. This first collected edition of Haydn's piano works, in twelve volumes, included not only compositions for piano solo but also piano trios, vocal works for one and more parts with piano accompaniment, and duos for piano and violin. Four of these duos were, in fact, contemporary arrangements of piano sonatas. Apart from such works, thirty-four piano sonatas were included in the *Oeuvres complettes,* and all subsequent "complete" editions of Haydn's piano sonatas consisted of these works. Five further works were added by Hugo Riemann in his edition of Haydn's piano works published by Augener (London) in 1895. Finally, the collected edition of Haydn's sonatas which was published by Breitkopf & Härtel and excellently edited by Karl Päsler (three volumes, from 1918) contained no less than fifty-two sonatas.

The discrepancies between these numbers must be explained. Haydn had requested a thematic catalogue from his Leipzig publishers and from this he removed not only spurious works but also, as the foreword goes on to say, "those works of my early youth, which are not worth preserving". In other words, Haydn was concerned not only with expunging spurious works but also with limiting the edition to his more mature compositions. Though we can understand the composer's attitude, our own point of view is bound to be different. Only an edition which contains, so far as is possible, all the works of a composer in chronological order can form the basis for studying that composer's development, as well as illuminating his relationship to his contemporary musical world. To this one must add that the early works of a master often contain moments of such beauty that they should be kept alive by performance and not be allowed to fall into oblivion.

The actual text of the *Oeuvres complettes* can hardly be regarded as "the master's last will and testament". The ageing Haydn, at this time preoccupied with other work, had little or nothing to do with the revision.

Breitkopf & Härtel carried out this revision simply by taking the sources at their disposal and bringing them into line with the musical taste at the turn of the century. The editor was probably August Eberhart Müller, who in 1800 became assistant of the *Thomaskantor* Johann Adam Hiller and then himself became Cantor of St. Thomas in Leipzig in 1804. Although Müller revised the sonatas with relative care, he did not hesitate to make his own changes and additions, and in this "revised" form the sonatas have survived through most editions until the present day. Päsler rendered a great service in preparing the first critical and complete edition, for he attempted to give us as authentic a text as possible, based upon the available autographs, contemporary manuscript copies, and the first and early editions (these latter sometimes of doubtful textual validity). Päsler's edition has unfortunately long been out of print and the recent reprint by Lea Pocket Scores, besides omitting Päsler's long foreword to the first volume and his notes to all three volumes, is in miniature score format and therefore unsuitable for practical use.

It is not only for these reasons, however, that a new edition is needed. As a result of Jens Peter Larsen's new direction in Haydn research, a new standard in the critical evaluation of sources has been introduced which provides the basis for authenticity, chronology, and establishment of the text. Although the editing of the sonatas may not require changes as extensive as those in the symphonies, the appearance of then unknown autographs and contemporary manuscript copies also plays a part in making a new edition desirable. The new sources — that is, those not used by Päsler — were found largely in Austrian and Moravian libraries and archives. Of all the sources used by Päsler, only some for early sonatas which were in the German castles of Altjeßnitz and Gotha* were destroyed in the last war. These would seem to have derived from the copies advertised by Breitkopf in 1766 and 1767. On the whole it might be said that Päsler tended to attach too much importance to printed editions and manuscript copies based on these editions. Even when good sources were at hand he gave too much emphasis in his critical notes, and to some extent in the musical text itself, to readings from such editions. Though the variants were distinguished in his edition by smaller print and other means, this not only cluttered the page but also left the danger

---

* Recently the Gotha copies have reappeared.

that the player would unconsciously be influenced by them. This is perhaps the place to stress that when in Haydn research the autograph is not available, one must, with very few exceptions, give preference to a copy independent of printed editions and closer in time and place to Haydn himself. The prints were all too often issued without the composer's knowledge, based on inferior sources or even containing specious alterations introduced by the publisher.

AUTHENTICITY AND CHRONOLOGY

In addition to the fifty-two sonatas that Päsler included in his edition, he also recorded eight sonatas thought lost and the themes of which were entered by Haydn himself in the catalogue he kept of his own works, the so-called *Entwurf-Katalog* (published in facsimile by Jens Peter Larsen). Päsler included these eight works in his foreword but did not insert them into his chronological list of the fifty-two. This chronological arrangement of the Breitkopf & Härtel Haydn edition was subsequently taken over by Anthony van Hoboken in his Haydn Catalogue (Mainz, 1957), so that the Hoboken numbers (added for convenience in our present edition) are in every case identical with those of Päsler.

Of the sixty sonatas (the fifty-two plus the lost eight), three cannot be retained: Hob. XVI/No. 15, which is a dubious arrangement for piano of the Divertimento in C (Hob. II/No. 11); Hob. XVI/No. 16, whose authenticity is extremely doubtful; and Hob. XVI/No. 17, which was probably written by J. G. Schwanenberg.

Of the remaining works, apart from the eight "lost" sonatas listed by Päsler, the following may be considered as indubitably genuine on the basis of an extant autograph, an entry or reference in the *Entwurf-Katalog* or the existence of an authentic printed edition: No. 9 (Hob. XVI/No. 4), No. 13 (6), No. 14 (3), No. 16 (14), No. 20 (18), No. 29 (45), No. 30 (19), No. 31 (46), No. 33 (20), Nos. 36—41 (21—26), Nos. 42—47 (27—32), Nos. 48—52 (35—39), Nos. 54—56 (40—42), Nos. 58—59 (48—49), No. 62 (52), and Nos. 60—61 (50—51). The reference in Haydn's London catalogue of works included in the fourth London notebook is probably, if not explicitly, to the last three works. On the basis of the sources and on stylistic grounds the following sonatas may also be considered genuine — although in the case of the early works, leaving aside the inferior sources for some sonatas, the determination of authenticity on grounds of style is severely handicapped by our comparative ignorance of the music of the period: No. 1 (Hob. XVI/No. 8), No. 2 (7), No. 3 (9), No. 6 (10), No. 8 (5), No. 10 (1), No. 11 (2), No. 12 (12), No. 15 (13), No. 32 (44), No. 34 (33), No. 35 (43), No. 53 (34), Nos. 19 and 57 (see Hob. XVI/No. 47).

In addition to the sonatas published by Päsler, from which we have excluded the three sonatas mentioned above, the present three-volume edition offers the following works:

(a) The fragment of a sonata in Haydn's autograph, sold at auction from a private collection by the Marburg firm of J. A. Stargardt in 1961. This fragment, one of the eight sonatas previously thought to be lost, at one time belonged to the Viennese collector Wilhelm Kux and is included in our list as No. 28 in D major. Hoboken mistakenly listed it under *Mehrstimmige Divertimenti mit Klavier* (XIV/No. 5). Through the fortunate reappearance of this work it now seems possible that one or more of the remaining "lost" sonatas may someday come to light. We have therefore included all eight works in our new thematic list. (Their numbering follows the order in the *Entwurf-Katalog*. Since Haydn entered these and other works, presumably *en bloc*, in his catalogue about 1767/68, and since some of the others were written before or during this time, the numbering of the eight works is not necessarily chronological.)

(b) A version in E of the three-movement Sonata No. 57 in F (Hob. XVI/No. 47) issued by Artaria in 1788. Jens Peter Larsen found this version, No. 19 in our list, in the archives of the Gesellschaft der Musikfreunde in Vienna, where it is in a manuscript containing other Haydn piano works as well. This version is also in three movements but does not contain the rather curious opening movement of the printed version (a movement which is, stylistically, strikingly at odds with the rest of the work). The version in E begins with the "Larghetto" (here marked "Adagio", and in E minor) and continues with the "Allegro" (here in E major). The final movement is a hitherto unknown "Tempo di Menuet" (E major). It appears that we are dealing with a work which was composed in the 1760s and which was altered later by Haydn for Artaria, or by Artaria himself. Even the two transposed movements show considerable textual divergencies. The printed version is no doubt a potpourri, utilizing a single piano piece in F as an opening movement.

(c) Two sonatas in E flat major (Nos. 17 and 18), mentioned for the first time by Georg Feder, which are part of a manuscript of early Haydn sonatas copied in the former Benedictine Monastery of Rajhrad (Raigern) in Moravia.*

(d) Finally, it seems justifiable to include two additional works among the piano sonatas: a work marked "Divertimento" (our No. 4, Hob XVI/G 1) and the "Variazioni" (No. 7), included as D 1 among the *Klavierstücke* (Hob. XVII), which, because of its three movements, seems closer to the sonata than to the *Klavierstücke*. The movement that appears as the first movement of Sonata No. 5 (Hob. XVI/No. 11) in our edition also appears as the Finale of Sonata No. 4 (Hob. XVI/G 1), where it seems to be more appropriate. Therefore we must consider Sonata No. 5, which was also included by Päsler, to be merely a combination of three unrelated movements.

Incidentally it is hardly likely that all Haydn's early piano — or rather "keyboard" — compositions have come down to us. They were intended for his pupils rather than for the general public, and those remaining have survived by happy accident.

A chronological order for Haydn's piano sonatas,

* First edition also by Georg Feder, G. Henle Verlag.

especially his early works, can only be suggested, not definitively established. Too many factors, of importance not only for chronology but even for the works' authenticity, are problematical. We need to know much more about the Viennese copyists and "copy shops" of that time and we lack precise details about the exact period in which any given copyist worked. For instance, not one of the extant copies of Haydn's piano sonatas can be established as "authentic" — that is, as having been supervised by Haydn himself. Nor do we have a catalogue of pre-classical and classical keyboard music, such as Jan LaRue (New York) has already compiled for the eighteenth-century symphony; such a catalogue would be of vast importance for the origins and development of the sonata in the classical period. It is not enough merely to establish that the young Haydn was naturally first influenced by the contemporary Viennese musical world — by Wagenseil, for example — and later turned to C. P. E. Bach, who most profoundly influenced his musical thought. The situation is obviously much more complex and we are faced here with an area of research of which only the surface has been touched.

Haydn's development from the simple partitas of the 1750s to the mature works of his London period can be dependably traced only through the dated material at our disposal. The way leads through the *Sturm und Drang* period to the works of 1773 dedicated to Prince Esterházy (although these do not quite carry forward the stylistic line of the previous sonatas), the sonatas of "Anno 1776", the Artaria Sonatas, published in 1780, the Bossler Sonatas (1784), the two-movement Sonata in C for Breitkopf (1789), and the E flat Sonata for Marianne von Genzinger, written in 1789/90 and containing subtle Mozartian touches. We end with the last three sonatas, the first of which is close to Beethoven, while the first movement of the D major has an almost Schubertian melodic line. The chronological order of these last sonatas cannot be precisely determined. While we assume that all three were written during Haydn's second London sojourn (a first version of the second movement of Sonata No. 60 was printed by Artaria in Vienna in 1794), we know that the autograph of No. 62 is dated 1794.

The principal differences between our chronological list and that of the Breitkopf & Härtel collected edition are as follows: No. 29 (Hob. XVI/No. 45), which was issued in 1788 together with Nos. 31 and 32 (46, 44), was known to exist in autograph, dated 1766, after the Breitkopf & Härtel chronology had already been established. Nos. 31 (46) and 32 (44) must also be placed much earlier, for stylistic reasons and also because No. 31 (46) was entered in the *Entwurf-Katalog* about 1767/68, near No. 29 (45) and No. 30 (19, autograph 1767). The editor believes, moreover, that Sonatas Nos. 34 and 35 (33 and 43) probably date from the early 1770s, whereas No. 53 (34) seems to have been written after 1780. But in the early sonatas too our list differs from that of the collected edition. The establishment of an exact chronology here becomes especially difficult because while Haydn was striving to evolve new and more personal musical forms he apparently continued to compose *galant* pieces for the *dilettanti*.

In our edition each sonata has been given its known or presumed date of composition. Since the search for new sources may be expected to continue, it is entirely possible that the order of those works which cannot be exactly dated may be changed by the discovery of new sources or documents. The seven sonatas still lost could certainly help to fill the apparent lacunae in development and chronology. One or more of them might provide a link in the development up to the Sonata No. 29 (Hob. XVI/No. 45) of 1766, and another will perhaps continue the sudden outburst of *Sturm und Drang* whose culmination appears in the C minor Sonata No. 33 (Hob. XVI/No. 20).

The term "sonata" first appears — as far as we know from authentic sources — in this C minor Sonata (1771), while the earlier works are termed either "divertimento" (as in the *Entwurf-Katalog*) or "partita" (as in the autograph of Sonata No. 13, Hob. XVI/No. 6). The contemporary copies also continue to employ the title "divertimento" in works written after 1771. Since a strict separation of these various designations is not possible, we have given the principal title "sonata" to all these works.

CHOICE OF INSTRUMENT AND INTERPRETATION

It is not always possible to decide with certainty which of the sonatas was conceived for harpsichord and which for clavichord or already for the *Hammerklavier*. Of those works surviving in autograph, the holograph fragment of Sonata No. 20 (Hob. XVI/No. 18, written c. 1766?) contains a single dynamic marking, but a variety of dynamic markings is first revealed in Sonata No. 33 (Hob. XVI/No. 20), dated 1771, where we find *forte, piano, sforzato,* and *f-p* effects. A *crescendo,* which would point to the use of a *Hammerklavier,* appears first in the Artaria edition of this C minor Sonata, published in 1780, in a passage not preserved in the fragmentary autograph; the *crescendo* is possibly a later addition. The autograph fragment requires "Clavi Cembalo" — *i. e.* harpsichord — which description is in contradistinction to the dynamic markings and must be regarded as a *genre* description for keyboard instrument. In Sonatas Nos. 36—41, written in 1773, there are only two dynamic markings, one of which is merely an echo effect. The autograph and the authentic first edition continue to specify harpsichord. It is not until Sonata No. 44 (written between 1774 and 1776) that we again find dynamic markings. Certain reliable copies even indicate *crescendo,* but none of these is confirmed by the autograph fragment. The Artaria Sonatas of 1780, however, show many dynamic effects including *crescendo* and these works, Nos. 48—52 (and 33) of our edition, are marked on the title page of the authentic first edition "Per il Clavicembalo, o Forte Piano", a description which, incidentally, one finds on the title pages of very late works, obviously to increase their sales appeal. A *perdendosi* turns up in Sonata No. 53, probably written in the early 1780s.

The entire question of what instrument to use seems to the editor to be primarily of historical interest and one whose importance is generally exaggerated. The essential musical substance of a masterpiece is quite independent of such considerations, which in themselves will always vary with changing taste and local acoustic conditions. When there is any doubt about which instrument is advisable for works not explicitly composed for the *Hammerklavier,* the editor would recommend performance on a fortepiano or clavichord (or, of course, a modern piano) rather than a harpsichord. It should be added that such dynamic markings as are preserved, which were conceived with the sound of the older instruments in mind, are not necessarily to be taken too literally. Eighteenth-century notation gave free rein to the performer's fantasy and imagination, and in many cases the dynamic changes are to be considered as gradual rather than sudden. Only much later did the composer indicate precisely the way in which a given piece was to be performed. Even tempo changes, for instance, need not always be executed too abruptly. The "adagio" in the first movement of Sonata No. 43, for example, may very well be introduced by a *ritardando,* whereas the re-introduction of the *tempo primo* must follow immediately. In Sonata No. 52, published by Artaria in 1780 and intended for wider distribution, we already find such a *ritardando* implicitly marked. It should be further remembered that Haydn's sporadic articulation signs should stimulate the imagination of the player even in the places not marked, so as to reveal the true underlying meaning of the music. One can learn a great deal about how Haydn rendered his musical text ever more precise by comparing the first version with the final version of the second movement of Sonata No. 60. (See Volume III and its appendix.)

The *sforzato* sign so frequently used by Haydn — and often falsified in print as an *f* or even *ff* — has a varied significance which may even include emphasizing the formal structure of a particular passage. The manifold possibilities for performing this sign comprise not only the execution of a sharp rhythmic accent — especially in fast movements — but also that of a highly expressive, hesitating, or even soft attack of the key. Not only in slow movements but even in fast movements as well, this sign may often indicate the application of *rubato.*

APPOGGIATURE AND ORNAMENTS

The Editor's Report published as a companion to this edition also deals with the vexing question of ornaments and grace notes. Even those works of which we have the autographs present problems, but these difficulties inevitably proliferate when our sources are only manuscript copies or printed editions. C. P. E. Bach's *Versuch über die wahre Art das Clavier zu spielen* can be of only limited help to us here, for Haydn modified and extended in his own way the precepts of his North German master in accordance with the South German and Austrian tradition, as exemplified by Leopold Mozart in his *Violinschule.* Concerning the execution of grace notes, the theoreticians recognized with few exceptions only the accented ones, whose character of suspension cannot be denied even in the quickest tempo. In his *Beitrag zur Ornamentik,* published by Universal Edition, Heinrich Schenker says of the short grace note: "There is nothing that can be regarded as the ultimate upper limit of the short *appoggiatura* until one comes to the long *appoggiatura,* and so the broad realm of the former ends only where the latter begins." It is in the light of this quotation that our suggestions on the performance of grace notes must be regarded.

Haydn uses the following ornaments in his piano works: *tr* , ⟍ , ∼ , ⚹ , ✛ , and also ⌒⌒ and ⟋⟍ , as well as ♪ and ♪ or ♪. Some trills are to be played with, and some without, suffix; those with suffix are often written out in the figure ♪♪♪ and its modifications, and in ⟋⟍ the suffix is included in the sign itself. Whether the trill begins with the note above or the main note must be determined by the flow of the music. In certain cases, the trill must be started with the note below, as in the signs ♪♪, ♪♪ or ⌒⌒. The sign ⟍ (*Pralltriller* or short shake) often appears together with descending seconds and especially in connection with *appoggiature,* but also is found where a long trill may be assumed. In a letter to Artaria, Haydn specifically differentiates between ∼ and ✛ (= ⚹ ?) , calling the latter a "half-mordent". We have definite autograph evidence, however, that in parallel passages Haydn placed ✛ instead of ∼ , or vice versa. Passages containing proof of Haydn's intention for one possibility in executing this manifold ornament (✛) are to be found in autographs or in other reliable sources, where, for instance, ♪ is later abbreviated as ✛. It is hardly possible to create a rule from such evidence, but Haydn seems to have preferred ∼ in connection with the figure ♪♪, and ✛ together with ♪♪, on repeated notes or on notes entering without preceding notes. In those passages in the late works which still make use of a sign for diminution, the sign ✛ is almost entirely replaced by ∼. The signs ⚹ and ✛ are used almost interchangeably in the autographs, and the latter often seems to be a hasty abbreviation of the former. Haydn did in fact use the mordent in the usual sense, as can be seen at the beginning of the B minor Sonata, No. 47, where the ornament is at first written out in small notes and, in the course of the movement, abbreviated by a sign. Therefore we have another variant of this diverse sign.

To summarize, the sign ✛ is in the majority of cases equal to a turn (∼), which generally starts with the note above and consists of three notes. On the other hand, it can be a mordent (⚹), which in its usual execution consists of two notes — the main note and the note below. In the present edition we have attempted to differentiate between these signs, but we must point out again that ⚹ and ✛ can barely be distinguished in the sources. Thus both executions may be equally justified. The *geschnellte Doppelschlag* ♪♪♪, wherein the grace note is, as it were, incorporated into the ornament proper, also appears as follows: ♪♪♪.

It should be stressed that the player must select, from among the varying possibilities for the execution of ornaments, the one most suited to the musical content of the passage in question, the tempo and character of the movement itself being decisive. Here one should remember Philipp Emanuel Bach's admonition to exercise the most exacting good taste in addition to the rules.

EDITING PRINCIPLES OF THIS EDITION

In view of the varying reliability of the sources, our editing principles have necessarily been flexible. Certain ones have however to remain fixed. In order to avoid cluttering the printed page, articulation signs which had to be added have not been bracketed. Such signs have in any case been added solely on the basis of parallel passages and only in very few cases, where the player might be led astray, has the editor added slurs not found in the sources. Ornaments, with their pertinent accidentals, not found in the principal sources, however, as well as added notes and dynamic markings, have been placed in brackets. Where appropriate authority was lacking by reason of absence of the autograph, the sign that may be presumed to be correct has been added. Where the ornament was manifestly false, the apparently suitable sign has been inserted. Added ties have been bracketed except when based upon parallel passages. The Editor's Report contains a detailed list of all important textual divergencies, further additions by the editor, and description and evaluation of the sources used. The accidentals have been placed in accord with modern usage, and doubtful ones, not found in the sources, have again been bracketed.

The "long" *appoggiature* have been reproduced as in the sources, but if they appeared incorrect their value was changed to correspond with the actual value as played. On the other hand, the so-called "short" *appoggiature* have been left as semiquavers, according to Haydn's notation. Where the notation is likely to mislead the present-day performer, the execution recommended by the editor has been added to the musical text upon its first occurrence in the movement. A slur from the *appoggiatura* to the main note has been added throughout, which emphasizes its indivisibility.

The graphic appearance of the sources, *i.e.* the distribution on the staves, the change of clef, and the disposition of the cross-beams — except in those cases where the transposition from the soprano to the G clef

made it meaningless — has been preserved as closely as possible. We have kept Haydn's notation in "parts"* where understanding of the musical content appeared to be clarified thereby.

Triplets and sextuplets, which Haydn indicated by 3, 3 (6, 6) or only by a slur, have been printed in our edition as 3 and 6. Particularly in slow movements, it is sometimes difficult to distinguish the slur used for a triplet or sextuplet from an articulation sign, but in the majority of cases this sign should be taken to indicate a triplet, etc.

Only in two places has Haydn's authentic fingering come down to us (Nos. 29 and 56). The fingering added by Oswald Jonas might at first glance seem rather unorthodox, but on closer association the player will discover that it will help to lead him to the right interpretation. This fingering is designed to express the articulation, and though it may appear to increase the difficulties from the technical point of view, it will soon become clear that it actually lightens the task and facilitates the appropriate position of the hand. The fingering will in itself indicate musical separation and connection where the player has little else to guide him.

By way of conclusion, I should like to quote a sentence written by Hermann Abert when in 1920 he reviewed the first volume of the Päsler complete edition and which unfortunately is just as applicable today: "Up to now," writes Abert, "the sonatas have been treated just like the symphonies; that is, one clung with touching devotion to a few tried and trusty warhorses. Some people seem to think that Haydn is outmoded as a keyboard composer. This is mere prejudice. Here is the chance to discover the sonatas in all their abundance. Let us not neglect this opportunity."

Vienna, 1963   Christa Landon

---

* *i.e.* instead of

176

DOCUMENTS AND COMMENTS TO VOLUME I

The sonatas contained in this volume reveal a phenomenal development in Haydn's style. It is a development that gradually sheds the *galanterie* of the early classical era with its partita-divertimento forms and leads to a deepening of content in the piano sonata — an entirely new keyboard writing which found its continuation only in Beethoven.

The major stages of what was at first a slow evolution are marked by three groups of works, the order of which, especially within the first and third groups, is complicated by the lack of documentation: the early works (Sonatas Nos. 1—15), the transitional works (Sonatas Nos. 16—19, 28), and the mature works (Sonata No. 20 and from Sonata No. 29 onwards).

Very few biographical clues to Haydn's early creative period exist. Most of the early keyboard compositions that have survived were probably written before 1761, the year in which Haydn entered the service of Prince Esterházy. They were apparently composed for teaching purposes and to meet commissions. Certainly the young Haydn had to earn a part of his livelihood by teaching, before taking up his first post as *Kapellmeister* to Count Morzin in 1759. Since Haydn himself never received formal theoretical instruction, he was forced to acquire the "science of composition" by his own effort. This may explain the young Haydn's relatively slow development, as may the fact that Vienna, during this transitional period, had no really outstanding composers. At first, Haydn probably carried on existing local traditions. Gradually, from about the mid-1750s onwards, he was able to arrive at a more personal style. Perhaps it was at this time that he first came into contact with the works of Philip Emanuel Bach. Bach's influence can be noticed in the transitional works and even in a few of the early works; it is unmistakably present, however, in the works that mark the breakthrough to maturity. In judging the period of transition to the new style with its prodigious intensification of expression, it is possible that we lack one or another of the seven missing sonatas. These could perhaps explain the rather sudden maturity which appears to start with Sonata No. 29, composed in 1766. This transformation, above all in Haydn's keyboard writing, is already evident in the Capriccio in G major (Hob. XVII/No. 1) from the year 1765, while the Divertimento in C major with accompaniment of two violins and bass (Hob. XIV/No. 4, 1764), — the autograph of which is also preserved — still continues distinctly in the *galant* style, since it is an ensemble piece for entertainment. The Trios of the Minuets in particular, even those of the earliest solo keyboard works, show a great wealth of invention. One is almost tempted to say that the contrast between the Minuet and the Trio spurred the composer on to new ideas. The D minor Trio in Sonata No. 28, for example, is quite unique and virtually a drama in miniature.

The most significant of the sonatas from the second half of the 1760s — and indeed one of the greatest of all the Haydn sonatas — is No. 31, which is not preserved in autograph and therefore cannot be dated with certainty. On the other hand, Sonata No. 30 which, according to the autograph, was composed later than No. 29, is somewhat less profound in expression than the works surrounding it. The sonatas of the late 1760s are followed by another high point, the great Sonata No. 33 in C minor. Sonatas Nos. 34 and 35, the dates of composition of which can only be surmised (we have placed them in the early 1770s), perhaps exhibit the lighter aspects of his style, as can be seen in Sonatas Nos. 36—41, composed in 1773 and dedicated by Haydn to Prince Esterházy.

THE SONATAS BEFORE 1766

There are no autographs of the early works apart from an undated autograph of the first three movements of Sonata No. 13. An authentic date for this work might have offered opportunity for stylistic comparison within the group of early works. According to Georg Feder's convincing method of dating early Haydn autographs, based on Haydn's writing habits as can be deduced from his dated autographs (particularly the change in the notation of *appoggiature* from quavers to half the value of the main note, as well as the alteration of "Minuet" to "Menuet"), Sonata No. 13 could not have been composed later than 1760*. With works preserved only in manuscript copies, this method can of course be applied only conditionally due to the unreliability of the preserved sources.

The autograph fragment of Sonata No. 28 begins in the recapitulation of the first movement. Thus the date of composition which Haydn, from about 1760 onwards, usually wrote at the beginning of each work, is lacking here as well.

The earliest evidence of the distribution of a solo keyboard composition under Haydn's name is the advertisement of Sonata No. 8 in the Breitkopf Catalogue of 1763. Other works obtainable from Breitkopf in manuscript copies were Sonatas Nos. 1, 2, 3 and 13 together with the Variations Hob. XVII/No. 7, listed in the Breitkopf Catalogue of 1766, as well as Sonatas Nos. 5, 6, 12, 15 and 16 in the Breitkopf Catalogue of 1767. These dates can of course only be regarded as an upper limit. Furthermore, the distribution of two series of five works each does not necessarily indicate a chronological connection between the individual works. Nothing is known of contacts between Haydn and Breitkopf at that time, either direct or through an intermediary. The compilation of the works is certainly accidental, so that a chronological rearrangement is justified.

To add a presumed date to the not yet distinctive works before the middle of the 1760s seemed of little point to the editor; hardly any such clues exist with regard to the keyboard works. The chronological order in our edition can be regarded merely as an attempt. It is possible that a smaller part of the early works belongs to the earliest Esterházy period. The dating "before 1766" in our text is understood to mean that we have in Sonata

* Cf. Georg Feder, "Zur Datierung Haydnscher Werke" in *Anthony van Hoboken, Festschrift zum 75. Geburtstag*, Mainz 1962, pp. 50—54.

No. 29 — which, according to the autograph, was composed in 1766 and which already shows a distinct individual style — the first real possibility for stylistic comparison in Haydn's keyboard sonatas. (An exception is Sonata No. 8, advertised by Breitkopf in 1763, which may, however, not be a work of Haydn's at all — see below.)

When writing the general preface to this edition — it went to press in 1963 — only a part of the autograph fragment of the hitherto unpublished Sonata No. 28, then in private possession, was known to the editor. Only after this autograph fragment was purchased by the Stiftung Preußischer Kulturbesitz could it be examined *in toto*. It was then found that the work is perhaps placed too late in our chronological list and should appear with the preceding complex of the seven missing Sonatas Nos. 21—27, following No. 19.

In the general preface attention has already been drawn to Sonatas Nos. 4 and 5. The Minuet of Sonata No. 5 appears in altered form, with another Trio, in the Baryton Trio Hob. XI/No. 26. Except for the dubious Trio, the other movements of this apparently compiled sonata seem to be authentic. The "Presto", at once the opening movement of Sonata No. 5 and the final movement of Sonata No. 4, appears as a single movement in a manuscript of miscellaneous compositions. Sonata No. 4 is the more convincing in its sequence of movements. Two of the extant sources do not contain the Finale; in one of them, however, a page has been cut out following the Trio. In one of the two sources that do contain the Finale, the soprano clef has been replaced by the treble clef, which fact points to a later date for this manuscript; the other source has a string accompaniment (that can hardly be attributed to Haydn), as was occasionally the practice with other early works. Incidentally, almost all the later Haydn sonatas were also published as arrangements, particularly with violin accompaniment. The 18th century was still geared to the requirements of the musical *dilettanti* and *ad libitum* practice, a fact illustrated by the vast variety of arrangements printed by enterprising and clever publishers. On the other hand, several early accompanied divertimentos have been transmitted without the accompanying parts, since the independent character of the harpsichord part permits playing without instrumental accompaniment.

The authenticity of Sonata No. 8, advertised by Breitkopf in 1763, is most doubtful. The primitive setting with its succession of unrelated phrases and the puerile modulations does not suggest Haydn's authorship, even in view of the few opportunities we have for comparison. Although this sonata belongs to those works summarily acknowledged by Haydn in 1803, when going through the thematic lists for the *Oeuvres complettes* (see also the general preface), it can scarcely have been possible for the ageing Haydn to recall each and every composition of such early date. It should be mentioned here that this work was published with violin accompaniment about 1790 by J. Cooper in London, under Pleyel's name. It appeared together with Sonatas Nos. 6, 12, 15 and 16, *i. e.* with those works advertised by Breitkopf in 1767. Sonata No. 5, however, also published by Cooper, but under Haydn's name, was replaced by

Sonata No. 8, also distributed by Breitkopf. The Minuet and Trio of this sonata are contained in a manuscript miscellany. This movement seems the most likely of the three to be genuine Haydn.

The Finale of Sonata No. 13, three movements of which exist in autograph (see above), has been preserved in manuscript copies only. The last three bars of the Adagio are notated in the autograph at the beginning of a new page; otherwise, the page contains only the designation "Finale", the clefs and key signature. Haydn seems to have started the Finale again on a new sheet. The version for piano trio (*cf.* Hob. XV/No. 37), traceable in editions from 1767 onwards, does not contain the Finale. This arrangement was done by an expert musician, but most probably has nothing to do with Haydn. In the autograph, the work is designated "Partitta per il Clavicembalo Solo", and is entered as a solo work in Haydn's holograph catalogue of his works.

The problems arising in connection with Sonata No. 19 and with regard to the other version in F published by Artaria (*cf.* Volume III, Sonata No. 57, as well as the general preface) could be solved only if authentic source material were to come to light. The Finale is contained in only one of the two sources known to exist so far. The authenticity of this "Tempo di Menuet" cannot be doubted, nor in all probability the fact that it is indeed a Finale. A "Tempo di Menuet" is in Haydn's works usually a concluding movement. In some passages of the Adagio the texture seems unlike that intended for a keyboard instrument, and one might almost be inclined to believe that we are dealing with an arrangement rather than an original setting for the keyboard. The source containing the Finale is found in a manuscript which includes a number of keyboard works by Haydn, mainly from the 1760s (among them Sonatas Nos. 14, 16 and 30). It should be pointed out that two works, the Variations Hob. XVII / Nos. 2 and 3, appear there transposed. This fact could be of importance in solving the problem of the original key of Sonata No. 19, resp. No. 57. In any event, this source contains several errors. The second source, which does not include the Finale, is also by no means devoid of errors. The writer was a professional Viennese copyist whose hand is known to us first and foremost from copies of keyboard music. His copies, partly from printed editions, seem to date mainly from the 1780s. Several of Haydn's keyboard works exist in his handwriting, among them Sonatas Nos. 20 and 29—32, contained in this volume. Apart from his copy of Sonata No. 19, the Kremsier Archives possess his separate copy of the first movement of Sonata No. 57, which is not copied from the printed edition. The title page of this single movement carries the copyist's note "1.tes Stük". Corresponding notes by this copyist are found in his copy of Sonata No. 19: in the first movement, "2tes Stük. aus F mol"; in the second movement, "3tes Stük. F. dur". These comments quite obviously refer to the printed version (*cf.* Sonata No. 57). The question remains whether these remarks relate directly to the printed edition or perhaps to a version in F which existed before the published version, or whether they even have some connection with the engraver's copy.

Four works (Sonatas Nos. 7, 9, 17 and 18) have survived in one source only. Two of them, Nos. 17 and 18, were recently located and published by Georg Feder. Among the works preserved in a single source is one confirmed by Haydn's holograph catalogue of his works (Sonata No. 9). It can be proved that the manuscript itself cannot have originated earlier than 1772, a fact which demonstrates the element of mere chance in the preservation of Haydn's early keyboard music. In this connection it is curious that no manuscript copy of Sonata No. 28, a work of a later period, has so far come to light (the autograph has unfortunately not been completely preserved — see above).

The textual value of the individual sources varies of course, but the generalization can be made that the sources are, for the most part, rather late copies in relation to the dates of composition. The sonatas distributed by Breitkopf from the 1760s onwards, are also preserved in sets. Only recently, a further set of Sonatas Nos. 5, 6, 12, 15 and 16 (Breitkopf Catalogue of 1767) was auctioned in London. Of particular importance for the text of several "Breitkopf" sonatas were sources made independently of the Breitkopf copies, and which are, moreover, of Austrian or in some cases Moravian origin.

Two manuscripts contain a number of Haydn's keyboard compositions; the manuscript already mentioned in connection with Sonata No. 19, in the archives of the Gesellschaft der Musikfreunde, Vienna; and a manuscript from the former Benedictine Monastery at Rajhrad (Raigern) in Moravia, which contains Sonatas Nos. 11, 15 and 16, in addition to the afore-mentioned Sonatas Nos. 17 and 18 found by Georg Feder. Further copies, not known to the editor of the first critical complete edition of Haydn's piano sonatas, Karl Päsler, are preserved in the Austrian National Library, and also in the Kremsier Archives, where keyboard music in general is present in extraordinary quantity. A large number of copies in those episcopal archives were written by professional Viennese copyists, a fact pointing to close contact with Vienna. In the monastery archives of Lower Austria — otherwise so rich in Haydn's works — only a very few keyboard sonatas are found.

A comparison of the autograph first three movements of Sonata No. 13 with the extant manuscript copies of that work deriving from the Breitkopf series provided an interesting elucidation of the latters' source value: the actual musical text of these copies is less corrupt than one would suppose, but it is significant that numerous ornaments and ties contained in the autograph are missing. In several works, the octave bass progressions typical of the early works have been falsified, due to the abbreviated notation employed by the copyists (e. g., ♪♪♪); thus the octaves are often discontinued or shifted to the wrong register.

Because of the uncertain source situation it appeared necessary, for musical reasons, to prepare the text of the early works from a combination of the sources. To avoid the danger of a subjective selection of readings, but also to make it possible for the player to have versions from other sources before him, an exception has been made by giving, as footnotes, important readings not taken into the main text, even when such readings seemed suspect to the editor. In many cases, a decision as to the priority of the readings simply cannot be made. Sources not mentioned by name in the footnotes, as well as the further divergences between the sources, are discussed in the Editor's Report on our edition.

The uniform notation of *appoggiature* as quavers, as is customary in the early works, was not retained when the main note is of equal or lesser value, since nowadays the notation ♪♪♪ instead of ♪♪♪ , or ♪♪♪ instead of ♪♪♪ , is confusing to the player.

The editing of Sonatas Nos. 17 and 18, which works, as we have mentioned, are preserved only in the manuscript from Raigern, caused particular difficulty. The text of the five sonatas in this manuscript appears to derive from trustworthy sources, but the one immediate source for the Raigern manuscript was probably faulty. In addition, the hasty writing, typical of the entire manuscript, indicates that part of the errors did not arise from a faulty source but must rather be blamed on the local writer (*cf.* also the reproduction): the noteheads are inaccurately placed; chords are abbreviated to figures; repeated but not always quite identical phrases are placed in ‖: :‖ , giving rise to incorrect continuations; ornaments, notated with a "standardized" sign, are often in the wrong place and appear occasionally instead of *appoggiature* and even instead of triplet signs; ties are almost entirely lacking, notes have been left out, and so on. Especially noticeable are rhythmic errors which arise in part from incorrect drawing of beams; in our text, therefore, the rhythmic alterations suggested by the editor are added in brackets above the stave. It is possible that a third movement of Sonata No. 18 is lacking. (In this manuscript, the Trio of Sonata No. 15 is omitted, and in Sonata No. 11 the second and third movements appear in reverse order.) It is to be regretted that Sonatas Nos. 17 and 18, which probably originated in that so little illuminated transitional period in Haydn's keyboard writing, are preserved only in such a corrupt form.

THE SONATAS FROM 1766 ONWARDS

Sonatas Nos. 20 and 29—32, all of which were probably composed in the late 1760s, were issued at the latest in 1788 together with the Sonata Hob. XVI/No. 17. These six works were published in two groups of three sonatas each by Artaria & Comp. in Vienna as Opus 53 and 54, and at roughly the same time by Longman & Broderip in London as Opus 53. In the editions, the works are printed in the following order: Hob. XVI / No. 17, then Nos. 30, 20, 32, 29 and 31 in our numbering. Hob. XVI / No. 17 appears to be by Johann Gottfried Schwanenberg (Schwanenberger? 1737 or 1740—1804), and may also be eliminated from the list of genuine Haydn works by reason of stylistic criticism. Of the five genuine works, two are preserved complete in autograph (No. 29, 1766, and No. 30, 1767). Of Sonata No. 20 — probably too early in our chronological list — only an autograph fragment is extant, beginning at bar 40 of the second movement. Manuscript copies exist of these three works and also of the other two sonatas, Nos. 31 and 32. These copies belong to the most important new findings among the sources for Haydn's piano sonatas.

Karl Päsler established that the editions of those sonatas still preserved in autograph, particularly that of Sonata No. 30, repeatedly diverged from the autograph versions. Here the question remained open as to whether the revision of works composed some twenty years before publication can be traced to Haydn himself, although reasons of a musical nature argued against it. The extant manuscript copies (unknown to Päsler) which give, in the case of works preserved in autograph, the version of the autograph and not that of the editions, helped to clarify this problem but could not resolve it completely.

In Sonatas Nos. 31 und 32 as well as in the parts of No. 20 not preserved in autograph (particularly the first movement), the printed version also deviates from the manuscript sources. Thus we have, for all five works, two more or less divergent versions. The manuscript copies are preserved in various archives and libraries, and some of them bear a date (the earliest is 1781). The Kremsier Archives contain the complete set, including Hob. XVI / No. 17. All six works were written by the professional Viennese copyist mentioned in connection with Sonata No. 19: here again his sources appear in some way to be connected with those of the printed versions. Curiously enough, Haydn's name has been made indiscernible in all six copies. Divergences between the manuscript copy and the printed version could also be established in the unauthentic work Hob. XVI / No. 17; these indicate that here again a reviser was at work. This fact alone must rule out the authenticity of the printed version of Sonatas Nos. 20 and 29—32; Haydn would scarcely have made alterations in the work of another composer, handing it to a publisher in his name, together with works of his own.

Why it is that precisely these five genuine works appear with an unauthentic one can only be surmised. In order to make a complete set of six sonatas, a Viennese copyist, by accident or design, probably added the sonata not composed by Haydn. It cannot be established who was responsible for the printed versions. As it happens, manuscript copies of works by the Brunswick Court *Kapellmeister* Schwanenberg were distributed in Vienna, as can be seen from an advertisement by the Viennese copyist and later publisher Johann Traeg in the *Wiener Zeitung* of December 21st, 1782. There is as yet no documentary evidence of a possible connection between the assiduous Traeg and the sources for the printed editions.

The Artaria edition is advertised in the *Frankfurter Staats-Ristretto* of May 2nd, 1788; on the other hand, the *Wiener Zeitung*, in which Artaria usually announced their new editions, contains no advertisement. This could be taken as an indication that the publisher had come into possession of the sonatas unlawfully, that is, without Haydn's knowledge. Longman & Broderip registered the first series at Stationers Hall on April 23rd, and the

second series on May 20th, 1788. The legend in the English edition, "Engraved from the Authors original Manuscript", was probably intended to give the public the impression that the publishers had the sole rights of publication. The question of priority in these two editions is of little importance, but Artaria's edition seems to have appeared earlier. There exist some textual divergences between the two editions which cannot be explained as errors in engraving or as arbitrary alterations. Several deviations appear between the manuscript copies which are not necessarily due to errors in the sources. These deviations are too complex to be discussed here and must be reserved for the Editor's Report. It may be mentioned that in Sonata No. 30 the tempo marking for the second movement appearing in the editions, "Adagio ma non troppo" instead of "Andante", is also verified by the manuscript copies, a fact which could point to an authentic intermediary source. A few other readings deviating from those of the autographs are found both in the manuscript copies and editions and leave open the possibility of such an intermediary source.

The autograph of Sonata No. 30, which contains no corrections whatever, has the character of a fair copy, while in Sonata No. 29 the legibility of several articulation signs and ornaments caused difficulties even when the original in the British Museum was examined.

Sonata No. 33 is the "SONATA VI" of the six sonatas dedicated to the von Auenbrugger sisters, and published as Opus 30 by Artaria & Comp., Vienna, in 1780 (*cf.* Volume II, Sonatas Nos. 48—52, as well as the preface to that volume). Haydn sent the sonata to the publisher on January 31st, 1780, and described it in his accompanying letter as the "longest and most difficult" of the six sonatas. Of this work only an autograph fragment dated 1771 has been preserved. Thus Haydn, in order to complete the set, reverted to an earlier work, since all the other sonatas to be considered for publication appear to have been already circulated as copies. This extant autograph, which cannot be identical with the engraver's copy for Artaria, contains, of the opening movement, only the beginning of the first draft. It comprises two separate double sheets. The exposition is complete; there follows a sketch of the first nine bars of the development; the next page is blank, and on the fourth page are sketches for the conclusion of the first movement. Of the second double sheet, the first page is blank; the other three are fully written on and contain the Finale as far as bar 130.

We do not know when Haydn completed the work. We also do not know whether it was only upon publication of the sonata that Haydn made the alterations disclosed by comparing the preserved parts of the autograph with the Artaria edition. The alterations are a matter of refining and clarifying (for example the beginning of the first movement, bars 1 and 5, where the figure in the bass is corrected from ♪♩ to ♫♩) as well as of additions applying especially to the articulation. These additions and alterations have been taken over from the Artaria edition in our text. As is the case with the other sonatas of Opus 30, Artaria's source has not survived.

We have assumed the period of composition of Sonatas Nos. 34 and 35 to be the early 1770s. Of Sonata No. 34 manuscript copies have been preserved which bear the date 1778. This date refers to the copying of these almost identical sources; they seem to have come from the same copyists' workshop, and the date can thus be regarded only as an upper limit. Both sonatas were published fort the first time in London, probably without the composer's knowledge, as "Sonata I" (No. 35) and "Sonata II" (No. 34) of a series begun jointly by Beardmore & Birchall; the third work in the series was Sonata No. 53 (cf. the preface to Volume III). The first sonata (No. 35) was entered under the names of both partners at Stationers Hall on July 26th, 1783, and the second (No. 34) under Robert Birchall's name on November 27th of the same year, probably after the partnership had already been dissolved. The edition published by Le Duc (Paris) in 1785 contains, apart from Sonatas Nos. 34 and 35, Hob. XVI/No. 15 (an arrangement for keyboard — probably not by Haydn — of the Divertimento Hob. II/No. 11).

The no doubt gradual transition from the harpsichord style to the dynamically differentiated style of the fortepiano probably explains why works with prescribed dynamics appear alongside works with no dynamic markings. As mentioned in the general preface, the designation "per il Clavicembalo", which continues to appear even in later works, should rather be understood as a general term for keyboard instruments. Most of the works previous to 1766 seem to have genuine harpsichord character, while the later ones exceed more and more the capacity of that instrument. The new instrument, the fortepiano, only gradually came into its own among music lovers. Even Marianne von Genzinger, for whom Haydn had written Sonata No. 59, did not yet own a fortepiano in 1790, but only a harpsichord.

The *piano* in the second movement of Sonata No. 20 (verified by the autograph) permits the assumption that the dynamic markings in the first movement are also authentic. Bars 16/17 (and 91/92) are particularly differentiated: the *piano* is not to be understood as a *subito piano*, but rather in the sense of a dynamic flow as the termination of a *decrescendo*, the preceding *forte*, in its turn, as a *sforzato* marking the third and final recurrence of the descending phrase (bars 13/16 and bars 88/91).

Nothing is known about the practice of repeating the second part of a movement. Problems arise in those movements with an embellished fermata or with a suspension at final cadences. Only in the rarest instances, in all probability, will players nowadays repeat the second part, particularly in a slow movement. If, however, the second part is repeated, the embellishment must of course be varied; as a rule, it will be more lavish than in the *prima volta*. The embellishments we have proposed in Sonatas Nos. 30 and 31 would, accordingly, apply to the *prima volta*; in the repeat, the player may — and should — expand them (cf. in this connection both suggestions for embellishment in the third movement of Sonata No. 13). The player should proceed with

imagination and in accordance with his own taste, once he has realised that an embellished fermata must in fact be embellished. As regards the suspensions at final cadences, which appear principally in triple metre, the resolution of the suspension on the third beat should be reserved for the *seconda volta*. In the second movement of Sonatas Nos. 29 and 31, the concluding bar is already written in *seconda volta* execution; in the event of a repetition, the *prima volta* should be played like the conclusion of the first part. In the second movement of Sonata No. 20, the final resolution is even more delayed (cf. bar 45 and bars 109/110). To stress the effect of conclusion on the strong beat of a bar, the formulas in the bass (particularly typical of early works) may also be altered at the final recurrence:

for example:

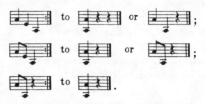

In so doing, the preceding part writing, the register and the upper parts must of course be taken into account. An altered concluding formula is written out in several of the works (cf., for example, Sonata No. 2, third movement; Sonata No. 3, first movement; Sonata No. 6, Finale; Sonata No. 20, first movement).

Judging by the autograph of Sonata No. 13, the conclusion can be reached that other early works were also far more generously embellished than is evident from the preserved sources. (The embellishments in the later works are, to an increasingly larger degree, no longer abbreviated, but are written out as an immutable part of the music.) Therefore, the editor has added ornaments in brackets where they would seem to be required. Of course the player may, at his own discretion, additionally enrich the ornamental components, among other ways by varying the ornamentation when repeating a section. Naturally, the ornamentation is also dependent on the kind of instrument used. The trill in particular, with its scarcely perceptible suspension effect gained from the reiterated alternation of upper neighbouring note and main note, enlivens the character of timbre of the harpsichord. Playing on this instrument requires far more extensive ornamentation than playing on the *Hammerklavier* or clavichord. On the *Hammerklavier*, a short trill (*Pralltriller*) or a turn may, at suitable passages, be played instead of a trill. Some of the ties added in brackets by the editor also apply only to the *Hammerklavier*. On that instrument it is not necessary to attack a sustained note anew, due to the longer duration of its sound. Such sustained parts present in the musical structure, above all in the bass but in the upper and middle parts as well, do of course exist latently when playing on the harpsichord. For, as Philip Emanuel Bach puts it so perfectly: "In music after all many things occur which one must imagine without actually hearing them."

INDEX

Hob. = Anthony van Hoboken: *Joseph Haydn. Thematisch-bibliographisches Werkverzeichnis.* B. Schott's Söhne, 3 Bände, Mainz, 1957/1971/1978

DOCUMENTS FOR VOLUME II

The "Sei Sonate per Cembalo" with which this volume begins were written in 1773 and printed in typeset a year later by the Viennese bookseller and printer Joseph Kurzböck, with a dedication to Prince Nicolaus Esterházy. The autographs of the first and third sonatas — Nos. 36 and 38 of our new edition — are no longer complete, while those of Nos. 39 and 40 are missing entirely. Apart from a few easily discernible misreadings of the autograph and allowing for the mechanical placing of the slurs which this kind of musical typeset necessitates, the Kurzböck edition proved, when compared to the existing holograph manuscripts, to be thoroughly reliable. It retains, incidentally, the notation "in parts" and the soprano clef as it is in the autograph. Kurzböck's is the first authentic printed edition of sonatas by Haydn, and the first edition of any of his works for which Haydn was personally responsible. Both the composer and the publisher took the greatest pains with it. Soon afterwards, Johann Julius Hummel (Berlin—Amsterdam) issued an edition of the works as Opus 13, no doubt without Haydn's knowledge or approval. The false readings and changes of Hummel's edition, where the soprano clef is replaced by the G clef, were faithfully carried down in later prints, including the *Oeuvres complettes*.

In the case of the next six sonatas (Nos. 42—47), we must be dealing with the "6 Sonaten von Anno 776 [1776]" which Haydn entered without the *incipits* in the *Entwurf-Katalog*. All six works are preserved in copies written by one and the same copyist and dated 1776; the "Anno 776" would seem to mean the date when the set was finished. We have an autograph fragment of Sonata No. 44 in F, dated 1774, which breaks off after the exposition of the first movement. This autograph does not contain the dynamic markings found in the copies, though it is the only one of the six works that has any dynamic markings at all. We must conclude that the extant autograph is probably a first draft of the sonata, of which the final version has disappeared. The first printed edition of these six sonatas was made by Hummel (Opus 14, issued in 1778), again in all probability without Haydn's authority.

The five last works in this volume (Nos. 48—52) appeared together with the C minor Sonata No. 33, begun in 1771 as Opus 30, published by Artaria & Comp. in Vienna in 1780, and dedicated to the von Auenbrugger sisters. This was Haydn's first venture with the firm that was later to become his principal publisher. From Haydn's correspondence with Artaria we can see that the sixth sonata of Artaria's edition (our No. 33) was sent from Eszterház on the 31st January 1780, while the "fifth and last" (No. 52) was sent on the 8th February. The others must therefore have been finished previously, and were probably composed in the late 1770s. On the 25th February 1780, Haydn sent back the proofs of all six sonatas, and by April 12th Artaria had already announced their publication in the *Wiener Zeitung*. The autographs of the five works contained in our volume are lost, and all the extant copies — even those in which Artaria's G clef is transposed "back" to the soprano clef, as it would have been in the autograph — can be proved textually to have been taken from Artaria's print. In addition, Artaria's edition eliminates to a great extent the notation of the individual parts that was usual with Haydn. On the whole, it contains so many mistakes that one is inclined to wonder how thoroughly Haydn read his proofs. It would also appear that Artaria was remiss in carrying out the corrections indicated by Haydn in his letter of 25th February. It is obvious, too, from the mistakes that the transposition from soprano to G clef was left to the publisher. Hence, the loss of the autographs is, from the textual point of view, most regrettable indeed.

As early as the 9th September 1780, Hummel announced his edition of the six sonatas in the *Berliner Nachrichten*; they appeared as Opus 17. Hummel corrected some of Artaria's mistakes and changed the order of the sonatas. Nevertheless, it can be shown that Artaria's edition served Hummel as the basis of his print. We must therefore conclude that Hummel's Opus 17 is not, as has been suggested, an independent edition.

The thematic similarity between the second movement of No. 49 and the first movement of No. 52 prompted Haydn to make the following note in the Artaria edition:

"Avertimento. Tra queste sei Sonate vi si trovano due Pezzi che cominciano con alcune battute dell'istesso sentimento, cioè l'Allegro scherzando della Sonata No. II, e l'Allegro con brio della Sonata No. V. L'Autore previene averlo fatto a bella posta, cangiando però in ogn'una di esse la Continuazione del Sentimento medesimo."

In the letter to Artaria of 25th February 1780, Haydn explains as follows:

Incidentally, I consider it necessary, in order to forestall the criticisms of any witlings, to print on the reverse side of the title page the following sentence:

"*Avertissement. Among these 6 Sonatas there are two single movements in which the same subject occurs through several bars: the author has done this intentionally, to show different methods of treatment.*"

For of course I could have chosen a hundred other ideas instead of this one; but so that whole opus will not be exposed to blame on account of this one intentional detail (which the critics and especially my enemies might interpret wrongly), I think that this *avertissement* or something like it must be appended, otherwise the sale might be hindered thereby.

Christa Landon

INDEX

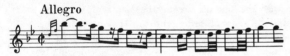

Hob. = Anthony van Hoboken: *Joseph Haydn. Thematisch-bibliographisches Werkverzeichnis.* B. Schott's Söhne, Mainz, 1957

DOCUMENTS FOR VOLUME III

Only two of the ten sonatas contained in this volume, Nos. 59 and 62, are preserved in autograph. The establishment of the text of the other works proved to be extremely difficult owing to the quite inadequate sources. With the exception of Sonata No. 53, these sonatas were no longer distributed in manuscript copies but only in printed editions. Even those editions which seem to be based on authentic sources show a number of errors and inaccuracies. That Haydn corrected the proofs of any of these editions — which in the case of Sonatas Nos. 33, 48—52 is shown through his correspondence with the publisher Artaria (see Volume II) — is not supported by any documentary evidence. For these reasons the establishment of the text of those works not preserved in autograph can be considered only as an attempt to reconstruct Haydn's intentions. Perhaps another autograph of one of the last sonatas may some day come to light. It will be recalled that the previously unknown autograph of Sonata No. 62 was acquired in 1933 by the Library of Congress, Washington. The textual problems caused by the lack of good sources for most of the sonatas in this volume render it especially necessary to use the separately published Editor's Report.

Sonata No. 53, which for stylistic reasons we assume was composed in the early 1780s, was first brought out in London as "Sonata III" of a collection called "A Fifth Sett of Sonatas", containing also Sonatas Nos. 35 and 34. This collection had been started under the publishing partnership of Birchall with Beardmore (Beardmore & Birchall) in 1783. The third sonata (No. 53) was entered in Stationers Hall by Robert Birchall on January 15th, 1784. The first edition seems to have used a copy from a Viennese "copy shop" and replaces the soprano clef by the G clef. It is doubtful if this edition was made with the composer's knowledge. Sonata No. 53, published together with Sonatas Nos. 54—56 by Le Duc (Paris) in 1785, is based on the London edition; the edition brought out by J. André (Offenbach/Main) in 1786 contains only Sonata No. 53 and cannot claim independent source value either. None of the preserved MS. copies, all of which retain the soprano clef, may be considered as a primary source.

The next three sonatas, Nos. 54—56, are dedicated to the wife of the later Prince Nicolaus II, Princess Marie Esterházy, neé Princess Liechtenstein. Bossler (Speyer) published the first edition of these sonatas (advertised in the *Frankfurter Staats-Ristretto* on August 31st, 1784). It was taken into the inventory of the Viennese bookseller Rudolf Gräffer, as can be seen from Gräffer's advertisement in the *Wiener Zeitung* of February 5th, 1785. All further editions from 1785 on — Bland (London), Le Duc (Paris), Hummel (Berlin-Amsterdam), etc. — are based on the Bossler edition. A copy of the Bossler edition (which uses the G clef), once in the possession of P. Werigand Rettensteiner and preserved in Michaelbeuern Monastery near Salzburg, shows the following note in P. Rettensteiner's hand: "Folgende 3 Sonaten sind mir vom Herrn Joseph Haydn zu Esterhasz den 3ten Junj 1785 bey einem stundigen und unterhaltenden Besuche zur Verehrung gegeben, und von ihm vorgespielt worden." ("The following three sonatas were given to me as a present by Joseph Haydn during a delightful visit in Esterhasz on June 3rd, 1785 and were played for me by him.") The Bossler edition, the only source for the three sonatas, proved to be extremely careless, above all in the placing of slurs, ties and dynamic indications. In the first of the sonatas (No. 54), all of which were provided by Haydn with an abundance of dynamic effects, no differentiation is yet made between *sforzato* (also appearing as *ff*) and *forte*. Not until the second sonata (No. 55) does one find a special designation for *sforzato* ("forz"), but here, and especially in the third sonata (No. 56) an intermingling of the signs is still encountered. The interpretation of these designations (an exact description may be read in the Editor's Report) brought with it many difficulties. In the present edition it was decided not to encumber the musical text with brackets or with references. The editor's hope of finding corrections in P. Rettensteiner's copy proved to be false: the copy contains not one alteration.

In 1788 a version of these three sonatas for string trio — violin, viola and violoncello — was published by Franz Anton Hoffmeister in Vienna. The Editor's Report discusses in more detail the vexing question as to whether the trio version is an arrangement of the piano sonatas, or whether the sonatas are arrangements of the trios. The kind of musical setting of the sonatas, with the conspicuously high register of the bass, could lead to the supposition that the three pieces were not originally conceived for the keyboard. The editor believes that the extant trio version is an arrangement based on the Bossler edition and is perhaps by Hoffmeister who was himself a composer and arranged works by other composers. It is likely that this edition was not done without Haydn's knowledge; one can imagine that Haydn may have had a trio version in view, leaving the execution of the project to the composer and publisher Hoffmeister for lack of time or that an original trio version is lost. It may be added that all of Haydn's genuine string trios, which admittedly date from an earlier period, are written for two violins and violoncello. The fact that Haydn played the piano sonatas for his visitor seems to support the contention that the works are genuine piano pieces.

Sonata No. 57 belongs to the works for piano published in 1788 by Artaria & Comp. in Vienna, virtually all of which were probably composed in the 1760s (Hob. XVII, No. 1; Sonatas Nos. 30, 20, 32, 29 and 31; Hob. XVII, Nos. 3 and 2 as well as Hob. XVIIa, No. 1). Apparently none of these editions may be considered as an authentic edition. In any event, one of the three sonatas eliminated by us (Hob. XVI, No. 17) appeared in this series. Questions with regard to the doubtful authenticity of the first movement of Sonata No. 57 and the further problems of this version in relation to the version in E printed as No. 19 in Volume I of our edition have not yet been resolved satisfactorily and are discussed in the Editor's Report. The first movement of the Artaria version in F (No. 57) is also preserved in manuscript copies.

Christa Landon

Sonata No. 58 appeared in September, 1789, in the first volume of a "Sammlung neuer Klavier-Sonaten... von verschiedenen beliebten Komponisten" called "Musikalischer Pot-Pourri", published in a typeset edition by Breitkopf in Leipzig. Haydn's relations with this publishing house, which lasted until his old age, were established towards the end of 1786 during a visit to Vienna by Christoph Gottlob Breitkopf. Two years later, on January 10th, 1789, Breitkopf asked Haydn to contribute an as yet unpublished piano sonata to a collection compiled by himself. Breitkopf was to receive the sonata by March of the same year. On March 8th Haydn reported to Breitkopf through his go-between, the Vienna music dealer Johann Traeg, that "the new pianoforte Sonata shall be finished by the coming week". At the beginning of April Haydn asked to be excused, since he had to look through the work again. On April 5th Haydn informed the publisher that he was sending the sonata through Traeg, "fully hoping that it will meet with the musical world's approbation". The work arrived in Leipzig on April 25th. It can not be said with certainty whether this sonata really was composed at this time or somewhat earlier, or whether our Sonata No. 58 was, as has been suggested, "a Sonata for pianoforte alone" which Haydn had offered to the London publisher William Forster in a letter of April 8th, 1787. An error in the second movement of this sonata could indicate that the manuscript sent by Haydn still used the soprano clef. The earliest autograph evidence for Haydn's employment of the G clef in piano writing is the autograph fragment of the Trio in G major, Opus 40, No. 3 (Hob. XV, No. 5) which is one of the trios Haydn sent to Forster in October 1784. In the works for piano solo the G clef is authenticated for the first time in Sonata No. 59, written in 1789/90.

Other piano sonatas commissioned by Breitkopf were not supplied by Haydn. On November 18th, 1789, Haydn presented the new collection, "a little musical vegetable pot" as he called it in his accompanying letter, to his friend Marianne von Genzinger.

An edition was issued by John Bland in London around April 1st, 1791, with the publisher's note: "This is the first Sonata that has been printed since his [Haydn's] arrival in England." Despite Bland's personal relations with Haydn this cannot be considered as an authentic edition with regard to the text. It derives from the Breitkopf edition in spite of a number of divergent readings (given in the Editor's Report for our edition). The derivation is perhaps not so direct as in the case of Sonata No. 59 where the Artaria first edition or a copy thereof obviously served as the source of the Bland edition. Neither can a Viennese manuscript copy of Sonata No. 58 claim independent source value and is, with the exception of "corrections", identical with the Breitkopf edition. The editing of this sonata was made difficult by the mechanical placing of the slurs in the first edition, which this kind of typesetting necessitates. Dynamic markings are also inaccurately placed.

Sonata No. 59 was composed by Haydn for Marianne von Genzinger. According to Haydn's correspondence with Frau von Genzinger, the date on the title page of the preserved autograph, June 1st, 1790, certainly does not refer to the start of the composition of the sonata, since the first and third movements were written one year earlier. The attribution of the work stands in apparent contradiction to Haydn's own dedication on the autograph: "Composta per la Stimatissima Signora Anna de Jerlischeck". It can clearly be seen in the letters, however, that "our Mademoiselle Nanette" had commissioned Haydn "to compose a new pianoforte Sonata four Your Grace [Frau von Genzinger, to whom this letter of June 6th, 1790 is addressed], but which should not be permitted to get into other hands". In his Haydn Catalogue, Anthony van Hoboken discusses "Mademoiselle Nanette" at length and assumes that she is identical with "Anna de Jerlischeck" (Maria Anna Gerlischek). She was apparently in charge of the Esterházy household and was probably married in 1790 to Jean Tost, to whom Haydn had dedicated the Quartets Opus 64, composed the same year. This sonata is mentioned frequently in Haydn's correspondence with Frau von Genzinger. Haydn recommended that his friend acquire a fortepiano made by the Schantz workshop (which he preferred to those made by Anton Walter), because "everything may be better expressed... I know I ought to have composed this Sonata in accordance with the capabilities of your Clavier [= harpsichord], but I found this impossible because I was no longer accustomed to it." Frau von Genzinger wished that the passage might be changed "in the second part of the Adagio, where the hands cross over" "if by so doing it does not detract from the beauty of the piece" (cf. second movement, bars 57ff.). Although Haydn promised that "Your Grace shall receive the alteration in the Adagio" he seems not to have altered this passage in the sonata as far as we know from the sources at our disposal.

The first edition of this sonata was published by Artaria & Comp. as Opus 66 in August 1791. It carries no dedication on the title page — the dedication on the autograph seems incidentally to have been pasted over — and was probably brought out without the knowledge of the composer, who was in England at the time. This may be referred to in the following passage of a letter to Frau von Genzinger from London (March 2nd, 1792): "I was not a little shocked to hear the unpleasant news of the Sonata. By God! I would rather have lost 25 ducats than to hear of this theft, and no one except my own copyist can have done it." The sincerity of Haydn's annoyance should perhaps be taken with a grain of salt; in an earlier letter Haydn had asked Frau von Genzinger to purchase two works of his from Artaria, have them copied and sent to him in London for further publication, all of this without Artaria's knowledge. Moreover Sonata No. 59 was already published c. February 1792 by John Bland in London also as Opus 66 ("J. Haydn's 4th Sonata Published since his arrival in England") and was derived from the Artaria edition.

The relationship between the autograph and the Artaria edition could not be elucidated. Disregarding the customary errors or incorrect readings of the source (which even lead one to suspect that the autograph, or a direct copy thereof, served as the engravers' copy), the Artaria edition contains, on the one hand, versions diverging from the autograph and additions not contained in it; on the other hand, in passages altered in the autograph, the Artaria edition gives the original version. A manuscript copy of the sonata came to light some years ago in the antiquarian trade; unfortunately, only three pages in microfilm (the first page of each movement) were at the editor's disposal. This copy is not from the hand of a typical Viennese copyist but possibly stems from the Genzinger circle. It is clearly based on the autograph and not on the Artaria edition. But none of those passages is contained in these three pages which would contribute to a clarification of the relationship of autograph and first edition. Our text follows the autograph except at a few indicated points. In certain instances the Artaria version appears in a footnote. Most of the ties in brackets are present in Artaria.

All of the three sonatas, Nos. 60—62, were probably composed during Haydn's second London sojourn, 1794/95. Since the reappearance of the autograph of Sonata No. 62, which is dated London, 1794 and bears the dedication: "Composta per la Celebre Signora Teresa de Janson", it is certain that at least two of these three works (Nos. 60 and 62) were written for Therese Jansen. On May 16th, 1795, Haydn was one of the witnesses at the wedding of Therese Jansen to the engraver (Kupferstecher) Gaetano Bartolozzi in London. The title pages of the English first editions of Sonatas Nos. 60 and 62 state that the works were expressly composed for Mrs. Bartolozzi. With regard to Sonata No. 61, we do not possess conclusive documentary evidence. There is a discrepancy between the two contemporary Haydn biographers, Griesinger and Dies, concerning the transcription of Haydn's London catalogue of works contained in the missing fourth London notebook. Griesinger lists "Zwey Sonaten für Miss Janson", while Dies, retaining Haydn's original English entry, mentions "3 Sonates for Ms. Janson" which is probably correct. Here the question remains open whether this entry does not refer to the Piano Trios Hob. XV, Nos. 27—29, also written for Mrs. Bartolozzi (Therese Jansen) and published in 1797. As was customary at the time, they too were entitled sonatas. It is reasonably certain, however, that the third sonata (No. 61) was in fact composed for Therese Jansen. "An Andante and Finale which Haydn had composed in England for a lady who kept the original manuscript", one of the three works Haydn offered Breitkopf & Härtel around 1804, is without doubt Sonata No. 61.

In an exhaustive article written by W. Oliver Strunk on the reappearance of the autograph of the E flat Sonata, a new chronology of the last three sonatas was also suggested: E flat major (No. 62), D major (No. 61) and lastly No. 60 in C major which, incidentally, is the only sonata in which the range is extended to a''' in contrast to the upper limit of f''' in Haydn's other piano works.

Since a chronological order based on stylistic criteria alone is rarely entirely satisfactory, the present editor decided to retain the chronology of the Breitkopf & Härtel collected edition. Thus our edition closes with the E flat major Sonata, which is a fulfilment of the classical sonata and at the same time points the way to the future.

The first edition of Sonata No. 60 published in 1801 by J. & H. Caulfield (London) seems to have used the autograph or a copy thereof as engraver's copy. In editing this sonata difficulties arose particularly on account of the inaccurately placed dynamic marks and the interpretation of these signs. The earlier version of the second movement (which appears as an appendix to this volume) was published as a single "Adagio" by Artaria & Comp. in Vienna in June 1794 in a rather inaccurate edition. The Oeuvres complettes (Cahier XII) included it in this form. It must be regretted that better sources are not available for a comparison of the two versions.

Sonata No. 61 was published by Breitkopf & Härtel in 1805 separately from the Oeuvres complettes but appeared again in Cahier XI. Obviously not the original manuscript (in possession of the English lady) but a rather unreliable manuscript copy served as the source for the first edition. It is most questionable if the editor of the Oeuvres complettes used again the source of the first edition. But we have made an exception in our text and have referred to additional dynamic markings in the Oeuvres complettes.

Sonata No. 62 was first printed in December 1798 by Artaria & Comp. and is dedicated to Magdalena von Kurzböck, the daughter of the Viennese bookseller and printer Joseph von Kurzböck, with whom Haydn had brought out his first sonata edition (Nos. 36—41) in 1774. This dedication is probably not by Haydn but by Artaria. It is also to be doubted whether this edition was made with the agreement of Haydn, who surely must have been bound by contract to Mrs. Bartolozzi. Artaria shows additions to the autograph and divergencies from it, the authenticity of which must be questioned. They were therefore not included in our text but are mentioned in the Editor's Report. The reproductions in this volume make possible a comparison of an autograph page from the second movement of this sonata with the corresponding page of the Artaria edition. The English first edition, advertised in "The Morning Chronicle" of December 27th, 1799, was published by Longman, Clementi & Co. (London). It proved to be an almost exact reproduction of the autograph which must have remained in Mrs. Bartolozzi's possession. Directions for the engraver in English contained in the autograph seem to point to the fact that this edition was engraved from the autograph. On the title page the piece is expressly described — perhaps with an eye towards Artaria's edition — as "A New Grand Sonata".

INDEX

PREFACE

Background to the Work's Composition

In 1938 Paul Hindemith made his home in Switzerland to escape from the increasingly menacing situation in National Socialist Germany. Two years previously performances of his music had been banned (although curiously enough his compositions were still allowed to be published); and to make matters worse his wife had been classified as 'half Jewish'. Five months after the outbreak of the second world war, in February 1940, he gave in to the entreaties of his friends and resolved to emigrate to the United States. On no account did he wish to live on the West Coast, in proximity to the numerous European émigrés in and around Los Angeles, nor did he relish the thought of earning a living playing the viola in public (he was widely reputed to be one of the foremost viola players of his day). Consequently Hindemith accepted Buffalo University's offer of the chair of music theory. At the same time he was invited to lecture at a number of other universities, including the prestigious Yale University in New Haven, Connecticut. So successful were these guest lectures that Yale offered him a permanent faculty post. *This first place I have come across here in which it seems to me that one could feel a bit at home*, he wrote to his wife[1], who was still in Switzerland. When the Yale authorities declared themselves willing to adopt Hindemith's proposals for the reorganisation of the music syllabus[2] he accepted their offer, arranged for his wife to join him and began to acquiesce in the American way of life which he had initially derided with sarcastic perplexity. According to one of his students at the time, Howard Boatwright[3], the next few years saw Hindemith emerge as the most sought-after composition teacher for miles around, although Hindemith himself was convinced that 'composition' could not be taught and always tried to educate his students as musicians in a broad sense. He owed his growing fame and prestige largely to his phenomenal ability to compose on the blackboard during classes: complete pieces — works for string trio, choral settings with instrumental accompaniment, fugues for piano — which were throughout rationally explicable. These compositions were performed on the spot and, to everyone's surprise, always 'sounded like Hindemith'. In 1940 he produced a number of major works, including the cello concerto, the *Symphony in E flat* and the ballet *Die vier Temperamente* for piano and string orchestra, which were immediately resounding successes.

It was only when the United States entered the war in 1941 that Hindemith's fortunes took a turn for the worse. As an immigrant from a country with which the USA was at war his freedom of movement was subject to limitations. Moreover, in the prevailing wartime mood of hysteria and chauvinistic solidarity émigré composers found themselves being forced to the sidelines by their indigenous colleagues who were turning out music felt by the public to be genuinely American. This spirit of solidarity extended to those countries with which the United States was allied in the war, first and foremost the Soviet Union. And so it happened that the American première of Dmitri Shostakovitch's Seventh Symphony, intrepidly smuggled out of besieged Leningrad and performed by Toscanini and the New York Philharmonic on July 19th 1942, proved nothing short of a sensation[4]. More than two hundred radio stations relayed the original concert, and by the end of the year the work had received a further sixty performances. Against this background, Hindemith withdrew more and more from public life. He wrote theoretical treatises for his students and composed chamber music and songs. It was also at this time that he conceived the idea of the *Ludus tonalis* for piano. One of his most challenging compositions, he regarded its realisation as nothing short of a *moral conquest* which he contrasted with the above-mentioned Shostakovitch symphony. Incensed and profoundly embittered, he wrote to his American publisher on November 24th 1942: *On the other hand it seems to me that precisely at the present time, when every half-baked adolescent is turning out symphonies and every conductor is performing the most despicable rubbish just because it is either American or Russian and has nothing going for it except that it is written for orchestra, and when a work's quality is apparently assessed purely in terms of the impact it has on the vulgar sensory organs from the pineal to the prostate gland — that at just such a time something needs to be published to remind those who have not completely succumbed what music and composition really are. [...] and I am also aware that given the present world situation it is a matter of complete indifference whether the siege of Leningrad as portrayed in symphonies is set against a moral conquest (albeit one that is fully appreciated only after the lapse of 50 [...] years).*

On August 29th 1942, after completing his sonata for two pianos which ends with one of the most grandiose fugues he ever composed, Hindemith began writing out a number of small-scale fugues for piano. He had finished six fugues (Nos. 6, 5, the first version of 11, 7, 4 and 12) when he wrote to his publisher on September 9th 1942: *In addition there is a volume of light, genial and enjoyable three-part piano fugues.* At this stage Hindemith was evidently not yet planning an extended composition for piano closely bound up with the theoretical principles expounded in his *Unterweisung im Tonsatz*[5]. In all probability what he had in mind was no more than a set of twelve fugues in chromatic sequence: in his autograph catalogue[6] he refers to the piano fugues merely as *Kleine dreistimmige Fugen für Klavier*, and in a fragmentary index to the sketches they are listed in chromatic sequence.

We cannot ascertain when Hindemith made up his mind to extend the work to its final dimensions. The way he laid out the manuscript in which he first wrote out the work in full does, however, provide sufficiently conclusive evidence for us to deduce the date. The manuscript in question comprises two distinct parts. He initially laid out the second part in such a way as to provide room for all the fugues that he still planned to compose. It was only after he had completed fugues Nos. 8, 2, 1 and 10 — that is, after September 15th 1942 — that he inserted additional sheets of score paper in the second part on which to write out the interludes and the *Praeludium — Postludium*. Thus we can conclude that he first finished composing the set of twelve fugues, the revise No. 11 and finally wrote the *Interludes* and the *Praeludium — Postludium*. He clearly found the composition of this latter piece very arduous: he was able to write as many as three of the *Interludes* in a single day, but completing the *Praeludium*

---

1 Letter dated April 12th 1940. All letters are quoted from the copies in the collection of the Hindemith-Institut in Frankfurt am Main.

2 L. Noss: *A History of the Yale School of Music 1855-1970*, New Haven 1984.

3 H. Boatwright: *Paul Hindemith as a Teacher*, in: *The Musical Quarterly* L, 1964, pp. 269ff.

4 K. Meyer: *Dimitri Schostakowitsch*, Leipzig 1980, pp. 123f.

5 *Theoretischer Teil*, Mainz 1937, ²1940.

6 In the collection of the Hindemith-Institut, Frankfurt am Main.

— *Postludium* appears to have taken him two weeks. Not that Hindemith felt he was stretched to his limits by this work, strenuous though it was: while he was composing the first of the fugues he was still finishing the fair copy of the sonata for two pianos, and having written out the first six fugues he composed two piano *Lieder* on September 9th and 10th 1942, *Envoy* (F. Thompson) and *La belle dame sans merci* (J. Keats). The table below gives the dates of composition of the individual pieces which make up the *Ludus tonalis*:

Fuga in D sharp: August 29th 1942 — *Fuga in E*: August 30th 1942 — *Fuga in B*: September 3rd 1942 (first version) — *Fuga in A flat*: September 6th 1942 — *Fuga in A*: September 8th 1942 — *Fuga in F sharp*: September 8th 1942 — *Fuga in D*: September 13th 1942 — *Fuga in G*: September 14th 1942 — *Fuga in C*: September 15th 1942 — *Fuga in D flat*: September 15th 1942 — *Fuga in F*: September 16th 1942 — *Fuga in B flat*: September 16th 1942 — *Fuga in B*: September 17th 1942 (revised version) — *Interludium* between the fugues in B flat and D flat: September 18th 1942 — *Interludium* between the fugues in E and E flat: September 18th 1942 — *Interludium* between the fugues in E flat and A flat: September 19th 1942 — *Interludium* between the fugues in B and F sharp: September 20th 1942 — *Interludium* between the fugues in D flat and B: September 20th 1942 — *Interludium* between the fugues in D and B flat: September 21st 1942 — *Praeludium / Postludium*: October 4th 1942 — *Interludium* between the fugues in F and A: October 10th 1942 — *Interludium* between the fugues in A flat and D: October 11th 1942 — *Interludium* between the fugues in G and F: October 12th 1942 — *Interludium* between the fugues in A and E: October 12th 1942 — *Interludium* between the fugues in C and G: October 12th 1942.

Hindemith had not yet decided upon the work's final title *Ludus tonalis* when he completed it. He informed his publisher merely of a *Klavierbuch*. It was not until October 26th 1942 — a fortnight after the completion date — that he told his publisher of the definitive title, explaining: *I thought I would call the whole thing 'Ludus tonalis' on account of the somewhat didactic (not to say sophisticated) impression that evokes. Our Latin specialists thoroughly approve of the title. I can think of nothing better in English or in German which conveys so unequivocally (and yet so equivocally) what it is and at the same time suggests it belongs to the same category (by genus only, not in terms of quality!) as the Well-Tempered Clavier and the Art of Fugue. The full title would be: 'L.T. Studies in Counterpoint, Tonal Organisation, and Piano Playing.' Okay? Okay.*

By the time Hindemith wrote that letter he had already embarked on the second — calligraphically meticulous — fair copy of the work. He was planning to publish it as a facsimile edition of his autograph manuscript, for two reasons. In the first place, he wanted it to appear as soon as possible, and his experience to date with American music publishers suggested that the process of engraving the score would take too long. Secondly, he was apprehensive that too many errors would creep into a printed edition during the engraving. Nevertheless he left the choice between facsimile or engraved edition to the publisher's discretion[7]: *So you decide, on the strength of your publisher's conscience, enhanced in its sense of responsibility as it is by your awareness of musical history and hounded as it is up hill and down dale by the present shortages of metal and manpower. What Pub [i. e. Associated Music Publishers] says is good enough for me.*

The publisher decided on an engraved edition of the *Ludus tonalis*. Hindemith's misgivings proved partially justified. The work did not appear in print until a year later, in

August 1943, and the published score severely mutilated some aspects of the notation, like the supplementary accidentals which Hindemith has taken such care to insert in his manuscript. The American first edition was promptly sent to the German Schott publishing house in Mainz — via Santiago Kastner in Lisbon, because there were no direct postal connections between the United States and Germany. In the closing months of the war Schott managed to publish an edition based on the American first edition, but with further changes to Hindemith's score and with the English tempo and expression marks supplanted by Italian terms. The musical text which Hindemith definitively stipulated in the manuscript designed for facsimile publication was not published until the Complete Edition of 1981. This edition, which also contains information on the background to the composition and the sources of the work, was compiled by Bernhard Billeter[8]. With one exception[9], the musical text given in the present edition is identical with that of the Complete Edition (cf. Critical Notes, 'Evaluation of Sources').

Hindemith and the Fugue

The description of the *Ludus tonalis* as a *moral conquest* points to a radical transformation in Hindemith's aesthetic thinking. This is in its turn reflected in his response to the music of Johann Sebastian Bach.

The new trend in music which emerged during the 1920s rejected the nineteenth-century concept of 'absolute music' divorced from every manifestation of functionality and transported into the realm of artistic sanctity. The composers concerned largely pursued artistic goals defined in the terms 'functional music' or 'occasional music'[10]. They took Bach's sacred cantatas to be the epitome of functional music at its most sublime. Or more exactly: they rediscovered the occasional or functional nature of the music by Bach which serves non-musical ends. And they scorned as a nineteenth-century distortion any attempt to impute aesthetic autonomy (Carl Dahlhaus) to such music.

Hindemith's early development as a composer radically reflects this paradigmatic change. It is most clearly seen in his fugues and fugati[11]. The younger Hindemith could not avoid parody when he made use of these 'period' techniques which had originated in 'renaissance ideals' and found their way into the music of Brahms, later of Reger and finally of his own teachers Arnold Mendelssohn and Bernhard Sekles. A fugato in the opening movement of his *Lustige Sinfonietta* opus 4 (1916) bears the heading *Das große Lalula*, an allusion to a poem by Morgenstern; while the analogous fugato in his 2nd string quartet opus 10 (1918) is marked *...completely apathetic, numb*. In the viola sonata opus 11/4 (1919) the players are instructed to perform the fugal variation movement with *bizarre ungainliness*; and the cycle of piano pieces entitled *In einer Nacht* opus 15 (1919/20) closes with a rumbustious fugue immediately preceded by a foxtrot. The choral fugue in the one-act opera *Das Nusch-Nuschi* opus 20 (1920) prompted Hindemith to add an explanatory note in the score: *The following 'choral fugue' (with all mod cons — augmentations, diminutions, stretto, basso ostinato) owes its existence solely to a stroke of bad luck, in that it occurred to the*

---

7 Letter dated November 24th 1942.

8 Paul Hindemith: *Sämtliche Werke*, Volume V, 10, *Klaviermusik II*, edited by B. Billeter, Mainz 1981, pp. 160ff.

9 *Fuga septima in A flat*, bar 16: wrong alinement.

10 Term coined by Henrich Besseler; cf. St. Hinton: *Musik nach Maß. Zum Begriff der Gebrauchsmusik bei Paul Hindemith*, in: Musica XXXIX, 1985, pp. 146ff.

11 G. Schubert: *Paul Hindemith und der Neobarock*, in: *Hindemith-Jahrbuch* 1983/XII, pp. 28ff.

composer. All it sets out to do is to fit elegantly into its context and afford the 'experts' an opportunity for a querulous tirade against the vulgarity of its creator. Hallelujah! The piece should first and foremost be danced (wobbled) by two eunuchs with voluminous bellies. Finally, Hindemith's *Ragtime (well-tempered)* for large orchestra (1921), a piece in burlesque style which transcends the borderline between serious and light music, is based on the subject of the C minor fugue from the first volume of Bach's *Well-Tempered Clavier*. Hindemith prefaced the score with the following remarks: *Do you think that Bach is turning in his grave? On the contrary: if Bach had been alive today he might very well have invented the shimmy or at least incorporated it in respectable music. And perhaps, in doing so, he might have used a theme from the Well-Tempered Clavier by a composer who had Bach's standing in his eyes.*

The parodistic element in the above-mentioned pieces hits out at 'autonomous aesthetics' and their view of Bach and the 'period' techniques but not at Bach or these techniques themselves. In the course of the 1920s Hindemith's artistic aspirations became more ambitious, although he came no nearer to embracing a concept of 'absolute music'. The *Suite 1922* for piano opus 26 (1922), made up of the movements *Marsch, Shimmy, Nachtstück, Boston* and *Ragtime* sets out to imitate the baroque dance suite in contemporary idiom; it was an occasional work permeated by a polemical opposition to the realm of unapproachable music justified by its own self-reference. The two sections of the *Klaviermusik* opus 37 (*Übung in drei Stücken*, 1925, and *Reihe kleiner Stücke*, 1925/26) are strongly reminiscent of Bach's *Clavier-Übung* and pursue didactic goals. The numerous fugues and fugati which his extremely diverse compositions from that period contain — most notably the double fugues in the fifth string quartet opus 32 (opening movement) and in the first string trio opus 34 (final movement) — are highly elaborate and devoid of any trace of parody. On the other hand they also have nothing to do with the kind of music which is self-justifying. Their purpose is to regulate and impose order on the unbounded, overflowing impetus of the playing.

It was not until Hindemith came to compose the sonatas dating from the thirties that his aesthetic stance underwent one last modification. The double and triple fugues which close such works as the third piano sonata (1936), the fourth violin sonata (1939) or the sonata for two pianos (1942) form the immensely intricate culminations to each piece. The fugues themselves are neither stylistic imitations nor do they represent a deliberate quotation of the 'period' style. Rather, we should see them as the embodiment of a mould of musical thinking[12] which has its roots in polyphony and is harmonically permeated; a mould of thinking founded in the art of thematic writing (August Halm) and in which the functional aspects of the work are neutralized. The paradigm of Hindemith's mould of musical thinking at the time was to be the *Ludus tonalis*, a modern-day equivalent of the 'Kunstbuch' although it would go beyond the scope of superficial craftsmanship and constitute an engrossing, concentrated, highly expressive work of musical art. Thus, the various pieces which make up the *Ludus tonalis* exist in their own right and conform to rigid intrinsic principles, and yet at the same time they are embedded in an overall functional context which transcends the scope of the work as such. As the subtitle suggests, Hindemith visualized the *Ludus tonalis* as illustrating certain problems relating to musical theory, composition technique and pianistic technique. This means that the *Ludus tonalis* is conceived as belonging to the sphere of 'autonomous music' but not to that of 'absolute music'. The problems relating to musical theory

with which the work deals point to Hindemith's *Unterweisung im Tonsatz*, a treatise on the relations between notes perceived to be independent of any given stylistic context and proceeding from a concept of the 'nature' of musical sound. Those aspects of the work which deal with composition technique are enshrined in a systematic exposition of the fugue as a mould of musical thinking supplemented and extended but also contrasted and highlighted by the *Interludes*. The use of the ambiguous term 'ludus' implies that a treatment of these matters can be enjoyable and devoid of pedantry or tortuous didacticism. At the same time the term also serves as a reminder that a piece of music, however rigidly organised and functionally defined it may be, transpires in reality to be a 'game' — albeit one invested with substantial meaning.

Music theory and Composition technique

In his *Unterweisung im Tonsatz. I: Theoretischer Teil* Hindemith goes back as far as possible to what he terms *the natural state of tones*. From the overtone series intrinsic to every sounding note he derives the relations of the twelve notes of the chromatic scale, which has at the same time subsumed all the other scales: the major and minor scales or the church modes. He represents these relations by a sequence of notes which he calls *Row 1*[13]. With c^1 as a starting point (the fifth produces the closest affinity between notes, the tritone the most remote affinity), *Row 1* is as follows:

By incorporating the compound tones which always occur when two notes sound simultaneously Hindemith derives *Row 2*[14]. This systematically orders the intervals in terms of their distinct value and tension. Hindemith makes use of *Row 2* to formulate a *Phenomenology of all musical sounds*, which arranges all conceivable forms of chord in six categories[15]. *Row 2* is as follows:

Hindemith terms the different values and tensions resulting from the sequence of different *sounds harmonic gradation*[16] (*'harmonisches Gefälle'*), while he calls the sequence of ground-notes which make up a larger harmonic context *step progression*[17] (*'Stufengang'*).

Several of Hindemith's compositional principles strictly speaking go beyond the scope of the above theoretical exposition as formulated in the *Unterweisung im Tonsatz*. His term *generic two-part writing*[18] denotes a composition technique in which the bass part combines with the next most important part to form *immaculate two-part writing intelligible without any addition*. The term *sequence of seconds*[19] designates a principle involved in the structure of a melody whereby the primary notes of a melody should relate to one another in second steps. Finally, Hindemith sees three-part writing as marking the limits of the direct perception of independent part writing[20], while at the same time he regards three-part writing as a prerequisite for the unequivocal representation of harmonic relations.

Fundamental theoretical assumptions such as this left their mark on the *Ludus tonalis*, not merely indirectly but al-

12 H. Danuser: *Der Klassiker als Janus?*, in: *Neue Zürcher Zeitung* of January 1st/2nd 1986, No. 1, p. 29.

13 *Unterweisung im Tonsatz* ²1940, p. 78.
14 Op. cit., p. 80
15 Op. cit., p. 129
16 Op. cit., pp. 144ff.
17 Op. cit., pp. 173ff.
18 Op. cit., p. 142
19 Op. cit., pp. 228ff.
20 Op. cit., p. 140

so directly: even in its external form the *Ludus tonalis* is closely bound up with Hindemith's basic theoretical principles.

1. Hindemith ignores the polarity of key relationships etc., recognizing only the relationship between a given note and the ground-note: he thus composes just one fugue for each of the twelve steps of the chromatic scale, designating each fugue by reference to the ground-note: *in C, in G* etc.

2. Hindemith arranges the twelve fugues in a sequence determined by the relationships between the ground-notes, in other words on the basis of *Row 1* (see above).

3. All the fugues are three-part fugues.

Having thus established the layout of the *Ludus tonalis* on the lines of his fundamental theoretical assumptions, Hindemith inserts the *Interludes* as planned. With a few exceptions, they modulate from one key to the next, progressing from a given ground-note to that which follows it in *Row 1*. Technically speaking they are absolutely free and untrammelled.

Within this overall context of theoretical premises directly determining the external form of the *Ludus tonalis* Hindemith then sets out to investigate a number of complex problems relating to composition technique. He evolves technical paradigms of polyphonic thinking as articulated by a certain choice of theme.

Each of the *Interludes* is conceived as a character piece, although Hindemith gave only three *Interludes* titles designating them as such: *Pastorale* (*Interludium* 2), *Marsch* (*Interludium* 6) and *Walzer* (*Interludium* 11). The pianist Franzpeter Goebels[21] lists the following designations: 1 — *Improvisation*; 2 — *'Pastorale'*; 3 — *Moment musical*; 4 — *Etude*; 5 — *Intermezzo*; 6 — *'Marsch'*; 7 — *Funeral march*; 8 — *Capriccio*; 9 — *Elegy*; 10 — *Ostinato*; 11 — *'Valse'*. Other designations are, of course, perfectly conceivable. The pianist Emma Lübbecke-Job, for instance, who was closely acquainted with Hindemith from his earliest years as a composer, noted in her copies of the *Ludus tonalis*[22] the following descriptions or expression marks: 1 — *taut, rounded, energetic, concise*; 2 — *delicate poetry, beautiful, not flabby, flowing;* 3 — *light jazz rhythm, all very concise, not stopping on the way, no lingering or delaying anywhere*; 4 — *toccata-like*; 5 — *very flowing, regular and precisely co-ordinated playing*; 6 — *very cheerful*; 7 — *absolutely regular*; 8 — *like a pistol shot*; 9/10 — no description; 11 — *rhythmic, temperaments, gently forwards, not elegaic.*

While the *Interludes* evince the greatest possible diversity in technique, form and expression, in the *Praeludium — Postludium* and the fugues Hindemith combines the most stringent discipline in his composition technique with a formal diversity[23] reminiscent less of the *Well-Tempered Clavier* than of the *Art of Fugue*. We should remember, though, that Bach did not write the *Art of Fugue* with a specific instrument in mind and did not therefore address those problems of translating notes into sound which Hindemith emphatically deals with.

The toccata-like *Praeludium* breaks down into three components: a prefatory section (Prelude) whose 'preludizing' as it were explores the compass of the instrument (bars 1-14); a two-part *Arioso* (bars 14-25/25-32); and an Ostinato (bars 39-47) preceded by a transitional passage (bars 33-39) which introduces the two elements to be dealt with in the Ostinato itself. The Prelude and the *Arioso* are largely in C major, while the transition to the Ostinato leads quite

abruptly to F sharp which is then established in the Ostinato. Thus, the *Praeludium* delineates the tonal dimensions of the work as a whole.

Hindemith derives the *Postludium* from the *Praeludium* by means of a special type of cancrizans inversion: the score of the *Praeludium* is rotated by 180°. In tonal music which generally takes into account the different values of the intervals this variant of the cancrizans inversion is particularly difficult to execute, because of the displacement of the intervals in relation to each other and because enharmonic modulation is not possible (which explains why pieces of comparable dimensions and significance employing this inversion technique are very rare). By rotating th page the major second c^2-d^2 becomes the leading note step B-c; the tritone f sharp^1-c^2 is transformed into the augmented fifth c-g sharp etc. In his quest for solutions to these extremely complex technical problems Hindemith arrived at two fundamental insights without which the piece could not have been written: a) c as a sound value remains c even when the page is rotated; and b) there are five scales which encompass all the original sound values after they have been turned upside down, so that the available notes are the same either way up[24]:

Hindemith proceeds principally from the scales of A flat, A and C. Bars 15-18 of the *Arioso*, for example, relate to A flat, bars 18-19 to C, bars 19-23 to C, bars 25-31 to A flat and bars 31-32 to C.

With the exception of *Fuga septima* in A flat und *Fuga octava* in D, the fugues vary widely in the way they are realised (cf. the relevant passages in the 'Detailed Notes' on the interpretation of the work.

However distinctly Hindemith may have lent the individual components of *Ludus tonalis* their own identity in terms of both the composition technique and the character of the pieces, he also employed a number of musical techniques to invest the work as a whole with a cyclical continuity. The composer's intentions can therefore be conveyed fully only by a performance of the entire *Ludus tonalis* (because the majority of the *Interludes* modulate, they are anyway unsuitable for performance on their own). Not that, given thoughtful preparation, a partial performance of the work is completely out of the question. The *Praeludium — Postludium* provide a framework whose two parts relate absolutely coherently to each other and which delineate the tonal poles of the work (C-F sharp), G sharp-C. *Row 1* quoted in the *Unterweisung im Tonsatz* lays down the tonal progression which is apparent principally in the *Interludes*, while the three-part writing of all the fugues lends the composition regularity and homogeneity. Moreover, some of the fugues and *Interludes* are closely linked in terms of the sound qualities of the harmonic structure and — less frequently — the-

21 *Interpretationsaspekte zum „Ludus tonalis"*, in: *Hindemith-Jahrbuch* 1972/II, pp. 156f.

22 In the Hindemith-Institut, Frankfurt am Main.

23 Cf. G. Metz: *Melodische Polyphonie in der Zwölftonordnung*, Baden-Baden 1976, pp. 450 ff.

24 D. Neumeyer: *The Music of Paul Hindemith*, New Haven and London 1986, p. 230.

matically. The *Fuga sexta* in E flat, for instance, ends on D sharp (= E flat); *Interludium* 6-7 begins and ends in E flat — in other words, it does not modulate. *Fuga septima* in A flat immediately takes up the principal theme of *Interludium* 6-7 and is thus thematically rather than harmonically linked to the preceding *Interludium*. *Fuga septima*, in its turn, surprisingly does not close in A flat but in C. The expected A flat does nor occur until the beginning of *Interludium* 7-8. In this way Hindemith creates coherent musical correlations between the individual pieces by setting up a network of direct and indirect relationships which avoids any suggestion of schematic rigidity.

Giselher Schubert

THE INTERPRETATION OF THE WORK

1. General remarks

An indispensable prerequisite for an intelligible and persuasive performance of a piece of music is a comprehensive understanding of the work in all its subtlety. That means reading and studying the musical text thoroughly. Yet literal compliance with the written instructions is by itself not enough. The intrinsic musical meaning will emerge from the playing only if the performer has understood the relative significance of the printed signs and the correspondences between the notes. What is entailed in understanding a score? What is the score and what does it convey?

The score is the more or less successful attempt to formulate the products of the musical phantasy (ideas, dreams, feelings) in musical notation. A painting or a sculpture is always present in its unique and definitive manifestation. The score of a musical composition is waiting to be interpreted, awakened to life, translated from notes on the printed page into audible, living music. The score of a composition may precisely define the external scenario of a piece of music, but it can only hint at its inner life. Grasping the diverse planes on which a good piece of music exists requires an adequate capacity for intellectual and emotional understanding.

We will be able to read the meaning of music between the lines of the score only if we approach it with alertness to both intuitive insight and intellectual discernment. When we adopt the stance of purely rational analysis, we are inevitably missing the overall point. We will be sensitive to the tonal blending of a chord, the vibrations of the music's pulse or a subtle nuance in a *cantilene* only if we are ourselves in tune with the music. The very first time we read the score or play it through we need to summon up our capacity for enthusiasm, our open-mindedness and our emotional responsiveness. However gratifying it may be to read a score, it can never be wholly satisfying, because music needs to express itself in sound and to communicate aurally.

How does one approach a fugue? Step one: intuitive comprehension, grasping the subject (the invention). Step two: understanding the subject's intrinsic potential for growth and development. This leads to a study of the formal structure. It is not the formal principles as such which need to occupy us, but the way in which the musical phantasy is articulated and made intelligible through the organisation of the musical substance.

2. Detailed Notes

The following notes are intended purely to help the reader formulate an approach to the music, in terms of both an intellectual understanding and a practical mastery of its difficulties. A player who spends enough time studying this score will arrive at his or her own interpretation. The fingering given here is intended as a guideline, particularly the first time the score is played through. The player will later work out fingering which suits his or her fingers best. On the use of the pedals I have offered only general suggestions. The use of the pedals will depend on a large number of considerations like the volume of the instrument, the acoustics, the dynamics, the tempo, the action and not least the player's own imagination.

The focus — in a sense the axis — of the whole work is the set of twelve three-part fugues in each of the keys. The sequence of the keys corresponds to Hindemith's *Row 1*, as explained in detail in the Preface. The eleven *Interludes* provide — each in its own way — an opportunity to relax after the concentration required in following the fugues. They also serve to link the fugues by modulating from the final key of one to the opening key of the next fugue. The exceptions to this are: *Interludium* 2-3 in G; *Interludium* 3-4 in F (which does not need to modulate because the next fugue begins in F); and *Interludium* 6-7 in E flat (again, the next fugue begins in that key). The *Praeludium* and the *Postludium* frame the composition, the latter being an exact mirror inversion of the former.

The *Praeludium* falls into three sections and leads from C to F sharp. The player can afford to invest this music with improvisatory freedom, bringing out the expansive and ecstatic nature of the music. A crucial point in the musical argument is the build-up to the ₁F sharp in bar 33.

Fuga prima in C. The first, three-bar subject ascends from C to D flat in one breath. The fifth-motif also proves to be the nucleus of the counterpoint. The second subject likewise derives from the fifth. After only ten bars the third subject follows. At the marking *very quiet* the three subjects are played simultaneously. Given the gentle flow of this fugue the player can afford a slightly faster tempo than that suggested by the composer (♩72 instead of ♩66). This makes the *cantabile* easier. Bars 24 and 27 are rather awkward to play. Because of the wide intervals the legato requires great smoothness — something which most players will be able to achieve only with the help of the pedal.

Interludium 1-2 is resolute and dynamic. It progresses in what is really free metre, with 2/4 time predominating. The *Interludium* leads from C to G. If the player takes his bearings from the harmonic centres a meaningful and plastic structure emerges almost by itself. The basic character of the piece is certainly robust, but to avoid it sounding pedestrian it is advisable to observe greater nuances of dynamics and articulation than the composer specifies. The present editor plays *crescendo* rather than the prescribed *decrescendo* in bar 4 and bar 12.

The five-bar subject of the *Fuga secunda in G* is reminiscent of Rameau's *Hen*. There are two stretti, one in E, the other in B flat. The recapitulation contains abbreviated stretti, rudimentary canons and shifting accents. The piece requires precise and carefully differentiated articulation, graduated dynamics, rhythm and a much humour as well as the lucid structuring of the broad sections. I suggest a slightly faster tempo. Reaching the ninths takes a supple hand.

Interludium 2-3, poco rubato; the music needs to breathe.

The piece is in G; for once this *Interludium* does not act as a transition to the key of the ensuing fugue.

Fuga tertia in F. The six-bar *cantabile* subject contains almost every note in the chromatic scale. The syncopation in the second bar subsequently also provides the rhythmic impulse for the development (from bar 19). The coherence of the music is more easily brought out at a rather more measured tempo (♩ 104). Some chords (bars 42/44) can only be played *arpeggio*. From bar 30 onwards the fugue proceeds retrogressively.

Interludium 3-4. This slightly eccentric piece is technically straightforward. The humour is best conveyed by structuring and phrasing unschematically. The nuances of dynamics and articulation should be carefully observed. This *Interludium* is in the key of F throughout; no modulation is necessary because the following *Fuga quarta* opens in F. The key of A is established only at the second entry of the subject.

Fuga quarta in A. The fourth forms the focus of this fugue. It is laid out in large-scale three part form. The slow central section (preferably *Andante*) contains the second subject which is used in the third section in what amounts to a double fugue. The player can afford to employ stark dynamic contrasts but must bring out the structure clearly and interpret the music *con fuoco*. Difficult part writing in bars 61-63.

Interludium 4-5, fast and impulsive, leads from A to E. Informal structure and no beat accentuation. In the lower register it is preferable to play *non legato* (semiquavers) — including the double runs. The left-hand passages require very good finger technique.

Fuga quinta in E. Play this fugue *quasi Gigue e gioccoso*. In the second episode (bars 27ff.) the basic form of the subject is followed by its inversion, while in the third episode (bars 51ff.) the inversion is followed by the basic form.

Interludium 5-6. I suggest a rather more measured speed: in free tempo, *poco rubato*. This *Interludium* leads from E to B flat (the dominant key of the next fugue).

Fuga sexta in E flat. If the player feels this piece in crotchets the *cantabile* subject has more freedom to breathe and the music's coherence is easier to bring out. In the second episode (bars 21ff.) the subject appears in its inversion.

Interludium 6-7 is a vivid piece infused with biting humour. Note the shift of accentuation between bars 9 and 15. In bars 18-19 I double every note in octaves. The central section (bars 21-30) needs to be played with black humour and in a relentless tempo. This *Interludium* is in E flat throughout because the fugue which follows opens in that key.

Fuga septima in A flat. The opening is centred around E flat, while the fugue closes in C! A flat is not reached until the start of the ensuing *Interludium*. The beginning of the fugal subject is derived from the opening of *Interludium 6-7*. A second idea occurs in bar 18 but is not developed (as it were, a second subject). Trills should not be terminated with a 'Nachschlag'. I recommend a slightly more measured tempo.

Interludium 7-8 is orchestral and majestic. I take the opening at about ♪63, from bar 5 at a more leisurely pace. This *Interludium* modulates from A flat to D.

Fuga octava in D. The subject is dominated by the fifth and extends over five crotchets, which is why I recommend counting in 5/4. The episode in bars 12-15 is in free metre.

Interludium 8-9 is turbulent, alternating between *staccato* and *legato*. Given the density of the writing I suggest playing all the chords from the beginning to bar 12 *staccato*, possibly with half pedal. In accordance with the shifting accentuation I count in bars 34-40 as follows: 3-6-6-4-4-5 beats (based on a dotted crotchet). This *Interludium* modulates from D to B flat.

Fuga nona in B flat requires carefully observed nuances of dynamics and articulation — *molto capriccioso*. The variant in bar 40 (a^1 rather than a^2) is not very appealing. I suspect that it was inserted as a slightly more easily playable option. But a^2 is barely more difficult and is certainly more attractive. Hindemith uses not just the four basic forms of the subject but also augments it and subjects it to a wide variety of stretto treatments.

Interludium 9-10, quasi Nocturno, dolce espressivo. This piece modulates from B flat to G flat.

Fuga decima in D flat is in two equal parts, the second the inversion of the first — with the exception of the closing bars of both sections. The two-bar subject is best played in one breath.

Interludium 10-11. The danger of the music sounding pedestrian can be avoided if it is played with lightly-sprung accents, a vibrating tone and an informal strucuring of the piece. It modulates from C sharp to B.

Fuga undecima in B is actually a two-part canon at the fifth with a fundamental bass part. It is made up of two sections of roughly equal length. In the second section the canon begins a minor second lower, but the fugue then develops differently. The whole piece should be played *piano* and *pianissimo* with only slight *crescendo*. The *legato* in the leading part can in places (e. g. bar 9) be played only *arpeggio* and with the help of the pedal.

Interludium 11-12. Tempo rubato e con sentimento. This piece modulates from B to C sharp (the dominant key of F sharp).

Fuga duodecima in F sharp, to be played with flowing movement, allowing the music to breathe, as if there were no bar lines. Tranquil as the music is, I play it at ♩. 46. Hindemith here makes consistent use of the stretto principle.

Postludium begins in G sharp and leads back to C, the key in which the work began. The music comes full circle. The key of C is reached as early as bar 15. It is therefore not easy to maintain the tension to the end. The *Postludium* is the cancrizans inversion of the *Praeludium*. This means that inevitably the tonal relations (as well as the tension between the lines, the dynamics and so on) are not identical in detail with the equivalent specific aspects of the *Praeludium*. The tension has its own way of building up here, and that is how it should be felt. The C sharp in the bass is tied from bar 26 to bar 27 (cf. *Praeludium*, bars 21-22).

Günter Ludwig

INDEX

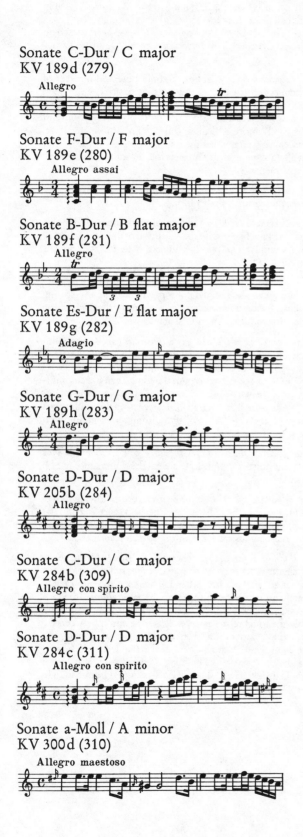

K V = *Chronologisch-thematisches Verzeichnis sämtlicher Tonwerke Wolfgang Amadé Mozarts . . . von Dr. Ludwig Ritter von Köchel, bearbeitet von Franz Giegling, Zürich, Alexander Weinmann, Wien, Gerd Sievers, Wiesbaden, Breitkopf & Härtel, Wiesbaden, 1964.*

PREFACE

"At a time so rich in productive minds, when new works of music are constantly supplanted by still newer ones, it is surely worth taking the trouble to look back at those works which will never suffer the fate of being pushed aside. Mozart's genius, which moved in all regions of musical composition so felicitously as to erect in each a model such as his time had not seen — Mozart's genius created, in piano music too, a marvellous cycle of works which, although infinitely diverse in nature, all bear the stamp of the highest perfection."[1]

Mozart's piano sonatas continue to enjoy a universal and undiminished popularity which time cannot touch. They are among those works which are played with just as much pleasure as they are listened to; actually, whether an audience is present or not is immaterial, since the player is his own best listener, with his profit doubled. Less in number than the sonatas of Haydn or Beethoven, Mozart's sonatas nevertheless form their own cosmos, in which there is no place for repetition. No two sonatas resemble one another; in them Viennese influences are mixed with German and Italian; their line of stylistic descent proceeds from Scarlatti and Bach's sons Carl Philipp Emanuel and Johann Christian; they anticipate Beethoven and Schubert, and bring in a new and individual tone which does not disavow Mozart the dramatist. As Nissen aptly puts it, "The way the hands behave makes the music similar to a dialogue; one constantly takes up the train of thought of the other, putting its case with still greater eloquence..."

Thematically and in the way the instrument is used, the first six sonatas composed in 1774 in Salzburg (or at the beginning of 1775 in Munich, according to the most recent research) are still indebted now and then to the "gallant style." Mozart's "Clavierl," the instrument he took with him when travelling, was a clavichord, and later he continued to be fond of using it for composing. But even in these early sonatas — and still more in the next seven, composed in Mannheim and Paris in 1777/78 — the "Hammerklavier," with its clear cantabile tone, touch-controlled dynamic shadings from *forte* to *piano* (without extreme dynamic levels) becomes the true instrument for Mozart's piano music. "Affect" dynamics and thematic contrasts now seem to be born of the sounding tones themselves, and Mozart uses those affects and contrasts like a dramatist; more and more, the last six sonatas (composed in Vienna) raise expressiveness to a level that is individual and

improvisatory. In all of Mozart's late works — on the threshold of the Romantic age, a generation after the pinnacle of Bach — the miracle happens again: a consummately balanced blend of all musical components into an art of "musical composition," of which counterpoint, as it is generally understood is only a single aspect.

Mozart's first five and last three sonatas were not published during his lifetime. Three of the eleven sonatas which did appear in print while the composer was alive were published in Paris, presumably in 1782; seven of the other eight were printed in Vienna in the short space of two years, 1784 and 1785. The majority of them had been written nearly a decade before. Only three works, K 475, 457 and 533/494 (and perhaps a fourth, K 315c), were published soon after they were composed. This circumstance is the origin of a number of editorial problems.

Further on in these introductory remarks we will discuss the source situation in detail. We should, however, anticipate that discussion by a resumé here, for Mozart's works are a special case as regards editorial policy and the reasoning behind it. And this in turn cannot be separated from the meaning and function of a critical edition in general.

It is the urgent and understandable desire of busy musicians and music lovers nowadays to be given a critical text — prepared after protracted examination and thought — which can be correctly grasped in all details at a first glance. There are several ways of providing such an edition. Let us look at the two most prominent. One way is for the editor to solve all the problems and thus to take the full responsibility. Without in the least intending to question the authority of an editor who works from strictly philological considerations, this method is acceptable only when the source situation is relatively uncomplicated (*e. g.* a single, clear and authentic source) or when the musical object itself can be described as unusually difficult (*e. g.* an edition of works by Arnold Schoenberg). If, however, the source situation is more or less confused — as in Bach, Haydn and Mozart — and additionally complicated by the absence of autographs and carefully made contemporary editions, the other method will almost certainly prove to be better: namely, to inform the reader about two (or more) traditional readings and to compare them, especially when it can be assumed that a later reading is definitive — conclusions made on the basis of analogy and musical quality having to substitute for documentary evidence. To present this critical edition of Mozart's sonatas properly, the second path had to be taken. We have considered it obligatory to mention diver-

[1] Georg Nikolaus von Nissen: *Anhang zu Wolfgang Amadeus Mozart's Biographie,* Breitkopf & Härtel, Leipzig, 1828, p. 147.

gent readings in the musical text (especially when a clear decision as to preferability cannot be made), since experience has shown that only very few musicians ever bother to read the Critical Notes. By doing this we have renounced a right which is usually tacitly usurped by editors in a similar position, namely the right to suppress, for the sake of one reading, another reading which in quality and "philological" backing may be just as acceptable. The student of the present edition will find that he is confronted with problems to which he will have to give a certain amount of attention; this means that he will be expected now and then to decide for himself, which is admittedly less convenient than having the editor decide for him. We note with satisfaction, however, that the younger (and youngest) generation is more receptive to information nowadays, and more ready to make its own decisions than ever before.

Among the significant textual divergencies which are mentioned on the spot in the musical text are (in addition to the divergent readings mentioned above) readings whose authorship must remain disputed; there are also occasional comments on the correction of errors which became widespread thanks to late 19th-century editions; finally, the editor has made — relatively sparingly — suggestions on interpretation. This latter point leads to another difficulty met in presenting a musical text which — as we have said — can be correctly grasped in all details at a first glance. The question as to what is necessary in the way of notation to put music down on paper so that there will be no mistaking what is intended has been answered individually by every composer not only in terms of his epoch, but differently at different creative periods — and a decisive role has been played by the constantly changing relationship of the composer to the interpreter. The editor of a critical edition must first investigate the notational technique of the classic composers (which is by no means an open book any more) if he wants to comply both with the intentions of the composer and the wishes of the player. In the course of our remarks we will try to point out, using concrete examples, a few essential facts which are still too little heeded.

Dynamic markings must always be thought of as relative, both as regards the degree of intensity and the duration of validity. The musical context always dictates whether, for example, a *forte* written by Mozart is to be viewed as the culmination of a *crescendo* or as a *subito forte* — not forgetting that markings like *crescendo* or *diminuendo* (or others) may have been omitted by the composer for the simple reason that he could expect such an execution as a matter of course[2]. We may consider it a rule

that until the onset of subjectivism in music composers wrote down only those indications which were not self-evident at their time, *e. g. piano* at the beginning or end of a piece, staccato markings, etc. The question of the extent to which something is "self-evident" is one of the most difficult of all, for the editor as well as for the player — and presumably for the composer too; the fact that in later creative periods composers as a rule are much more precise about notation than in earlier periods is surely not due solely to the increasing complexity of their works. (We are forced to say "as a rule," since Mozart's last three sonatas contain very few markings, and the slow movements none whatever.) The placement of dynamic markings should likewise not be taken too literally by the player. Over and above their more secondary function as execution signs, dynamic markings have a primary function, especially in the music of Viennese Classicism: they express the compositorial and structural aspect of the piece — and this is the basis from which any and all playing indications proceed.[3] Although Mozart's notation is quite precise, it may be taken for granted that he intended a gliding scale of dynamic values even when markings are few and far between, or are lacking entirely (whatever the reason: it may be, as we have mentioned, that dynamic execution was so obvious that detailed markings would have cluttered the notation undesirably; it may also be that Mozart did not write down everything he should have after all). In any event, the first editions, which diverge from the autograph in these particulars, show that Mozart counted on a gliding scale of dynamic values[4]); in addition to varied recapitulations and embellishments, the revisions for the press contain an abundance of dynamic markings, including several in passages where even an experienced editor would hesitate before recommending them[5]). At this point

---

[2] A few examples: in K 475, b. 8/9 and 164/5, a *diminuendo*

can be read in between *forte* and *piano;* the same can probably be done in b. 19, 168 and 171, if the player decides in favour of the other possibility mentioned in the Critical Notes, namely to assume that *forte* begins a semiquaver later, in which case *piano* is reached via a *diminuendo* at the beginning of the next crotchet. The example of b. 5 and 28 in the 2nd movement of K 189h (283) is instructive: here Mozart places the *piano* marking in such a way that a *diminuendo* is absolutely taken for granted; likewise in K 284c (311), 2nd movement, b. 24 and 74, and 3rd movement, b. 138.

[3] *Cf.* Critical Notes on K 457, 3rd movement, b. 211 ff., and the pertinent footnote. The case described there also includes an example of gliding dynamics: it is obvious that a *diminuendo* must be played between the *f* in b. 211 and the *p* in bar 213.

[4] *Cf.* Critical Notes to K 205b (284), 3rd movement; K 300k (332), 2nd movement; K 457, 2nd movement. (300k, however, has no *crescendo* or *diminuendo* markings.)

[5] *Cf.* K 457, 2nd movement, which according to Ernst Rudorff (see below) is too abundantly marked in the first edition: "All expressive markings are those of the oldest edition; the autograph contains them practically only in the variations of the theme."

we may perhaps be permitted a short digression on the subject of divergencies. Basically these are nothing other than additions which are not out of place in the improvisatory, "re-creative" playing that was still the practice at Mozart's time. The question which arises in this connection is whether the interpreter, following the composer's example, should likewise be ready to "impr ise," *i. e.* to embellish. The question can be answered affirmatively for the piano concertos, works written by Mozart for his own use as a soloist; only rarely is the improvisatory aspect set down in hard and fast terms. As regards the piano sonatas, however, the question may be answered in the negative. We may rest assured that Mozart put in all the necessary finishing touches[6]); the little evidence we have gives us insights profound enough to confirm Mozart's authorship from the quality and function of these (not very numerous) additions. Another proof of authenticity cannot be produced, since engravers' copies — not to mention proof sheets — have rarely been preserved.

The musician who is familiar with the notational habits of master composers will not have too much trouble distinguishing between authorized alterations and publishers' additions. What we find in the Sonata K 315c (333) are certainly first and foremost publishers' additions; therefore the supplementary dynamic markings in the first edition have not been adopted in the musical text of the present edition. In Sonatas K 300h (330) and 300k (332) this could not be established quite so definitely; Artaria, so far as we know, did not make any editorial additions, at least not on its own initiative — in contrast to other publishers, for example André, Hoffmeister, Torricella and Hei (one of the least inhibited), not to mention the œuvres complètes" begun after Mozart's death. But we do know that Josepha Auernhammer, who was Mozart's pupil beginning in the summer of 1781, "looked after the engraving by Messrs. Artaria of many of Mozart's sonatas and varied ariettas"[7]); it should not be too difficult, however, to distinguish between Mozart's additions and those of his overly zealous pupil. The additional dynamic markings found in editions which appeared during Mozart's lifetime (of works for which an autograph still exists) are treated in two ways here. We decided to adopt them into the musical text only in the case of Sonatas K 300k (332) and 475 and 457, and to mention them otherwise in footnotes or in summarized form in the Critical Notes. In a few instances, the editor has supplied dynamic markings; these appear in brackets and are likewise

mentioned in the Critical Notes or — if their importance demands it — in footnotes to the musical text. To avoid having two kinds of brackets in the music, other editorial additions — usually made on the basis of parallel bars — also appear in round brackets. One last point: in the autograph and often in the first editions, separate dynamic markings are given for the left and right hand; where differentiation of this sort between the two hands does not seem necessary, the marking has been placed in the middle, between the staves.

In aiming at an interpretation faithful to the work, a not insignificant role is played by a circumstance which should be kept in mind more consistently than it usually is: the nature and characteristics of the instrument at the time the work was written. Only when one has played a Mozart piano does one realize with astonishment how intimately united are the material and intellectual tonal structure in Mozart (and not only in him), and how cogently the specific sound determines the interpretational moulding of details, thus reducing to irrelevancy many things which have become interpretational and editorial problems for our time. Here we can only state that this circumstance exists, and hope that a comprehensive discussion from a competent quarter may soon follow. The decisive role of *legato* playing in the piano music of Viennese Classicism has become still more decisive today, in view of the utterly different conception of sound. To ward off misunderstanding: when the classical masters write *legato,* they do not mean a merely mechanical *legato* but rather an articulating *legato* that leads the player to certain hand reflexes which will produce an articulation that corresponds logically to the musical content.[8]) Obviously, the countless passages where Mozart writes no slurs likewise demand variegated articulated playing, from *legato* to that typically Mozartian *non legato* which agrees with the ideal of the "svelte" sound, especially in passage work.[9]) A word on editorial policy in this respect: articulation given only at the beginning of a passage in the autograph, and not continued, is not supplemented in the musical text of this edition. The articulation of parallel bars which are not immediately adjacent (or are far removed, as in exposition and recapitulation) has, however, been matched up as a general rule. The passages in question are mentioned in the Critical Notes.

---

6) The only exception is perhaps b. 62/63 of the 2nd movement of K 576; see Critical Notes.

7) From a report from Vienna dated 29 January 1787, which appeared in the *Magazin der Musik,* Hamburg, edited by Karl Friedrich Cramer.

8) From Oswald Jonas' Preface to C. P. E. Bach, *Kurze und leichte Stücke mit veränderten Reprisen,* Universal Edition, Vienna, 1962.

9) A splendid example of Mozart's nuances is the differing articulation in bars 24/25 — 26/27 and 148/149 — 150/151 in the 3rd movement of K 315c (333); this would not come out at all if the editor — as editors are prone to do — were to supply the slurs "missing" in b. 27 and b. 151. A further example is found in b. 54/57 and 141/144 in the 1st movement of K 300h (330).

It can be assumed that the execution of Mozart ornaments is generally known today. Apart from a few cases when an attempt to establish the metrical value of an appoggiatura may be welcome, we have limited suggestions to the possible executions of trills, which vary quite a lot in Mozart. Generally, trills begin with the upper neighbouring tone, but sometimes they begin with the principal tone; decisions must be made on the basis of the music itself. As to appoggiaturas, we remind the student that Mozart very frequently writes them ♪ (*i. e.* ♪). The player will not go wrong if, in cases where an appoggiatura is not either clearly "long" (♪ ♪♪ = ♪♪♪♪) or "short" (♪♪♪ = ♪♪♪), he executes it as non-anticipating and somewhat shorter than a "long" appoggiatura. Only one recommendation can be made today about a matter which until well into Mozart's time could be left to the musical understanding and taste of the player: sterile uniformity should be avoided and every decision prompted by what happens in the music. Let it be emphatically stated that none of our comments on interpretation can be exhaustive; all of them are to be considered solely as suggestions. At a future time a comprehensive examination of questions of interpretation and notation may be forthcoming. Until then, we must make do by explaining typical examples, drawing general conclusions in terms of particular cases, in the hope that — the other way round — the particular can come to be recognized within the framework of the general.

In preparing the critical musical text, autographs and first editions were used, as were other editions published during Mozart's lifetime, and whatever contemporary MS. copies happen to be extant. Information on the uneven quality of the first editions is given from case to case in the Critical Notes.

Other problems involved in preparing the musical text should be mentioned briefly:

First there were the divergencies between the autograph and first edition, more precisely, in those passages where it was suspected that a subsequent alteration or addition had been made by Mozart; if the alteration in question was an added dynamic marking, we incorporated it into our text (footnotes or the Critical Notes give particulars); when the divergency was a diminution, an embellishment or another kind of alteration (*e. g.* a change of octave as in K 457), the autograph reading was adopted.

The source of a second problem is the fact that many first editions, primarily those by Heina and Artaria, are faulty in the extreme. Further, some of the sonatas, whose autographs were lost before the end of World War II, did not appear in print until after Mozart's death. Fortunately, the existence of an authentic source for the first movement of the Sonata in C major K 189d (279) could be proved (see below); here the Critical Notes had to be more extensive than is usually necessary in an edition such as ours.

A final problem — more "philological" than anything else — arises from the existence of two differently engraved impressions of the first edition of the Fantasy and Sonata in C minor K 475 and 457, with the same title page, the same publisher's number and the same amount of pages, that is, the same spatial distribution. For easier comparison we have reproduced a page of each impression. Which of the two is the impression published at the end of 1785 cannot be conclusively proved. Some of the pages of one impression show distinct signs of cracks in the plates. Dr. Alexander Weinmann suspects that this was the reason for the new engraving being made. Certain features of the engraving (French-style crotchet rests and the slanted sharps) point to the engraver and publisher Anton Huberty, who often worked for Artaria at the time. Huberty was an excellent musician; his work is therefore less faulty than the impression engraved by Artaria's own man, whom we meet again and again in other Artaria Mozart editions. Huberty's engraving, then, would be the first impression. There exists, however, an authentic MS. copy of K 457, namely the dedication copy for Therese von Trattner; it must have been made shortly after the composition was finished — in any event, the slow movement does not contain any diminutions, which were probably added by Mozart only when the work went to press (as presumably happened with K 300k [332] too). Curiously enough, the rhythmic disposition in bar 19 (a variant of bar 3 — see Critical Notes) agrees with that of the impression of the first edition which in our opinion is the later of the two. It is of course conceivable that such an agreement is purely coincidental (Huberty augments the two notes of the 2nd semiquaver, right hand, by augmentation dots; this, like so many other things, could have been overlooked by Artaria's engraver, who went on to put the missing demisemiquaver value into the 4th quaver of the bar on his own authority). The faultiness of the Artaria engraving could also provide the simplest explanation for the absence of many ornaments — without our having to search for a connection with the dedication copy, or an unknown intermediary source, or the autograph. On the other hand, it is conceivable that plates engraved at a later date could, for some reason, crack sooner than plates engraved at an earlier date; but this would dispose of the imperative reason for a new engraving, unless one wants to suppose that Mozart demanded it because of the faultiness of Artaria's engraving and did in fact get his way. Instinctively, one is inclined to believe that the more correct and painstakingly engraved impression must be the later of the two. Even so, we consider the opinion of Dr. Weinmann — whom we wish to thank at this point for his help — more convincing, and after taking into account all the arguments mentioned above, we have denoted the Huberty engraving as the earlier one in the Critical Notes on this work.[10]

In addition to the contemporary sources we have mentioned, an edition in two volumes (10 sonatas each) by André of Offenbach was also used. Published *c.* 1841 (publisher's numbers 6421 ff.), its title reads "Billigste und correcte Original-Ausgabe/ Sonaten für Pianoforte allein/componirt/von/ W. A. Mozart". The edition, which contains all the sonatas in unchronological order, plus an arrangement of K 547 and an unauthentic Sonata in B flat, shows by and large what is evidently the levelling hand of a reviser; but in at least a few instances it demonstrably goes back to authentic sources or to the autograph itself. In sonatas whose critical texts had to be prepared without the benefit of an autograph, the readings of André's edition are quoted principally when readings in the early editions are suspected of being erroneous or of being

publisher's alterations; cases are likewise mentioned in which the André edition agrees with the extant autograph but disagrees with the early editions. For the first movement of K 189d (279) it had, as we have mentioned, to be used as the primary source in the absence of any authentic source. The "Akademische Ausgabe" edited by Ernst Rudorff in 1900 (Breitkopf & Härtel, Leipzig), was also used for purposes of comparison whenever its text derives from authentic sources which today are lost or — for one reason or another — are not generally accessible.

We were also able to use photograph copies of sonata autographs lost at the end of World War II; they are located in the Salzburg Mozarteum, and we wish to thank the Mozarteum for making them available. Our thanks also go to the following libraries which supplied source material: the Musik-sammlung der Österreichischen Nationalbibliothek, Vienna; the collections of the Gesellschaft der Musikfreunde, Vienna; the Vienna Stadtbibliothek; further, to Dr. Anthony van Hoboken, Ascona; the libraries of Melk and Göttweig Abbeys in Lower Austria; the British Museum, London; and the Bibliothèque du Conservatoire, Paris. Finally, we would also like to express our gratitude to Christa Landon, Dr. Alexander Weinmann and Paul Badura-Skoda, Vienna, Dr. Wolfgang Plath, Neue Mozart Ausgabe, Augsburg, and David Whitwell, USA, for their help and ready information.

Heinz Scholz
Karl Heinz Füssl

[10] In the collections of the Gesellschaft der Musikfreunde, Vienna, there is a printed copy in which 12 of the 22 pages have already been replaced by the newly-engraved impression. Thus the new engraving must have been made by degrees, beginning with a page at a time. All the pages engraved by Huberty show signs of cracks in the plates.

Notiz zur dritten Auflage:

Die Entstehung der ersten fünf Sonaten dieser Ausgabe dürfte laut neuestem Forschungsergebnis etwas später als bisher angenommen anzusetzen sein. Der Datierungsvermerk für KV 189d—h (279—283) — wie auch für KV 205b (284) — hat daher *vermutlich Anfang 1775, München* zu lauten. Es dürfte auch KV 315c (333) nicht 1778 in Paris, sondern 1783/84 in Wien entstanden sein. Vgl. Wolfgang Plath: *Zur Datierung der Klaviersonaten KV 279—284* in „Acta Mozartiana", Heft II, August 1974.

K. H. F.

Note to the third edition:

The dating of the first five sonatas in this edition is, according to the latest scholarly research, rather later than was previously believed to be the case. The listed sating for K 189d—h (279—283), and also for K 205b (284) ought, therefore, to read: "probably beginning of 1775, Munich". K 315c (333) was probably not written at Paris in 1778 but at Vienna in 1783/4. See Wolfgang Plath: *Zur Datierung der Klaviersonaten KV 279—284* in: *Acta Mozartiana*, Heft II, August 1974.

K. H. F.

Wolfgang Amadeus Mozart: Piano Pieces

INDEX

Fantasie [Präludium] KV 300g (395) [284 a]
Fantasia [Prelude] KV 300g (395) [284 a]

Fantasie und Fuge KV 383a (394)
Fantasia and Fugue KV 383a (394)

Fantasie d-Moll KV 385g (397)
Fantasia D minor KV 385g (397)

Rondo D-Dur KV 485
Rondo D major KV 485

Rondo a-Moll KV 511
Rondo A minor KV 511

Adagio h-Moll KV 540
Adagio B minor KV 540

KV = *Chronologisch-thematisches Verzeichnis sämtlicher Tonwerke Wolfgang Amadé Mozarts . . .* von Dr. Ludwig Ritter von Köchel, bearbeitet von Franz Giegling, Zürich, Alexander Weinmann, Wien, Gerd Sievers, Wiesbaden, Breitkopf & Härtel, Wiesbaden, 1964. Sechste Auflage / Sixth impression

PREFACE

This volume contains six of the more extensive individual piano pieces which Mozart wrote partly for his sister, partly for the instruction of his pupils. The letters written during the journeys to Mannheim and Paris include two references to the *"Praeambula"*, and Mozart still sent his sister works of this kind when he was in Vienna. There is still no certainty today about the date of composition of the small Fantasia in C major KV 300g (395). In 1826, Nissen, Constanze's second husband, prepared a copy from the autograph, which belonged to Mozart's sister Nannerl, and he inserted the following note, presumably based on a statement that Nannerl had made: *"Von WA Mozart dem Vater für seine Schwester komponiert wahrscheinlich im April 1782"* (*"Composed by W. A. Mozart the father for his sister, probably in April 1782"*). Nannerl, however, could have easily confused this piece with the other Fantasia in C major which Mozart sent, together with a fugue, to Salzburg on 20th April, 1782. As it does not really fit the description of that *"Capriccio"* which Mozart enclosed in a letter to his sister from Paris (20th July, 1778), there remains the possibility that it might belong to the *"4 Preambele"* which the composer despatched to Nannerl from Munich on 11th October, 1777. An earlier rather than a later date has to be assigned to this modest piece.[1] The autograph, which came to light again a few years ago and which is now located in the Pierpont Morgan Library, New York, could be used, therefore, in the preparation of this new edition of the piece.

In a letter from Vienna, dated 20th April, 1782, Mozart gave a detailed account of the larger Fantasia in C major with the fugue. He called it *"Praeludium"* and, according to the letter, he was inspired to write this piece through his association with Baron van Swieten, in whose Sunday concerts he performed works by Bach and Händel. Mozart referred to the fugue in this letter: *"I have put the direction Andante Maestoso above it deliberately, so that it will not be played quickly — because, if a fugue is not played slowly, the entries of the subject can not be articulated clearly, and, consequently, the effect is lost."* He also reported: *"The Prelude should precede the Fugue — I had already conceived the Fugue and written it down while I was still thinking about the Prelude."* Only the first version of the fugue has survived in autograph. Constanze Mozart probably sent this autograph to André in Offenbach on 26th November, 1800, after Breitkopf & Härtel had used it for their edition in Cahier VIII, 1.

There is no known evidence regarding the composition of the Fantasia in D minor, KV 385g (397). Its first appearance is in the edition of the Bureau d'Arts et d'Industrie (1804) which is incomplete, however, in that the final 10 bars are missing; these were first supplied by the editor of the Œuvres complettes (A. E. Müller). In the first edition, therefore, the Fantasia ends on the A seventh chord in bar 97. The initial impulse for this Fantasia, as well as for the other Fantasias, came from Mozart's knowledge of the works of Carl Philipp Emanuel Bach which he had acquired through his father.

It would seem that Mozart wrote the Rondo KV 485, dated 10th January, 1786, in the autograph, for a lady pupil. A dedication on the autograph has been erased, but some of it is still recognisable: *"Pour Mad*belle*: Charlotte de Wü . . ."* Perhaps the lady in question was a Mademoiselle Würben or Würm, as both these names appear in a list of subscribers for Mozart's concerts in 1784. Mozart borrowed the theme of this Rondo from the Rondo of his Piano Quartet KV 478. Perhaps the grace notes before the crotchets in the theme are to be taken as signifying Lombard rhythm in accordance with French taste (Z. Sliwinski, *Ein Beitrag zum Thema: Ausführung der Vorschläge in W. A. Mozarts Klavierwerken* in Mozart Year Book 1965/66, p. 179 ff.).

Mozart could have written the Rondo in A minor KV 511, which bears the date 11th March, 1787 in the autograph, specially for the collection of piano pieces published by Franz Anton Hoffmeister, in whose Volume X of the *Prénumeration pour le Forte Piano ou Clavecin pour le Mois d'Aoust 1786* it appeared. Mozart also wrote Variations for Hoffmeister's volumes (letter of Constanze Mozart to André, 31st May, 1800).

It is not known what motivated Mozart to write the Adagio in B minor KV 540, which he entered in his own catalogue of works on 19th March, 1788. The work, which is written in sonata form, was probably included in the *"most recent piano pieces"* which Mozart sent to his sister on 2nd August, 1788.

I have to thank the Pierpont Morgan Library, New York, the Gesellschaft der Musikfreunde, Vienna, the Music Section of the Staatsbibliothek Preußischer Kulturbesitz, Berlin, the Musicological Institute of the Johannes Gutenberg University, Mainz, the Musicological College of the Rhenish Friedrich Wilhelm University, Bonn, the Bibliothèque Nationale, Paris, the Stiftelsen musikkulturens främjande (R. Nydahl), Stockholm, the Royal Library, Copenhagen, and the National Museum, Prague, for their readiness to place copies and films of the autographs, manuscripts and printed music at my disposal.

---

[1] As W. Plath points out in the Preface to the volume "Einzelstücke für Klavier (Orgel, Orgelwalze, Glasharmonika)" in the Neue Mozart-Ausgabe, series IX, group 27, volume 2, pp. XII—XV, this composition can be identified as the "Vier Präludien für Klavier" KV 284 a, dating from 1777.

Hans-Christian Müller

Wolfgang Amadeus Mozart: Works for Piano Four Hands

INDEX

PREFACE

The present edition contains not only Mozart's completed original compositions for Piano Duet (four-hand) but also the fragmentary Sonata K 497a (357) which was published by J. André, Offenbach/Main, with additions by Julius André in 1853. Furthermore, the following works were included in this edition in an arrangement for four hands: the Fugue in g minor, K. 375e (401), which seems to be a study in counterpoint, and two works written for a mechanical organ. All these works are contained in the collections of Mozart's four-hand compositions since the early 19th century.

Both magnificent compositions for a mechanical organ can be performed only by means of an arrangement, the most obvious being that for an organ. Needless to say, this requires an instrument which does justice to the polyphonic structure and the late Mozartian style embodied in these works. A setting for orchestra would perhaps give the most satisfying result but it is in the four-hand arrangement that these works can find their widest circulation. Our edition presents for the first time an arrangement of both these works which differs from that of the *Œuvres complettes* version. K 594 was altered only slightly while an entirely new arrangement had to be made of K 608. The text is based on the extant sources, i.e. copies of the scores supplied for the clock maker – whose range had to be in agreement with the limited number of pipes. For a piano version this range certainly had to be extended. There is little reason for publishing these works in a so-called "original version", such as recently appeared within the frame of an *Urtextausgabe* of the four-hand works by Mozart in which the score for the clock maker, which consisted of four staves, is simply divided into two halves in a mechanical fashion, with two staves each for Primo and Secondo. This kind of "original version" meets neither the demands of an *Urtext* nor that of the practical executant.

Mozart's four-hand compositions span his creative output ranging from childhood to his mature style. In number, the works which Mozart composed in this genre are rather small: K 19d composed 1765 in London takes the lead to be followed only in 1772 and 1774 by the two next works, K 123a (381) and K 186c (358), both written in Salzburg. The ensuing works are already of the rather late Vienna period. From 1786, we have K 497 and K 501. After these comes the last of the four-hand compositions, the Sonata in C major, K 521, dating from 1787. The unfinished sonata K 497a (357), which does not bear any date, is placed after the sonata in F major, K 497, for stylistic reasons.

This edition rejects the procedure of strict chronological order. It was felt that more homage would be paid Mozart by starting the volume with the more mature works, the Sonatas in D major and B flat major instead of the relatively unimportant work of his childhood, K 19d, which was placed at the end.

The text was primarily based on the holograph manuscripts insofar as they are extant and, in addition, the first prints were consulted. Works which have not survived in authentic sources are based on sources which were the nearest ones with regard to distance and time.

The lack of documentary evidence that Mozart proof-read his first editions is in fact of importance mainly in connection with the F major Sonata*. In the third movement of this Sonata the divergencies between autograph and first edition are essential and the question remains open whether these alterations were made by Mozart himself or at least approved by him. The added dynamic markings in the Artaria first edition which are not to be found in the autograph are not really convincing and quite suspect. However, the changes in part-writing, which to a certain degree simplify the execution, are done in too masterly a way to stem from an editor's hand. They may have been a concession to the publisher and common taste since the original version, as Haydn said, seems to have been "for too learned ears". It was decided to maintain the autograph's version in our main text.

In the remaining works whose autographs have survived, the first editions were not of too much help in clarifying certain textual problems since, with the exception of a few additions in phrasing and dynamics, they represent a more or less correct engraved reproduction of the autographs. Those divergencies in the G major Variations K 501 between the autograph and the first edition published by Hoffmeister which mainly concern phrasing and dynamic markings, give the impression of being arbitrary alterations and additions of the publisher. Therefore, it was here also decided to follow the holograph manuscript.

The following principles were applied in this edition. It was decided not to burden the musical text with brackets because the editor's additions are based on parallel occurrences. Exceptions are some purely editorial additions such as the "decresc." in the third movement of K 497, Primo bar 110 or the dynamic marks in the second movement of K 497a, Primo bars 107 and 108, accidentals of ornaments not appearing in the sources as well as questionable accidentals and added appoggiaturas. In only a few cases have we distinguished between a staccato dot and a staccato stroke. The latter appear as elongated or thickened strokes in Haydn's and Mozart's autographs which should be executed with a slight accent. The graphic evidence in the autographs is far too inconsistent and, furthermore, the editor came to the conclusion that such differentiations in the manuscripts are largely a result of the procedure of writing. Even at places when the exterior picture in writing seems to confirm the musical contents we are dealing less with matters of strict execution indications and more with subtle suggestive factors which will at most influence the execution. The grace notes are reproduced in the text as they appear in the manuscripts. With a few exceptions the distribution of the two staves is in accordance with that of the sources. In the musical text the sign × indicates where the left hand of the Primo coincides with the right hand of the Secondo. A slur from grace note to main note has been added throughout.

---

* A contemporary document may be of importance with regard to the question of the textual differences between manuscript and first edition. The Hamburg *Magazin der Musik*, published by Karl Friedrich Cramer prints a letter from Vienna, dated 29th January 1787, in which the following statement is contained: "... Madame Aurenhammer (sic) is an excellent master on the piano, on which she also gives lessons ... She is the one who dealt with and corrected the engraving of many sonatas and varied ariettas of Mozart at the Mess" Artaria." Whether this notice of Cramer's informant is according to the facts cannot now be determined for lack of supporting evidence. But it is entirely possible that Josepha Auernhammer, Mozart's pupil who played in many of his concerts, was authorized by Mozart to deal with engraving corrections.

Christa Landon

INDEX

Band 1 / Volume 1

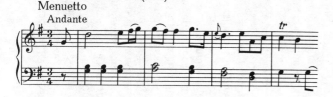
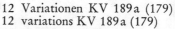
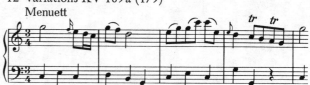

KV = *Chronologisch-thematisches Verzeichnis sämtlicher Tonwerke Wolfgang Amadé Mozarts . . .* von Dr. Ludwig Ritter von Köchel, bearbeitet von Franz Giegling, Zürich, Alexander Weinmann, Wien, Gerd Sievers, Wiesbaden, Breitkopf & Härtel, Wiesbaden, 1964. Sechste Auflage / Sixth impression

PREFACE

This edition contains W. A. Mozart's fourteen sets of variations for piano which have survived in their entirety. Together with the two sets of variations for violin and piano (KV 374 a, 374 b) and the variations for piano duet (KV 501) they constitute, beside the other piano works, a comparatively extensive group of works in the composer's total output. Conceived as occasional compositions for his own concerts, in which it was customary to improvise and perform variations, and for the instruction of his pupils, the variation sets are based mainly on themes which were already well known and popular in those places where Mozart was concertizing. Mozart wrote many variation works during his concert tours. Thus the ten-year-old boy wrote his first two sets of variations on Dutch songs in The Hague and in Amsterdam during his great concert tour through Europe in 1766. The next work was written in 1773 during his stay in Vienna — on an aria from Salieri's opera "La fiera di Venezia", which had been performed in Vienna shortly before. Mozart probably wrote four sets of variations in Paris in 1778 (KV 299 a, 300 e, 300 f, 315 d), including the set on the song "Ah, vous dirai-je Maman", which was very popular in Paris at that time. The later works of this type were conceived in Vienna, with the exception of the Variations KV 573, written in Potsdam in 1789 and based on a Minuet by Jean-Pierre Duport, the director of the royal chamber music. Mozart composed the Variations KV 374 c in 1781 at the same time as the two variation works for violin and piano, probably for the instruction of Countess Rumbeck. On the other hand, Mozart improvised two other sets (KV 416 e and KV 455) for the first time in a concert which he gave on 23rd March, 1783 in the presence of Gluck, in whose honour Mozart played variations on "Unser dummer Pöbel meint" from his Singspiel "Die Pilgrime von Mekka". It is possible that Mozart played his last variation work (KV 613), composed in March, 1791 on a song from the Singspiel "Der dumme Gärtner" by Benedikt Schack/Franz Gerl, which Schikaneder performed in 1789, in his final public concert in Vienna on 4th March, 1791.

The improvised performance of the variations in the concerts — Mozart wrote down at least two sets of variations (KV 416 e and KV 455) only after performance — is reflected in the often very free cadenzas and embellished Adagios, particularly in the works from the Vienna period. From a formal-istic point of view, all the variation works, with the exception of KV 416 e, have in common an "Adagio" tempo marking in the penultimate variation (in the final variation in KV 299 a). Of the variations before the Vienna period, KV 299 a and 315 d stand out because of their particularly varied designs. They already foreshadow the later variation works in the order of the individual variations with a variation in the minor and change of time signature in the final variation (KV 315 d), as well as the repeat of the theme at the end.

The appearance in print without exception of Mozart's variations during his lifetime could probably be explained by the fact that variations were decidedly fashionable at that time and that, in particular, Mozart's mature variation works were regarded as models. The first two works were printed in Amsterdam and The Hague respectively already in 1766, Mozart had three more published (KV 173 c, 189 a, 299 a) by Madame Heina in Paris in 1778, KV 300 e was published by Torricella in Vienna in 1785, Artaria announced publication of KV 300 f, 315 d, 374 c, 416 e, and 455 in Vienna in 1786, Hoffmeister published KV 500 in Vienna in 1786, Hummel printed KV 573 in Berlin in 1789, and KV 613 was published by Artaria again in Vienna in 1791. These editions have survived "in toto". The first print of KV 573 was lost until recently, however, it was discovered by K. Hortschansky in 1963. Consequently, this present new edition has been the first to be able to draw on this source for the editing of the musical text.

The complete autograph is available for KV 455 only, and the autographs of two other works (KV 300 e and 300 f) have survived in fragmentary form. On the other hand, contemporary or later copies of most of the works are available to us; many copies have been preserved in Melk, also in Vienna, Kremsier, Graz, Göttweig, Salzburg, Kremsmünster, Prague, Krumau, Berlin, and Donaueschingen. As far as they were important for the edition, they have been specified in the Critical Notes.

Obvious writing or printing mistakes have been tacitly amended in the new edition; information about musically important variants is given in the notes. Adjustments to parallel passages, particularly with regard to slurring, have been made sparingly. Additions to the text have been placed in brackets or appear in small print.

Hans-Christian Müller

SUGGESTIONS FOR INTERPRETATION

No prudent player will be led to the false conclusion that he would be doing justice even to the most unpretentious of the variation works contained in this volume if he merely performed what was notated in the text. It is fatal for Mozart's music to a particular degree, when it is performed only cleanly, neatly, and harmoniously, without sensitivity. It requires the most delicate shading in dynamics, rhythm, and tempo.

Ideally, an interpretation will arouse the impression that the piece being performed must be played in this and no other way. This is not the only correct interpretation, however. Everyone who begins work on one of these compositions should study the conditioning factors of style in Mozart's time, should read Mozart's letters, and should, above all, listen to his great instrumental works, his operas in particular, and try to really get to know them. The more comprehensively he has studied Mozart's music, the more he may venture to trust his imagination in his own playing, and the more certain he will be to overcome the danger of violating the character of this always sensitive and exceedingly delicate music.

To play Mozart's music, which was written for quite different instruments, authentically on a modern piano is extremely difficult! The following recommendations are made for a satisfactory rendering:

1. Good mastery of "classical" technique (i. e. above all, a precise but always light finger technique, without pressure, from 'legato' through 'leggiero' to 'non legato') and of touch technique (as far as it is required; also without any sluggishness, mainly from the wrist);

2. Mastery of the most subtle use of the pedal (the "normal pedalling" viz. the consistent use of only the following pedal is not satisfactory in Mozart);

3. Liveliness and flexibility in expression and dynamics (dynamic inflexibility must always be avoided);

To perform the embellishments customary in Mozart's time, which, understandably, appeared in profusion, is difficult even on old instruments, with their light mechanism and shallow key-action. This should not lead one to be overawed by the ornaments, however. There will be many passages, nevertheless, in which both amateur and professional pianists, confiding in the old maxim that it is better to play a piece well without embellishments than to play it badly with them, may act accordingly.

The artistic conscience of the player must determine, in each case, which of the often very numerous ornaments can be dispensed with.

The fingerings should lighten the task of the player and help him also to realise clearly the articulation recommended in each piece.

It will be attempted in the following to give p o s s i b i l i t i e s of interpretation for the separate variation works. These directions should be understood only as examples. At all events, the occasional general comments on the character of the works and the demands made on the player resulting therefrom are to some extent obligatory.

Eight Variations on the Dutch song "Laat ons Juichen, Batavieren!" by Christian Ernst Graaf, KV 24

The work as a whole has a happy character. So that the performance may also give pleasure to the listener, the smoothest execution and the greatest possible dynamic variety are required. A few suggestions follow:

Allegretto	c. $\quartnote$ = 63. *mp* to *mf*
Var. I—II	*p* to *mp*
Var. III	*mp* to *mf*, but, for example, the dynamic level could be *p* from the third quaver of bar 56 to the third quaver of bar 60
Var. IV	Stronger, about *mf*, brilliant; perhaps *p* again and *non legato* from the third quaver of bar 72 to the third quaver of bar 76
Var. V	*f*; play everything crisply, almost *staccato*
Var. VI	*p*; light and airy
Var. VII	c. $\eighthnote$ = 92, almost a little *pomposo*; *espressivo*, but the basic character is certainly not to be gentle. A *p* is recommended from the third quaver of bar 120 to the second quaver of bar 124
Var. VIII	Bright, playful, but *cantabile* in the upper part, nevertheless; *mf* to *f* from the third quaver of bar 136 to the second quaver of bar 140, reverting to the original dynamics thereafter and ending *p*

The sign ⤸ which appears in this and the following works should be played, in accordance with the tempo, either as a simple or double mordent, or also as a trill on the lower note.

Seven Variations on the Dutch song "Willem van Nassau", KV 25

Allegro	c. ♩ = 72. It should certainly be begun *mf*, in which case the repeat can be played *p* or also *più f*
Var. I	The first part could be played *p* and the repeat *mf*; *mf* in bars 25—30, *p* in bars 31—36
Var. II	Very light, somewhat akin to the sound produced by a lute stop on the cembalo. First part *p*, *pp* in the repeat; *p* to *pp* in the second part
Var. III	Brilliant, perhaps *un poco più mosso*. First part *p*, *mf* in the repeat. Second part *p*, return to *mf* again from the third beat of bar 66
Var. IV	Play with some bravura, *non legato*, almost *staccato*! First part *mf*, *f* in the repeat. In the second part, three bars *p*, then three bars *mf*, and *f* again with the fourth beat in bar 84; *poco rit.* at the end. Short pause!
Var. V	c. ♩ = 92. *Cantabile*
Var. VI	*Tempo primo*. Brilliant, but not *forte*! First part *mf*, *pp* in the repeat. Second part *p*, *mp* from the fourth beat of bar 117, and *mf* from the fourth beat of bar 120
Var. VII	First part *f*, *p* in the repeat. Second part *p*, *mf* from bar 136, and *f* from the fourth beat of bar 138; *un poco rit.* in the final bar

Six Variations on "Mio caro Adone", from the finale of Act II of Antonio Salieri's opera "La fiera di Venezia", KV 173 c (180)

The metrical compression from the crotchets of the theme through the quavers of the first variation, the triplets of the second, and the semiquavers of the third to the trills and octaves of the fourth should be reflected in performance both in the dynamics and in the increase in intensity of expression. This *affection* should be at its most clear in the interpretation of the Adagio variation (V). The rich figuration in the upper part of the latter should not be interpreted as trifling; on the contrary, the quick scale passages are a token of intense feeling. The closing Allegretto radiates cheerfulness; it should not be played very quickly, but should be dance-like and flexible.

Menuetto	c. ♩ = 96. The *fp* effect, which is required often, provides clear proof that this variation work is to played with particular feeling
Var. I—III	c. ♩ = 104
Var. IV	With a little more restraint c. ♩ =

96—100. The demisemiquavers after the trills are written-out after-notes; the trills should flow into them without a break, therefore

Var. V	c. ♪ = 104
Var. VI	c. ♩ = 108. Very dance-like, in the style of a merry final dance. The last 4½ bars certainly *f*

Twelve Variations on a Minuet by Johann Christian Fischer, KV 189 a (179)

The harmonic structure of these variations is unusually simple. The use of different types of touch and of a great variety of dynamics is particularly necessary for a lively performance of the work. The following dynamic marks represent only the dynamic basis in each case. There must be the greatest flexibility of performance within the bounds set by them.

Minuet	c. ♩ = 112. *mf* in bars 1—8, *pp* in the repeat, perhaps; *p* in the second section, *cresc.* from bar 15, *f* from bar 18 (!); *mf* at first in the repeat, *decresc.* from bar 15, and *p* from bar 16 to the end
Var. I	c. ♩ = 116. First section *f*, *p* in the repeat; second section *p* first time, *cresc.* from bar 36, and *f* from bar 43; begin the repeat *mf*, *cresc.* at bar 36, but *decresc.* from bar 40, and *p* from bar 43
Var. II	The crotchets should be played *legato* throughout, in contrast to the *staccato* quavers. First section *p*, *mf* in the repeat; begin the second section *p*, *cresc.* to bar 68, *f* from here right to the end; begin the repeat *mf*, *cresc.* only to bar 64, *dim.* from bar 66, and *p* from bar 68 to the end.
Var. III	Remain in the same tempo, but play very *legato* and *cantabile* First section *p*, *mf* in the repeat; second section *mf*, *dim.* from bar 91, and *p* from bar 93 to the end; begin *p* in the repeat, *cresc.* to bar 91, a little *dim.* to bar 93, *cresc.* again from bar 96, and *f* to the end A small break
Var. IV	c. ♩ = 126—132. The semiquavers are to be played with a precise *non legato* touch and brilliantly First section *f*, *pp* in the repeat (play the bass crisply, but not without resonance, somewhat like a cello *pizzicato*); second section *p*; *cresc.* from bar 122 to the end

mf with *cresc.* in the repeat, but *dim.* in bar 117, and *p* from bar 118, *pp* from bar 122 to the end

Var. V   First section *mp* to *mf*, *f* in the repeat; second section *mp*, *cresc.* to bar 141, begin a *dim.* here, and *p* from bar 143; begin the repeat *p* and *cresc.* to bar 143, *f* from here to the end

Var. VI   A little more gently, melodious and with feeling in the upper part, the left hand very light, even, and without sharing in the declamation of the right hand
First section *p*, *pp* in the repeat; second section *pp*, gradual *cresc.* to bar 168, *mf* from here to the end; *mp cresc.* in the repeat, *dim.* from bar 167, and *p from* bar 168 to the end; last bar *poco rit.* The other variations can be disposed dynamically in a similar manner

Var. VII c. ♩ = 120. It would be better if one played a turn instead of a trill; the basic character of the variation should not be gentle, in contrast to the next variation

Var. VIII c. ♩ = 116. The variation is certainly to be played *p cantabile*

Var. IX   c. ♩ = 120

Var. X   c. ♩ = 126. Both variations (IX and X) are to be played with glittering virtuosity, with *f* as the basic dynamic level

Var. XI   c. ♩ = 60. *Con affetto, cantabile* with a very flexible *espressivo;* the more active the movement in the upper part, the more intensive the expression

Var. XII c. ♩ = 120—126. Virtuosic, bright; not too cautious dynamically; basic dynamic level *f*, very precise and resilient in the left hand with flexible accents

Twelve Variations on the Romance "Je suis Lindor" from Beaumarchais' comedy "Le Barbier de Séville", music by Antoine-Laurent Baudron, KV 299 a (354)

Air   c. ♩ = 84. *Amabile*, basic dynamic level *mp*, *cantabile*, also *espressivo*, but without any heaviness

Var. I   *p* as basis, *pp* in the repeat; second section *pp*, *più f* from bar 34, still more from bar 39; the reverse pro-

cess in the repeat, *più p* from bar 39 and *dim.* to the end

Var. II   Begin *pp*, repeat *p;* second section *p* to *mf*, *f* from bar 62; *pp* in the repeat, *meno p* from bar 57, *mf* from bar 62

Var. III *poco meno mosso;* very elegant and with playful brilliance
Further disposition of dynamics according to previous procedure. Avoid standardisation! Maintain a clear sound

Var. IV   Certainly in the first tempo again at least! The quavers melodious, the triplet semiquavers very exact, with the greatest lightness and unobtrusiveness

Var. V & VI c. ♩ = 100. *più mosso*, definite virtuosic character; beware of playing them mechanically, as if they were studies! Remain dynamically flexible

Var. VII *un poco maestoso,* to be played with great brilliance and majesty; *poco rit.* at the end of the repeat of the second section. Short pause!

Var. VIII c. ♩ = 120. Very dance-like; virtuosic and improvisatorial cadence

Var. IX   c. ♩ = 60—63. *meno mosso,* to be played with great feeling

Var. X & XI c. ♩ = 80. With great virtuosity, but without a rough *f*; elegant; *Poco rit.* at the end of Var. XI. Short pause!

Var. XII c. ♩ = 46. The rule that precisely the quick figurations are to be played *espressivo* in such Adagio variations is applicable again here

Allegretto (bar 311). In the opening tempo, but more peaceful, like a charming reminiscence

Twelve Variations on the French song "Ah, vous dirai-je Maman", KV 300 e (265)

Theme   c. ♩ = 126. First section *p*, *pp* in the repeat; second section *p*, *più f* from bar 13; *mf* in the repeat, *p* from bar 13; still *dim.* to the end

Var. I   Same tempo, a good finger *legato* of classical technique in the right hand; possibly *pp non legato* in the repeats

Var. II   First section *poco f*, repeat *p;* second section *pp*, *p* to *mp* from bar 65; *p* in the repeat, *mp* from bar 61, *più f* from bar 65

Var. III First section *f*, repeat *p;* second section *pp*, *p* from bar 85, *mp* from bar 89; *mf* in the repeat, *p* from bar 85, *mf* from bar 89

Var. IV First section *f*, repeat *p;* second section *pp*, *mp* from bar 109, *mf* from bar 113, repeat *mf*, *pp* from bar 109, *mf* to *f* from bar 113; final bar *poco rit.* Short break!

Var. V c. ♩ = 132. Play very lightly and with great delicacy; dynamic disposition similar to that in the preceding variations, but basically a little gentler here

Var. VI Not loud, even if more brilliant now; play the semiquavers, those in the left hand in particular, very clearly *(non legato)*

Var. VII c. ♩ = 138. Must be played with sparkling virtuosity; the echo *(e. g.* bars 181—184) to be executed with a spring *non legato* touch, *poco rit.* in bars 191—192 in the repeat. Short pause!

Var. VIII c. ♩ = 116. Simple, *cantabile*, between *mp* and *pp;* the editor recommends the use of a *legato* touch throughout, with the exception of a few obviously original *staccato* dots

Var. IX c. ♩ = 138. Not loud, although the final two bars of each section should be played *mf* or even *f*

Var. X To be performed with virtuosity, between *p* and *f; poco rit.* at the close of the second section in the repeat

Var. XI c. ♪ = 80—84. With much feeling, very flexible in dynamics

Var. XII High-spirited last dance; with virtuosity, but never producing a powerful sound; reaching *f*, clear, and sprightly in rhythm, nevertheless

Twelve Variations on the French song "La belle Françoise", KV 300 f (353)

The performance of this entire work should be characterised by charm, elegance, and the most subtle shading *amabile, con amore* . Precision is also necessary here, naturally, but brilliant virtuosity takes second place to sensitiveness

Theme c. ♩. = 63

Var. I—VIII The same basic tempo, but avoid inflexibility

Var. IX & X c. ♩. = 52 or 48. *meno mosso*

Var. XI c. ♪ = 96

Var. XII c. ♩ = 144. *poco rit.* in bars 172/173. Short pause!

Tempo I (upbeat to bar 174). Very simply, *p* to *pp*

Carl Seemann

INDEX

Band 2 / Volume 2

9 Variationen KV 315d (264)
9 variations KV 315d (264)

8 Variationen KV 374c (352)
8 variations KV 374c (352)

6 Variationen KV 416e (398)
6 variations KV 416e (398)

10 Variationen KV 455
10 variations KV 455

12 Variationen KV 500
12 variations KV 500

9 Variationen KV 573
9 variations KV 573

8 Variationen KV 613
8 variations KV 613

KV = *Chronologisch-thematisches Verzeichnis sämtlicher Tonwerke Wolf-*
gang Amadé Mozarts . . . von Dr. Ludwig Ritter von Köchel,
bearbeitet von Franz Giegling, Zürich, Alexander Weinmann, Wien,
Gerd Sievers, Wiesbaden, Breitkopf & Härtel, Wiesbaden, 1964.
Sechste Auflage / Sixth impression

SUGGESTIONS FOR INTERPRETATION

No prudent player will be led to the false conclusion that he would be doing justice even to the most unpretentious of the variation works contained in this volume if he merely performed what was notated in the text. It is fatal for Mozart's music to a particular degree, when it is performed only cleanly, neatly, and harmoniously, without sensitivity. It requires the most delicate shading in dynamics, rhythm, and tempo.

Ideally, an interpretation will arouse the impression that the piece being performed must be played in this and no other way. This is not the only correct interpretation, however. Everyone who begins work on one of these compositions should study the conditioning factors of style in Mozart's time, should read Mozart's letters, and should, above all, listen to his great instrumental works, his operas in particular, and try to really get to know them. The more comprehensively he has studied Mozart's music, the more he may venture to trust his imagination in his own playing, and the more certain he will be to overcome the danger of violating the character of this always sensitive and exceedingly delicate music.

To play Mozart's music, which was written for quite different instruments, authentically on a modern piano is extremely difficult! The following recommendations are made for a satisfactory rendering:

1. Good mastery of "classical" technique (i. e. above all, a precise but always light finger technique, without pressure, from 'legato' through 'leggiero' to 'non legato') and of touch technique (as far as it is required; also without any sluggishness, mainly from the wrist);

2. Mastery of the most subtle use of the pedal (the "normal pedalling" viz. the consistent use of only the following pedal is not satisfactory in Mozart);

3. Liveliness and flexibility in expression and dynamics (dynamic inflexibility must always be avoided);

To perform the embellishments customary in Mozart's time, which, understandably, appeared in profusion, is difficult even on old instruments, with their light mechanism and shallow key-action. This should not lead one to be overawed by the ornaments, however. There will be many passages, nevertheless, in which both amateur and professional pianists, confiding in the old maxim that it is better to play a piece well without embellishments than to play it badly with them, may act accordingly.

The artistic conscience of the player must determine, in each case, which of the often very numerous ornaments can be dispensed with.

The fingerings should lighten the task of the player and help him also to realise clearly the articulation recommended in each piece.

It will be attempted in the following to give possibilities of interpretation for the separate variation works. These directions should be understood only as examples. At all events, the occasional general comments on the character of the works and the demands made on the player resulting therefrom are to some extent obligatory.

Nine Variations on the arietta "Lison dormait" from the Singspiel "Julie" by Nicolas Dezède, KV 315 d (264)

The work is to be played with polished elegance, and with pronounced virtuosity in some variations. If the repeat of the second section is omitted each time — which would appear to be justifiable in this work — the written-out repeats in Variations IV, VIII, and IX must, by analogy, either be deleted, or an amalgam of both versions of the second section be played. The editor ends Var. IV at bar 161. In the Adagio (Var. VIII), the written-out repeat seems more attractive to him, and so he jumps from bar 312 to bar 336 and plays from there to the end of the Adagio. In Var. IX, one can jump directly to bar 386 after the repeat of the first section

Theme	c. ♩ = 120
Var. I—IV	c. ♩ = 126. A small *rit.* at the end of Var. IV. Short pause!
Var. V	c. ♩ = 104. A small break again at the close
Var. VI & VII	c. ♩ = 132
Var. VIII	c. ♩ = 69
Var. IX	c. ♩. = 92. A trill on the highest note of the chord is recommended in bar 413, its after-note leading into the cadenza. Play the cadenza improvisatorially and with virtuosity. The parallel sixths are best executed *glissando*

The overall dynamic disposition should be similar to that in the earlier variation works, for which possible patterns were provided. Always remain flexible!

Eight Variations on the choral piece "Dieu d'amour" from André-Ernest-Modeste Grétry's opera "Les Mariages Samnites", KV 374 c (352)

The numerous *forte* indications in the theme are, without a doubt, not to be regarded as strong expressive accents, but they should be understood from the "dance-like" movement as particular stressings of the march rhythm.

With regard to dynamics, their disposition in performance should correspond approximately with that provided for the earlier variation works.

Theme	c. ♩ = 116—120
Var. I & II	c. ♩ = 120
Var. III	c. ♩ = 126—132
Var. IV	c. ♩ = 120
Var. V	c. ♩ = 96. *meno mosso*
Var. VI	c. ♩ = 120. Brilliant
Var. VII	c. ♩ = 58
Var. VIII	c. ♩. = 88

Six Variations on the aria "Salve tu, Domine", from Giovanni Paisiello's opera "I filosofi immaginarii", KV 416 e (398)

This unjustly neglected work is distinguished for its amazing compositional inventiveness.

In spite of the technical and metric variety, the serious *legato* character of the theme should have some bearing on the performance of each variation.

Theme	c. ♩ =96. Certainly begin *mf*, *p espressivo* from 3rd quaver of bar 12, *f* from bar 17 to the pause, then *p*
Var. I	c. ♩ = 120. Maintain melodic interest, in spite of the playful broken chords in the upper part
Var. II	c. ♩ = 120. Not *f*, *legato*, *cantabile* from 2nd crotchet of bar 56, *f* from bar 61, *meno f* after the pause
Var. III	c. ♩ = 112. Basic character *f*, but *p* and certainly also *poco rit.* in the last 2½ bars
Var. IV	c. ♩ = 96. *meno mosso*, with feeling, basically *legato*, *p* to *mp*; *cresc.* from bar 112, the cadenza free and with much expression
Var. V	In the tempo of the theme; this variation should also be distinguished from the theme in character, chiefly by means of a more intensive expression; the trills at the end should lead into the next variation without a *diminuendo*

Var. VI	c. ♩ = 96—100. Basically *f*, but never a powerful sound; careful pedalling! Play the cadenza brilliantly and imaginatively
[Theme]	(bar 156) *mf* at the beginning, *p* from bar 160, *mf* in bar 164, *pp* in bar 166, *pp* to *mp* from bar 168 to the end, almost no *rit.*

Ten Variations on the arietta "Unser dummer Pöbel meint" from the Singspiel "Die Pilgrime von Mekka" by Christoph Willibald Gluck, KV 455

The richness of invention and the abundance of the most diverse instrumental possibilities place the work in the proximity of the great piano concertos. Compared with the other sets of variations for piano, it attains a unique position from the beginning of the 7th variation at the latest. Great demands, both from a technical and an artistic point of view, are made on the player.

Theme	c. ♩ = 120. Vary the specified dynamics in the repeats
Var. I—IV	Same tempo, as varied dynamically as possible
Var. II	The appoggiaturas exactly on the beat
Var. V	c. ♩ = 104. *meno mosso*, careful realization of the different articulation marks
Var. VI	c. ♩ = 126. Not loud, but with pianistic brilliance throughout
Var. VII	c. ♩ = 132. Agitated, but by no means restless, also not loud
Var. VIII	Brilliant, the semiquavers to be played very clearly; like a cadenza from bar 152
Var. IX	c. ♩ = 63. Expressive, not quiet basically, but, of course, very flexible in dynamics
Var. X	c. ♩. = 84. With elegant accentuation; virtuosic, but without any forcefulness; rich in dynamic contrasts, but without hardness; play *rubato* in bars 315—322
Tempo I	(bar 323). Certainly begin *p*; c. *mf* from bar 333 at the latest, and *crescendo* to *f*

Twelve Variations on an Allegretto, KV 500

The work is to be played very much in the style of a dance, with charm and subtlety in dynamics.

Theme	c. 𝅗𝅥 = 63; likewise Var. I—IV

Var. V	c. $\d = 58$
Var. VI	c. $\d = 66$
Var. VII	c. $\d = 60$
Var.VIII—X	c. $\d = 66$
Var. XI	c. $\d = 58$
Var. XII	c. $\d. = 80$. Play the cadenza (bar 146) before the reprise of the theme freely, not too quietly, but *dim.* towards the close
Tempo I	(upbeat to bar 147) *p* to *pp, grazioso*

Nine Variations on a Minuet by Jean-Pierre Duport, KV 573

Theme	c. $\d = 116$
Var. I—V	c. $\d = 116$
Var. VI	c. $\d = 88$. *meno mosso*
Var. VII	c. $\d = 126$—132. Brilliant
Var. VIII	c. $\d = 50$. Strong, but guarded expression
Var. IX	c. $\d = 138$. Very playful and dance-like; the same applies to the coda (bar 241), in which, moreover, a virtuosic and almost improvisatory interpretation is necessary

Tempo I	(bar 267). Certainly *p* to the first crotchet of bar 274 or even bar 276

Eight Variations on the song "Ein Weib ist das herrlichste Ding" from the Singspiel "Der dumme Gärtner" by Benedikt Schack/ Franz Gerl, KV 613

As many of Mozart's other variation works as possible should be studied, before one ventures to embark upon this work, which makes the greatest artistic demands on the player.

Theme and Var. I—III	c. $\d = 132$
Var. IV	c. $\d = 126$. left hand brilliant, with the greatest precision, but without inflexibility
Var. V	c. $\d = 132$
Var. VI	c. $\d = 108$. *meno mosso;* careful realization of the phrase markings specified in the minor section
Var. VII	Bars 328—335, c. $\d = 132$, Adagio c. $\d = 52$—54
Var. VIII	c. $\d = 132$—138
Tempo I	(bar 454) very colourful, and with flexibility in dynamics; play the final four bars quite simply

Carl Seemann

Modest Mussorgsky: Pictures at an Exhibition

INDEX

Promenade

Nr. 1 Gnomus
Der Zwerg
The Gnome

[Promenade]

Nr. 2 Il vecchio castello
Das alte Schloß
The Old Castle

[Promenade]

Nr. 3 Tuileries
(Dispute d'enfants après jeux)
(Streit der Kinder nach dem Spiel)
(Children's Quarrelling at Play)

Nr. 4 Bydło

[Promenade]

215

Nr. 5 (Originaltitel russisch)
Ballett der nicht ausgeschlüpften Küchlein
Ballet of the Unhatched Chicks

Nr. 6 Samuel Goldenberg und Schmuÿle
Samuel Goldenberg and Schmuÿle

Promenade

Nr. 7 Limoges
Le marché (La grande nouvelle)
Der Marktplatz (Die große Neuigkeit)
The Market Square (The Big News)

Nr. 8 Catacombae (Sepulcrum romanum)
Die Katakomben (Eine römische Totengruft)
Catacombs (A Roman Sepulchre)

Con mortuis in lingua mortua
Mit den Toten in einer toten Sprache
With the Dead in a Dead Language

Nr. 9 (Originaltitel russisch)
Die Hütte auf Hühnerfüßen (Baba-Jaga)
The Hut on Hen's Legs (Baba-Yaga)

Nr. 10 (Originaltitel russisch)
Das Bogatyr-Tor (in der alten Hauptstadt Kiew)
The Bogatyr Gate (at Kiev, the Ancient Capital)

PREFACE

Modest Mussorgsky composed the piano cycle *Pictures at an Exhibition (Kartinki s wystawki)* within a short period of time, between 2nd and 22nd June 1874. At the instigation of the art critic Vladimir Stassov a commemorative exhibition was put on of drawings, watercolours, designs etc. by the composer's friend Viktor Hartmann (1834–1873), who had died unexpectedly. Mussorgsky decided to pay his own tribute to Hartmann in the form of a succession of piano pieces portraying some of the artist's work in music. The original title given to the cycle was *Hartmann*.

It was probably in 1870 and through Stassov that Mussorgsky had first made the acquaintance of Hartmann, who had studied at the art college in St. Petersburg and was actually an architect. For the piano cycle Mussorgsky selected mainly drawings and watercolours which Hartmann had produced during his travels abroad – in Italy, France and elsewhere. Exactly which pictures Mussorgsky drew on can only partially be ascertained today, because not all the paintings and drawings are extant.

Hartmann's best known work reflects his professional aspirations to become the founder of an indigenous Russian style of architecture. His designs thus incorporate elements derived from the traditions of folk art, wood carving and ethnic ornamental work. However, some of his designs, like that for the Great Gate of Kiev, were never built.

In June 1874 Mussorgsky wrote to Stassov[1]: *My dear généralissime, Hartmann is bubbling up inside me like "Boris" did, the air is full of sounds and thoughts, I devour and am devoured, I am barely able to put pen to paper . . . My physiognomy can be seen in the interludes. So far I think it is working . . .*

The titles are strange: "Promenade (in modo russico)"; No. 1. "Gnomus", Intermezzo (the intermezzo has no heading); No. 2. "Il vecchio castello" – Intermezzo (likewise without a heading); No. 3. "Tuileries" (Dispute d'enfants après jeux); (immediately followed by) No. 4. Sandomirzsko bydlo (Le télègue) (Le télègue is not intended as a heading, but that in confidence). How well the work is going . . .

In the catalogue of works which Mussorgsky drew up for Stassov[2] (*. . . in memory in Mussoryanin, August 26th 78, Petersburg*) the cycle is listed as opus 11. Although Mussorgsky had intended *Pictures at an Exhibition* to be printed immediately (cf. Critical Notes), the cycle was published only in 1886, five years after the composer's death, by W. Bessel, St. Petersburg. The second edition, with a preface by Stassov, was issued by the same publisher. In both cases the editor was Nikolay Andreyevitch Rimsky-Korssakov who – with the best of intentions – felt obliged to emend some of Mussorgsky's more daring touches, with the result that the work was not printed in its original form.

Some sections of the cycle were orchestrated by M. Tushmalov, and in 1922 Maurice Ravel produced the orchestral version which had been commissioned by Serge Koussevitzky. The American conductor Leopold Stokowski also made a well-known orchestration.

It was not until 1931 that *Pictures at an Exhibition* was published in its original form, in the complete edition of the works of Mussorgsky as volume VIII, separate edition 2, by the two publishers Musgis-Moscow and Universal Edition Vienna. The editor Paul Lamm produced a musicologically correct edition on the basis of the autograph manuscript, and reprints followed in the Soviet Union and in other countries.

The cycle's programmatic content is outlined by Stassov in the first of the above-mentioned editions as follows:

The introduction is headed "Promenade".
No. 1 "Gnomus" – the drawing shows a tiny gnome clumsily waddling on bow legs.
No. 2 "Il vecchio castello". A medieval castle, in front of which a troubadour is singing.
No. 3 "Tuileries. Dispute d'enfants après jeux". Avenue in the Tuileries Gardens, with many children and governesses.
No. 4 "Bydło". A Polish farm cart on huge wheels, drawn by oxen.
No. 5 "The ballet of the unhatched chicks". An illustration by Hartmann for the performance of a picturesque scene from the ballet "Trilbi".
No. 6 "Two Polish Jews, one rich, one poor".
No. 7 "Limoges. Le Marché". French women arguing furiously in the market square.
No. 8 "Catacombae". The picture shows Hartmann himself looking at the Paris catacombs by the light of a lantern.
No. 9 "The hut on hen's legs". This drawing by Hartmann depicts a clock in the form of a witch's hut on hen's legs. Mussorgsky added the ride of Baba-Yaga (the witch) on the mortar.
No. 10 "The Bogatyr Gate in Kiev". Hartmann's drawing is the design for a city gate in Kiev, in the old-Russian massive style, with a dome in the form of a Slav helmet.

The present edition is based on a printed facsimile of the autograph manuscript (cf. Criticals Notes), for the acquisition of which I am indebted to Jürgen Köchel in Hamburg.

Manfred Schandert

[1] Letter from Mussorgsky to W. W. Stassov, dated June 12th or 19th 1874, in: Alexandra Anatolyevna Orlova, *Works and Days of M. P. Mussorgsky, Chronicle of his Life and Work*, Moscow 1963 (in Russian), p. 393 (translated by Manfred Schandert).

[2] Published in: Michael Dimitri Calvocoressi, *Modest Mussorgsky, His Life and Works*, London 1956, pp. 10f.

SUGGESTIONS FOR PERFORMANCE

Perhaps the most important and crucial point in understanding this piece is that although it was conceived initially as a programmatic cycle, the result is music that not only goes far beyond mere descriptive qualities but in fact gives us a penetrating insight into the dark and brooding spirit of Mussorgsky – or for that matter of Russia itself. Indeed everything in his music – including *Pictures* – is seen through and by the eyes of a human being in the midst of the narrative. If the potential performer keeps this in mind and realizes how much good and evil, tragedy and triviality, fairy tale and stark reality are contained in this opus, he will be on the path of realizing the composer's intentions. Conversely, if he treats it simply as a piece of entertainment, then his hard work (and it *is* a difficult piece!) will be in vain and he is doomed to failure.

Having said that after this introduction, I shall leave the rest to the imagination of the individual performer and will limit myself only to dealing with some practical observations which hopefully may be of help to some and of interest to others.

Promenade. Make sure the upper voice is clear and distinct in bars 3 and 4 and indeed keep the melodic line very well projected. Attention to dynamics is especially advisable considering the relative monotony of the material: bar 9 could be *mf,* then bars 11–12 *crescendo* and bar 13 *forte;* then perhaps *dim.* in bars 14–15–16, the *crescendo* starting in bar 17 culminating in *forte* at the end of bar 21 and then *ff* in bar 23, fourth beat.

Gnomus. Articulation is the essence of the basic motive. Therefore the tempo should be dependar͏ how fast the low register can "speak". Bear in mind that there is more fear than aggressiveness in this piece; it migh͏ help in creating the right atmosphere. Rests and fermatas are of great importance therefore; the silence should be potent and frightening. I usually play the repeat of bars 19–28 softer and with different colours but there could be other solutions. I tend to play bars 38–44 rather *piano* or *mezzo-piano* so that the contrast with *ff* is greater. Some fingering suggestions in bar 87 and the last passage:

The next *Promenade* should be reflective and transparent, leading into the mood of

Il vecchio castello. There is no disputing the predominance of the beautiful sad melody – unrequited love of a troubadour? – but do not forget the accompaniment, the repeated g ♯ in the left hand; here lies the secret of the continuity of the piece and ultimately the attentiveness of the listener largely depends on it. In bars 23, 24, 25, 26 I play with the left hand the lower notes printed in the right hand part to enable the right hand to be as free as possible for the sake of the melody.

Tuileries. Due to the famous Ravel orchestration this piece is often played rather slow simply because it would not sound very good in a faster tempo in that particular instrumentation. The result is often rather sleepily elegant whereas what one needs is scherzando and excitement. Children argue when they argue and really run when they run. Find a tempo which allows you to articulate all the sixteen notes but these passages should be full of energy, descriptive of running children rather than of a prim Sunday school outing. The tiny middle section (from bar 14) sounds better *meno mosso* but you should be getting back into the original tempo gradually from bar 22 onwards. I sometimes make a *crescendo* in bar 10 and *subito piano* in bar 11 (it is fun).

218

Some fingering suggestions:

Bydło. Note *ff* at the beginning as opposed to the complete misconception in Ravel's score (*pp* and tuba solo). Try *meno forte* in bar 21, *più forte* in bars 25–30, then *diminuendo* and *crescendo* to return to the original tune.

Promenade should sound very sad indeed.

Ballet of the Unhatched Chicks. Perhaps a slight *crescendo* in bars 5–8 and back to *pp* in bar 9. I have heard a small *accelerando* in bars 17–21 – it can work well but it is not essential. Note *ppp* in the trio – shimmering trills and a distant left hand.

My fingering suggestions:

If you have doubts about how to do uninterrupted trills in bars 3 and 4 of the Trio here is one idea:

It works with me often. But if you can do it unmeasured and without accents and really shimmering then it is wonderful.

Samuel Goldenberg and Schmuÿle. I think the opening should be played with a lot of *rubato* but not too much so to lead to distortion. One needs a touch of false rhetoric. In the fourth bar I make a *sf* on the third beat (an arrogant Fa) but this is personal and if the performer feels against it I would not recommend it. The passage describing the poor man's trembling *(Andantino)* should be played in one sweeping line – (no gaps between beats) – try also to achieve a near unity of tempo when you come to *Andante* and *Grave*. In any case I do not think there should be an abrupt change of tempo there. I play the four final notes very slow and in an exclamatory way.

Limoges. A very difficult piece pianistically. Make sure you do not approach it as a study. If you begin to play it as a toccata, because of the many repeated notes, it is fatal. The left hand should be balanced in favour of the right hand and if one begins to hear a lot of the left hand, something is wrong! The left hand should be a continuous and active rythmic support but this should be in the background. The *crescendo* should be very strong in this piece, with the *sf*'s sharp and played with real bite. Elemental vitality is what one needs here. If it makes life easier play the long notes printed in the left hand part with the right hand in bar 5. In bar 8 I play this:

and in the same way in parallel places, bars 18, 19, 21, 33, 34, 35. Some fingering ideas:

Catacombs. Treat the first two bars as exclamation and echo. The same in bars 4–5 and 6–7 and 23–24, the greatest being bars 23–24. Imagine a distant trumpet in bars 19–21. To get maximum sonority in bars 13–14 I actually keep the pedal from bar 12 into bar 13 just shaking the foot in order to make the harmony clean. And I keep bars 13 and 14 on the same pedal. Before you begin the tremolo (the opening of the next number) imagine it already sounding and then try to match what is in your mind – then you might begin it really as if coming out of nothing. The tremolo should be absolutely uninterrupted. Find different colours in the left hand between the chords and the low octaves.

Baba-Yaga. The witch on a broom is a scary thing. This should sound evil, satanic and powerful. The rythm should be very good, relentless, but not metric and wooden. The middle section offers beautiful fairy-tale colours in the tremolos, so do not pass them by.

The Bogatyr Gate. My suggestion is that the beginning should not sound overwhelming – (leave the greatest sonority for the closing bars) – but rather like decorative accompaniment to a royal procession. The dynamics of the piece should be graded so as to lead into the final blast. Try to keep the bells in tempo (bells are not known for making a lot of *rubato*). With strong accents in the right hand in bars 89–96 and especially bars 97–106, and with the boomy bells in the left, the effect can be magical and devastating. The descending scale should be practically on one pedal – vibrate the foot somewhat to be able to hear the individual notes clearly but get a wave of sound – I treat it as a build up for the tune that follows. Note the dynamics in the next section *Meno Mosso.* They are very useful and help to build up to the last few bars. In the closing bars *(Grave)* again use pedal over the bar lines and shake the foot. Bars 50–51 are awkwardly written – I suggest this:

Vladimir Ashkenazy

Franz Schubert: Complete Dances for Piano

PREFACE

Franz Schubert's numerous dance compositions, which in most instances have come down to posterity as "Pianoforte" pieces, must be considered in terms of the musical practise of the period. A few words on that practise may be in order. Even masters of the calibre of Haydn, Mozart and Beethoven were not reluctant about writing dance pieces for practical use; in some cases, indeed, their position demanded that they do so. For the most part, such compositions were printed in an edition for piano, and often for small orchestra as well. For social events of a more intimate nature there were, in addition, arrangements for a tiny ensemble consisting of three violins and bass, which could be augmented by a few wind instruments when the occasion called for them.

At the turn of the 19th century a number of specialists in dance music composition appeared on the scene, some of whom were subsequently employed for balls held by the nobility and the court. These composers carried on an already existing practise by mass-producing sets of 12, 18, 20 and more dance pieces; countless sets by composers like Pamer, Faistenberger, Wilde and others have been preserved. A more well-known colleague, Johann Nepomuk Hummel, composed and published such sets of dances year after year for the Apollosaal, perhaps Vienna's most famous dancing establishment at that time. We still find editions of these pieces for piano and for two or three violins and bass.

In performance, as we can imagine, these dance pieces were treated quite freely. The parts at hand, sometimes printed but more often in manuscript, served merely as a general basis; any additional instrumentalists were more or less forced to improvise, a talent which was second nature to all good musicians. In this respect, incidentally, little has changed in dance music down to the present day.

Franz Schubert's relationship to dance music was undoubtedly intimate, too; it was, however, rather differently circumstanced. Schubert's sphere of activity hardly extended to the nobility and still less to court circles, but was limited to the middle class. It is generally known that, when among friends, Schubert never had to be coaxed to play for dancing. Although — like Johann Strauß, the Waltz King — he himself did not dance, his piano playing was apparently received with the greatest satisfaction by his friends who did. This is not so self-evident as it may seem. Many outstanding pianists, past and present, were and are incapable of playing properly for dancing. Even Chopin, by his own testimony, was, to his regret, unable to bring off a real waltz for dancing during his stay in Vienna. Schubert, a middling pianist, managed it out of hand. Dance music is and remains an applied art; its practical execution, however, seems to be inherent and not learnable.

The music Schubert played on these occasions must also be taken into account. Nowhere do we find a statement to the effect that Schubert was asked to play current "hit tunes" (these, of course, have always existed); therefore, we have every reason to assume that he gave full play to his imagination, drawing on the vast resources of his art of improvisation. If one or another theme happened to please himself or his friends, he seems to have written it down later. In time, a quite impressive repertoire materialized in this way, and may have induced his friends to recommend to Schubert or his publishers that it be printed. Several such sets were in fact published in engraved editions during Schubert's lifetime or shortly after his death. The majority of the dance pieces, to be sure, exist only in autograph, large sets as well as single pages with two or three dances which may have been quickly noted down for special occasions. Some decades after Schubert's death these pieces began to interest publishers and editors, one of whom was no less a personality than Johannes Brahms.

Whereas our great classicists on the one hand and the dance music specialists on the other took the trouble to make and publish arrangements of their works for large or small orchestra, Schubert showed no ambition whatever in this direction. Lack of time, or a better use for it in creating works of a less ephemeral nature, seem to have kept him from doing so.

In view of these circumstances it may be understood, and not be considered a sacrilege, that one is not prepared to apply to Schubert's drafts of dance music the measuring-stick of his other, great and stylistically formative, piano music. Only in the rarest instances did he take the path later entered upon by the Romantic era with its idealized forms, the patterns for which no one other than Schubert himself had designed.

In his dance compositions, then, Schubert quite consciously kept within the bounds of applied art. He apparently showed little interest in seeing these works through the press, unhesitatingly leaving to his publishers the final formation and choice of pieces for the sets, as is conspicuous in the often arbitrary order. The nature of the sketches also argues against applying musicological methods in all their exactitude. Often enough, the same musical ideas are found in widely different versions with regard to key, metre and phrasing. It is obvious that a careful revision of these pieces, many of which were jotted down in great haste, was urgently required. The practise itself suggests that Schubert by no means played these dances at the piano with complete fidelity to the text, but rather that he was accustomed to suit his interpretation to the occasion. All these points lead to a conclusion which, in the interest of the music, we hope can be accepted without hesitation: not to consider the whole body of Schubert's dance music as definitive in form, but frequently to regard it as a sort of sketch and only as that.

Schubert's own disinterest in arranging his dances for orchestra or small ensemble was due, as we have suggested, to a lack of time and opportunity. On examining more closely the musical contents of the dances, one discovers that many of the pieces gravitate away from the relatively dry timbre of the piano and towards an arrangement for strings and winds. Several decades later, musicians like Otto Bach in Salzburg did set groups of dances for orchestra, thereby confirming the need at which we have hinted. In our own time, Anton Webern arranged the German Dances of 1824 for orchestra. An attempt of my own, three LPs with Waltzes, Ländlers and Ecossaises arranged in the old Viennese manner for four to eight players, had a success that far exceeded our expectations, largely due to the consummate interpretations by the Willy Boskovsky Ensemble. We are thus perhaps justified in assuming that these magnificent dance pieces will in many instances be heard to better advantage in performances by small or large ensembles than in performance by piano alone.

These and similar considerations may be regarded as the guide-lines of the present edition of Schubert's dances. If we cannot consider them stylistically formative in the domain of piano music, we can delight all the more in the musical contents of this treasure chest left to posterity by Schubert. In view of the intellectual, practical and artistic background, this edition may prove its value and justification.

Alexander Weinmann

Franz Schubert: Fantasy in C major "Wanderer-Fantasie" (D 760)

PREFACE

The Fantasy in C Major, called "Wanderer Fantasia", occupies a special position among Schubert's piano works. It is without doubt his most monumental piano piece and belongs to those works written during the period of crisis 1822—23, which are distinguished by enormous emotional tension, dramatic power, and concise, bold formal construction. Composed in 1822 (the same year in which Beethoven added the final block to the edifice of his sonata œuvre with his Op. 111), the Wanderer Fantasia points to the future in a manner scarcely equalled by any other work of the period and contains the seeds of the whole symphonic development of the 19th century. The four movements are developed from a single thematic cell, a rhythmic motive taken from the song *Der Wanderer*. One line of this song ("Die Sonne dünkt mich hier so kalt...") forms the basis of the gripping central variation movement; hence the title "Wanderer Fantasia", which is not, however, of Schubert's invention. It is possible that Schubert himself was not aware of the revolutionary nature of this composition. Not only are all themes (with the exception of the first subsidiary theme of the Scherzo) developed from a single *Leitmotiv* as in the symphonic poem of a later era; of even more importance is the creation and sovereign command of a new formal design. Here the classical symphonic order of movements — Allegro, Adagio, Scherzo, Finale — corresponds simultaneously to the principal sections of one larger sonata movement (exposition, development, recapitulation, coda). Within this framework the Adagio functions as a free development, the Scherzo takes on the character of a varied recapitulation in the sub-mediant, and the final Allegro section presents a grand closing climax and a strengthening of the basic tonality (similar to the final sections of many Beethoven symphony or sonata movements).

The Wanderer Fantasia stands as a guidepost to the future not only in the matter of form, but also in its grandiose "orchestral" use of the piano. In this feature the work surpasses all piano compositions of that period. The modernity of such a use of the instrument in certain respects leaves even Beethoven behind: in its exhaustive use of the various sonorities a piano can produce, in its audacious octave passages which demanded a way of playing from the shoulder that was completely new at the time, this work finds an equal only as late as Liszt*. This fact is all the more notable, as Schubert himself was by no means a virtuoso pianist.

That the Wanderer Fantasia was recognized as a masterpiece immediately after its appearance speaks very highly for music criticism at the time (*Wiener Zeitung*, February 24th, 1823). Another review in the *Allgemeine Musikalische Zeitung* (April 30th, 1823) also spoke enthusiastically about the work, but the critic found that Schubert had gone "too far" in certain chord progressions.

The present edition is the first to be based on the autograph, which appeared recently in the United States, and to which previous editors apparently did not have access. In addition, the first print of 1823 (Cappi & Diabelli, Vienna) was used for the purpose of comparison. Additions in round brackets and in small print are by the editor.

My warmest thanks go to my friends Alfred Brendel and Jörg Demus, who helped me in preparing this edition. They assisted me in revising the musical text and gave me valuable suggestions concerning the fingering.

Paul Badura-Skoda

---

* Not only in his use of the piano is Liszt greatly indebted to Schubert: his many transcriptions (among them one of the Wanderer Fantasia as a piano concerto) testify to his intensive Schubert studies. The form of his symphonic poems as well as the new harmonic language using tonalities related by the third can be traced back clearly to Schubert. Liszt was also one of the first to assemble material for a biography of Schubert, which did not, however, proceed beyond the sketching stage.

INDEX

4 Impromptus D 899, Opus 90

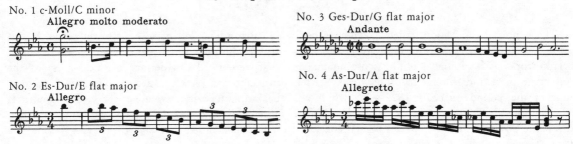

No. 1 c-Moll/C minor
Allegro molto moderato

No. 3 Ges-Dur/G flat major
Andante

No. 2 Es-Dur/E flat major
Allegro

No. 4 As-Dur/A flat major
Allegretto

6 Moments musicaux D 780, Opus 94

No. 1 C-Dur/C major
Moderato

No. 4 cis-Moll/C sharp minor
Moderato

No. 2 As-Dur/A flat major
Andantino

No. 5 f-Moll/F minor
Allegro vivace

No. 3 f-Moll/F minor
Allegretto moderato

No. 6 As-Dur/A flat major
Allegretto

4 Impromptus D 935, Opus post. 142

No. 1 f-Moll/F minor
Allegro moderato

No. 3 B-Dur/B flat major
Andante

No. 2 As-Dur/A flat major
Allegretto

No. 4 f-Moll/F minor
Allegro scherzando

3 Klavierstücke / 3 Piano Pieces
(Impromptus) D 946

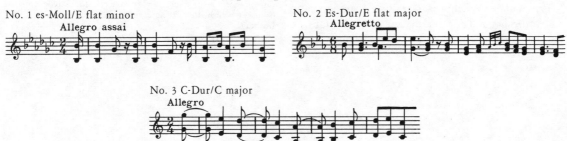

No. 1 es-Moll/E flat minor
Allegro assai

No. 2 Es-Dur/E flat major
Allegretto

No. 3 C-Dur/C major
Allegro

D = Otto Erich Deutsch: Schubert, Thematic Catalogue of all his Works in
Chronological Order. J. M. Dent & Sons, London, 1951

Motto: If only he could have known the renown that now is his, he would have been inspired to the highest achievements. But since he is long since at rest, let us carefully collect and register what he has left to us. There is nothing among it that does not testify to his spirit; it is a rare life-work that bears so clearly the stamp of its creator as does his.

Schumann, Collected Writings, Vol. II

PREFACE

The present volume contains the 8 Impromptus, the 6 Moments musicaux and the 3 Klavierstücke of 1828, *i.e.,* all the late sets of piano pieces by Schubert. Further, the sketch of the first Impromptu, located in the Vienna Stadtbibliothek, is reproduced for the first time since it appeared in the Tonger Edition, which long has been out of print. The sketch is printed at the end of this volume as an appendix of the *Kritische Anmerkungen.* A comparison of the sketch and the final version of the Impromptu affords interesting insights into Schubert's method of working.

It is curious that Schubert, the master of the *Lied,* should have turned only relatively late to the individual piano piece, many of which could be called "Songs Without Words". Almost all the earlier piano pieces, as the most recent Schubert research has established, are sonata movements which were divorced from their original context. Schumann's wish and (incorrect) supposition expressed in connection with the Impromptus D 935 (Op. 142), has been fulfilled in another way. "But I hardly believe", wrote Schumann, "that Schubert really entitled these movements 'Impromptus'; the first is so obviously the first movement of a sonata, so perfectly executed and concise, that no doubt whatever can arise; ... titles and headings are of little importance; on the other hand, a sonata is such a mark of honour in a composer's work that I would like to credit him one more, in fact with twenty more such works." As it happens, the order of pieces in both of Schubert's sets of Impromptus brings them quite close to being a sonata.

Painstaking examination of all available autographs and first editions has produced a musical text which we believe agrees by and large with Schubert's intentions. Of particular interest in this regard were the many inspections of the autograph of the Impromptus D 935, which is at present in the collection of Walter Hinrichsen, New York. In the present volume attention is drawn for the first time, in footnotes and in the *Kritische Anmerkungen,* to several obvious slips of the pen on Schubert's part. Musicological aspects have been coupled with practical considerations. The question of fingerings has been approached with the greatest con-

scientiousness. The directions for playing ornaments are intended primarily for use by teachers. Additions in round brackets are by the editor.

Several special problems of Schubert interpretation may be touched on here:

Dynamics: In Schubert, the marking *fp* — is often to be interpreted *f*——*p* (*e.g.,* the beginning of the Impromptu in F minor D 935/1). At the end of the *dim.* wedge there is often a new *p* or a *dim.* marking which would otherwise be devoid of meaning, *e.g.,* in the "Wanderer Fantasia" D 760, 1st movement, m. 34—35, 40—41.

Rhythm: Schubert used the notation ♪.♪ not only in the customary sense, but also to mean ♪.♪ = ♪³♪ . (I have not yet encountered the notation ♪³♪ anywhere in Schubert.) In the song "Erstarrung" from "Die Winterreise" Schubert even wrote this combination:

In this volume, triplets are clearly intended in the second episode of the Kavierstück in E flat minor D 946/1 and in the third variation of the Impromptu in B flat major D 935 (Op. 142), No. 3. Until about 1860 all Viennese publishers took this into account in the graphical layout of their editions. Anton Diabelli even went one step further in his first edition of the Impromptus (1838), and printed:

(The duplets were probably intentional, *cf.* m. 19 of the same variation, where Schubert certainly would have written ♪.♪♪.♪ otherwise.)

Re-grouping as triplets does not apply, however, in the Impromptu in C minor D 899 (Op. 90), No. 1, in which the march-like dotted rhythm of the introduction is doubtlessly meant to be retained throughout. There is a doubtful instance in the Klavierstück in E flat minor D 946/1, where both rhythmic executions are possible.*)

Compass of the instrument: As is generally known, Schubert's Piano had a compass extending from FF to f⁴. The editor has no qualms about using the lower octave occasionally (down to CC), e.g., at the end of the Impromptu in E flat major D 899/2, in the Impromptu in G flat major D 899/3, m. 31/32 and 48—50, or in the Impromptu in A flat major D 935/2, m. 68, first note 8va. Exceeding the upper limit of the compass, however, can be recommended only with the greatest reservation, for it easily can produce an unwanted shrill tone. It would seem to be required in one instance only: in the Impromptu in F minor D 935/4, m. 41, 82, 376, 417, where the piping sound is little short of intentional. I play g⁴ as the top note, analogous to m. 43.

Embellishments:

a) Appoggiaturas: In his songs, Schubert often writes long appoggiaturas in the vocal part, but he always writes out the same appoggiaturas in large notes in the piano part. This means that appoggiaturas in Schubert's piano music (and his music for other instruments) are to be played short as a matter of principle. There is a possible exception in the Impromptu in F minor D 935/4, m. 3, where the appoggiatura, analogously to the parallel passages (m. 47, 338 etc.), can also be played long and accentuated. (The editor plays it short.)

b) Turns always begin with the upper note and are to be played like the written-out turn in the Impromptu in A flat major D 935/2, m. 27.

c) Trills: The question as to whether the trill begins with the principal note or with the neighbouring note must be left open. The written-out trill in the first movement of the Sonata in B flat major D 960, m. 19, and the figuration at the trills in the Largo of the Fantasy in F minor D 940, would seem to suggest that trills in these late works begin with the principal note. For Pralltriller (inverted mordents), the notation in the Sonata in A minor Op. 42, D 845, where Schubert alternately writes them out and abbreviates them, demonstrates that they were started with the main note.

Tempo, agogics, stress: In general, Schubert's

tempo is to be strictly retained throughout**), but occasional modifications of tempo are not only permissible but often even necessary (cf. the authentic minute changes of tempo in "Gretchen am Spinnrad" and many other songs). In the Impromptu in A flat major D 935/2, for example, the player will increase the tempo quite unconstrainedly in m. 65—68 and broaden it again in m. 75—78. Likewise, on makes a *ritard.* in m. 50—51 of the Impromptu in E flat major D 899/2 and in the Trio of the Impromptu in A flat major, m. 137—138, after which *poco meno mosso* is recommended beginning at m. 139 and *accel. al Tempo I* beginning at m. 147. In the Klavierstück in C major D 946/3, which is reminiscent of Slavic folk dances, the middle section should be somewhat slower than the outer sections (i.e., the ♩ of the Trio is somewhat calmer than the ♩ of the Allegro), with *rit.* before the Trio and *accel.* after it.

To judge from the original metronome markings in several of the songs, Schubert preferred flowing tempos, which on no account must be allowed to drag in slow movements. Applied to the Impromptus D 899 (Op. 90), the following tempos — to be taken *cum grano salis* — would result, assuming that one may make *a posteriori* conclusions:

I   ♩ = 88—92, from m. 41 onwards = c. 104
II   ♩ = c. 200
III ♩ = c. 76—84
IV ♩ = c. 152

Declamation, period structure

The importance of correct musical declamation must be strongly emphasized, for today it is often noticeable by its absence. Arsis and thesis must be brought out in much the same way as in a spoken poem. In the Trio of Moment musical No. 4, for example, the last quaver must always be dropped without accentuation, but the first semiquaver must be accented lightly, so that it does not sound like an upbeat. The Trio of the Klavierstück in C major D 946/3 is a model of interesting, irregular period structure; this must consciously be brought into relief.

It is my pleasant duty to thank my esteemed colleagues Alfred Brendel and Jörg Demus for valuable advice; Karl Heinz Füssl and Hermann Nordberg for constructive collaboration in matters of edition and revision. I am grateful to Mr. Walter Hinrichsen of New York for the opportunity of examining the autograph of the Impromptus D 935 (Op. 142), which is now in the Pierpont-Morgan Library, New York City (communication from Christa Landon), and to the Musiksammlung der Österreichischen Nationalbibliothek and the Vienna Stadtbibliothek for providing me with valuable source material.

Paul Badura-Skoda

---

*) Cf. a letter written by the editor to the *Musical Times*, London, printed on p. 873 in the issue of December 1963.
**) Cf. a letter of May 13, 1828, from Schubert to the publisher Probst: "... and have a care that the tempo remains the same at the change of metre." (Piano Trio in E flat major, Op. 100, last movement.)

PREFACE

Robert Schumann's Album for the Young is one of the few works in the piano literature that successfully manages to combine pedagogic intentions with artistic demands; one might compare it with Bach's Inventions, or the Clavierbüchlein for Wilhelm Friedemann, or in more recent times, with Debussy's Children's Corner and Bartók's Mikrokosmos. Schumann's Kinderszenen (Scenes from Childhood) Op. 15, on the other hand, is such a piece in name only, since in this case, the pedagogic element is completely subordinate to the "poetic" element — Schumann's primary aesthetic category. But in the Album for the Young, composed ten years later, the essentially pedagogic intentions are constantly in evidence, even in the ordering of the pieces. Yet Schumann didn't simply sacrifice higher artistic standards to pedagogic intentions — at least, not in the majority of the pieces, which are naturally of variable artistic quality: these pieces are also based on "poetic ideas", as can be seen in the titles given to some of them (titles which actually have no programmatic implications). Moreover, Schumann changed many of his original titles so as to give them a more general character; this is enough to show that they shouldn't be misunderstood as having extra-musical, programmatic connotations, not even when they seem to explain the pieces' contents. The brief, mainly easily-grasped forms (many of them 'ternary') that Schumann has given the pieces likewise prohibit one from viewing them as little pieces with a concrete programme. In a letter to his friend the composer Carl Reinecke, written on October 6th 1848, Schumann himself characterised the two works as follows: "The 'Scenes from Childhood' are reminiscences by an adult for other adults, whereas the Christmas Album (this was Schumann's initial title for the Album for the Young) looks forward, contains presentiments and anticipations of what is to come for young people."

Like some of the works mentioned above, the Album for the Young first arose through personal, family considerations, and then rapidly combined these with broader perspectives: for the 7th birthday of his eldest daughter, on September 1st 1848, Schumann wrote a few Stückchen fürs Clavier. Zu Marie'chens 7tem Geburtstag..., gemacht vom Papa (Little Pieces for the Piano, for little Marie's 7th birthday..., made by Daddy); from Schumann's household accounts, we can see he did this on August 31st. In the entry for the same day we find the remark "Idea of a Children's Album", and the entries for September show the Album taking shape in Schumann's hands: on September

9th he believed that "the Album is pretty well finished", but as the next few weeks went by, scarcely a day passed without "new little pieces" being added. Schumann soon got the sketches, hastily jotted down, mainly incomplete in detail, but often complete as far as their musical substance is concerned, in order, and made a fair copy, partly with Clara's assistance; by September 27th he was able to send them to his publisher as models for the engraver. "I couldn't remember ever having been in such a good mood as when I wrote these pieces. They flooded out one after another...", "I felt as if I were starting to compose all over again", he wrote to Reinecke on the 4th and 6th October: optimistic witness to starting composition afresh after the strength-sapping, tedious work on the opera Genoveva, finished shortly before. By the middle of December, the Album for the Young was already in print.

It is not just the length of the work as originally planned that grew during composition; the whole conception of the work shifted away from personal, family, and pedagogic considerations, to a more general artistic intention. We have already mentioned the numerous changes of titles of individual pieces, which tend in this direction. The fact that Schumann had originally included pieces by older masters (Bach, Händel, Mozart, Beethoven, Schubert and Weber) in Marie's little birthday book, and partly even copied them into the fair copy of the Album for the Young, but then excluded them, shows the growing tendency, during work on the set, to make the Album for the Young a work with an artistic substance of its own. This tendency is emphasised still further by more ambitious homages to Bach, Beethoven and Mendelssohn in some pieces (No. 2, 21, 28 and 39), taking the form of thematic or stylistic references. The exclusions of some excessively simple little pieces (e. g. Appendix, No. 1), further illustrates the raising of his ambitions in the course of composition.

As with all of Schumann's musical works, there has not been a critical edition of this work up to now, despite the quite extraordinary number of editions of this work in particular. In the Complete Edition brought out by Clara Schumann during the years 1880—1887 — partly in collaboration with Johannes Brahms — one has come to notice some smoothing-out and interferences with the text that Clara believed herself obliged to make, but without mentioning it. Despite the general mistrust of Clara's edition which soon arose from this kind of interference (often only discovered by chance), the very existence of this edition, and the weight accorded to it by the name of its editress, has remained one of the greatest barriers to making a new, critical Schumann-Edition. From our comparison of sources, it turned out that Clara had also made arbitrary alterations to the text of the Album for the Young, especially as far as expression marks were concerned. In addition, over and above the mistakes in the first edition, numerous other mistakes have crept into her edition, and these mistakes have mainly survived into more recent editions of the work. A new edition which seeks to live up to the requirements of an "Urtext-Edition" should naturally depend only on the original sources — in their entirety. Comparison and critical evaluation of these sources, which diverge sharply at times, resulted in a text that is often very different from the customary picture of the work sanctioned by Clara's edition.

It wasn't always easy to decide which of the many variants in the original sources should be taken for our text, and in some cases, a brief justification has been necessary. The user of this book will find them in our Critical Notes, along with more details on the basis for our edition, the sources referred to, and the genesis of the individual pieces. Since our edition is the first attempt at an authentic text making critical use of the sources, these notes were, inevitably, rather more extensive than is normal in editions of this kind.

In the Appendix we have reproduced a few pieces of Schumann's that are found in the handwritten sources for the Album for the Young, but weren't used in the printed edition; the necessary information concerning these will also be found in the Critical Notes.

The famous *Musikalische Haus- und Lebensregeln* (Musical Rules for Life and the Home) were actually penned at the same time as the Album for the Young; it wasn't until the Second Edition (1850) that Schumann included them in their entirety. The pedagogic import of some of these proverbs is such that one couldn't agree with it unreservedly nowadays; still, it won't do the young reader any harm, and the more mature users of the volume may find it an instructive documentation of Schumann's educational and musical outlook, as well as of the tricky balance between pedagogic intentions and artistic requirements that Schumann successfully maintained in the Album for the Young.

Klaus Rönnau

PREFACE

At the end of September in 1838 Robert Schumann moved from Leipzig to Vienna in order to establish a new centre of activity there as a writer on music and composer. For various reasons, however, his plans did not materialise, and in April 1839 Schumann returned to Leipzig. Nevertheless, amongst the fruits of his months spent in Vienna were the composition of a number of new works, as well as the discovery of the manuscript of Schubert's Great C major Symphony. He evidently found here much to inspire and stimulate him, for he wrote the *Arabeske* Op. 18, the *Blumenstück* Op. 19, the *Humoreske* Op. 20, parts of the *Faschingsschwank aus Wien* Op. 26 and the final movement of the *Sonata in G minor* Op. 22. All of these were compositions for the piano, which since 1828 had occupied him almost exclusively. But we now see the composer in a new light: in particular the *Arabeske* and the *Blumenstück* reveal both his mastery of a light-hearted, serene elegance and his ability to produce perfect, extremely clear piano-writing. The former demonic quality of *Kreisleriana* Op. 16 and penetrating intensity of the *Fantasie in C* Op. 17 recede into the background. We look rather to the *Kinderszenen* Op. 15, composed in the spring of 1838, for the kind of intimate grace and delicate dream-atmosphere of this new musical conception, where dark passions are excluded, and even struggles with problems of form, harmony and structural technique have no place. "At the present time I am composing prolifically, and I should very much like to become the favourite composer of the ladies of Vienna"[1] writes Schumann to the pianist Joseph Fischhof at the end of 1838, obviously referring to the *Arabeske* and the *Blumenstück*. This rather uncharacteristic remark is, however, offset in a sentence in a letter of 15 August 1839 to Ernst Adolph Becker (both works, together with the *Humoreske* Op. 20, had just been published by Mechetti in Vienna), where he writes laconically: "Op. 18 and 19 are rather slight works, more to the taste of the ladies; Op. 20 is far more substantial and significant"[2]. Even in the preliminary sketch for the first 22 bars of the later *Blumenstück* there is an ironic comment at the end: "Written in the absence of anything more inspiring." We should, however, not take too seriously Schumann's deprecatory remarks (of which there are quite a few more) about his own works. As Schumann was in general well aware of the value and importance of his compositions, these comments can better be interpreted as attempts to create a distance between himself and his music, enabling him to consider it objectively: he had been so often totally involved in it. In a letter of 11 August 1839 to Henriette Voigt his assessment is similar, and here he goes into more detail. He is almost apologetic: "Three new compositions have been sent from Vienna, and await your judgment. One is a *Humoreske,* which is actually rather melancholy, and there is also a *Blumenstück* and an *Arabeske* which are less significant. Even the titles give this away, and I can't take any blame for the delicacy and slightness of the lines and contours."[3] That Schumann dedicated both works to a woman does not therefore seem strange, indeed it seems almost mischievous. The dedicatee was the wife of Major Friedrich Serre, whom Schumann and his fiancée Clara Wieck had often visited in Maxen, a small spot near Dresden, where they had also lived from time to time. As late as 1849 Schumann and his family found refuge for a time in her house during the violent upheavals of the May revolution. We learn from a later letter to Clara (13 March 1839[4]) that only the *Blumenstück* was originally to be dedicated to Major Serre's wife; the *Arabeske* was meant for the composer Julie von Webenau, née Baroni-Cavalcabò, a pupil of Mozart's son Franz Xaver. Instead Schumann dedicated the *Humoreske* Op. 20 to her, which was originally to have no dedication.

As to the dating of the two works, there is some discrepancy in the different reference books, biographies and editions. The *Arabeske,* assigned in most reference works to the year 1839, dates from the year 1838 (i.e. composed in Vienna between October and December of that year) according to a letter from Schumann to his admirer Simonin de Sire of 15 March 1839[5]. He dates the *Blumenstück* from 1839 (it must therefore have been composed in Vienna between January and the middle of March). On the other hand the above-mentioned sketch is signed "Vienna. October 1838". At all events it is certain, according to the letters of 13 March and 15 March 1839 to Clara and Simonin de Sire respectively, that both works were completed by that time.

The titles *Arabeske* ("arabesque") and *Blumenstück* ("flower piece"), used here for the first time as designations for musical compositions, are closely connected with a principle of Romantic art theory which Schumann also seems to have adopted here. He writes: ". . . for the painter a poem becomes a painting, the composer converts the painting into sound. E[usebius].–The aesthetic process of the one art form is the same as that of the other; only the raw material differs. F[lorestan]."[6] "Arabesque", an ornamental term used with reference to oriental painting and architecture, and *Blumenstück,* "flower piece", belong in the first instance to the sphere of visual art, as Schumann's letter to Henriette Voigt, quoted above, seems to indicate. But on a different, hidden level these titles hark back to literature, which underlay almost all Schumann's early piano works. While, however, we must not overestimate the influence on Schumann's *Arabeske* of the "Arabesques" of W. Sihler, which according to his diary[7] served as Schumann's "night-reading", the literary reference of the *Blumenstück* is quite apparent: Jean Paul's novel *Blumen-, Frucht- und Dornenstükke oder Ehestand, Tod und Hochzeit des Armenadvokaten F. St. Siebenkäs im Reichsmarktflecken Kuhschnappel* ("Flower, fruit and thorn stories, or the marriage, death and wedding of the poor-lawyer F. St. Siebenkäs . . ."), (First edition Berlin 1796/7, 3 vols.), a work by his favourite writer, whom he idolized, which he had known since boyhood (as we again see from his diary[8]), was here very much in evidence. Jean Paul for his part – and we hereby come full circle – had been inspired by painting. In a letter to Christian Otto (Hof, 16 September 1795) he writes: ". . . I have to finish colouring in the Dornenstücke – a mad biography in my usual style"[9]. The faithful Schumann disciple Stephen Heller chose for his Op. 82 the complete title of the novel: *Blumen-, Frucht- und Dornenstücke.* We also come across arabesques later, amongst others the *Deux Arabesques* (1888) of Debussy and Reger's *Aus meinem Tagebuch* Op. 82, vol. IV, No. 4, 1912. In this way these two such different and contrasting composers both gave creative expression to their admiration for Schumann.

Joachim Draheim

---

[1] Robert Schumanns Briefe. Neue Folge. Ed. F. Gustav Jansen, Leipzig ²1904, p. 146.

[2] ibid., p. 169.

[3] ibid., p. 167.

[4] Robert Schumann in seinen Schriften und Briefen, ed. W. Boetticher, Berlin 1942, p. 233.

[5] Jansen, p. 150.

[6] Robert Schumann, Gesammelte Schriften über Musik und Musiker, ed. Martin Kreisig, Leipzig ⁵1914, vol. 1, p. 26 (Aus Meister Raros, Florestans und Eusebius' Denk- und Dichtbüchlein).

[7] Robert Schumann, Tagebücher, vol. 1 (1827–1838), ed. Georg Eismann, Leipzig 1971, p. 128.

[8] cf. Tagebücher, p. 82.

[9] Die Briefe Jean Pauls, ed. Eduard Berend, vol. 2, München 1922, p. 105. Cf. Hans Dahler, Jean Pauls Siebenkäs. Struktur und Grundbild, Bern 1962,

INDEX

Des Abends / Evening

In der Nacht / In the Night

Aufschwung / Soaring

Fabel / Fable

Warum? / Why?

Traumes Wirren / Restless Dreams

Grillen / Whims

Ende vom Lied / The End of the Story

Anhang / Appendix

Des Abends. In der Fassung nach Schumanns Abschrift für Ernst Adolf Becker
Evening. In the version according to Schumann's manuscript copy for Ernst Adolf Becker

PREFACE

Schumann composed the *Fantasiestücke* Op. 12 in the Spring of 1837, at a time when he was separated from his bride, Clara Wieck. The pieces and the descriptive titles added later reflect Schumann's changeable moods during this time. He dedicated them to the Scottish pianist, Miss Anna Robena Laidlav, who gave concerts in Leipzig in July 1837, although Schumann was not inspired by her to write the pieces. Schumann had already offered the *Fantasiestücke* for publication on 22. May 1837 and sent them to Breitkopf and Härtel on 7. August, where they appeared in February 1838.

The autograph which Schumann presented to the Weimar music teacher Karl Montag, now the property of Hans Schneider in Tutzing, was not made available. An autograph copy of the first piece *Des Abends*, presented by Schumann to his friend, Ernst Adolf Becker of Freiberg, as a farewell gift, was also used in preparing the new edition. Becker had travelled to Leipzig for a concert given by Clara Wieck on 13. August. With his help, Schumann and Clara Wieck came together again on this occasion, after her father had succeeded in separating the two a year previously. It is therefore understandable that Clara's personal dedication is added on the manuscript: "With love and discretion from Clara Wieck." In this manuscript the piece contains a number of variants to the final version, so that it seemed advisable to reprint the earlier version in an appendix.

Schumann has mentioned the *Fantasiestücke* on several occasions in his letters. As early as 22. December 1837, that is before the edition came out, he writes to Clara that he considered *In der Nacht* particularly suitable for recitals; he also recommended *Des Abends* to her later. He was continually preoccupied with *In der Nacht*. On 22. April 1838 he writes to his friend Krägen that "'Nacht' is my favourite, too. Later I found the story of Hero and Leander in it. Look it up. Everything fits surprisingly well". And to Clara on 21. April: "When I play *Nacht*, I cannot forget the picture — first how he dives into the sea — she calls — he answers — through the waves happily to the shore — then the cantilena, until night envelopes all in darkness again ... Tell me whether this picture fits the music for you too."

In the letter to Krägen, Schumann also mentions: "Liszt, who is in Vienna, is said to have sight-read the *Fantasiestücke* to the delight of everyone; the *Ende vom Lied* in particular." On 13. March 1838, he writes to Clara about this piece: "I meant, now, at the end, all to resolve in a merry wedding, but in the final bars the painful longing for you returned too and now it sounds like the intermingling of a wedding and dying."

Hans-Christian Müller

SUGGESTIONS FOR PERFORMANCE

Des Abends

In order to preserve the ²/₈ time, the triplet movement in the left hand must be strictly maintained. Extensive *rubati* are to be avoided in playing the melody. The fingering makes possible an unbroken *legato*.

Aufschwung

The editor's metronome marking is ♩. = 100—108. A reliable stretch of a tenth in the right hand is desirable for the performance of the principal motive. The following possible alternatives will be of help to those with smaller hands:

Bars 1—3

and in parallel passages.

After the B flat major section  and at the end of the piece.

The semiquaver figures in the D flat major and A flat major section are to be played as clearly as possible so that the short crescendi may be heard distinctly. In practising the last 22 bars of the B flat major section, particular attention should be paid to the opposite dynamic markings in the right and left hands.

Warum?

The instruction "Slowly and tenderly" clearly points to the piano opening of the piece. The dynamic changes must be carefully observed; the beginning and end of ⟨ and ⟩ are particularly important. The *p* in bar 13 is to be played as a sudden *p* (piano subito). The *rit.* in bar 30 applies to the second crotchet only.

Grillen

The editor's metronome marking is ♩ = 184. Bars 1—8 of the principal motive are marked *mf* at the beginning but always *f* thereafter; the *f* should always be treated carefully, however. The required accent on the third crotchet in bar 24ff. is best achieved by means of pedalling:

The shifting of stresses in the G flat major section will be made clear only by very rhythmical playing.

In der Nacht

This piece was Schumann's "favourite" — "Later I found the story of Hero and Leander in it" (Letter to Karl Krägen, April 1838). The restlessness of the semiquavers is important as far as the interpretation is concerned. The dynamic contrasts should not be exaggerated: only the climax of the process of intensification in Tempo I before the return of the main idea and the closing bars are marked ff. Schumann's fingering in bars 11/12 requires agility but is extremely effective. Etwas langsamer ($\flat$ = 108): the semiquavers must flow evenly. The execution of the bass corresponds for the most part with that of the melody; the crotchets at the beginning of the second part are to be lightly emphasised. The direction *Tempo I* is clearly meant to take effect from the second bar of the new semiquaver figuration onwards. An *accelerando* is possible in the previous bar; the mood of tension produced by the *crescendo* is intensified, however, if the slower tempo is maintained. The first eight bars of the canonic passages are still to be kept strictly in time. After the *accelerando,* the original tempo can be resumed either four or two bars before the entry of the main idea. A *stringendo* in the closing bars does not intensify in any way the unrelenting drive towards the end.

Fabel

The exact tempo relation in the Clara Schumann edition "Slow ($\flat$ = 48) — Fast ($\flat$ = 48)" keeps the piece together well. The fermata lengthen the value of the notes about half as much again. The composer's careful notation of the requested attack should be well studied.

Traumes Wirren

The danger of the piece becoming a mere study can be avoided if the melodic flow is skilfully stressed. It would be advisable to begin softly. The fingering of the semiquaver figure is generally 3 4 3 1; deviations from this depend on the shape and size of the hand. When crossing hands, the left hand always goes over the right hand. The crotchets in the middle section are to be played *molto legato* and without *rubato* throughout. The crotchet six bars before the end is not a printing mistake!

Ende vom Lied

The editor's metronome markings are $\flat$ = 144 and $\flat$ = 168 in the *Etwas lebhafter* section. The indication "Mit gutem Humor" ("with good humour") forbids any suggestion of pathos in the interpretation of the piece. It is particularly important that a thick sound should be avoided and that a light articulation should be adopted in playing the accented notes on weak parts of the bar. To depress the pedal during the passage from the end of the principal section to the 10th bar of the Coda is hardly satisfactory as far as the sound is concerned. Instead, a type of half-pedalling may be adopted, so that the pedal changes between two-bar groups can be somewhat disguised.

Gerhard Puchelt

PREFACE

Robert Schumann completed his *Scenes from Childhood* in March 1838. In a letter to Clara, written on 17th March, 1838, he described the origin of this work: *"Was it an echo of what you once said when you wrote to me 'I often seemed like a child to you' — in short, I felt as if I were in pinafores again and then I wrote thirty quaint little things, about twelve of which I have selected and called Scenes from Childhood. You will enjoy them, but you will certainly have to forget that you are a virtuoso."*

Already in the following winter the *Scenes from Childhood*, a cycle of thirteen pieces, appeared in print as Opus 15; they were published in 1839 by Breitkopf & Härtel in Leipzig. The title of this work and, in particular, the superscriptions of the individual pieces have provided many a motive for misinterpretation. Schumann wrote as a subtitle: *Easy Pieces for the Pianoforte. Composed 1838.* This should not mislead one into underestimating the intellectual and technical difficulties, however; rather should it encourage one to preserve the inner lightness and gentle buoyancy of these small pieces. Let us pay attention to Schumann's own words: *"As regards the difficult question of how far instrumental music should go in the representation of thoughts and events, there are many who appear to be too apprehensive. It is certainly erroneous to suppose that composers avail themselves of pen and paper with the ignoble intention of expressing, describing, painting this or that. Yet we must not too lightly estimate fortuitous influences and impressions from without. Without our being conscious of it, an idea often develops simultaneously with the musical image, the eye is busy as well as the ear, and this ever-active organ retains, amidst all the sounds and tones, certain outlines which can crystallise and assume definite form as the music itself takes shape ..."*

The original edition, which Schumann prepared with exemplary care, is rich in subtle aids to understanding and performance. The clarity of notation, the delicacy of phrasing, the directions regarding dynamics, articulation and agogics should be observed. The original notation has been retained in the new edition; a few additional staccato dots have been made clearly distinguishable through small print. Clara Schumann, in her new edition for amateurs made substantial alterations, particularly with regard to the metronome specifications. — She herself indicated *"important differences of interpretation"* in one of her diary entries. — The double metronome specifications in the musical text may encourage one, therefore, to make comparisons as to effect.

This ever youthful work of Schumann fulfills effectively the requirement once made by the composer: *"... there should really be something of Spring in every piece of music."*

Franzpeter Goebels

Robert Schumann: Papillons Op. 2

PREFACE

The "Papillons" are among the earliest pieces Schumann composed. Sketches of them are contained in the third sketchbook, and the first versions of Nos. 2 and 9 already appear in the first sketchbook. Schumann wrote them between 1829 and 1831, partly in Heidelberg. The sketchbooks contain further "Papillons" and "Waltzes", some of which later found their way to "Carnaval" and others to Opp. 99 and 124. In the third sketchbook, No. 1 is marked "Waltz 6," and Nos. 6 and 7 are entitled "Waltz 4" and "Waltz 5," that is, the "Papillons" do not yet appear in their final order. No. 2 and the beginning of No. 9 were written in doubled note values at first; similarly, the second section of No. 7 was still notated in doubled values in the definitive fair copy.

The "Papillons," which Schumann himself interpreted as "butterflies" or "flying slips of paper," were inspired by the last scene of Jean Paul's "Flegeljahre," a costume ball. Schumann underlined several passages in his copy of the novel, relating them to the individual "Papillons." In letters he emphasized, however, that he put the words to the music only subsequently. To Henriette Voigt in Leipzig he wrote: *"I want to mention that I put the text to the music and not the other way around; for me, that would have seemed a foolish undertaking. Only the last one, which playful chance made an answer to the first, was evoked by Jean Paul."* The passages marked in Jean Paul read, for example, as follows: No. 2: *"Punch room ... ball room ... full of zigzag figures moving towards each other"*; No. 3: *"sliding about, a gigantic boot wearing and carrying itself"*; No. 4: *"simple nun with a half-mask and a sweet-smelling bunch of auricula"*; No. 7: *"hot desert dryness or dry feverish heat ... most earnest supplications ..."*; No. 6: *"Your waltzing ... good mimical imitations, partly in the carter's horizontal, partly in the miner's vertical ..."*; No. 10: *"exchange of masks ... floatingly gliding up and down ... butterflies of a faraway island. Like a rare lark's song in late summer ..."*
Schumann dedicated the "Papillons" to his three sisters-in-law. The edition was fresh from the press when Schumann sent it to his family in Zwickau on 17 April 1832, with the accompanying lines: *"... then I would say to them (the butterflies), bear the Papillons along to Therese, Rosalie and Emilie, flutter and exult around them as lightly and blissfully as you wish ... Then beg them all to read the final scene of Jean Paul's 'Flegeljahre' as soon as possible, and tell them that the Papillons actually were supposed to translate that costume ball into tones, and ask them then if perhaps something of Wina's angelic love, of Walt's poetic nature and of Vult's sharply flashing soul is correctly reflected in the Papillons; say and ask all this and still more, still more."*

Schumann attempted to explain the connection with Jean Paul's "Flegeljahre" in other letters and notes too. On 19 April 1832 he wrote to Ludwig Rellstab in Berlin, the editor of the magazine "Iris": *"Not so much for the editor of Iris, but for the poet and spiritual relation of Jean Paul, I permit the Papillons to add a few words about their origin, since the thread that is supposed to twist them into one another is scarcely visible. You certainly recall the last scene of 'Flegeljahre': costume ball — Walt-Vult — masks — Wina — Vult's dancing — exchanging masks — confessions — anger — unmasking — dashing off — final scene and then the departing brother. I turned over the last page often, for the end seemed only a new beginning to me; I was at the piano almost unconsciously, and one Papillon after another was born."*

Despite such explanations in all directions, Schumann's title was taken literally ("Butterflies") almost from the very first, and the composition was thus completely misunderstood.

Even though Schumann may have selected appropriate texts for the individual pieces only subsequently, the "Papillons" as a whole are inspired by Jean Paul; a musical ballroom scene, a succession of waltzes and polonaises rounded off by the reappearance of the first waltz in the last piece, in which Schumann quotes the "Großvatertanz."

Hans-Christian Müller

SUGGESTIONS FOR PERFORMANCE

The markings in Robert Schumann's piano works are always intended for the "thinking performer". For that reason fingerings are rarely found. Schumann's notation of touch is unequivocal but often incomplete. Slurs can mean either simply *legato* or the demarcation of a melodic phrase; they can also indicate a subtle declamation. Dynamics are clearly marked. Accents are frequently shown by *f* instead of the more customary *sf;* in addition, the marking ⊳ is used to indicate a light stress, and ∧ or ∨ for a heavier accentuation. Tempo markings often elucidate only the character of the composition; the performance tempo is left to the player's own empathy. For a present-day sense of tempo, the traditional metronome markings are surprising in many instances. Tempo changes are indicated in the simplest way (Etwas lebhafter, Più lento); accelerations and retardations are precisely delimited, but they are seldom expressly cancelled. The marking *rit.* often applies only to the bar in which it appears, and sometimes to a single note; the execution is then comparable to a *rubato* or *tenuto*. In the case of arpeggiated chords or appoggiature, Schumann requires that the melody note coincide with the last tone of the broken chord. Concerning pedalling, Schumann wrote to Henselt in 1837: "... *I write nothing more than 'Pedal' at the beginning of my compositions, unless it should happen that new effects are wanted which require the pedal to be depressed at precisely the right second.*" Schumann marks such passages clearly and unequivocally.

Introduzione
The *p* in bar 5 must be strictly observed.

No. 1
The melody in octaves must be played *molto legato*. The g in bar 12—14 can only be sustained by using the pedal.

No. 2
An exercise for accuracy in the falling octaves in bar 2 and 3:

It is important that the semiquaver rests in the melody at bar 5 and 6, and 9 and 10 (in contrast to the uninterrupted *legato* of the other bars) be strictly observed.

No. 3
Schumann writes ♩ = 120; the editor plays ♩ = 160. Entitled "Riesenstiefel" (Gigantic Boot) by Schumann. (Jean Paul: "sliding about, a gigantic boot wearing and carrying itself.") The accentuation of the crotchets applies to the whole piece. No *ritardando* at the end.

No. 4
♩. = 69 is better suited to the declamation of the melody, which is to be played *portato*. The *accelerando* at the beginning of the second part must be started cautiously and then continued until the *ritenuto* is reached.

No. 5
The editor plays *p;* this makes the *pp* four bars before the end more understandable. The arpeggio appoggiature in bar 6 must begin simultaneously in both hands. The *sf* in bar 9—11 should sound bright and clear. Bar 13 can begin softly; the middle part in the right hand forms a chain of sixth-chords with the thirds in the left hand. The editor plays bars 23/24 *(pp)* more calmly, resuming the tempo in the *portato* closing bars.

No. 6
The A major episode (bar 7—14) should not be played with the soft pedal, so that the bright sound is retained. The bar-by-bar alternation of *staccato* and *legato* in the *leggiero* (bar 25—32) must be strictly observed. The supporting chords in the left hand must resound as long as possible without pedal.

No. 7
Bars 1—8 require caution in the use of the pedal. The waltz character of the second part can be nicely supported by clear articulation of the lower part in the right hand. A pretty tone-colour effect will be produced in the last bar if the pedal is not used.

No. 8
♩ = 168. *Staccato* and *legato* must be clearly distinguished. The melodic middle part in the right hand (bar 5 ff.) must be brought out carefully. The *ritenuto* in bar 17 does not extend beyond bar 20. Here both hands must play the melody and the arpeggios quasi unisono. The a-flat" in the last bar should die away without pedal.

No. 9
♩ = 112 is quite in order. The staccati must coincide precisely and evenly in the two hands. The soft

pedal should be used for gradation of tone (bar 10 ff., last *pp* in both sections), but not generally to attain the *pp*.

No. 10

The editor plays Vivo ♩. = 96, Più lento ♩. = 72. The accentuation of the third crotchet (bar 25 ff.) only emphasizes the lilting waltz rhythm, and must be played very lightly; the left hand plays groups of two bars *molto legato*. The left-hand broken chords in *mf* following the repeat sign forms a continuous succession of quavers with the melody. According to Schumann's markings, the *mf* in the closing section is to be played *subito,* as is the *ff* eight bars later. If the pedal markings in the last bars are observed strictly, the chord that dies away will be a pure C major.

No. 11

The brilliant and festive Polonaise corresponds to the earlier custom of a closing procession by the dancers. In the Più lento the accents are not so much for the sake of emphasis as they are an indication that the tones must be sustained their full value; this also explains why they are replaced by the marking *sempre legato.* The right-hand appoggiature are to be thought of as binding the succession of octaves.

No. 12

The editor begins ♩ = 184; in 2/4 ♩ = ♪; Più lento ♩ = 138 (like No. 1), resuming the initial tempo at the pedal point D. The pedal point must be sustained until the last bell-stroke dies away, but only by the damper pedal. Neither a change of pedal nor the use of the sustaining pedal agrees with the composers written intentions. The *poco a poco diminuendo* should begin in the left hand. The bell-strokes should be played without *diminuendo.* The final arpeggio is to be played without pedal, very softly and with a very slight *crescendo* to a'. The fingers are then raised evenly, one after the other. The last three notes should be played very softly and very short.

Gerhard Puchelt

Robert Schumann: Forest Scenes Op. 82

INDEX

PREFACE

"As they entered they saw Dorian Gray. He was seated at the piano, with his back to them, turning over the pages of a volume of Schumann's *Forest Scenes*. 'You must lend me these, Basil', he cried. 'I want to learn them. They are perfectly charming.'" The second chapter of Oscar Wilde's novel, *The Picture of Dorian Gray* (published 1890)[1] begins with this scene and bears witness to the great popularity which had already been attained even outside Germany by Schumann's *Waldszenen* Op. 82 forty years after the composition of the work. "I enclose the *Waldszenen* – a piece which I have greatly cherished for a long time. May it bring you profit, if not an entire forest, at least a small stem to new business"[2], Schumann himself wrote full of confidence from Düsseldorf to the publisher Bartholf Senff in Leipzig on 8 October 1850. The new work, which was published by Senff in November 1850, was enthusiastically received not only by the public but also by the experts. The critic of the *Berliner Musik-Zeitung Echo* wrote, on 5 January 1851: "Our poets and musicians have preferred to escape into woodland solitude for some time now, and so these new piano pieces are like Gustav Pfarrius's excellent Songs of the Woods. The observant critic would perhaps find some brushwood in both, but he does not look for it; he is delighted with the mysterious rustling, the melodies sounding in the distance, and the mystical flowers of the musical magic forest, and hopes that the composer will find many players who will penetrate to the essence of his nature and perform his work with skill and understanding."[3]

Schumann, who was always interested in politics and had republican sympathies, paid a great amount of attention to the revolutionary events of 1848/49. Unlike his contemporary Wagner, however, he did not desire to become actively involved. He shielded himself from the stormy happenings of the time by steeping himself in composition. After finishing the opera *Genoveva* Op. 81, Schumann composed various works of different kinds in Dresden towards the end of 1848. These include the music to Byron's *Manfred* Op. 115, the *Album für die Jugend* Op. 68, the *Bilder aus Osten* Op. 66 for piano duet, and another series of piano pieces described as follows in the Household Book: "24 December 1848 Forest Scenes. Very cheerful . . . 29 December 1848 A Forest Scene (Flowers) . . . 31 December 1848 Inn from the Forest Scenes. Merry."[4]

The forest as a specifically romantic area of imagination also plays an important part in Schumann's work. Weber's *Freischütz* and Eichendorff's poems which he valued highly are the models and sources of inspiration here. Schumann has given impressive proof of his affinity with this sphere in *Liederkreis* Op. 39 (settings of Eichendorff, 1840), the second part of *Das Paradies und die Peri* Op. 50 (1843), Act 4 of the opera *Genoveva* (1848) and

Part 1 of the choral ballad *Vom Pagen und der Königstochter* Op. 140 (1852). Their continually recurring themes – rustling trees and springs, singing birds, lone wanderers, hunting and the sound of horns, darkness and the silence of night – and that mysterious mixed feeling of security and danger stimulated Schumann's imagination as well. Thus, the composition of a series of character pieces for piano, in which this theme could be developed, was always in the air, so to speak. The musical realisation did not cause Schumann any effort and was accomplished without sinking into cliché. The changing pictures are united to a cyclic form by means of a schematic key sequence[5] and thematic relationship between the individual pieces[6].

Nevertheless, a few of the *Waldszenen* also became famous very quickly as separate pieces, particularly *Vogel als Prophet*, one of the rarest gems in Romantic piano music. This was one of Hermann Hesse's favourite pieces, and he sometimes asked Clara Haskil to play it for him.[7] *Verrufene Stelle* (with a poem by Hebbel as a motto), in which the combination of Bach style counterpoint[8] and a bold, richly dissonant harmony produces an oppressive effect, and *Jagdlied*, a gay virtuoso piece, also became very popular at an early date. The influence of Mendelssohn's musical style, which can be seen again and again in Schumann's later works and, particularly, in *Waldszenen*, is most noticeable in the final piece, *Abschied*. Besides *Erinnerung* (Op. 68 No. 28), it is the finest memorial to his friend who had died too early. The first section seems to be like the evocation of a "Song without Words". Schumann's unmistakeable style breaks through again in the middle section with its gentle polyphonic interweavings.

Schumann had originally intended to preface not only *Verrufene Stelle* but also five other pieces, namely *Eintritt*, *Jäger auf der Lauer*, *Vogel als Prophet*, *Jagdlied* and *Abschied* with literary mottos taken from lines and verses by Eichendorff as well as from two popular collections of poetry at the time: Heinrich Laube's *Jagdbrevier* (Leipzig 1841) and Gustav Pfarrius's *Waldlieder* (Cologne 1850).[9] Schumann's intention, which he expressed on frequent occasions, was that these mottos, as well as the super-

---

[1] Complete Works of Oscar Wilde. With an Introduction by Vyvyan Holland, London and Glasgow 1967, p. 27.

[2] Robert Schumann in seinen Schriften und Briefen, ed. W. Boetticher, Berlin 1942, p. 470. The publishing house Bartholf Senff was founded in 1850.

[3] Berliner Musik-Zeitung Echo, Erster Jahrgang, 1850, No. 1, p. 5. Further very appreciative reviews of *Waldszenen* appeared in: Signale für die Musikalische Welt, Achter Jahrgang, 1850, No. 51, p. 489–491; Neue Berliner Musikzeitung, Fünfter Jahrgang, 1851, No. 19 (7 May 1851), p. 145–146.

[4] Robert Schumann in seinen Schriften und Briefen, loc. cit., p. 447.

[5] B flat major / D minor / B flat major / D minor / B flat major / E flat major / G minor / E flat major / B flat major.

[6] Cf. Richard Hohenemser, Formale Eigentümlichkeiten in Robert Schumanns Klaviermusik, in: Festschrift zum 50. Geburtstag von Adolf Sandberger, Munich 1918, p. 23: "In No. 4, *Verrufene Stelle*, however, the principal motif from No. 3, *Einsame Blumen*, is used in spite of the clearly contrasting moods of the two pieces." Sandberger refers to the connection between the flower which has sprouted from the blood of a murdered person, as referred to in the Hebbel verses which are quoted as the motto of *Verrufene Stelle*, and *Einsame Blumen*, and also writes: "We are also aware in *Verrufene Stelle* of a relationship with No. 2, *Jäger auf der Lauer*, in that both seem to close in D major but then return to D minor by means of a G sharp diminished seventh chord. It is clear that this is the reason for the mood of mystery and suspense in the music in both cases."

[7] Cf. Hermann Hesse, Musik. Betrachtungen, Gedichte, Rezensionen und Briefe, Frankfurt am Main [2]1977, p. 206–207 (Hesse describes *Vogel als Prophet* here as a "beautiful and mysterious" piece), p. 221.

[8] The critic referred to above (Berliner Musik-Zeitung Echo loc. cit., p. 5) remarked that "its legato is derived from Joh. Seb. Bach's 'Well-Tempered Clavier'".

[9] These texts are printed in full for the first time in the Critical Notes.

240

scriptions in many of his pieces, were to be regarded not as definite programmes but as poetic hints for both the listener and the player to illustrate the character of the music. They were always chosen after the composition was finished. Further examples can be found in the *Intermezzi* Op. 4 (No. 2), the *Davidsbündlertänze* Op. 6, and the *Fantasie* Op. 17. It says much for Schumann's assured artistic instinct that he decided to use only one motto – Hebbel's

expressive verses – in the printed edition of *Waldszenen*. The occasionally rather trite rhymings of Laube and Pfarrius, no matter how well they fit the titles of the pieces here and there, would have brought Schumann's *Waldszenen* dangerously near that type of honest, rustic "field, wood and meadow" Romanticism with which his music must not be associated.

Joachim Draheim

SUGGESTIONS FOR PERFORMANCE

Eintritt

The relatively high metronome number suggests that Schumann was thinking more of a rustling wood than of woodland tranquillity. In bar 8 (both first time and second time) of the Clara Schumann Edition, *pp* is purposely written again.
Clara Schumann Edition ♩ = 132.

Jäger auf der Lauer

The required tempo is very quick; in spite of the recommended metronome number, the four crotchets should always be counted, so that the triplets and, particularly, the numerous note and chord repetitions can be clearly articulated.
Clara Schumann Edition ♩ = 76.

Einsame Blumen

Above all there must be a clear distinction between the two voices in the duet. The portato touch in the left hand in the first two bars is to be retained for similar bars throughout the piece.
Clara Schumann Edition ♩ = 96.

Verrufene Stelle

Particular attention should be paid to the Hebbel verses: this is the only piece in the entire cycle which Schumann prefaced with a motto in the final version. The player must consistently make a clear rhythmical distinction between the demisemiquaver upbeats and the semiquavers (see particularly bars 8/9 and 21/22) and must observe exactly the many different types of touch required (legato, portato, staccato). The player should take particular care over the lengths of the melodic phrases in the rather complicated polyphonic texture. The crescendo in bar 34 is important: it refers once again to the horror of the scene.
Clara Schumann Edition ♩ = 60.

Freundliche Landschaft

The triplets should be played as cantabile as possible. The metronome marking in the Clara Schumann Edition is appreciably slower than that in the original edition and is

probably intended to underline the cantabile nature of the theme.
Clara Schumann Edition ♩ = 144.

Herberge

The tempo is certainly to be taken "moderately", but a certain momentum is to be maintained throughout. The great number of musical motives which are meant to follow one another as characteristically as possible depicts a very lively scene.
Clara Schumann Edition ♩ = 132.

Vogel als Prophet

Although Schumann did not mark the demisemiquaver triplets, the printing shows the rhythmical structure clearly (cf. bar 9). The piece must be played with the most delicate touch possible and with a sense of flow throughout. The rests are to be observed exactly (count quavers!). There is no change of tempo in the middle section.
Clara Schumann Edition ♩ = 63.

Jagdlied

The tempo is brisk, not quick. The pulsating quavers must remain continually even and clear throughout the piece. The player must take particular care to ensure that Schumann's almost excessive accents and sforzati in the main section are expressive aids to sonority and not mere explosions in the rhythm. The A flat major middle section was clearly intended by the composer to provide a contrast in texture and dynamics; it should be played very lightly and "piano" throughout.
Clara Schumann Edition ♩. = 120.

Abschied

The broad melodic arches require a great amount of articulation and a high level of concentration from the player. The accompanying triplets must be played very evenly but lightly. It is recommended that the *mf* of the opening be taken again for bars 21–28. There should be no ritardando in the coda (bar 46 to the end) which is to be played "more and more faintly".
Clara Schumann Edition ♩ = 80.

Gerhard Puchelt